THE BOOK OF GUTSY WOMEN

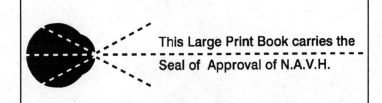

This Large Print Book carries the
Seal of Approval of N.A.V.H.

THE BOOK OF GUTSY WOMEN

HILLARY RODHAM CLINTON AND CHELSEA CLINTON

WHEELER PUBLISHING
A part of Gale, a Cengage Company

**LIBRARY OF CONGRESS CIP DATA ON FILE.
CATALOGUING IN PUBLICATION FOR THIS BOOK
IS AVAILABLE FROM THE LIBRARY OF CONGRESS**

ISBN-13: 978-1-4328-7207-6 (hardcover alk. paper)

Published in 2019 by arrangement with Simon & Schuster, Inc.

Printed in the United States of America
1 2 3 4 5 6 7 24 23 22 21 20

*For everyone
looking for inspiration
to live their own gutsy life*

CONTENTS

Colvin • Coretta Scott King • Dolores
Huerta • The Peacemakers • Victoria
Mxenge • Ai-jen Poo • Sarah Brady, Gabby
Giffords, Nelba Màrquez-Greene, Shannon
Watts, and Lucy McBath • Nza-Ari
Khepra, Emma Gonzàlez, Naomi Wadler,
Edna Chavez, Jazmine Wildcat, and Julia
Spoor • Becca Heller

Storytellers 519

Maya Angelou • Mary Beard • Jineth
Bedoya Lima • Chimamanda Ngozi
Adichie • America Ferrera • Ali
Stroker • Amani Al-Khatahtbeh

Elected Leaders 557

Bella Abzug • Shirley Chisholm • Ann
Richards • Geraldine Ferraro • Barbara
Jordan • Barbara Mikulski • Ellen Johnson
Sirleaf • Wilma Mankiller • Michelle
Bachelet • Danica Roem

Groundbreakers 627

Frances Perkins • Katharine Graham •
Constance Baker Motley • Edie Windsor
• Ela Bhatt • Temple Grandin • Ellen
DeGeneres • Maya Lin • Sally Yates •
Kimberly Bryant and Reshma Saujani

Women's Rights Champions 693

Rosa May Billinghurst • The Suffragists
• Sophia Duleep Singh • Fraidy Reiss •
Manal al-Sharif • Nadia Murad

INTRODUCTION

When CNN published the eye-catching headline "Rare blue pigment found in medieval woman's teeth rewrites history," we both read the article, then immediately sent it to each other. It explained that researchers examining burial remains at a women's monastery in Germany had come across the skeleton of a woman who had died as early as 997 AD. As they looked at the skeleton, they noticed something strange: There were flecks of blue in her teeth. Those blue flecks turned out to be a rare, expensive pigment made from crushed lapis lazuli stones, once as expensive as gold. Only the most talented artists were permitted to use it. So how — in a time when artists were presumed to be men — did it find its way into this woman's teeth? According to the scientists, she was most likely a painter, dipping her brush in her mouth after each stroke.

"That the discovery was made in a rural German monastery is no surprise; books were being produced during this time in monasteries across the country," the article explains. "But women were not known to be the illustrators of such prized creations. . . . In fact, the writers and illustrators often didn't sign their work, as a gesture of humility — and if women were those writers and artists, the practice would effectively erase them from history." Reading the story brought to mind Virginia Woolf's famous work *A Room of One's Own:* "I would venture to guess that Anon, who wrote so many poems without signing them, was often a woman."

Power has largely been associated with — and defined by — men since the beginning of time. Yet women have painted, written, created, discovered, invented, and led for just as long. It's simply that their work is more likely to go unrecognized — sometimes for centuries. We believe it is past time for that to change.

Take the women on the cover of this book, civilian firefighters pictured during a training exercise at the Pearl Harbor Naval Shipyard circa 1941. The photo was published countless times before a librarian and writer named Dorothea Buckingham came across it on a website and looked it up in the Hawaii War Records Depository. Seventy years after the photograph was taken, the public learned who the women were: Elizabeth Moku, Alice Cho, Katherine Lowe, and Hilda Van Gieson. "We were rugged," Katherine, then ninety-six years old, remembered fondly. "We carried heavy stuff, oil drums, bags, anything that needed to be stored."

By now it's a familiar idea, beautifully echoed by Sally Ride: "You can't be what you can't see." But many of the women in this book set out to become *exactly* what they couldn't see. They had no route to follow, no guarantee they'd ever reach their destination — whether that destination was freedom, the right to vote, the chance to be a doctor, or the opportunity to compete in sports or in anything else. But every time someone has the courage to try, she shows the way. And that helps little girls and boys alike to know that girls' dreams are equally as valuable, valid, and important as those of their brothers, their friends, and most of the faces they see in their history books. Each of us has seen — first in her own life, then through the eyes of her daughter — just how powerful representation can be.

That's what drove then ten-year-old Marley Dias to start the campaign #1000blackgirlbooks after she noticed that there were no characters in the books she read who looked like her. It's what inspired Chelsea to write *She Persisted* and *She Persisted Around the World,* and to include inspiring women in *It's Your World* and *Start Now!,* her books for young activists. It's why movies like *Hidden*

13

Figures, about three black women working in the space program, and *On the Basis of Sex,* about Justice Ruth Bader Ginsburg, are so important. It's why it's so thrilling to cheer for female athletes around the world, from ice hockey players in India to synchronized swimmers in Jamaica to the four-time World Cup champion women's soccer team in the United States. It's why the leadership shown by Prime Minister Jacinda Ardern after the mosque massacre in New Zealand and the significant speech against misogyny by former Australian prime minister Julia Gillard are so powerful. It's why we love hearing from girls — and boys — about who their favorite female heroes are and sharing our own favorites. And it's why we loved writing this book.

Throughout history and around the globe, women have overcome some of the toughest and cruelest resistance imaginable, from physical violence and intimidation to a total lack of legal rights or recourse, in order to redefine what is considered "a woman's place." That is the great achievement of the women featured in this book. And thanks to their talents and guts, we have all made progress.

So how did they do it? The answers are as unique as the women themselves. The writers Rachel Carson and Chimamanda Ngozi Adichie named something no one had dared talk about before. Civil rights activist Dorothy Height, LGBTQ trailblazer Edie Windsor, and swimmer Diana Nyad kept pushing forward, no matter what stood in their way. Labor Secretary Frances Perkins and tennis stars Venus and Serena Williams had laser focus despite a storm of sexism made even more challenging because each was a "first" in her own way. Harriet Tubman and Malala Yousafzai stared fear in the face and persevered. Pioneering nurse Florence Nightingale and organizer Ai-jen Poo relied on seemingly endless reserves of compassion. Wangari Maathai, who sparked a movement to plant trees, understood the power of role modeling. Early women's rights advocate Sojourner Truth and Clara Barton, founder of the American Red Cross, saw how one cause was linked to another. Teenage climate activist Greta Thunberg remained fiercely true to herself even when she was ignored or belittled. Every single one of their lives was or is optimistic — they had faith that their actions could make a difference.

Before we had even finished writing, we were seized with regret that we couldn't include every woman who has inspired us with her tenacity and commitment to improving our world, whether she defined that as her own family or our global community. We initially included a courageous DREAMer fighting for comprehensive immigration reform, but she told us that doing so would likely expose her family to retribution. And we could have written an entire book about our friends who have proven, through their own bravery and brilliance, that one gutsy woman can spark a chain reaction within her community.

The list went on and on. What about Babe Didrikson Zaharias, who shattered nearly every athletic barrier in the early 1900s and, when asked whether there was anything she *didn't* play, answered, "Yeah, dolls"? What about artists like Mary Cassatt, Georgia O'Keeffe, Frida Kahlo, Carrie Mae Weems, and the rest of the page-long list we came up with? What about Laverne Cox, whose courage has changed hearts, minds, and laws — not to mention television? What about Zainab Bangura, the first woman to run for president of Sierra Leone and someone who has dedicated her life to speaking out against the atrocity of rape used as a tactic of war? What about fearless journalists like April Ryan, who are standing up for freedom of the press despite personal attacks from the president of the United States? What about the three mighty women on the United States Supreme Court, or the 127 in Congress? What about Joy Harjo, who became the first Native American U.S. poet laureate as we handed in our final manuscript? What about the six — six! — women running for president of the United States in mid-2019? We are living through a time of upheaval and tumult around the globe, but we're also living in an era of gutsy women from all walks of life.

We hope this book will be the beginning of a conversation, or the middle — but certainly not the end. If reading about these women sparks your curiosity, we encourage you to go out and learn more about them. We hope you'll go to your local public library and check out a book; we used to go to the library across the street from our church in Little Rock on Sunday after services, and it was there that Chelsea first discovered some of the women she writes about here. If the book you want to read doesn't yet exist, maybe you're the one to write it. Maybe there's a woman you think is missing from the pages of history. Maybe it's your mother, your grandmother, your aunt, or your daughter. Maybe it's you. Heroes are everywhere. It's up to each of us to seek them out, tell their stories, and celebrate the women who inspire us every day — and then, even more important, to take their example to heart by finding our own unique way to make our mark on the world.

Ensuring the rights, opportunities, and full participation of women and girls remains a big piece of the unfinished business of the twenty-first century. Finishing it is going to take all of us standing shoulder to shoulder, across the generations, across genders. This is not a moment for anyone to leave the fight, or sit on the sidelines waiting for the perfect moment to join. We are reminded of Gloria Steinem, who described being asked repeatedly when she planned to "pass the torch." Her answer summed it up perfectly: "I'm not giving up my torch. I'm using it to light others. That's the only way there can be enough light."

So, to borrow from a well-known quote: Here's to gutsy women. May we know them, may we be them, may we raise them. And may we thank and celebrate them. We're grateful every day to the women in this book, and to all the gutsy women of yesterday, today, and tomorrow.

■ ■ ■ ■

EARLY INSPIRATIONS

■ ■ ■ ■

FIRST INSPIRATIONS

HILLARY AND CHELSEA

Hillary

As a young girl growing up outside Chicago in the 1950s, I personally did not know any woman who worked outside the home, except for my public school teachers and our town's librarians. My mother, like the mothers of all my friends, was a full-time stay-at-home mom. She and the other mothers I knew lived lives like the ones I saw portrayed in the television shows of that era, tending children and the house while trying to keep life on an even keel. My mother may never have vacuumed in a dress and pearls like I saw on *The Donna Reed Show,* but to a child's eye, there were more similarities than differences between her and Donna Reed. When I went to a friend's house, the mother was usually there. I might be offered a peanut butter and jelly sandwich by my friend's mom, just like at home or like I saw June Cleaver doing on *Leave It to Beaver.* The images I saw on TV comfortably and

DOROTHY RODHAM
(GRANDMA DOROTHY)

VIRGINIA KELLEY
(GRANDMA GINGER)

predictably reinforced the roles and behaviors I saw around me.

CHELSEA

I still remember telling you, Mom, when I was probably seven, that my best friend Elizabeth's mom was my second favorite mom — after you — followed by Donna Reed. When I was at Grandma and Pop-pop's, we watched lots of Nick at Nite. Donna reminded me so much of Grandma Dorothy and how she took care of me. (As I got older and saw more of my friends' moms making different, loving choices for their families, Donna Reed fell far down the leaderboard — in the best possible sense — while Grandma Dorothy stayed at the top of her own category!)

HILLARY

I remember that, too! Clearly, Donna's appeal was intergenerational.

I loved my mother and respected the other moms I knew who took good care of their kids and treated me like a member of their own families. I watched and learned from them. As a young girl, I knew that my mother loved her family and home but felt limited by the narrow choices in her life. It can be easy to forget now how few choices there were for women in her generation — even for white, middle-class women who had far more options open to them than most black women did. With my mother's encouragement, I wanted more choices in my life than she'd had and was always looking for inspiration to believe that was possible. She nourished my interest in school and books, and took me to our local library every week, where she helped me pick out books and discussed the characters with me.

Early on, I looked to women in fairy tales and myths, on television, in books, and in the pages of *Life* magazine. The women I discovered there did things and had adventures unlike anything I saw around me, planting seeds in my imagination and widening my view of what women could do. I was also an avid reader of the cartoon strip about Brenda Starr, the flaming-red-haired, beautifully dressed reporter, and her far-flung global adventures. She was the only character in the comics I identified with and was inspired by as a young girl. Fictional though she was, Brenda became one of my first professional role models.

All through school, I had dedicated, challenging teachers who inspired me, but my sixth-grade teacher, Mrs. Elizabeth King, stood out. She drilled us in grammar, encouraged us to think and write creatively, urged us to try new things, and pushed us to excel. She often paraphrased a verse from the Gospel of Matthew: "Don't put your lamp under a bushel basket, but use it to light up the world." She assigned me and four of my classmates to write and produce a play about five girls taking a trip to Europe, a place none of us had ever visited. We dove into the project and were so proud when we presented it on the stage in our elementary school auditorium, complete with our energetic Parisian cancan dance performance.

Also at the behest of Mrs. King, I wrote my autobiography. In more than twenty-nine pages filled with my scrawly handwriting, I described my parents, brothers, pets, house, hobbies, school, sports, and plans for the future. Because of my parents' encouragement and expectations from teachers like Mrs. King, I knew a few things: I wanted to go to college and then have a job and family. My mother didn't have the chance to attend college when she was young, and my dad went to Penn State to play football, which wouldn't apply to me. So I'd have to figure it out along the way. To do that, I would need guidance from as many courageous women as I could find.

Almost instinctively, I found myself leafing through books, eagerly looking for girl characters I could root for. I was delighted when I found Louisa May Alcott's *Little Women* with the March sisters and their mother, Marmee — captivating, complex characters. Free-spirited Jo was my favorite. I couldn't help but identify with the tension she felt between a fierce love and loyalty for her family, and an equally fierce desire to throw herself into the world. "I want to do something splendid before I go into my castle," she vowed, "something heroic, or wonderful, that won't be forgotten after I'm dead. I don't know what, but I'm on the watch for it, and mean to astonish you all, someday."

I also adored Nancy Drew, the intrepid sixteen-year-old high school graduate who solved mysteries. Nancy inspired my friends and me to no end. We pretended to be her as we played around our neighborhood, looking for made-up criminals we wanted to catch. We weren't old enough to drive a "roadster," and our parents wouldn't have let us travel around chasing bad guys, but we loved imagining. We knew we weren't detectives, but we wanted to be more like Nancy Drew: smart, brave, and independent. And, of course, I admired the way Nancy would sometimes do her detective work in sensible pants. ("There's only one thing left to do," she said before climbing up into the rafters of a building in pursuit of a fleeing cat in *The Clue of the Tapping Heels*. "I'm glad I wore pants.") Many women who grew up in the 1950s, from Supreme Court Justices Sandra Day O'Connor and Sonia Sotomayor to Laura Bush and Gayle King, have said that this imaginary character was an important influence on them.

CHELSEA

Nancy Drew was the first literary hero you, Grandma Dorothy, and I shared. She was indomitable — a word I learned because of her! Grandma had saved some of your original books, so I got to read the same books you read when you were my age. The stories were later shortened, and Nancy changed to be more "ladylike" and deferential to the men in her life. I adored the original Nancy, and it felt magical to hold the books I knew had so inspired you.

After I'd read the first ten or so original books, I asked my grandmother if we could one day take a trip to River Heights, Nancy Drew's hometown. She gently told me it wasn't a real place, and no, she said, there was no Nancy Drew museum to visit, either. But she reassured me that what was real and important about Nancy was her curiosity, unapologetic smarts, and doggedness. She never gave up on a case even when her life was in danger. I knew that Nancy was completely improbable — what sixteen-year-old had the financial freedom and wherewithal to travel the world solving mysteries? How did she always manage to escape danger? It was absurd, yet still inspiring.

In addition to Nancy Drew, I was thrilled when I came across a book about Athena, the Greek goddess of wisdom and war, and

Artemis, the goddess of the hunt and wild animals. They had special powers and presided over activities and places I had always associated with men being in charge. I took their examples to heart.

There were lots of kids in my neighborhood, and when we weren't in school, we were outside playing in all kinds of weather. We were always dividing ourselves into teams and making up elaborate games like one we called "chase and run," an elaborate version of hide-and-seek that included capturing prisoners. Because I had read the Greek myths that featured strong female figures, I felt comfortable taking leadership roles, planning our strategy and speaking up when I disagreed with the boys. I even asked my mom if I could get a bow and arrow like the hunter Artemis. She wisely refused, despite my best argument that the Roman name for Artemis, Diana, was like my middle name, Diane.

Chelsea

I was captivated by Ancient Egypt for the same reason: the stories of Nefertiti, Cleopatra, and Hatshepsut were all examples of strong, brave, and fearless women leaders. In fourth grade, I wrote my then longest report ever on Hatshepsut, one of the first female pharaohs, and the woman who would sit longest on Egypt's throne. A couple of years earlier, in 1987, my mom and I had gone to the

Ramses II exhibit in Memphis, Tennessee, and while I wanted to know more about the real-life pharaoh Yul Brynner portrayed in the movie *The Ten Commandments,* I spent most of the two-and-a-half-hour drive from Little Rock chatting incessantly about women in Ancient Egypt. As pharaoh, Hatshepsut commissioned construction on a scale that Egypt had never before seen — building temples, obelisks, and more, some of which still stand today. She also expanded trade routes and supported agricultural experimentation. She sent a powerful message to Egyptian women when she insisted on ruling as her young son's equal — a statement that resonated with me thousands of years later.

Like my mom, I looked for inspiring women everywhere. When at the age of nine or ten I took a summer class on medieval Europe, Joan of Arc stood out against the backdrop of histories and legends dominated by men. She was committed to driving the English out of France and never wavered in the face of sexist skepticism (what young woman could lead an army?!), doubts about her sanity, and even death; she was burned at the stake by her English captors for "insubordination and heterodoxy." As soon as I learned about Joan, I immediately knew what I would be for Halloween months later. My Grandma Dorothy made me a beautiful costume; I spent most of my time trick-or-treating explaining who I was.

About thirty years later, I learned of Joan's mother, Isabelle Romée, from the play *Mother of the Maid,* which imagined the history of her life. In the play, Isabelle supported Joan and cared for her in her final days in prison. After Joan was burned at the stake, Isabelle spent more than two decades working to exonerate her daughter. She taught herself to read and to speak in public, journeying as far as Rome to plead her case to the Vatican; she was over seventy years old at the time. Finally, in Paris twenty-five years after Joan's execution, a religious court overturned the earlier verdict. Talk about a mother-daughter pair of determined, gutsy women.

My love of history and fascination with the ancient world, particularly Ancient Egypt, has continued into adulthood. In 2008, I picked up a copy of *Crocodile on the Sandbank* at a secondhand bookstore and instantly fell in love with the writing of Barbara Mertz. Under her pen name, Elizabeth Peters, she created a delightful heroine in turn-of-the-century archaeologist Amelia Peabody. From the moment I started the book, I couldn't put it down. I laughed so hard that friends and strangers — anyone nearby — kept asking me what was so funny. As soon as I finished it, I shared it with my grandmother and then my mom. Our book club of three was born. My grandmother and I later read and loved Barbara's more scholarly books on Egyptology, and my mom and I both wrote Barbara fan letters before she passed away, thanking her for the joy she brought us.

Hillary

By the time I started Wellesley College in the fall of 1965, the women's movement had started, popularly catalyzed by *The Feminine Mystique,* a book by Betty Friedan published in 1963. We didn't often buy books in my family, we checked them out of the library, and that's what my mother did. She brought home a copy of Friedan's book to read and found so much of interest in it that she then bought a copy she could underline. And she talked to me about it. I've read many valid criticisms of *The Feminine Mystique* in the years since, but for women like my mother, it was revelatory, even revolutionary. She had felt guilty about feeling unfulfilled and regretful about being at home full-time until Friedan described her feelings as "the problem that has no name." She, along with millions of other women of her time, didn't know what ailed her until Betty Friedan named it. She didn't agree with all of the arguments in the book and always insisted that being a mother, especially after her own unhappy childhood, was the best thing she'd ever done, but suddenly, she felt like a veil had been lifted from her eyes. When I met Betty Friedan many years later, I thanked her for writing a book that meant so

31

much to my mother. "What about you?" she replied.

And, of course, what about me? Although *The Feminine Mystique* didn't affect me in the same way it did my mother, I appreciated how impactful the book had been and agree with Gail Collins, the *New York Times* columnist who wrote the introduction to its fiftieth-anniversary edition. It deserved to be on the list of the most important books of the twentieth century. As Collins pointed out, it "also made one conservative magazine's exclusive roundup of the '10 most harmful books of the nineteenth and twentieth centuries.' Which if not flattering is at least a testimony to the wallop it packed." It motivated me to read widely in feminist literature, including Mary Wollstonecraft's *A Vindication of the Rights of Woman* (1792) and Simone de Beauvoir's *The Second Sex* (1949). My feminist reading continued well after college, from the writings of Gloria Steinem to Margaret Atwood's *The Handmaid's Tale* (1985) to Roxane Gay's *Hunger* (2017) and the many others whose work inspired me to think harder about women's roles and rights.

When I became a mom, I saw the search for role models through Chelsea's eyes. She would page intently through her books, looking for the girl characters, and her face would light up when she found them. Like me, she was captivated by fictional heroines. But everywhere Chelsea looked, she saw real-life examples of women who were pursuing dreams that would have been unimaginable when I was a little girl. I loved watching her pepper our family friends and fascinating women she met with questions about what they did and why they loved it. In the span of a single generation, so much of what once seemed impossible had become not only possible but commonplace.

Chelsea

Growing up in Little Rock, I was surrounded by inspiring women: my mom and my grandmothers; my teachers at school, Sunday school, and ballet; my pediatrician, Dr. Betty Lowe; for a time, our mayor, Lottie Shackelford; the historical women I learned about; and the fictional girls and women I fell in love with when reading and watching their stories. I've also been blessed to have wonderful female friends throughout my life; my oldest friend, Elizabeth Fleming Weindruch, is the daughter of a woman my mom met in Lamaze class. I have known and loved her my whole life. My friends have provided support, community, shared love, and adventures. They, too, have been an important source of inspiration — as women, friends, leaders, professionals, mothers, and citizens.

In some ways, the cascade of inspiration started before I can remember: my grandmothers and mom talking to me about their lives, my mom reading me *The Runaway Bunny* — a clear lesson in the power of a mother's love as well as the power of determination, from parent and little bunny alike. Or, arguably, the inspiration started somewhere between Kansas and the Emerald City.

I will always be grateful to my first-grade teacher, Dr. Sadie Mitchell, for the gift of helping me conquer my first chapter book, *The Wonderful Wizard of Oz.* It took our class a month, maybe longer, to get through L. Frank Baum's classic about Dorothy's magical adventures and realizing "there's no place like home." I was in awe of Dorothy's refusal, at an age not much older than I was, to give up on herself or her friends.

HILLARY

The Wizard of Oz was also the first movie I ever saw in a theater, and I remember feeling the exact same way. I also remember being scared of the flying monkeys!

At the end of the year, our class, along with Mrs. Tabitha Phillips's class across the hall, put on a *Wizard of Oz* play for our classmates and families. I was the Wicked Witch of the West and determined to have the most spectacular melting scene possible on our Forest Park Elementary stage. My mom was supportive but not enthusiastic when I declared

I would temporarily dye my hair green and paint my face green for the role. Her lack of enthusiasm was warranted — it took about a week for my hair, washed daily, to turn back to its normal color.

Dr. Mitchell cheered me on every step of the way and told me my melting scene was perfect. While Dorothy was one of my first imaginary heroes, Dr. Mitchell was one of my first real-life heroes beyond my family. She spent time with every student. When we'd had a rough day, she would tell us the next morning, "That was yesterday. Today is a new day." She never treated me differently because I was the daughter of the governor of Arkansas. She expected me to be a good student and a good person — it's what she expected of everyone to the best of our abilities. Dr. Mitchell was unfailingly patient, kind, and fair in doling out praise and punishment alike. She set the standard for what an excellent teacher is.

HILLARY

Having wonderful teachers sparked a lifelong love of learning in each of us. And while our teachers introduced us to inspiring women and role models, we both wish we had learned more about the sung and unsung heroines of history. (That's one reason why we're writing this book!) Still, we know how lucky we were to have had, more than once, extraordinary teachers who made us sit up a little taller as it dawned on us that we, too, could change the world.

After Dorothy, there was Meg Murry, the indomitable star of Madeleine L'Engle's *A Wrinkle in Time*. I remember talking nonstop to my parents about this book. Inspired by Meg, I practiced multiplication tables in my head to ward off any attempts at mind control. I would frequently ask myself: *What would Meg do?* If there had been a bracelet back then with that written on it, I'd never have taken it off. Alongside Meg, there was also Beverly Cleary's Ramona Quimby. When my Grandma Ginger asked me what I wanted for my eighth birthday, inspired by Ramona's efforts with her father, I said I wanted her to stop smoking. She said okay. Ginger never hid how hard it was for her to give up her couple-pack-a-day habit. Her candor and lack of self-pity impressed me as much as her success in quitting cigarettes. As inspired as I was by Meg and Ramona, Ginger inspired me even more.

Now, as a mother myself, I hope that my children understand why I was and am drawn to the girls and women who have long inspired me — some of whom are in these pages. I hope they will read a few of the books I loved so much as a kid. They certainly don't have to have the same role models, but I hope they understand why I have carried these women in my heart for so long.

Harriet Tubman

Hillary and Chelsea

The year was 1860. Charles Nalle, a fugitive slave, was getting ready to stand trial in Troy, New York. The authorities weren't letting any of the protesters who had gathered outside the courthouse into the proceedings. But an elderly-looking woman wrapped in a shawl, carrying a food basket, seemed innocuous. She had found a spot at the back of the room. When the judge announced that Charles Nalle would be sent back to Virginia, she suddenly rushed forward. She threw off her shawl, revealing that she wasn't an old woman at all — she was thirty-four years old. She grabbed Nalle and rushed him out of the room, taking advantage of the guards' surprise. As the two ran down the stairs, she fended off blows from policemen's clubs. Finally, she put her passenger onto a waiting ferry.

Victory was short-lived. The policemen waiting on the other side of the water brought him right back and shut him in the judge's office. But the young woman wasn't going to give up so easily. She rallied the people of Troy, and on her signal, the crowd stormed the office, freed Nalle, and put him on a wagon heading west. It was Harriet Tubman's first public rescue of a runaway slave.

Araminta Ross, as she was originally known, was born into slavery around 1820 in Maryland. Part of a big family, she was sent at age five to a neighbor who wanted "a young girl to help take care of a baby." She was so small she had to sit on the floor in order to safely hold the baby. One of her jobs was staying up nights to rock the cradle. When she fell asleep, she was whipped. She was homesick;

she missed her mother desperately. By the time she was returned to her family, she was sickly and weak. A few years later, an overseer threw an iron weight at a fleeing slave; it hit Harriet in the head, leaving her with a scar above her eyebrow and fainting spells that would last the rest of her life.

Living in the shadow of constant violence, cruelty, and racism, Harriet developed remarkable self-reliance and physical endurance. In her twenties, she married John Tubman, a free black man. Five years later, her master died, throwing her future, and that of her family, into uncertainty. Deeply spiritual, she prayed for guidance. Like Sojourner Truth, she decided passive prayer wasn't enough; to live out God's will, she needed to combine her faith with action. "I had reasoned this out in my mind," she said later. "There was one of two things I had a right to, liberty or death. If I could not have one, I would have the other."

That September, Harriet set out for unfamiliar territory, leaving behind her parents and her husband. Within weeks, her master's family was running ads in the paper, offering a reward to anyone who found her and brought her back. She followed the North Star, relying on an "underground railroad" of safe houses and hiding places she hoped were waiting for her. She offered a favorite quilt to a sympathetic white woman in exchange for directions to the first house as well as a piece of paper with two names of people who could help her written on it. Harriet was illiterate, so she couldn't read the names; she could only hand the paper to the next person she encountered and hope he or she would hide her.

Catherine Clinton writes in her biography *Harriet Tubman: The Road to Freedom:* "Since the earliest days of bondage, those captured and enslaved spent enormous reservoirs of energy trying to unchain themselves. The vast majority of slaves hoped in vain. They prayed for freedom but resorted to seeking salvation in the afterlife." Harriet risked everything to escape to freedom: the threat of bloodhounds on her trail, of slave catchers desperate to earn the bounty placed on her head, of danger and disease waiting for her in rivers and the woods, of the possibility that the door on which she knocked was not home to an abolitionist at all. She made her way almost entirely on foot, by night, across state lines. Most fugitive slaves, especially those who risked the dangerous journey on their own, were men; she was a young woman in her twenties.

When she arrived safely in Philadelphia, like many other freed slaves, she chose a new name to go along with her new life. There, she found a community of like-minded people, a network of black churches, and an open forum to discuss abolition. She spoke publicly about her personal experiences with slavery and found paid work to support herself.

Then one day, she heard a rumor that the wife of her former master was getting ready to sell Harriet's favorite niece, Kizzy. Here, her story goes from courageous to heroic. She made up her mind to turn around and go back, braving the dangers all over again, in order to try to rescue Kizzy and her two children. Though the details of the escape are unknown, we do know that Harriet succeeded. She brought the family to Baltimore and hid them there until she could find a way to transport them to the North.

In 1851, Harriet made her second trip back, rescuing not only one of her brothers but two of his coworkers. In the meantime, the U.S. had passed a fugitive slave law, making an already dangerous mission even more frightening: Even in free states, enslaved people were required by law to be returned to their masters. Anyone who aided an enslaved person could be thrown in jail or fined. Still, once again, Harriet was successful. But she had one more mission to undertake — this one deeply personal. On her third trip, Harriet sought out her husband, intent on persuading him to come with her. She made the unhappy discovery that he had remarried and had no plans to leave with her. At first, she said later, she thought "she would go right in and make all the trouble she could." In the end, she concluded, "if he could do without her, she could do without him."

Originally set on bringing her own family to safety, Harriet turned her attention to others who were in the same desperate situation. In December 1851, she officially became part of the Underground Railroad. "The Lord told me to do this," she said later. "I said, 'Oh Lord, I can't — don't ask me — take somebody else.'" According to her, the answer came back in no uncertain terms: "It's you I want, Harriet Tubman." So she went, bringing back a band of eleven fugitives that included another brother and several strangers. At this point, she decided to take her "passengers" to Canada, reasoning: "I wouldn't trust Uncle Sam with my people no longer." She settled there, eventually rescuing her entire family, including her elderly parents. She later moved the entire household to Auburn, New York, where she spent her later years.

All told, Harriet is credited with bringing hundreds of slaves to freedom. She traveled alone, risking her freedom and her life to liberate others. As word of her missions spread,

---

"I was a conductor of the Underground Railroad for eight years, and I can say what most conductors can't say: I never ran my train off the track and I never lost a passenger."

— HARRIET TUBMAN

---

she earned the nickname "Moses." She was single-minded, setting her own fear aside in order to bring her passengers on the "liberty lines." She carried a pistol, which she used more than once to frighten a fugitive on the verge of losing his or her nerve into staying the course. On one trip, she was distracted by a painful dental infection. She grabbed her pistol, knocked out the problem teeth, and kept going.

Harriet was also creative and a master of misdirection. Once she hid in plain sight in a town near her former Maryland home, covering her face with a sunbonnet and carrying two live chickens. When one of her former masters came toward her, she yanked the strings she had tied to the legs of the chickens, causing them to squawk and flap their wings. She rushed off, tending to the birds, and managing to avoid eye contact with the man. On another trip, she spotted another former master in a train car. Used to being underestimated or ignored, she passed herself off as an elderly woman, conveying instructions to hidden passengers through the spirituals she sang.

When the Civil War broke out, Harriet once again felt called. She had befriended the abolitionist John Brown (who called her "General Tubman") and was galvanized by his unsuccessful siege on Harpers Ferry. She believed her place was at the center of the battle. She traveled with Union troops to South Carolina, where she tended to sick and wounded soldiers, drawing on her knowledge of herbal medicine. In 1863, she was appointed head of an espionage and scout network for the Union Army. Even though she was a wanted woman, she went behind enemy lines in South Carolina, building a whisper network of scouts to help track Confederate operations. In 1863, she led the famous Combahee River Raid, resulting in the liberation of as many as seven hundred former slaves. She told the story of the raid again and again, thrilling audiences with her death-defying courage and making them laugh with her colorful observations. (After climbing into a boat to make her escape, she recounted, she would never again wear a skirt on a military expedition.)

In 1864, in failing health, she returned to New York to care for her aging parents. Though she was recognized by her fellow Union soldiers as a hero, her battle was far from over. On a train trip in 1865, the conductor refused to believe that a black woman could be carrying legitimately obtained soldiers' papers. He demanded that she give up her seat. When she refused, it took four men to remove her. They left her in the baggage car, where she stayed for the rest of the trip.

In Auburn, New York, she opened the doors of her home, taking in anyone in need of help. She channeled donations to orphans,

> *"Tubman never waited for a man to affirm her. Tubman reveled in defying men, defying governments, defying slavery, defying Confederate armies and slave catchers who put a $40,000 bounty on her head. This black woman who stood 5 feet tall was utterly and completely fearless."*
> — DENEEN L. BROWN,
> *THE WASHINGTON POST*

the elderly, and people with disabilities. She traveled the country speaking out in favor of women's suffrage, alongside her friends Frederick Douglass, Susan B. Anthony, and Sojourner Truth. She remarried, this time to Civil War veteran Nelson Davis, and they adopted a little girl named Gertie. She fought for decades to receive any compensation for her military service, though when community members offered donations, she immediately passed them along to anyone she believed was more in need than she was.

HILLARY

Years later, as senator for New York, I was proud to secure funding to restore the Harriet Tubman Home: a symbolic $11,750, which was the equivalent of the additional widow's pension she should have received after the death of her husband. I was delighted when

I learned that she would be depicted on the twenty-dollar bill — the first time a black person would appear on U.S. currency. However, it remains to be seen whether the current administration will follow through on this long-overdue recognition.

CHELSEA

When I was a little girl, one of the first heroes I remember my mom telling me about was Harriet Tubman. We also learned about her throughout elementary school, in history and social studies classes. Her courage, conviction, and lifelong belief in putting her faith into action represent the best of humanity, and her story is one every child should know.

The wisdom she shared with her passengers has stayed as relevant as ever. The rule for all of her Underground Railroad missions was to keep going. Once you started — no matter how scared you got or how dangerous it became — you were not allowed to turn back. On the path to freedom, Harriet had one piece of advice: "If you hear the dogs, keep going. If you see torches in the woods, keep going. If they are shouting after you, keep going. Don't ever stop. Keep going. If you want to taste freedom, keep going." Even in the darkest moments, that is what we all must do: Keep going.

Anna Pavlova, Isadora Duncan, Maria Tallchief, and Virginia Johnson

ANNA PAVLOVA

ISADORA DUNCAN

MARIA TALLCHIEF

VIRGINIA JOHNSON

Chelsea

Born in St. Petersburg, Russia, in 1881, Anna Pavlova was raised in poverty by her mother, a washerwoman. Anna and her mother always believed she was intended for greatness. As a child, Anna saw her first ballet, *The Sleeping Beauty,* and made up her mind: She wanted to be a dancer.

Accepted for training at the Imperial School of Ballet in St. Petersburg just a few years later, Anna was overjoyed. So was her mother, who must have felt validated having proof of her daughter's extraordinary potential.

From that moment on, ballet and dance took precedence over everything else in Anna's life. She matched her talent with her tireless work ethic and curiosity. As Anna supposedly said, "No one can arrive from being talented alone. God gives talent; work transforms talent into genius." By her midtwenties, she had become a prima ballerina, and danced the famously difficult role of Giselle with the Imperial Ballet.

At a time when most ballet dancers remained firmly within their discipline, Anna studied Polish, Mexican, Indian, and Japanese dances. When she did dance ballet, she focused on a simpler style than was in fashion, allowing her to show more emotion through her performances. She introduced new audiences to her version of ballet, traveling the world from New York to Tokyo, and on the silver screen as one of the first dancers ever to appear on film. Her most famous variation, and one she frequently performed on tour, was choreographed specifically for her: the Dying Swan. She is believed to have performed it four thousand times. Anna was renowned for her intensity and her grace. She should also have been known for the bravery it took to develop her own style and to eventually start her own ballet company — a rarity for any dancer at that time, particularly a woman.

Anna famously danced until her death — in fact, some argue she danced herself to death. As the star of her own company, she likely felt enormous pressure to keep performing in order to attract audiences and sell tickets to support herself, her dancers, and the orphanage for Russian refugee children she'd founded in Paris. Reportedly, a few weeks before she died, she refused surgery that might have saved her life though likely would have ended her career. One legend says that in her final performances audiences could see the blood seep through her pointe shoes onto the stage, proving her uncompromising dedication. I thought of Anna when I would wrap my toes at home, hoping to hide from my mom the toll that dancing was taking on my feet. I also knew I would never be as talented as Anna, so it would be highly unlikely that I would ever face a choice between my health and showing the world my ballet genius!

Born a few years before Anna and in San Francisco, Isadora Duncan, like Anna, was raised primarily by her mother after her parents' divorce. Unlike Anna, Isadora was largely self-taught — she had taken ballet lessons at nine years old before deciding the form was nothing more than "affected grace and toe walking" that produced "artificial mechanical movement not worthy of the soul." When I mentioned Isadora to my Grandma Dorothy, she remembered seeing old photographs of Isadora and thinking how glamorous and unbowed she looked. I had to look up "unbowed" in the dictionary. Once I had, I agreed.

Isadora wanted the world to return to an appreciation of classical lines and natural form, and based her dancing on those principles. In the late nineteenth century, American audiences largely rejected her early efforts, and, at twenty-one, Isadora used her scant savings to travel to England on a cattle boat, hoping to find a warmer reception.

European audiences quickly embraced Isadora's barefoot, corset-free, more relaxed style; American audiences would eventually do the same. In 1905, in St. Petersburg, Isadora gave a performance based on her manifesto, "Dancer of the Future." She believed dance needed "to become again a high religious art as it was with the Greeks," in part to ensure it never became "mere merchandise." Anna Pavlova was still living in St. Petersburg at the time that Isadora introduced her new interpretation, and as a young dancer, I desperately wanted to believe she was in the audience. (I've never found any evidence to support that hope, but still love to imagine it!)

Isadora's St. Petersburg performance was met with lavish praise and vehement condemnation — a success, since her goal had been to spark conversation. Isadora appeared to be neither overawed by the praise nor discouraged by the criticism; she simply continued to create.

Onstage and off, Isadora wanted to "dance a different dance." She lived her life fearlessly. Isadora never married the fathers of her children and declared herself a "revolutionist," as she said true artists are; all were uncommon choices for women in the early twentieth century. When a tragic car accident resulted in her two children and their nurse drowning in the Seine River in Paris, she channeled her grief into her work. She pushed her choreography, staging, and costumes into new territory, and opened dance schools around the world. She moved to Moscow in 1921, captivated by the social and political revolution unfolding in the Soviet Union and determined to translate her outrage over social injustice and human suffering into dance.

She later married Russian poet Sergey Aleksandrovich Esenin. Though she still objected to the institution of marriage, it was the only way he could travel with her on her newest United States tour. This time, she was greeted with hostility and false accusations that she and her husband were both Bolshevik spies. When she left, she vowed: "Good-bye, America, I shall never see you again!" Back in Europe, Esenin struggled with his mental health, eventually dying by suicide.

Isadora spent her final years in France. She was killed when the scarf she was wearing was caught in the wheels of a car. Both she and Anna died while still performing, and both far too young: Anna was forty-five and Isadora fifty. Anna brought ballet to the world and expanded the definition of what ballet could be. Isadora proved that other forms of dance besides ballet could be critically and commercially successful. They opened doors for classical and modern dancers alike, both helping to create the dance of the future.

Hillary

The first famous woman I ever saw in person who inspired me was Maria Tallchief, one of America's first prima ballerinas. Maria was born in Fairfax, Oklahoma. Her father was a full-blooded Osage Indian. When Maria was three years old, her mother enrolled her in ballet lessons; her sister, Marjorie, would later follow. Before long, they were dancing at county fairs and rodeos. ("Rodeos petrified me," Maria remembered. "Long-horned bulls lumbered by so close behind the grandstand I was sure I'd get gored waiting to go on.")

After her family moved from Oklahoma to Los Angeles, Maria experienced the feeling of not fitting in for the first time. Other students teased her about her name, made "war whoops" when they passed her in the hallway, and asked her if her father took scalps. That painful experience would stick with her the rest of her life. Throughout her dancing career and into retirement, she advocated for celebrating and preserving Native American history and culture.

Her big break came in 1942, when she was hired as an apprentice with the Ballet Russe de Monte Carlo, one of the most famous ballet companies in the world at the time. When the company director suggested that Maria change her last name to Tallchieva to sound less Native American and more Russian (a lot of American dancers adopted Russian stage names), she refused; she was proud of her name and her heritage.

Maria's star was on the rise at a critical time for American ballet. While living in New York, she met the choreographer George Balanchine. He would become her husband

and she his muse. Balanchine choreographed iconic roles that showcased Maria's extraordinary technique and artistry: Stravinsky's *The Firebird*, Tchaikovsky's *Swan Lake* and "Dance of the Sugar Plum Fairy" in *The Nutcracker*.

As for me, I started taking ballet at our local dance studio when I was seven. I liked to imagine myself becoming a real ballerina like Maria, whom I saw on television — probably on *The Ed Sullivan Show*, which my family watched every Sunday night. One day my mother told me that Maria would be dancing in Chicago; she hoped we could go. That was a big deal, since I had never been to a live professional performance of any kind. She had to ask my father, who totally controlled the purse strings, if he'd give her the money to buy two tickets. Somewhat surprisingly to me, he agreed to pay for the tickets and drive us back and forth to Chicago, since my mother didn't get her license until I was in high school.

Many years later, in 1996, Maria Tallchief came to the White House when she received a Kennedy Center Honor, and I had the chance to tell her how seeing her dance had inspired me.

Chelsea

I was lucky enough to meet Maria when I was a teenager, and to pay tribute to her years later at an event celebrating George Balanchine. The groundbreaking American choreographer is often credited with casting Maria in the roles that helped make her a star, though she was just as instrumental in shaping his career; without Maria, it's hard to imagine Balanchine. In her memoir, *Maria Tallchief: America's Prima Ballerina,* she vividly described the roles she danced and her travels around the world; she also took on complicated, difficult topics, including her relationships, her miscarriage, her feelings about being Native American, and aging.

Like Maria, I am thankful for the teachers I had who prized the best and also valued those of us who gave it our all while gently and consistently reinforcing that we had no professional future in ballet. At Washington School of the Ballet, where I started in the middle of eighth grade, our teachers rarely showed us old videos of variations or ballets. They wanted us to internalize their teaching and direction and then make it our own. They would share stories or impressions from their experiences and their favorite students and dancers. No one's name came up more frequently and to greater praise than Virginia Johnson's, an alumna of the school who broke barriers for black ballerinas and dancers. But Mary Day, the school's cofounder and still director when I studied there, had not always been supportive of Virginia. Back in the 1960s, she had given Virginia a scholarship, praised her dancing, and then abruptly told her upon graduation that she would never get a job in ballet, leaving it implied in big bright lights that it was because of her skin color. The racism was clear.

Virginia's parents expected her to go to college. Yet, not long into her freshman year, she realized how much she missed dancing and left, hoping to join the Dance Theatre of Harlem. It was the first classical ballet company started by a black American dancer, the extraordinary Arthur Mitchell, and centered on black American dancers. Mitchell had been the first black principal dancer at New York City Ballet and, after the assassination of Dr. Martin Luther King Jr., he decided to start a ballet company in the neighborhood where he had grown up. Virginia learned from Mitchell and then later went on to become one of Dance Theatre of Harlem's first stars.

Virginia danced everything from classical ballets to Balanchine. Her dancing career lasted far longer than many others because she was simply that good. After she retired, she founded and edited *Pointe* magazine, a publication that focused on ballet and preparing young dancers for professional careers. Eventually, she rejoined Dance Theatre of Harlem, ultimately becoming its artistic director at Arthur Mitchell's request. Virginia paved the way for a generation of dancers whose talent the world might have otherwise missed out on. Misty Copeland, the first black woman ever to be a principal dancer for American Ballet Theatre (and the first professional ballerina my daughter Charlotte was aware of) told Virginia: "There wouldn't be a Misty Copeland without a Virginia Johnson." Misty added that Virginia "gave the dance world this vision of what black dancers are capable of."

Anna, Isadora, Maria, and Virginia each captivated audiences with their brilliant performances. Not only that, they possessed the genius and boldness to redefine what dance could be. It is impossible to imagine ballet or modern dance without these trailblazers, for what they did and for the generations of dancers they inspired, including those of us (like me) who would never ascend to their heights and could only marvel at all they accomplished.

HELEN KELLER

HILLARY

Looking back, I realize that there weren't many lessons in elementary school about famous women. I remember my teachers mentioning Cleopatra, Queen Elizabeth I, and Joan of Arc. I found them interesting, but they didn't capture my attention the way Helen Keller did. It may seem surprising now, but all of my schooling took place before kids with disabilities had a right to accommodations that would allow them to attend public schools. From kindergarten to high school, I didn't have classmates with physical disabilities. But in 1957, when I was ten, I saw a production of *The Miracle Worker* on *Playhouse 90,* a television show that presented high-quality dramas. This dramatization of Helen's life as a deafblind young woman, and her journey with her teacher, Anne Sullivan, allowed me to imagine her struggles and rejoice in her achievements.

Helen Keller was born on June 27, 1880, in the small town of Tuscumbia, Alabama. At nineteen months old, she got sick. The illness was never diagnosed, but it left her both deaf and blind. She couldn't go to school or be left on her own. She developed a system of rudimentary signs to communicate basic needs to her family, but was isolated, frustrated, and prone to fits of rage in which she lashed out at anyone who came near her.

One day, reading Charles Dickens's *American Notes for General Circulation,* Helen's mother, Kate, came across the story of Laura Bridgman, a deafblind girl who was being educated at what is now known as the Perkins School for the Blind in Massachusetts. In

Laura's story, Helen's mother saw a glimmer of hope for Helen. Her parents applied to have a teacher sent to Tuscumbia.

Anne Sullivan arrived at Helen's home in Alabama on March 3, 1887, a day Helen later called "my soul's birthday." That beautiful turn of phrase has always stuck with me — what a perfect way to capture the moment of meeting someone who will go on to change your life for the better. Anne was a twenty-year-old Perkins graduate, herself visually impaired. She had her work cut out for her: "Virtually her first act on meeting the new teacher was to knock out one of her front teeth" reads one account in *The New Yorker*. But Anne recognized Helen's fierce intelligence. She taught Helen to communicate by spelling words into her hand, which Helen quickly memorized. On a fateful day in April 1887, Anne brought Helen to a water pump and spelled "water" into her palm. It clicked in Helen's mind that the words she was spelling corresponded to things in the world around her. "Somehow," Helen said later, "the mystery of language was revealed to me." Soon she was being celebrated in newspapers across America and Europe. At age eight, she met President Grover Cleveland at the White House. When Helen's dog died, contributions poured in from all over the country to replace her beloved pet. Instead, she asked the well-wishers to donate to a young boy who wanted to attend the Perkins Institute; they raised enough money to send him to the school.

From an early age, Helen was determined to go to college and was admitted to Radcliffe College of Harvard University. Anne went with her to every class, spelling out lectures as quickly as she could into Helen's palm, transcribing pages of text into Braille. In 1904, at the age of twenty-four, Helen graduated cum laude, becoming the first deafblind person to earn a bachelor of arts degree. (It seems not to have occurred to Radcliffe to give Anne a degree along with Helen, though she, too, had put in hours of work.) Helen wrote, gave speeches, and published her autobiography, *The Story of My Life,* all while still in college.

CHELSEA

In books and movies, Helen is often shown as a larger-than-life hero, almost impossibly determined in the face of suffering and obstacles — and she was. But Helen also had flaws, fears, and moments of longing, like anyone. "If I could see," she once said, "I would marry first of all." In response to the question of whether she ever wished she were not deafblind, she acknowledged that "perhaps there is just a touch of yearning at times. But it is vague, like a breeze among flowers. The wind passes, and the flowers are content." She also asserted: "Blindness has no limiting effect upon mental vision.

My intellectual horizon is infinitely wide. The universe it encircles is immeasurable."

Helen's story is usually told as that of one remarkable young woman who overcomes adversity through sheer force of will. It's also a story of the potential in every child — potential that too often goes unrealized because of circumstances out of the child's control. If Helen hadn't learned to read, communicate, and express her thoughts, if she had been committed to an institution, as many people with disabilities were in that time, we would have missed out on her brilliant mind and remarkable spirit. I thought of Helen when I played a small part as a young lawyer working for the Children's Defense Fund, helping convince Congress to pass legislation mandating that children of all abilities were entitled to a public education.

Helen's most thrilling adventures began where *The Miracle Worker* left off. After college, she set out to learn more about the conditions and lives of people with disabilities in America — a subject about which little was known — and quickly identified a connection between disability, exploitation, and poverty. At the time, the vast majority of people with disabilities were cut off from job opportunities or education, sidelined and marginalized in society. "For a time I was depressed," she said, "but little by little my confidence came back and I realized that the wonder is not that conditions are so bad, but that humanity has advanced so far in spite of them. And now I am in the fight to change things."

Contrary to some of the legends that surround her, Helen was not simply an inspiring individual focused on people with disabilities; she was an activist determined to build a more just, peaceful, and equitable world for everyone. She cofounded the American Civil Liberties Union (ACLU), in part to protect the rights of workers who were striking for better conditions and fair pay. Along with the other ACLU founders, she was a target of FBI surveillance. She was a socialist and a pacifist, a suffragist and a birth control advocate. ("The inferiority of women is man-made," she argued.) She spoke out against lynching and white supremacy and was a vocal supporter of the National Association for the Advancement of Colored People (NAACP).

Helen traveled the world, speaking out against fascism in Europe. In 1938, she wrote to the editor of the *New York Times,* urging the paper not to downplay or ignore Nazi atrocities. In 1948, she went to Japan as America's first goodwill ambassador after the war; there,

---

"Life is either a daring adventure, or nothing."
— HELEN KELLER

---

she helped bring attention to the country's blind and disabled population. At age seventy-five, she embarked on her most grueling trek yet: a forty-thousand-mile, five-month tour across Asia to bring encouragement and hope to people with vision loss and other disabilities.

Helen was famous from the age of eight until her death in 1968, and like most people in the public eye — particularly women — she was subject to criticism. She was accused of plagiarism, of being a mouthpiece for the views of the people around her, as though a young deafblind woman couldn't possibly hold and express her own opinions. When she spoke about her own life and struggles, she was celebrated. But when she spoke about politics and social issues, she was dismissed and belittled as being out of her depth. "So long as I confine my activities to social service and the blind, they compliment me extravagantly . . . but when it comes to discussion of a burning social or political issue, especially if I happen to be, as I so often am, on the unpopular side, the tone changes completely," she observed.

To some people, shocking though it may seem, she remains a controversial figure even today. I thought again about Helen's commitment to giving every child the chance to go to school when I heard in 2018 that the Texas State Board of Education had recommended eliminating lessons about both Helen and me

> *"I like frank debate, and I do not object to harsh criticism so long as I am treated like a human being with a mind of her own."*
> — HELEN KELLER

from American history classes in an effort to "streamline" the curriculum. I felt sorry that students in Texas would not be taught about Helen's extraordinary life and the impact she has had on so many others. When the board reversed its decision and reinstated us both, I was doubly happy. Her story deserves to be told again and again — the story not simply of an extraordinary little girl but of a woman who spent her life questioning why things were the way they were, and standing up for people who had no power.

MARGARET CHASE SMITH

HILLARY

When I was a little girl, my family subscribed to *Life* magazine, which came to our house every week on Friday. When I came home from school, I'd eagerly grab it and lie down on the floor in our living room to read it before I had to set the table for dinner. It was in those pages that I first encountered Senator Margaret Chase Smith, who was the first example I ever remember seeing of a woman elected official. Following her career — from the campaigns that led to her becoming the first woman to serve in both houses of Congress to her history-making candidacy for president of the United States in 1964 — shaped my understanding of politics and public service. She embodied the thrill of breaking barriers — and the challenges that come with being "the first."

Born and raised in Maine, Margaret discovered a passion for politics when her husband, Clyde Harold Smith, was elected to Congress. She campaigned for him and, after he was elected, joined him in Washington. During his first term, he became gravely ill, and Margaret stepped in to fill as many of his obligations as she could. She traveled back and forth between Washington and Maine, appearing at events on behalf of her husband. With Margaret's help, Clyde was reelected in 1938. His health, however, declined quickly. In the spring of 1940, he put out a statement urging his friends and supporters to stand behind Margaret if he could not run in the upcoming election. "I know of no one who has the full knowledge of my ideas and plans or is as well qualified as she is, to carry on these ideas and my unfinished work for my district." He died the next day.

Margaret easily won the special election to serve out her husband's unexpired term. At the time, most of the few women who served in office had been elected or appointed to fill a seat vacated by a husband or father. It was so common it even had a name: "the widow's mandate." Though she had never planned on it, Margaret was now the state's first woman member of Congress. ("Mrs. Smith Goes to Washington," read one headline.)

Taking office was one thing, but, as Margaret soon found out, *staying* there was another. The primary election for the next term was under way within a week of her taking office. She faced off against four male opponents, one of whom argued that, against a backdrop of the war in Europe and questions of America's role at home, there was just too much at stake to elect a woman to Congress. A local newspaper columnist agreed, sniping that the primary was at risk of hinging on a "question of sex" rather than "ability." But Margaret had already proved herself to the people of Maine, and she won.

Throughout her life, Margaret dismissed the idea that she was a feminist. She was a moderate, not a radical, and resented the idea that she or any woman should be treated differently because of their gender. "I never asked for any special privileges," she said later of her time in Congress. "And I can assure you I never got any." Still, she was a quiet and steadfast champion of policies advancing women's rights, equality, and dignity; I think she was a feminist even without claiming the label. Margaret voted again and again for the Equal Rights Amendment, even cosponsoring it in 1945. (What would she say about the fact that we still haven't passed it more than seven decades later?) Despite the critics who doubted that a woman could play a role in foreign policy, Margaret eventually served on the House Naval Affairs Committee. At the time, women who were part of the armed services were considered "volunteers" and didn't receive any benefits. Her signature piece of legislation was the Women's Armed Forces Integration Act, which led to the extension of benefits to all uniformed women in the military.

After eight years in the House, Margaret launched her campaign for the United States Senate. The Maine Republican Party was less than thrilled by her many votes across party lines, and they opposed her candidacy. Her opponents denigrated her in the press, suggesting that "the Senate was no place for a woman." She ran proudly on her experience in Congress, using the slogan "Don't trade a record for a promise." Right before the election, she was the victim of a smear campaign accusing her of being a Communist because she had supported the New Deal, the United Nations, the Truman Doctrine, and the Marshall Plan. With the help of a dedicated cadre of women volunteers who were the backbone of her shoestring campaign, Margaret Chase Smith won her election in a landslide.

When she entered the Senate, Margaret was clear-eyed about the reality of her humble position: She was a junior member and the only woman alongside ninety-five men. That didn't stop her from standing up for what she knew was right — even if it meant standing alone. When Wisconsin senator Joseph McCarthy used his position to launch a broad investigation of government employees and other Americans to root out Communists, whom he saw in every corner, Margaret was one of the first to sound the alarm over what she saw as dangerous demagoguery. His persecutorial tactics destroyed reputations and lives. Yet it became painfully clear that no other senator was going to speak out against him.

On the morning of June 1, 1950, she ran into Senator McCarthy on the "little Senate subway train" that would take her to the floor. She would remember their exchange for the rest of her life. Catching sight of her determined expression, McCarthy commented: "Margaret, you look very serious. Are you going to make a speech?" "Yes," she answered. "And you will not like it!"

> *"Mr. President, I speak as a Republican.
> I speak as a woman. I speak as a United
> States Senator. I speak as an American."*
>
> — SENATOR MARGARET
> CHASE SMITH

In her groundbreaking speech that day, she called out his hate and character assassination and the tactics he was using that became known as "McCarthyism." "Mr. President, I would like to speak briefly and simply about a serious national condition," she began. "It is a national feeling of fear and frustration that could result in national suicide and the end of everything that we Americans hold dear." She eviscerated McCarthy and called out her colleagues for their lack of courage in standing up to him. "I don't want to see the Republican Party ride to political victory on the Four Horsemen of Calumny — Fear, Ignorance, Bigotry, and Smear." She and six other Republican senators signed a statement expressing their concerns known as her "Declaration of Conscience." (McCarthy later mocked her and her cosigners as "Snow White and the Six Dwarfs." He would have been a natural on Twitter.) She continued to oppose McCarthy at personal and political cost for four more years, until 1954, when the Senate finally censured him for his conduct and ended his career.

With her seminal speech, Margaret captured the national spotlight. Reporters and prominent figures in Washington wondered whether she could run for vice president — or even president. Yet, as one reporter bemoaned, "It is considered doubtful that the country will see a woman head of state in the near or even distant future." (Unfortunately, they didn't know how right they were.)

Speculation mounted as to whether Margaret might launch an unprecedented run — would she or wouldn't she? In January 1964, her campaign manager drafted a speech to the Women's National Press Club with two endings: one announcing that she was in, one declaring she was out.

In her speech, she dryly detailed the reasons she had heard about why she should not run. "First, there are those who make the contention that no woman should ever dare to aspire to the White House — that this is a man's world and that it should be kept that way — and that a woman on the national ticket of a political party would be more of a handicap than a strength," she said that day. "Second, it is contended that the odds are too heavily against me for even the most remote chance of victory — and that I should not run in the face of what most observers see as certain and crushing defeat. Third, it is contended that as a woman I would not have the physical stamina and strength to run." (Ah,

> *"I have few illusions and no money, but I'm staying for the finish. When people keep telling you you can't do a thing, you kind of like to try."*
>
> — SENATOR MARGARET CHASE SMITH

memories!) She concluded with a twinkle in her eye: "So, because of these very impelling reasons against my running, I have decided that I shall." That day, she became the first woman to seek a major party's presidential nomination.

From the beginning, Margaret ran a scrappy, upstart campaign. Reporters were not kind to her: They commented on her hair, her figure, and her age. "Since my candidacy was announced, almost every news story starts off 'the sixty-six-year-old senator.' I haven't seen the age played up in the case of the male candidates," she pointed out.

At that year's Republican National Convention, she became the first woman to have her name put in nomination for the presidency. That night, delegates in the convention center carried signs reading "Smith for President" and "The Lady from Maine." Though Senator Barry Goldwater ultimately clinched the nomination, she sent a resounding message that resonated for many women, including me.

CHELSEA

One of my favorite fun facts about Margaret is that she wore a red rose in her lapel every day, gave them to her colleagues, and fought for years to have the rose declared the official flower of the United States. She faced staunch opposition from Senate Republican Leader Everett M. Dirksen, who argued that it should be the marigold. In 1987, long after her retirement, Margaret won this battle, and Congress designated the rose as the national flower.

Margaret lived to be ninety-seven years old. I included her in the video called "History Made" that played at the Brooklyn Navy Yard on June 7, 2016, when I reached the 2,383-delegate mark to become the Democratic nominee for president. I wanted more Americans to know about her. She has been on my mind even more than usual recently. I think often of her public example of courage in this time when her party seems to have lost its way. I can't help but think how much better off the Republican Party — and our country — would be if there were more like Margaret in public office today.

MARGARET BOURKE-WHITE

HILLARY

As I did with so many inspiring women from my childhood, I first met Margaret Bourke-White, the fearless photojournalist, in the pages of *Life*. From the moment I saw her photos and read the startling description of her as the "first female war correspondent," I was hooked. I wanted to learn more about the person behind the lens, who documented everything from Depression-era breadlines to the front lines during World War II.

Margaret was born in the Bronx just after the turn of the twentieth century, raised by parents who encouraged her to be brave and independent. Whenever her mother, Minnie, found out that one of her children had discovered a new interest, she would leave books on the subject around the house for them to find. Margaret's father, Joseph, an engineer, was interested in the burgeoning field of photography and printing. Margaret remembered him as "the personification of the absent-minded inventor. I ate with him in restaurants where he left his meal untouched and drew sketches on the tablecloth. At home he sat silent in his big chair, his thoughts traveling, I suppose, through some intricate mesh of gears and camshafts. If someone spoke he did not hear." As a little girl, Margaret followed him around while he took photographs, carrying an empty cigar box as her "camera" and helping him develop pictures in the family's bathtub. He brought her to factories and foundries, where she was awestruck by the heavy machinery and flying sparks.

Margaret was fascinated by her father's work. But she was more interested in looking at insects through a magnifying glass, collecting turtles and frogs, and poring over maps. "I pictured myself as a scientist," she said, "going to the jungle, bringing back specimens for natural history museums and doing all the things that women never do." After graduating from high school, she enrolled at Columbia University in New York to study art. That year, Minnie bought Margaret her first camera, a twenty-dollar Ica reflex with a cracked lens. Perhaps driven by her explorer's spirit, she bounced from school to school, never staying for long in one place or with one major: She studied art, swimming, dancing, herpetology, paleontology, and zoology. After six universities and one brief marriage, Margaret transferred to Cornell, her seventh; she chose it because she'd heard there were waterfalls on campus.

At Cornell, she discovered her calling. After struggling to find a part-time job to support herself, Margaret took the camera her mother had given her and used it to photograph the buildings on campus, selling the images to fellow students and the alumni newspaper. Soon she started getting calls from architects who wanted to know whether she was studying to become a photographer — something she had, up to that point, never considered. One day before graduation, she marched unannounced into the offices of York & Sawyer, a major architectural firm, with a folder full of her photographs, demanding an unbiased opinion of her work. She left assured that she had a future in architectural photography, if she wanted it.

After graduation, Margaret moved to Cleveland, her sights set on photographing the city's steel mills. Even though the mills were closed to women, she talked her way in with her camera. "Nothing attracts me like a closed door," she said later. "I cannot let my camera rest until I have pried it open." The same fascination with industrialization that she first experienced as a child was evident in her pictures, which provided an up-close look at a changing American economy.

Margaret's photos caught the eye of Henry Luce, the publisher of *Fortune* magazine, and she signed a part-time contract. The magazine eventually sent her to Germany, then to the Soviet Union. Though the latter was as closed to journalists as the Cleveland steel mills were to women, Margaret wouldn't take no for an answer. She lobbied the Soviet embassy in Germany for weeks, and the officials there finally relented; she became the first foreign photographer to gain unlimited access to the region in 1930.

Back in the United States, she signed on to a book project working with the writer Erskine Caldwell, who would become her second husband. It required the two of them to travel together for months on end. Margaret, used

> *"By some special graciousness of fate I am deposited—as all good photographers like to be—in the right place at the right time."*
> — MARGARET BOURKE-WHITE

to working on her own, didn't take kindly to Caldwell's instructions. They had barely left home when he tried to call off the trip because the two weren't getting along. Ultimately, Margaret felt the book was important and decided to do everything she could to make the project work. The end product was *You Have Seen Their Faces,* a book documenting people and families in the South.

In 1936, her photograph of Montana's Fort Peck Dam debuted on the first-ever cover of *Life* magazine. The stunning black-and-white image showed a towering concrete structure that looked almost like a castle, a symbol of economic revitalization during the Depression. Her photos were used not just as captivating images to supplement a story but to comprise the first photo essay. The issue sold out in hours, and the photograph would later become a postage stamp as part of a series about America.

While working as a staff photographer for *Life,* Margaret also spent time in Czechoslovakia and Hungary, photographing the rise of Nazism. She and Caldwell traveled through

Europe, recording the violence and anti-Semitism they saw. They worked in combat zones and, in 1941, traveled to the Soviet Union just as Germany was invading. As bombs exploded around them, Margaret and her husband hid from the officers who were evacuating residents, which allowed her to take the only photographs of the attack. Her book *Shooting the Russian War* is a candid behind-the-scenes look at her tour through China and the Soviet Union.

When Margaret returned to New York, she took a job at a local paper, at Caldwell's urging, that would allow her to stay close to home. But to her, the daily assignments and low-resolution snapshots were deeply un-satisfying. Though her husband pressured Margaret to have a child, she couldn't bear to give up her career or her independence, and she returned to *Life* (I'm grateful I didn't have to choose between my work and having Chelsea!). When she informed Caldwell that she was going back to England to photograph American B-17 bombers headed to war, he asked for a divorce.

Margaret became the first female war cor-respondent accredited by the U.S. military. When she learned about top-secret plans to invade North Africa, she sought permission to follow Allied troops. When the boat she was traveling on came under torpedo attack, Margaret escaped on a lifeboat, snapping photographs with the one camera she managed to rescue. She moved with American troops through Italy and Germany, reporting along the way. She later said she had never been as scared as she was on the front in Italy, with enemy fire raining down around her. When General Patton's troops marched across Germany in 1945, Margaret was there, too. She photographed the horrors of Nazi Germany and the liberation of concentration camps. She didn't tell anyone until after she returned that her father was Jewish, adding an even more painful dimension to what she saw. I recently came across this description of her by author Sean Callahan: "The woman who had been torpedoed in the Mediterranean, strafed by the Luftwaffe, stranded on an Artic island, bombarded in Moscow, and pulled out of the Chesapeake when her chopper crashed, was known to the *Life* staff as 'Maggie the Indestructible.'"

By the end of her career, she had photographed the Great Depression, the Dust Bowl, World War II, Gandhi in the midst of the struggle for Indian independence, and apartheid in South Africa. All told, she published eleven books.

Guided in part by her example, I declared in seventh grade that I wanted to be a journalist. I wrote a column for our school newspaper and visited the offices of one of the local Chicago newspapers for a school report. Although

I eventually decided on another path, Margaret's determination, her independence, and her fearless explorer's spirit left an impression that has stayed with me throughout my life.

Maria von Trapp

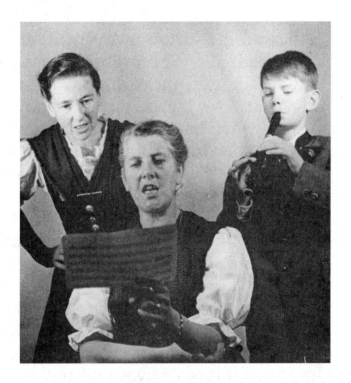

Chelsea

By the time I was five years old, I'd watched
The Sound of Music dozens of times. It was my
go-to when I wasn't feeling great, or if it was
my turn to choose our family Saturday-night
movie. From the opening scene, when Julie

Andrews as Maria is twirling about the hills, to the von Trapp family's escape over those same hills to freedom, I was mesmerized. By first grade, I knew all the words to every song and would often sing "So long, farewell, auf wiedersehen, goodnight" before going to bed. My dramatic flair wasn't confined to home. Playing on the playground at school, I would sometimes speak in an affected Maria/Julie Andrews voice. Thankfully, my best friend, Elizabeth, told me in the nicest possible way that I sounded silly. She probably saved me from untold amounts of teasing. I didn't stop imitating Maria — I just started to do it by myself, in my own backyard. (I still know the words to "My Favorite Things" and "Do-Re-Mi.") The more I learned about the real-life Maria, the more I looked up to her.

In the movie, although free-spirited Maria is committed to her life as a nun, the Mother Abbess suggests she might prefer life outside the walls of the abbey, and recommends her as a governess to Captain Georg von Trapp, a widower with seven children. Maria throws herself into her new job and life, bringing joy back into the children's lives and music back into their home. She stands up to Captain von Trapp, telling him that his children need fun and his love. And she fights for his love, too. Shortly after their beautiful wedding, filled with music from the nuns and smiles from all the children, the newly married von Trapps refuse to support the Anschluss, the German annexation of Austria. Though most Austrians supported their new occupiers, the von Trapps did not.

With every viewing I was on the edge of my seat. I don't think that's a metaphor — I remember actually being perched on the edge of our couch. I knew that in the end, the von Trapps would calmly sing their final concert, then hide in the abbey; that the sisters would take the oil out of the Nazis' cars; and that Rolf (erstwhile boyfriend of the oldest von Trapp daughter, Liesl) would do one right thing in his Third Reich uniform by not immediately exposing their hiding place. But I worried every time, hoping that this time, too, every member of the family would reach safety. Each time I watched the movie I thought of my friends whose grandparents had survived the Holocaust, and their family members who hadn't.

Inspired by Maria's bravery and the courage of the von Trapp children, as a child, I wrote President Ronald Reagan a letter in 1985. I had just turned five when I learned he was planning to visit a military cemetery in Bitburg on a trip to West Germany, to mark the fortieth anniversary of the end of World War II. I strongly believed an American president should not pay his respects on behalf of the American people at a place where Nazis were buried. So I wrote him a letter sharing my views, respectfully telling him that I knew the Nazis were "not very nice people" because I had seen *The Sound of Music.* (I also included a couple of my favorite rainbow and heart stickers on the letter and an entire additional sheet of my favorite stickers with the letter as a gesture of goodwill.) President Reagan never responded. I went to our mailbox every day for weeks to see if he had. I was so disappointed that no one wrote me back, but I was much angrier that President Reagan went to Bitburg. Afterward, he tried to justify his visit by explaining that he was there for only eight minutes. One was too many.

HILLARY

Because Chelsea didn't receive an answer, I made sure when we lived in the White House that we had a team of staff and volunteers dedicated to answering children's letters. I didn't want any other child to be disappointed like Chelsea had been. In fact, when Bill and I asked Chelsea in late 1992 what she hoped for from our move to Washington, the only thing she asked was for every child to get a response if they wrote to the president, the first lady, or the White House.

When I got older, maybe the summer after sixth grade, I read the real Maria von Trapp's book, *The Story of the Trapp Family Singers.* In some ways, the true story was even

86

more dramatic than the movie. The book described their unexpected encounter with Hitler while visiting Munich, and then their decision to flee. "We learned the shocking truth that 'home' isn't necessarily a certain spot on earth," she wrote. "It must be a place where you can 'feel' at home, which means 'free' to us." There was one development in which reality was slightly more mundane than the movie, though just as heroic: They left Austria not by trekking over the Alps but by boarding a train to Italy. "We did tell people that we were going to America to sing," said one of Maria's stepdaughters, coincidentally also named Maria. "And we did not climb over mountains with all our heavy suitcases and instruments. We left by train, pretending nothing." From the book, I learned that Heinrich Himmler, Hitler's head of the SS — the Nazi's elite paramilitary unit and the unit of some of those buried at the Bitburg cemetery — had later used the von Trapps'

"One of the greatest things in human life is the ability to make plans. Even if they never come true—the joy of anticipating is irrevocably yours. That way one can live many more than just one life."

— MARIA VON TRAPP

home as his local headquarters. Himmler also founded Dachau, the Third Reich's first concentration camp and the site where tens of thousands of Jews, homosexuals (as LGBTQ people were labeled then), political prisoners, Communists, and Jehovah's Witnesses were held and murdered.

The von Trapps' lives weren't all singing and heroism. In the book, Maria shared their family's financial struggles. "We are not poor," she wrote. "We just don't have any money!" Her children would later share that the real Maria wasn't always as sweet as Julie Andrews's character; in fact, she had a temper. "But we took it like a thunderstorm that would pass," said her stepdaughter Maria. "Because the next minute she could be very nice." The real-life love story was different from the movie, too. When Georg asked Maria to marry him, she was torn about whether to abandon her religious calling, until the other nuns urged her to follow what they saw as God's will and say yes. "I really and truly was not in love," she wrote. "I liked him but didn't love him. However, I loved the children, so in a way I really married the children . . . [b]y and by I learned to love him more than I have ever loved before or after."

My memories of Maria are now an amalgam of the movie, her memoir, and the time when Mom and I visited Salzburg the summer I was seventeen. In kindergarten and first grade, when I needed courage, I thought of Maria standing up to the Nazis, boldly risking so much in order to do what she knew was right and protect those she loved.

ANNE FRANK

HILLARY

On one of my regular visits to our local town library when I was around twelve years old, my favorite librarian told me I should read *The Diary of a Young Girl* by Anne Frank. She explained that Anne had been a Jewish teenager, not much older than I was, who wrote in her diary while hiding from the Nazis during World War II. I knew my father was a navy veteran of that war, that America and its Allies had defeated Nazi Germany and Imperial Japan, and that many millions of people around the world had been killed. I didn't know yet about the Holocaust and the deliberate plan by Hitler to exterminate Europe's Jews. Anne Frank's diary, and the 1959 movie based on it, were my first introduction to the horrors of the Holocaust.

Annelies Marie "Anne" Frank was born in Germany in 1929 but left with her family when she was four years old, after the Nazis took over. The family — her mother, Edith; her father, Otto; her older sister, Margot; and her cousin Buddy — settled in Amsterdam, but in May 1940, the Germans invaded the Netherlands, and the Frank family was trapped. The Nazis began to segregate and systematically discriminate against the Jews living there, forcing adults out of jobs and children out of schools. When Margot received a deportation

---

"The nicest part is being able to write down all my thoughts and feelings; otherwise, I'd absolutely suffocate."

— ANNE FRANK

---

order to a work camp in July 1942, the family went into hiding. They moved into rooms behind a door concealed by a bookcase in the building that held Otto's business. They couldn't take many possessions with them, but Anne brought with her a diary she had received for her thirteenth birthday and wrote in it throughout the two years of her hiding.

The Franks and the other Jews who joined them later in the "secret annex" were cared for and protected by a small group of Dutch citizens who had worked for Otto in his business. They provided food, protection, and news for two years. Anne called them "the Helpers" in her diary and wrote of their dedication in spite of the dangers they, too, faced if they were discovered.

The worst happened in August 1944: Anne and her family were betrayed, found by the Gestapo, and sent to concentration camps. The question of who tipped off the Nazis to the Franks' secret annex remains a mystery to this day. Anne and Margot were sent first to Auschwitz and then transferred to Bergen-Belsen, where they both died in early 1945.

Otto, the family's only survivor, returned to Amsterdam after the war and sought out the Helpers. One of them, his former secretary Miep Gies, gave him Anne's diary, which she had found and saved along with other papers. Otto worked to get the diary published first in Dutch and then in English in 1952.

What makes Anne's diary so special to me and millions of other readers is how honest she was. She described her sometimes ambivalent feelings about her parents and sister; her changing body and growing awareness of her sexual development; her first kiss with a young man in hiding with her; her frustrations at living in a cramped space and missing a regular life outside with her friends; her occasional fear and despair about the Nazis and the war. Anne's story became universal because she was an ordinary girl with extraordinary writing abilities who could connect with readers around the world.

Anne Frank's diary started out as a private record of her teenage thoughts and experiences and became one of the best-known accounts of facing the horror of war. Eleanor Roosevelt wrote the introduction to the first American edition and described it as "one of the wisest and most moving commentaries on war and human beings that I have ever read." John F. Kennedy spoke of her "compelling" voice. Nelson Mandela recounted how he had read the diary in prison and "derived much encouragement from it."

In 1999, *Time* magazine named Anne Frank one of "The Most Important People of the Century." "With a diary kept in a secret attic," they wrote, "she braved the Nazis and lent a searing voice to the fight for human dignity."

CHELSEA

During college, when friends would come and visit me in Washington, D.C., we always made a trip to the United States Holocaust Museum, where we would walk through every exhibit, then listen to the survivors' testimonies at the end. One of those friends was Mattie Johnstone Bekink. Many years later, Mattie was living in Amsterdam with her family when, tragically, she lost her four-day-old daughter, Elouisa. She found a renewed purpose when she began working with the Anne Frank House, supporting their mission of standing against anti-Semitism and all forms of bigotry, and championing human rights, freedom, and democracy. I'm inspired every day by her commitment to carrying on this important work in Anne's name — work she knows is vital to building the future she wants for her sons, and honoring the memory of their sister.

RIGOBERTA MENCHÚ TUM

CHELSEA

In fifth grade, my class read *I, Rigoberta Menchú: An Indian Woman in Guatemala*. Published in 1983, it's the first memoir I remember reading that had been written in my lifetime. Rigoberta writes of her experience as a young Quiché Indian in Guatemala who was exploited as a child in the fields and exposed to pesticides and horrific violence. We were lucky that we had teachers at Booker Arts Elementary in Little Rock who believed it was important that students knew about the daily injustice and horror faced in modern-day Guatemala by children, including Rigoberta.

Rigoberta's family couldn't afford food or other basic necessities. She watched her youngest brother die of malnutrition while the family was working for poverty wages on a coffee plantation. Motivated by her anger at his death, Rigoberta moved to Guatemala City and took a job as a maid in order to learn Spanish (and, later, other Mayan languages in addition to her native Quiché) and to understand more about her country and the world. Rigoberta believed that to be as powerful as she hoped to be for her community, she needed first to leave.

When she returned home, she learned that her father was in prison, accused of being part of a guerrilla force. She worked to free him and to help organize workers to fight for local indigenous rights, including protections and ownership of the land on which they toiled every day. After securing land ownership rights for her own community, Rigoberta advocated for indigenous rights across Guatemala. She also stood up against

> *"Only together can we move forward,*
> *so that there is light and hope for*
> *all women on the planet."*
> — RIGOBERTA MENCHÚ TUM

the gross human rights violations committed by the Guatemalan government and armed forces throughout the country's decades-long civil war. Even after one of her brothers was tortured and killed by the Guatemalan military and her father was killed during a protest, Rigoberta refused to give up her fight for human rights and meaningful reforms for indigenous people.

Forced into exile in 1981, Rigoberta went first to Mexico, then to France, where she met Venezuelan-French anthropologist Elisabeth Burgos-Debray. Elisabeth convinced Rigoberta to tell the story of her life; the tape-recorded interviews between the two of them became the basis for *I, Rigoberta Menchú*.

When her memoir was published two years later, Rigoberta wasn't yet twenty-five. While she had withstood immense personal loss — she would lose another brother to the regime's violence while in exile — and had already accomplished an extraordinary amount for someone so young, she knew her work wasn't finished. From exile, she continued to organize for indigenous rights and against the oppressive Guatemalan government. After the civil war ended in 1996, she worked to have the political and military leaders responsible for genocide against the indigenous community brought to justice; more than two hundred thousand people died over the course of the war, including many indigenous Guatemalans.

When Rigoberta's efforts were stymied in Guatemala, she looked to Spain, where the Rigoberta Menchú Tum Foundation filed a criminal complaint against former dictator General Efraín Ríos Montt and others. Finally, in 2005, a Spanish court ruled that genocide committed abroad could be prosecuted in Spain and called for the extradition of key members of the Guatemalan government during the civil war, including Ríos Montt. That gave momentum to efforts in Guatemala. In 2012, a Guatemalan court indicted and later convicted Ríos Montt of genocide, among other crimes. While that ruling was overturned, Rigoberta and her foundation continue to work to bring Ríos Montt and others to justice.

In 1992, while the civil war was still ongoing, Rigoberta was awarded the Nobel Peace Prize. As she was thrust onto the world stage, questions were raised about the authenticity of her autobiography. The *New York Times* reported that "based on nearly a decade of interviews with more than 120 people and archival research, the anthropologist, David Stoll, concludes that Ms. Menchú's book 'cannot be the eyewitness account it purports to be' because the Nobel laureate repeatedly describes 'experiences she never had herself.'" Scholars like Stoll suggested that the younger brother who had died of starvation never existed; that, contrary to her claim on the first page of the book that she "never went to school," she actually received a scholarship to earn the equivalent of a middle school education at a prestigious private boarding school.

The Nobel Committee dismissed the questions and said there was "no question of revoking the prize." Geir Lundestad, director of the Norwegian Nobel Institute, said "All autobiographies embellish to a greater or lesser extent." He explained that the decision to award the prize to Rigoberta was based not only on her autobiography but on her advocacy for Guatemala's indigenous people. Experts in the genre argued that her book was an example of *testimonio,* a method of blending personal and community history. *Testimonio* emerged out of common experiences between Latin America and solidarity movements in the United States. Its purpose was to help — even force — northern audiences, through storytelling, to understand a struggle they had not experienced firsthand.

At ten or eleven years old, I didn't know any of that; all I knew was what I read.

Rigoberta's book sparked an interest in Central America that never left me. Years later, in tenth grade, after we'd moved to Washington, D.C., I wrote my major research paper that year on the United Fruit Company's conspiracy with the United States Central Intelligence Agency (CIA) to overthrow Guatemala's democratically elected government under the guise of fighting the Cold War but really to protect United Fruit's banana monopoly. While the events in Guatemala in 1954 are not the origin of the phrase "banana republic" (coined decades earlier by the great short story writer O. Henry), they certainly could have been. The United States's actions in Guatemala were a particularly shameful chapter in American history (though in line with shameful behavior elsewhere at the time, from Iran to the Congo). I was proud of my dad when he apologized in 1999 on behalf of the United States for our country's role in the brutal Guatemalan civil war that took hundreds of thousands of lives from the mid-1960s onward, a war that might not have happened had democracy not been denied by U.S.-backed forces in 1954. I still cringe every time I am in Dulles International Airport — named after Secretary of State John Foster Dulles, whose brother, Allen Dulles, helmed the CIA in the mid-1950s.

Even with the criticism she faced, Rigoberta didn't retreat; she stayed in public life, returning to Guatemala to support Mayan communities and survivors of genocide and bring the perpetrators to justice. She went on to create WINAQ, the first indigenous-led political party. She ran for president of Guatemala twice, in 2007 and 2011. To this day, she continues to advocate for justice for the Mayan people in Guatemala and indigenous people everywhere.

JACKIE JOYNER-KERSEE AND FLORENCE GRIFFITH JOYNER

JACKIE JOYNER-KERSEE

FLORENCE GRIFFITH JOYNER

CHELSEA

When Jackie Joyner-Kersee was born in 1962, her parents named her after Jacqueline Kennedy. After all, as her grandmother announced: "Someday this little girl will be the

> *"I don't think being an athlete is unfeminine.
> I think of it as a kind of grace."*
> — JACKIE JOYNER-KERSEE

first lady of something." (Prescient words for the future first lady of track!) Her home in East Saint Louis, Illinois, was very different from the Kennedy White House in Washington, D.C. Jackie and her brother, Al, grew up across the street from a liquor store and a pool hall. At eleven years old, Jackie saw a man shot outside her house. Her parents wanted a different, brighter future for their children. Jackie focused on school, where she graduated in the top 10 percent of her class. And she didn't excel only in the classroom.

As a teenager, Jackie won the National Junior Championships in the pentathlon, a competition in five different track events. She would go on to win the title three more times. She set the Illinois high school girls' long jump record. In addition to track, she competed in volleyball and basketball. After graduation, she earned a scholarship to the University of California, Los Angeles. There, she competed in the long jump and on the basketball team. Even when she was a young woman, it was clear that Jackie's talent was bigger than any one event or even one sport.

In 1984, she made the Olympics, where,

despite a pulled hamstring, she won a silver medal in the heptathlon, her signature event. The heptathlon consists of seven events over two days: 100-meter hurdles, high jump, shot put, 200-meter dash, long jump, javelin, and 800-meter run. She would later become the first athlete to score over seven thousand points in the event. Jackie is the first person I remember watching throw a javelin or a shot put. It wasn't a man who defined these acts of precision and strength for me — it was Jackie.

Jackie's coach, Bob Kersee, believed in her, on the track and off. And in 1986, she married him. He told her, only half joking, that he wouldn't let her take his name until she set a world record. That year, at the Goodwill Games in Moscow, she did. At the 1988 Olympics, she set her fourth world record and won the gold medal in the heptathlon. At that same Olympics, Jackie's sister-in-law, Florence "FloJo" Griffith Joyner, broke the 100- and 200-meter world records. She still holds those records more than thirty years later; the men's record in the 100-meter, in the same period, has been broken twelve times. I cheered so hard for FloJo and Jackie from home in Little Rock that I went hoarse. Jackie's Olympic career didn't stop in 1988; four years later, in 1992, she became the first athlete to win the heptathlon in back-to-back Olympics.

Jackie and FloJo were both targets of those

who felt the need to demean the talent, skill, and strength of women athletes — particularly black women athletes — by suggesting they had resorted to steroids. Neither ever failed a drug test. FloJo passed eleven in 1988 alone. "I do not take steroids," Jackie said. In fact, having grown up around substance use disorders and addiction, she made it clear that she stayed away from drugs and alcohol altogether. In her journal the year she was publicly accused, she wrote that there was nothing she could do to change other people's opinions of her. "I questioned whether maybe it was the work of the devil, trying to distract me from what I can do, testing my faith. But deep down, I knew I didn't do anything wrong." In the meantime, she kept doing what she did best: working hard and competing. She refused to let others' doubts discourage her.

Before she became an Olympian, FloJo was asked by a teacher what she wanted to be when she grew up. She answered: "Everything." FloJo brought her everything to all she did, on and off the track. When she had to leave college to help support her family, she worked as a bank clerk and part-time hair stylist, training at night when she could. She qualified for two Olympics, winning her first medal, a silver, at the 1984 Los Angeles Games. She won three golds at the 1988 Seoul Games, running with her gorgeous six-inch-long nails painted red, white, blue, and gold. After she stopped racing, FloJo continued to support young athletes and became a fashion designer. Both were continuations of her life and work, since she'd started making her own track uniforms in high school. She died tragically young, at the age of thirty-eight, of an epileptic seizure. Her legacy is one of speed, style, and determination. And she remains, deservedly, to this day, the Fastest Woman in the World.

After Jackie retired from Olympic track, she played professional basketball, devoted even more time to the foundation she had started for at-risk youth, and encouraged other athletes to dedicate their time and talents, when not competing, to helping others. She understood that while talent is universal, opportunity is not, and she has spent her life trying to level the playing field so more young people can be "everything."

■ ■ ■ ■

EDUCATION PIONEERS

■ ■ ■ ■

SOR JUANA INÉS DE LA CRUZ

CHELSEA

When Juana Inés de Asbaje y Ramírez de Santillana, later known as Sor Juana Inés de la Cruz, was born in mid-seventeenth-century Mexico, at the time still part of Spain, educated girls were a rarity, even privileged ones like her. Still, as a girl, Juana was hungry for knowledge. She would hide in the chapel of her family's estate to read as often as she could, borrowing books from her grandfather's library next door; she would later claim to have read all the books he had.

While not much is known about Juana's early life, we do know that she wrote a poem at eight and, around the same time, was sent to live in Mexico City with extended family. She left behind her mother, who continued living more than thirty miles away. We also know that Juana always dreamed of going to college. As university degrees would not be awarded to women in Mexico for more than two hundred years, Juana begged her family to let her enroll dressed as a man. They refused.

When she was thirteen, Juana entered into service as a lady-in-waiting to the wife of the viceroy of New Spain. Juana's intelligence was

---

"Yo no studio para saber más,
sino para ignorer menos."

*"I don't study to know more,
but to ignore less."*

— SOR JUANA INÉS
DE LA CRUZ

---

unmistakable, and a year after she had joined the viceroy's court, a series of scholars tested her on questions of literature, history, math, and more. Juana so impressed them that she and her intellect became well known throughout Mexico.

Wanting to further her studies, and not wanting to get married, Juana took the only path available to her: She became a nun and joined the Convent of the Order of Saint Jerome. She seemed to struggle with the idea of blind faith, writing, "Can I not be saved while learning? Why would salvation need to come through the path of ignorance if that is repugnant to my nature?" In the end, she decided religious education was "the least disproportionate and most honorable decision I could make." In the convent, Sor Juana had a study and library of her own, and time to read, write poetry and plays, and talk with other scholars (all men) at the nearby university. She wrote essays, plays, and passionate love poems to María Luisa, the wife of the new viceroy. "Loving you is a crime," she wrote, "for which I never shall atone."

Like so many other outspoken women throughout history, she attracted her share of detractors. In 1690, more than twenty years after she entered the convent, Sor Juana wrote a letter criticizing a recent Jesuit sermon. The letter was published without her permission by a high-ranking bishop, and Sor

Juana was criticized both for the letter's contents and for focusing on nonreligious themes in her poetry. She responded to the furor with her now-famous "Respuesta a Sor Filotea de la Cruz" ("Reply to Sister Filotea of the Cross"), which is recognized today as the first articulation of a woman's right to education in the Americas.

Although she endured intense backlash for "Respuesta" and various priests demanded that she renounce her work and studies, Sor Juana continued writing. In her poem *Hombres Necios* (*Foolish Men*), Sor Juana responded, line by line, to the impossible double standards to which men hold women. ("You think highly of no woman," she wrote, "no matter how modest: if she / rejects you she is ungrateful, / and if she accepts, unchaste.") And in her poem "Primero Sueño" ("First Dream"), she described the soul's quest for knowledge, making clear that it's not only men whose souls thirst to understand more. As a nun, she also scandalized audiences with her lyric poems celebrating physical beauty: "I shall not play the slenderness / Of your fine, exquisite torso / For the bend of your waist is as / Troubling as a trill in the song."

Throughout her life, Sor Juana defied expectations. In her forties, she sold the four thousand books she owned, as well as her musical instruments, and donated the proceeds to charity. In 1695, while taking care of fellow nuns who were sick with the plague, Sor Juana fell ill and died.

In "Respuesta," she wrote that "God has given me the gift of a very profound love of truth." That love of truth and knowledge was a dangerous trait for a woman in the 1600s. Sor Juana was hundreds of years ahead of her time, something she may well have known then. Her extraordinary life has been the subject of multiple books, plays, and films, and people in Mexico see her face every day on the two-hundred-peso note, a constant reminder of a woman who believed her intelligence was something to be cultivated, valued, and admired — never downplayed or apologized for.

Margaret Bancroft

Chelsea

In mid-nineteenth-century America, there were few opportunities for young people with disabilities to go to school. Prejudice abounded, and the public and private schools that did exist were generally focused on more privileged white deaf and blind children.

One person who recognized these inequities was Margaret Bancroft. Born in 1854, Margaret always loved school. After she graduated from the Philadelphia Normal School, she became a fifth grade public school teacher. She was beloved by her students and took a particular interest in children who had trouble studying. Rather than write them off, she figured out why they were struggling; some had vision impairments, deafness, or cognitive challenges. She often consulted with doctors to identify the best way to tailor her teaching to the individual needs of her students. The way she saw it, it was a teacher's responsibility to find the best ways to educate children with disabilities — not a child's or a family's. When one of those same doctors suggested she start a school of her own, she boldly announced that she planned to resign in order to do so. Members of her school board tried to convince her to stay; one man told her that it was selfish for such a talented teacher to waste her potential on students who were less worthwhile. Margaret reportedly replied that every child deserved to learn.

Margaret fiercely believed in the potential of all students to learn, as long as they had the right environment, with dedicated attention, patience, and compassion. In 1883, she founded the Haddonfield Training School, which took an innovative approach, emphasizing nutrition, exercise, and sensory and artistic instruction — elements that were far from standard at schools for the deaf and blind, or even more "conventional" schools.

At a time when most children with disabilities were excluded from schools, hidden away by their families, and even institutionalized, Margaret's approach was radical. And while she was encouraged by others who shared her vision, she also faced derision from people who shared the sentiments of her previous board members: that some kids simply weren't worth the effort.

Margaret was undaunted, even when only one student enrolled for the first semester at her new school. Anxious though she must have been, she persevered. Enrollment quickly grew, and by 1892, she had to move to a larger space. Though it was a boarding school, Margaret did not keep students confined to campus. Haddonfield students went on nature

---

"Above all, we need a more optimistic spirit, a more affirmative point of view in handling our exceptional children. There is too much of a tendency to pronounce difficult cases hopeless, and to pack them off to the custodial schools."

— MARGARET BANCROFT

---

trips and visited museums and the circus. She wanted her students to see the world; she refused to believe any of them were "hopeless." Margaret provided a loving home, as well as methods of treatment that were years ahead of their time. And she got results: Children and adults with severe disabilities were able to get the support they needed to thrive in school, stay in their communities, and eventually get jobs.

In 1898, Margaret reincorporated her school as the Bancroft Training School. She didn't only teach students, she also trained teachers. Some of those teachers stayed at Bancroft, while most eventually left, taking Margaret's ethos and methodology to other schools across the country. Many of the subsequent leaders in the early twentieth century of special education trained under Margaret.

Beyond Bancroft, Margaret urged the medical establishment to change their approaches to treating patients with disabilities. At a speech to the Women's Medical College of Pennsylvania in 1907, she championed the idea that medical students had a responsibility to treat everyone regardless of ability. She advocated for schools for deaf and blind children to take a more individualized approach to education. In her writings, she also pushed for eliminating terms like "idiot" and "imbecile" completely, and for children and adults with disabilities to have a place in society.

She hosted the first meeting of the Haddon Fortnightly, a women's club, to help support women's educational and social interests beyond their homes. Haddon Fortnightly still exists. So does Bancroft, which continues to focus on serving a diverse population, from young learners through senior citizens, at outpatient, day, and residential programs. It has an especially illustrious history of producing many Special Olympians. Margaret Bancroft dared to reinvent the possible for children with disabilities — and the impact of her work continues to this day.

Juliette Gordon Low

HILLARY

The Girl Scout motto is simple: Be prepared. According to a version of the handbook published the year I was born, "A Girl Scout is ready to help out wherever she is needed.

Willingness to serve is not enough; you must know how to do the job well, even in an emergency." I couldn't have put it better myself. It's no wonder I found my way to the Girl Scouts.

Though it has been decades since I hung up my sash, I still remember all the songs. ("Make new friends, but keep the old. One is silver, and the other's gold.") Many of my most joyful moments on the campaign trail, as first lady, as senator, and as secretary of state have revolved around getting to spend a few minutes catching up with a gaggle of girls eager to show me their badges. Plenty of people who have never been a Girl Scout are familiar with the camping trips, the service projects, and, of course, the cookies. The Girl Scout cookie program is the biggest "girl-led business" in the world, with two hundred million boxes sold every season. (Thin Mints are the most popular variety, according to the organization's official reports — no surprise there. My mother always *loved* Thin Mints, and kept them in the freezer as a special treat.)

So just where, exactly, did it all start?

Juliette Magill Kinzie Gordon, better known to friends and family as Daisy, was born on October 31, 1860, in Savannah, Georgia. As a little girl, Juliette was sensitive, curious, compassionate, and adventurous. She suffered from ear infections and injuries when she was young, which left her hard of hearing.

On her wedding day, a grain of rice thrown by an overzealous guest got lodged in her "good" ear, leading to a painful infection. In the process of removing the rice, her eardrum was punctured, and she would spend the rest of her life almost completely deaf. (Later, she was known to exaggerate her deafness when friends tried to back out of their commitments to do work for the Girl Scouts.)

On a trip to England, Juliette met Lord Robert Baden-Powell, the founder of the Boy Scouts. He told Juliette that when he first formed the organization, six thousand girls registered. He wasn't about to have them traipsing across the country with his Boy Scouts, but he wanted to start a similar offering for girls. With Lord Robert and his sister, Agnes, Juliette helped set up some of the first troops of "Girl Guides" in Scotland and London. She showed characteristic foresight in a letter to her father, gushing: "I like girls, I like this organization and the rules and pastimes, so if you find that I get very deeply interested you must not be surprised!"

When she came home to America, Juliette made a fateful call to her cousin, Nina Anderson Pape, a teacher who would become the local commissioner of the Girl Scouts. Juliette didn't beat around the bush: "I've got something for the girls of Savannah, and all of America, and all the world, and we're going to start it tonight!" Over the next few weeks, they convened a small troop of eighteen girls who met at Juliette's house. As the girls mastered various skills (cooking, first aid, bicycling), they earned the coveted badges. Walter John Hoxie, a famous naturalist and a friend of Juliette's, helped organize one of the organization's first camping trips. A year later, the organization changed its name to the Girl Scouts and published a handbook, entitled *How Girls Can Help Their Country*. In the handbook were diagrams showing how to splint an arm, step-by-step instructions for how to extinguish a gasoline fire, lists of different knots, notes on civics, media literacy ("Wherever you go you will have the choice of good or bad reading, and as reading has such a lasting effect on the mind, you should try to read only good things" — that's advice that stands the test of time.), athletics, cooking, and more.

> " 'Stick to it,' the thrush sings. One of the worst weaknesses of many people is that they do not have the perseverance to stick to what they have to do. They are always wanting to change. Whatever you take up, do it with all your might, and stick to it."
> — *HOW GIRLS CAN HELP THEIR COUNTRY: THE 1913 HANDBOOK FOR GIRL SCOUTS*

Though she stopped short of getting involved in the budding suffrage movement, there is no doubt that Juliette believed in educating girls and giving them a sense of power. Years before women could vote, serve on juries, or open a line of credit in their own name, she wanted girls to learn career development, leadership, self-sufficiency, and financial literacy (described in an early handbook as "thrift"). She was an ardent supporter of sports for girls, believing that competition was not only healthy but necessary to development. She did a headstand and a cartwheel each year on her birthday just to prove she could still keep up with her Scouts.

When World War I broke out, Juliette got involved, and so did the Girl Scouts. They volunteered as ambulance drivers, rolled bandages, sold war bonds, planted gardens, and even stepped in for overworked nurses during the Spanish flu epidemic. Through it all, they kept growing. It was during the war years that the first Girl Scout cookies were sold. In 1917, they published their own magazine, called *The Rally.*

In addition to being a firm believer in the potential of every girl, Juliette was a prodigious fund-raiser. When attending a fancy luncheon, she would trim her hat with leftover vegetables from her garden, forgoing the traditional flowers. When her fellow guests raised an eyebrow, she would exclaim: "Oh, is my trimming sad? I can't afford to have this hat done over. I have to save all my money for my Girl Scouts. You know about the Scouts, don't you?" Even after she was diagnosed with breast cancer, she kept fund-raising and promoting the Girl Scouts.

Today, Juliette's family home is a historic landmark. There are schools, camps, and scholarships named after her. Her face has appeared on a postage stamp, and there was even an opera about her life. She was posthumously awarded the Presidential Medal of Freedom in 2012, a century after the Girl Scouts were founded.

CHELSEA

I loved being a Brownie and was honored to take part in the Girl Scouts' hundredth-anniversary celebration in 2012. There is no one better to lead the organization today than their current CEO, Sylvia Acevedo, who is a Brownie-turned-rocket scientist. She has used her background as an engineer to solve problems from disparities in education to lack of access to necessities like eyeglasses, toothbrushes, and books. Under her leadership, the Girl Scouts are creating new badges in the sciences, civics, and more. I'm excited to continue cheering on the Girl Scouts in their second century.

According to the organization, fifty-nine million American women alive today were part of the Girl Scouts growing up. Venus and Serena Williams are Girl Scout alums. So are Katie Couric, Barbara Walters, and Robin Roberts. My friend and fellow secretary of state Madeleine Albright was a Girl Scout. Former Girl Scouts are governors and astronauts. Fifty-eight percent of women elected to the 116th Congress were Girl Scouts. Juliette couldn't have known everything her Scouts would go on to achieve, but I like to think it's exactly what she had in mind. At a time when it was a radical concept, Juliette believed that girls really could help their country — that is, as long as they were prepared.

Maria Montessori and Joan Ganz Cooney

MARIA MONTESSORI

JOAN GANZ COONEY

Chelsea

Growing up in late nineteenth-century Italy, Maria Montessori was encouraged by her mother to pursue her studies, including in higher education — a rarity for Italian women at that time. Over the objections of her father, she studied medicine at the University of Rome. Although she confronted antagonism and harassment from her male colleagues and professors, in 1896 she graduated with the highest honors and became one of Italy's first women doctors.

A physician specializing in pediatrics, Maria was an early advocate for children's rights, including the right to an education. Refusing to accept the prejudice and cynicism of those who believed that differently abled children could never learn, Maria wrote to the relevant authorities to advocate for special classes and schools. Her persistence was rewarded in 1899 when she was appointed as a counselor to the newly created national league dedicated to the protection of children with disabilities. The following year, the league opened its first school to train teachers, complete with a laboratory classroom. Students in that first year's class passed the so-called normal school's year-end exam, and the new schools' efforts were deemed a success.

Over the next few years, Maria created

> *"Now, what really makes a teacher is love for the human child; for it is love that transforms the social duty of the educator into the higher consciousness of a nation."*
> — MARIA MONTESSORI

a new system of education and, in 1907, opened her first preschool, Casa dei Bambini (Children's House), in the low-income San Lorenzo neighborhood of Rome. The Casa's teachers would demonstrate a task, then encourage the students to complete the same task on their own. Rather than requiring children to simply listen, as other Italian schools did in the early twentieth century — Maria was a vocal critic of schools where "children, like butterflies mounted on pins, are fastened each to his place" — Casa dei Bambini helped children direct their own learning through "free choice." They were encouraged to explore using all their senses and to help clean up after they were finished, to leave the space clear for the next child's discovery.

"The world of education is like an island where people, cut off from the world, are prepared for life by exclusion from it," she said of traditional Italian education. It seemed obvious to Maria that allowing children to learn from their surroundings was a much better approach. Maria's pedagogy was not haphazard:

She had researched and analyzed how brains acquire and store information. For Maria, her strategy, heralded as being more humane and child-centered, was the clear outcome of science. The success of students in that first school inspired her to open many more schools, and the Montessori Method became a standard approach in Italian education.

In 1909, Maria published her first book, and it was quickly translated into many languages. (Its English title was succinct: *The Montessori Method*.) By 1911, there were Montessori schools across Western Europe and in the United States. At the 1915 Panama-Pacific International Exposition in San Francisco, she showed her approach to early education in a "glass classroom" that allowed passersby to watch young students making their own choices and working with intense focus. The following year, Maria expanded to elementary schools and explored how best to extend her method to older children.

In 1922, the Italian government appointed Maria the country's inspector of schools, quite a few of which were by then Montessori schools. In 1934, after years of growing fascism and the Italian government's alignment with Hitler's Germany, Maria left her beloved home country to live in Sri Lanka, Spain, and eventually, the Netherlands, where she died in 1952.

Today there are an estimated twenty

thousand Montessori schools around the world, including thousands in the United States. I went to a Montessori preschool and adored it. (My favorite lessons were about the cicadas and our careful — and respectful — explorations of their shed skin.) It took guts to revolutionize what education could mean, particularly for the youngest learners and differently abled children. It's not surprising that Maria won multiple recognitions in multiple countries and was thrice nominated for the Nobel Peace Prize. She pioneered an approach that, for the first time, embraced the idea that children are creative, curious, and eager to learn, and deserve to be treated as individuals. As she reportedly said: "The greatest gifts we can give our children are the roots of responsibility and the wings of independence."

Hillary

Born fifty-nine years after Maria and six thousand miles away in Phoenix, Arizona, Joan Ganz Cooney would also revolutionize children's education — through a very different means.

Joan started out in the early 1960s as a television producer, working on documentaries for educational station Channel 13 in New York. She later explained that she was influenced by Father James Keller's Christopher Movement, which called on people of faith to apply their principles to the world around them. "Father Keller said that if idealists didn't go into the media, nonidealists would," she recalled.

Joan's first programs were dedicated to teaching the public about major issues. One day in 1967, she went with her boss to a meeting at the Carnegie Corporation to discuss whether television could not only inform adults, but help prepare young children for school. When the idea of a study on the subject came up, Joan's boss answered for her: She wouldn't be interested in that. But Joan exclaimed, "Oh yes I would!" She traveled across America for her study, talking to experts and observing children. "Children all over the country were singing beer commercials," she said. "So it wasn't a question of 'could it teach,' the question was 'could it teach something of potential use to children.'" In her report, "The Potential Uses of Television in Preschool Education," Joan proposed a show like *Sesame Street*.

The report helped make a case for foundations and the U.S. Department of Education to contribute $8 million to fund a new company, the Children's Television Workshop. In the male-dominated fields of scholarship and television, people worried that the new project wouldn't be taken seriously with a woman in charge. Though it had been her study and her idea, Joan had to sit down and write a list of names of men who could be considered for the job. "I was told that if they chose one of them that I would be number two," she remembers. "And I said, 'No, you don't understand. I won't be number two.' It was absolutely what I was born to do, and I knew it." She successfully overcame the skepticism to become the executive director when *Sesame Street* premiered on PBS on November 10, 1969.

Sesame Street was a hit with kids and parents alike. The newspapers called her "Saint Joan" and said a miracle had occurred for children, who were learning their ABCs and 1-2-3s with the help of catchy songs and characters like Oscar the Grouch. Chelsea especially loved Big Bird as a little girl, and I loved watching her light up when she learned a new word thanks to *Sesame Street*.

Of course, even a beloved show like *Sesame Street* had its detractors. Six months after it premiered, a state commission in Mississippi voted to ban the show from airing on public television. One of the commission members leaked the story to the *New York Times,* explaining that "some of the members of the commission were very much opposed to the series because 'it uses a highly integrated cast of children'" and that those members felt that Mississippi was not yet ready for it. Joan called their decision "a tragedy for both the white and black children of Mississippi." After public outcry, Mississippi was forced to reinstate the show after banning it for twenty-two days.

Joan remained in her position until 1990 and served on the Children's Television Workshop board for years afterward. I served for a few years on the board alongside her, where I saw firsthand Joan's dedication to educating children. When asked about her "legacy" a few years ago, Joan scoffed, "A legacy is when something's over; this just keeps going." She's right: *Sesame Street* is still going strong, and so is Joan.

Joan helped revolutionize children's television in the 1960s, and she isn't finished yet. *Sesame Street* is now in more than 150 countries, and Sesame Workshop is bringing play-based learning to hundreds of thousands of children in refugee camps and communities around the world. In 2007, Sesame Workshop created the Joan Ganz Cooney Center, a research lab that is now studying how to design entertaining and engaging educational programming for children using digital media.

Both Maria and Joan had to fight for the chance to follow their passion into higher education and a meaningful career. It can't have been easy. But they were determined to do it anyway, and because they did, the world of education has never been the same.

MARY McLEOD BETHUNE

CHELSEA

By the time she was nine years old, Mary McLeod could pick 250 pounds of cotton a day; that would make about five hundred T-shirts today. Although Mary was born in

1875, after slavery, for many black Americans, bondage didn't end with the Emancipation Proclamation or after the Civil War.

Even after they were freed, Mary's parents, Patsy and Samuel McLeod, worked for years for their former master. Eventually, they earned enough money to buy five acres of the land made profitable only by their labor; on that land, Mary's father and brothers built the cabin in which she would be born. After Mary's birth, her parents continued to work in the fields; her mother also took in white people's washing, including that of her former master's family. Mary would go with Patsy as she made laundry deliveries. In white people's homes, Mary wondered about the toys and books white kids had, once asking herself if "the difference between white folks and colored is just this matter of reading and writing." On one visit, a white child told her that she wasn't supposed to read and should not touch the books. "When she said to me, 'You can't read that — put that down,' it just did something to my pride and to my heart that made me feel that someday I would read just as she was reading," Mary later said.

It wasn't until almost two decades after the Civil War that Mary's hometown of Mayesville, South Carolina, had a school open to black students. Emma Wilson, a black missionary who founded the school, asked the McLeods if they wanted to send their children. They could afford to send only one, and they decided on Mary. She walked five miles each way to make it to class and home again. After school, she would often teach her family what she had learned that day, then do her homework by candlelight.

Impressed by Mary, Ms. Wilson selected her to receive a scholarship to further her studies at Scotia Seminary in North Carolina. Mary left home when she was thirteen years old. After graduating from Scotia, she received a scholarship to the Moody Bible Institute in Chicago. Mary dreamed of being a missionary in Africa. But when she applied, the Presbyterian Mission Board rejected her application, informing her that there were no opportunities for black missionaries in their programs. Mary decided to return to Mayesville and took a job teaching at the school she had once attended. She would go on to teach at several schools across the South; while working in Augusta, Georgia, she met Albertus Bethune, whom she would marry in 1898.

The Bethunes moved to Florida in 1899, and Mary started selling insurance to support her family. Five years later, Mary realized a long-held ambition: She opened her first school, the Daytona Literary and Industrial Training School for Negro Girls. Without the support of a church or wealthy benefactor, Mary had to raise the funds to build and support the school herself, while working on its curriculum and hiring faculty. She purposefully opened her school in a poor neighborhood of a city where Jim Crow segregation was the law and a state where black Americans were routinely lynched. Surrounded by racist violence, she wanted to give black children a chance to get the education she believed all children deserved.

Initial enrollment at Mary's school was five girls, each of whom paid fifty cents a week. Within two years, there were 250 students. She also began offering night classes for black adults, particularly women, who wanted to learn to read and write. She would later focus on teaching exactly what was needed to pass the literacy tests required to vote.

As demand grew, Mary realized she needed more space — something that would

---

"There can be no divided democracy, no class government, no half-free county, under the constitution. Therefore, there can be no discrimination, no segregation, no separation of some citizens from the rights which belong to all. . . . We must gain full equality in education . . . in the franchise . . . in economic opportunity, and full equality in the abundance of life."

— MARY MCLEOD BETHUNE

---

require more money than she could raise through tuition, or selling homemade pies, another job she took on to support the school. She began raising money from wealthy white families, asking for donations from those who came to Daytona for the winter months. Looking for additional support, she also traveled the country; she won over the Gambles, the Rockefellers, and the Carnegie Foundation. Mary then leveraged her wealthy white supporters to fight for full accreditation so her school could offer middle and high school.

In 1920, the Ku Klux Klan threatened Mary, but she made it clear she and her school weren't moving. In 1923, Mary began the process of merging her school with the Cookman Institute for Men in Jacksonville to form what is now Bethune-Cookman University. Mary became the first black woman to serve as president of a historically black college and university (HBCU), and Bethune-Cookman remains the only HBCU founded by a black woman.

Even though she is best known for her work in education, Mary confronted racism and segregation anywhere she saw them. When hospitals in Daytona refused to care for black patients, she opened the McLeod Hospital and the McLeod Training School for Nurses. Not until the 1960s would black patients be legally integrated into Daytona's public hospital system. Even then, black patients continued to receive substandard care.

After the ratification of the Nineteenth Amendment, Mary led voter registration drives, working to register black women to vote. The hateful, racist attacks she encountered during her drives only made Mary more determined to work on a national level to champion black women. In 1924, she was elected president of the National Association of Colored Women's Clubs, where she was vocal in her support for expanding vocational training to black Americans. This put her at odds with Ida B. Wells, the great journalist, advocate, and anti-lynching activist, who criticized Mary's narrow focus. Wells argued that "to sneer at and discourage higher education would mean to rob the race of leaders which it so badly needed . . . all the industrial education in the world could not take the place of manhood."

In 1935, Mary founded the National Council of Negro Women to help connect black women and organizations across the country. In 1936, at Eleanor's encouragement, President Franklin Roosevelt appointed Mary as director of the Division of Negro Affairs at the National Youth Administration, a New Deal agency focused on providing work and education to young Americans. (By the end of her life, Mary would have worked for or served on committees under five American presidents.) In 1938, she helped organize the first National Conference on Negro Women at the White House, and two years later, she was elected the vice president of the National Association for the Advancement of Colored People (NAACP).

During World War II, Mary served as assistant director of the Women's Army Corps (WAC), which served to facilitate women's official involvement in the war effort. She ensured that the WAC would be open to black women and that units would be integrated — at least on paper. In practice, only some WAC units accepted black women. (The army itself wouldn't adopt a policy of integration until 1948, after the war, and wouldn't enforce that policy for many years to come.) Mary also fought to include black pilots in the Civilian Pilot Training Program, a government-sponsored effort to increase military preparedness, and lobbied government officials, including President Roosevelt, on behalf of black women who wanted to enlist in the military. She would later organize the first officer candidate schools for black women to provide the training needed to earn an officer's commission.

During this period, Mary was again the target of the Ku Klux Klan and other racists for championing black Americans' rights and opportunities. Once again, she ignored their attacks and continued her work. She cofounded the United Negro College Fund, which has since supported more than 450,000 college students.

Toward the end of her life, Mary wrote her last will and testament. The words are inscribed on the side of her memorial statue in Washington, D.C. I remember visiting the statue in high school and reading her words: "I leave you love. I leave you hope. I leave you the challenge of developing confidence in one another. I leave you a thirst for education. I leave you a respect for the use of power. I leave you faith. I leave you racial dignity. I leave you a desire to live harmoniously with your fellow men. I leave you a responsibility to our young people."

HILLARY

Her memorial statue was unveiled on July 10, 1974, which would have been Mary's ninety-ninth birthday. Approximately eighteen thousand people from all over the country came to witness this historic occasion. At the unveiling, Cicely Tyson read Mary's last will and testament, and Representative Shirley Chisholm spoke about how Mary had inspired her. The statue was the first monument of a black woman to be placed in a public park in Washington, D.C. — and, sadly, one of very few still to this day.

In 2018, amid a national outcry over the continued existence of monuments to Confederate traitors, the Florida legislature voted to replace the statue of Confederate General Edmund Kirby Smith in the National Statuary Hall Collection at the U.S. Capitol Building with one of Mary McLeod Bethune. She became the first black American chosen by any state to be commemorated in the collection.

ESTHER MARTINEZ

CHELSEA

Before Christopher Columbus arrived in Hispaniola in 1492, an estimated three hundred distinct indigenous languages were spoken across what is today the United States and Canada. But when Esther Martinez, a member of the Pueblo people whose Tewa name was P'oe Tsawa, was born in 1912, indigenous languages in the United States were already in steep decline — the consequence of purposeful efforts to eradicate them under a system of brutal colonization. After spending her early years in Colorado, Esther became one of the Native American children sent to schools with the objective of aggressive assimilation. At her school in New Mexico, Esther was punished harshly for speaking her native Tewa. The efforts to suffocate her Tewa didn't succeed. When she graduated from high school in 1930, Esther still knew that her native language had immense value.

After raising her ten children with her husband, and supporting her family by working as a janitor and in other service jobs, Esther went to work at a middle school in San Juan Pueblo — now known as Ohkay Owingeh — New Mexico. A chance meeting with linguist Randall Speirs in the 1960s helped her find her life's purpose. "He went up and spoke to her in our Tewa language," said Esther's grandson Matthew Martinez Jr. "She was stunned and taken aback, how this white guy could crisply pronounce the language."

Speirs encouraged Esther to document her language, and he taught her the fundamentals of linguistics. Working with Speirs and her

> *"Stories were told to teach us tips for survival and for socialization in the community. They were fun. Our whole life is about storytelling."*
> — ESTHER MARTINEZ

family, she helped compile the first Tewa dictionary. It was an involved, painstaking process. "When my grandfather said something that I didn't know," she said, "I would ask him and he would write it on a paper. It took me a long time." She also translated, for the first time, the New Testament into Tewa, and a traditional Tewa children's story, "Naughty Little Rabbit and Old Man Coyote," into English. She later wrote a book of many stories translated from Tewa.

Esther began teaching Tewa at Ohkay Owingeh Community School; she would eventually become its director of bilingual education. It was a very different environment from the schools she had attended as a girl in Santa Fe and Albuquerque decades earlier; its philosophy today is "Don't teach me my culture; use my culture to teach me." Esther's work as a teacher was widely recognized, and she won multiple awards, including from the National Council of American Indians and the New Mexico Arts Commission. In addition to her teaching, Esther embraced her role as a tradition bearer for her pueblo, giving advice to families, helping parents choose traditional names for their children, and sharing Tewa stories in their original language.

Her storytelling took her around the country, from schools to national parks. She also shared her knowledge generously with linguists, other academics, and anyone who believed in the importance of Tewa. In 2006, the National Endowment for the Arts made Esther a National Heritage Fellow. She was killed in a car accident shortly after the ceremony.

HILLARY

Less than three months after Esther's tragic death, President George W. Bush signed the Esther Martinez Native American Languages Preservation Act, providing new funding for the preservation of Native languages. I was honored to support the bill while I served in the Senate.

When Esther was just a child, the people who were supposed to educate her tried to take Tewa from her. It took bravery to defy those efforts, and a love of her culture to preserve Tewa and ensure that it didn't disappear. Thanks to her legacy, multiple efforts to preserve, document, and expand Native languages have received federal support through the Esther Martinez Native American Languages Preservation Act; it is a small fraction of what is needed to undo the centuries of targeted destruction. Today, approximately 150 Native North American languages remain actively spoken across the United States, but many of those languages are spoken by only a few thousand or a few hundred people. The best way to respect Esther's work would be for the United States government to fully fund all efforts to preserve Native languages, and revive those that haven't been spoken in decades or even centuries.

DAISY BATES

HILLARY

In her memoir, Daisy Bates wrote about learning as a young child that her mother, Millie Riley, had been raped and murdered by three local white men in the small south Arkansas town where they lived. Daisy was only a few months old at the time. Knowing about both her mother's murder and the failure of local police to pursue the killers fueled an anger inside Daisy, as well as a desire for vengeance that led her to identify and silently confront one of the men when she was just eight years old. He begged her to leave him alone, and later drank himself to death and was found in an alley.

After the murder of her mother, Daisy was raised by her father's close friends Orlee and Susie Smith. Her father fled town to protect his own safety; Daisy never saw him again. But her adoptive father saw something in Daisy that worried him. According to Daisy, he gave her this advice on his deathbed when she was a teenager: "You're filled with hatred. Hatred can destroy you, Daisy. Don't hate white people just because they're white. If you hate, make it count for something. Hate the humiliations we are living under in the South. Hate the discrimination that eats away at the South. Hate the discrimination that eats away at the soul of every black man and woman. Hate the insults hurled at us by white scum — and then try to do something about it, or your hate won't spell a thing." Those words guided her in the years to come.

Daisy married Lucius Christopher Bates, known as L. C., in 1942, when she was twenty-seven; together, they moved to Little Rock and started the *Arkansas State Press,* a weekly statewide newspaper. The paper quickly became a voice for civil rights, and in 1952, Daisy was elected president of the Arkansas Conference of the NAACP, a position she used to advocate strongly for the desegregation of schools. Even though the U.S. Supreme Court decided in the landmark 1954 case *Brown v. Board of Education* that segregated schools were illegal under the Constitution, schools in Arkansas refused to enroll black children. Owing to her position with the NAACP and her newspaper's strong stand for immediate desegregation, Daisy endured harassment and death threats, while the newspaper faced financial loss when white advertisers boycotted it.

During one of the racist assaults on her home, Daisy later recalled, "two flaming crosses were burned on our property. The first, a six-foot gasoline-soaked structure, was stuck into our front lawn just after dusk. At the base of the cross was scrawled: 'GO BACK TO AFRICA! KKK.' The second cross was placed against the front of our house, lit, and the flames began to catch. Fortunately, the fire was discovered by a neighbor and we extinguished it before any serious damage had been done." Despite the dangers, when the time came for courageous leadership, she was ready.

In 1957, Arkansas governor Orval Faubus defied a court order to desegregate Little Rock Central High School, and his defiance became the center of the nation's attention in the struggle over integration. In response to Faubus's actions, the *Arkansas State Press* printed a front-page editorial that read, "[I]t is the belief of this paper that since the Negro's loyalty to America has forced him to shed blood on foreign battle fields against enemies, to safeguard constitutional rights, he is in no mood to sacrifice these rights for peace and harmony at home."

Before the start of the school year in September, nine black students were selected to attend Central High School, and Daisy Bates became their guide and adviser. On September 2, Faubus called out the Arkansas National Guard to stop the Little Rock Nine, as the students were known, from attending their first day of school. Only white students were permitted entry, and the Little Rock Nine were told to go home. But one student, fifteen-year-old Elizabeth Eckford, had been separated from the other eight. She walked right into the mob that was threatening to kill the black students. I remember, as a child, seeing the photos of her calmly walking past screaming white protesters, some of whom were spitting at her.

Daisy quickly recruited local ministers to escort each student to school. She reassured their worried parents every day. She served as a sounding board for the students and continued to advocate for enforcing the federal court order and respecting the Constitution. Her home became a center of activity and was later designated a National Historic Landmark. As the Park Service explains in its description of her landmarked house, "[T]he perseverance of Mrs. Bates and the Little Rock Nine during these turbulent years sent a strong message throughout the South that desegregation worked and the tradition of radical segregation under 'Jim Crow' would no longer be tolerated in the United States of America."

The chaos at Central High School led President Dwight D. Eisenhower, in late September, to federalize the Arkansas National Guard, removing them from the governor's control, and send in troops from the 101st Airborne Division to enforce the court's order. Meanwhile, the Little Rock police arrested Daisy and other NAACP leaders and charged them with failing to provide information about other NAACP members, which they continued to refuse to do. They appealed the fines and arrests all the way to the Supreme Court, where they eventually won.

In a 1976 interview, Daisy said the most important contribution she made during the Little Rock crisis was the very fact that the kids got in, and remained at Central for the full year without being physically hurt. "That opened a lot of doors that had been closed to Negroes, because this was the first time that this kind of revolution had succeeded without a doubt," she said. Dr. Martin Luther King Jr., lauded her for adhering to nonviolence in pursuit of the goal of integrating schools. In a letter to Daisy, he wrote: "History is on your side."

But Daisy and her husband paid a price for her activism. The loss of advertising led to the closing of the *Arkansas State Press* in 1959. Daisy moved to New York City, where she wrote her award-winning memoir, *The Long Shadow of Little Rock*. She later worked in Washington, D.C., on anti-poverty programs during the Lyndon Johnson administration.

Daisy moved back to Arkansas in 1965 and retired a few years later. After L. C.'s death, Daisy revived the newspaper in 1984, and died in Little Rock in 1999. I met with Daisy throughout my years in Arkansas and as first lady; she always kept fighting to make a difference for young people, especially in her home state. On September 25, 1997, both Bill and I were honored to speak at the fortieth anniversary of the desegregation of Little Rock Central High; that was the last time I saw Daisy.

It took guts for Daisy to do what she did — to choose to hate injustice while having enough faith in people to hope that they would ultimately do the right thing. It was a loss when she passed, but her legacy lives on. Just last year, new audiences were able to see the Little Rock Nine's story in an off-Broadway play, *Little Rock,* that I went to with Bill and our friend Ernest Green, one of the Little Rock Nine. In 2019, governor Asa Hutchinson of Arkansas signed a bill to replace a statue of a white supremacist in the U.S. capitol building with one of Daisy Bates, making her the second black American chosen by a state to join the collection, alongside fellow education trailblazer Mary McLeod Bethune. As we continue to confront racism and segregation in our public schools, we must remember Daisy's example.

Patsy Mink, Bernice Sandler, and Edith Green

PATSY MINK

BERNICE SANDLER

EDITH GREEN

Believe it or not, when I was in high school, I played basketball. We didn't have an interscholastic league, but it was a big school — about five thousand students — so there was a lot of competition. But in those days, girls' basketball meant half-court basketball. We either played offense or defense, and could run only as far as the center line before we had to stop and go back in the other direction. The prevailing wisdom was that running back and forth the full length would be dangerous for girls' health and well-being.

Today girls not only play on the full court but have more opportunities than ever to excel in sports and in school. None of this would have been possible without Title IX. And Title IX wouldn't have been possible without three women who had one door after another closed in their faces, only to kick them wide open.

Patsy Mink was born in 1927 on the island of Maui, the granddaughter of Japanese immigrants who came to Hawaii to work the sugar plantations. Her father revered Franklin Delano Roosevelt, and Patsy used to sit under the mango trees in the backyard, listening to the president's fireside chats on the radio. She played basketball for Maui High School, though she was, of course, never allowed to play full court.

After the Japanese attack on Pearl Harbor

> *"No person in the United States shall, on the basis of sex, be excluded from participation in, be denied the benefits of, or be subjected to discrimination under any education program or activity receiving Federal financial assistance."*
>
> — TITLE IX OF THE EDUCATION
> AMENDMENTS ACT OF 1972

in 1941, local authorities began arresting prominent Japanese Americans and holding them for questioning. Patsy's father, a civil engineer, was taken away in the night. Though he returned home the next day, it cast a shadow over their family. More than one hundred thousand Japanese Americans would ultimately be forced into internment camps between 1942 and 1945. Patsy never forgot the sight of her father burning his Japanese mementos. "It made me realize that one could not take citizenship and the promise of the U.S. Constitution for granted," she later said.

As a high school senior, she became her school's first female student body president — the prelude to what would be a lifetime of firsts. After finishing high school as valedictorian, Patsy graduated from the University of Hawaii in 1948, then decided to apply to medical school. She received more than a dozen rejections, despite knowing she was just as qualified as any male candidate. "It was the most devastating disappointment in my life," she later recounted. She then decided to apply to law school, and was one of two women accepted to the University of Chicago. She later found out she had been accepted by mistake, designated as an "international student" despite the fact that Hawaii was a territory of the United States. After graduation, she returned home to learn that government officials would permit only Hawaii residents to take the bar exam required to practice law there. Though Patsy had been born and raised in Hawaii, her husband had not; her marriage perversely made her a nonresident. She fought for her right to take the exam and won.

Interviewing for jobs presented yet another hurdle. Patsy was turned away from one firm after another and advised to stay home with her young daughter. Frustrated, she decided to start her own practice. For her first case, she accepted a fish as payment. She never intended to run for office, but the indignity

---

"Women have a tremendous responsibility to help shape the future of America, to help decide policies that will affect the course of our history."
— REPRESENTATIVE PATSY MINK

---

of being denied a job simply because she was a mother changed her outlook. She won her first race for a Hawaiian territorial House seat by going door-to-door and talking to voters — something we might call "the old-fashioned way" today, though it was far from a common tactic at a time when many politicians were simply born and raised into political families. She eventually ran for the United States Congress and won in 1964, becoming one of thirteen women serving at the time.

When she arrived in Washington, Congresswoman Mink endured a barrage of sexist and racist stereotypes that still sound all too familiar today. Newspapers described her as "diminutive" and "exotic" and accused her of neglecting her child in order to pursue a career. She dealt with it head-on. When a reporter asked her how she balanced being a wife and a congresswoman, she calmly responded: "I think that's the most offensive question that's ever asked. I've never heard anyone ask a man, 'How has it been on your family?'"

In Congress, she saw herself as representing not only the people of Hawaii but also the women of America. Along with her small but mighty group of fellow congresswomen, she protested being barred from the all-male congressional gym. (Patsy later explained that what she really wanted was use of the swimming pool, where male members of Congress liked to swim nude. "Is it too much for the democratic process to ask you to put your pants on?" she asked.) She introduced the first federal child care bill, as well as legislation to support bilingual education, student loans, special education, and Head Start. She was an outspoken proponent of women's rights, civil rights, and the environment, and opposed the Vietnam War.

She knew from personal experience that what is right is not always popular. She lost her fair share of elections — for U.S. Senate, for governor of Hawaii, for mayor of Honolulu, even for president of the United States. Determined to serve, she sat on the Honolulu City Council, then ran for governor and mayor before winning back her congressional seat in 1990. Driving everything she did was the belief that government can and must make people's lives better. But of all her many accomplishments, the one she is perhaps best known for is being one of the principal authors of Title IX.

Like Patsy Mink, Bernice "Bunny" Sandler, who was born a year later in Brooklyn, New York, grew up hearing a chorus of voices telling her what girls should and shouldn't do. As she has said, she'd become so accustomed to it that she never would have called it upsetting or unfair — until the time came to apply for a job. Bernice had been teaching part-time at the University of Maryland while finishing her doctoral work in education. Yet she was informed that once she finished, she wouldn't be considered for any of the half dozen permanent positions in the department. Confused, she asked a faculty member why not. His answer stayed with her for the rest of her life: "Let's face it," he said. "You come on too strong for a woman."

His comment was laughable in its bluntness, but Bunny wasn't laughing. "I went home and cried," she said. At home, she recalled every time she had spoken out in class or in a department meeting. Over the next few months, she experienced a string of similar rejections: The research executive who spent nearly an hour explaining that he never hired women because when their children got sick, they wouldn't be able to come in to work. The counselor at an employment agency who glanced at her résumé and informed her that she was "not really a professional" but "just a housewife who went back to school."

It wasn't until her husband said the words that she realized what was happening to her had a name: sex discrimination. She started doing her research. One day, reading a report on the impact of anti-discrimination laws on racial discrimination, she came across an executive order from President Johnson prohibiting any federal contractor from discriminating on the basis of race, color, religion, or national origin. Then she noticed the footnote: It said that the executive order had been amended to ban discrimination based on sex.

"Even though I was alone, I shrieked aloud with my discovery," she said. "I had made the connection that since most universities and colleges had federal contracts, they were forbidden from discriminating on the basis of sex." So began a national campaign. In 1970, she filed a class action complaint against all universities and colleges in America, on behalf of all women in higher education. She pulled together eighty pages of background material. At the time, many colleges held women to a tougher admissions standard, or imposed a quota on how many they would accept — like the Cornell School of Veterinary Medicine, which admitted two women a year, regardless of the number of applicants. Some barred women altogether. Female students had a curfew, while male students could stay out as late as they wanted. At the time, all of this was completely legal.

At Bunny's urging, Representative Edith Green from Oregon held the first congressional hearings on the education and employment of women. As a young woman interested in science, Edith had been discouraged from pursuing a career as an electrical engineer because of her gender. Financial hardship led her to drop out of college (she would eventually return and graduate), so she was dedicated to making education affordable and accessible for all. Her background and passion for education, particularly as a former educator herself, led Edith's colleagues to affectionately refer to her as "Mrs. Education" and the "Mother of Higher Education." In her remarks opening the hearings, she got right to the point. "Let us not deceive ourselves," she said sharply. "Our educational institutions have proven to be no bastions of democracy."

For the next seven days, women members of Congress testified about the discrimination they had experienced. With the help of Representatives Mink and Green, Title IX was drafted, passed, and signed into law in 1972 by President Nixon, requiring equal opportunities for boys and girls in education. It would take nearly five more years before the law was enforced. In the process, they had to take on university administrators and their fellow congressmen who claimed the bill would force schools to build unisex locker rooms and admit equal numbers of male and female students. After the bill passed, Representative Green mused, "I don't know when I have ever been so pleased, because I had worked so long and it had been such a tough battle."

"A woman has to work twice as hard as a man to prove that she can do the job."
— REPRESENTATIVE EDITH GREEN

Nearly fifty years later, Title IX has transformed educational opportunities for generations of women and girls. In 1972, women comprised 9 percent of law school students; today they're more than half. Since the passage of Title IX, girls' participation in high school sports has increased by more than 900 percent. Before Title IX, there were only 700 girls participating in high school soccer programs in the United States; now there are more than 390,000. Anyone who loved cheering the U.S. women's national soccer team on to their fourth World Cup win has Title IX to thank. And Title IX has shaped the sport worldwide: The UK, Chile, Jamaica, New Zealand, Nigeria, Scotland, Spain, Thailand, and Canada all had players on their 2019 Women's World Cup teams who trained in the United States. Though the fight for fair treatment continues: Players on the U.S. women's team will earn about $250,000 each in prize money for winning the World Cup, while players on the men's team would have been paid $1.1 million. The message was unmistakable when, after the final match, the stadium erupted with the best chant of the game: "Equal pay! Equal pay!"

CHELSEA

We've definitely come a long way since your half-court basketball days, Mom! After the hundredth (or more) time my friend

Elizabeth and I had played basketball in her driveway as kids, and I had lost yet again, I finally accepted that I had no talent for the game. But that didn't diminish my later enthusiasm for the remarkable women of the Women's National Basketball Association (WNBA). In April 1996, during my junior year in high school, the NBA announced that it was launching a women's league, the WNBA, the following year. Players Lisa Leslie, Rebecca Lobo, and Sheryl Swoopes were all at the press conference. These three phenomenally talented women had won multiple awards in their college careers and would go on to be Olympic teammates that summer at the Atlanta Olympic Games. Less than a month into the new WNBA's inaugural season, Lobo became the first player to win one hundred consecutive games. Her streak would stretch to 102. I've always loved that Rebecca approached sportswriter Steve Rushin to ask him why he had mocked women's basketball in the pages of *Sports Illustrated*. (He "joked" that he'd snored through a WNBA game and thus had slept with 7,138 women in a single night.) Rebecca corrected him, pointing out that they got 15,000 fans at Madison Square Garden, and he admitted he'd never actually been to a game. She invited him to see the Liberty play; he accepted, and less than two years later, they got married.

Our work is far from finished. Women's sports still receive only a sliver of media coverage. The gains in participation still leave too many girls behind, especially young women of color, girls from immigrant families, girls with disabilities, and students from low-income families. And too many women athletes, even when they do have the opportunity to compete, are often paid much less or subjected to a damaging double standard when it comes to behavior. This is especially true of women of color — just ask Serena Williams. But the story of Title IX and the triumph of its "godmothers" remind us that strength in women is an asset to be cultivated, not a character flaw to be overcome.

Ruby Bridges Hall

Hillary and Chelsea

Hillary

Ruby Bridges was only six years old in 1960 when she was escorted by federal marshals past a crowd of angry, hate-filled white protesters into William Frantz Elementary School in New Orleans. She was the first ever — and, for the next year, the only — black student.

Ruby was born in Tylertown, Mississippi, the same year that the Supreme Court ruled in *Brown v. the Board of Education* that racially segregated schools were unconstitutional. In 1958, her family moved to New Orleans, where she attended a segregated school until the district was ordered by a federal court to integrate. Ruby was one of only six students to pass the "test" the district came up with to prevent black students from entering white schools. Ruby's mother encouraged her to take advantage of the opportunities that would be afforded her at the previously all-white William Frantz Elementary. Even though her father warned her that it would be daunting, Ruby showed up at her new school on a warm November day after having been forced to miss the first month of school because of the state legislature's efforts to keep schools segregated.

The picture so common in modern history books is in black-and-white, making it seem much older than a mere six decades ago: A small girl in a neat dress, carrying a book bag, her head held high, descends the steps of her new school surrounded by grown men in suits. Out of the camera's eye is a jeering crowd of white adults and children protesters, carrying signs reading "We Don't Want to Integrate" and "All I Want for Christmas Is a Clean

> *"Racism is a grown-up disease and we must stop using our children to spread it."*
> — RUBY BRIDGES HALL

White School." Instead of learning with the other students, Ruby spent most of that first day in the principal's office with her mother, prevented from getting to her classroom by the chaos in the halls. Norman Rockwell later depicted the moment in his painting *The Problem We All Live With,* considered an iconic image of the civil rights movement.

The rest of that first year wasn't much easier. Protests against integration continued across the city. Ruby's father eventually lost his job. Angry segregationists repeatedly showed up at Ruby's school, determined to drive her away; they never succeeded. Her mother was turned away from local stores, and her grandparents lost their land. Ruby remained determined to get the education she deserved. Only one teacher was willing to teach Ruby: Barbara Henry, who had moved from Boston to the South in hopes of helping to integrate the schools. They studied together, alone in a classroom.

Chelsea

Eventually, the protests died down. Other black students enrolled in William Frantz

Elementary over the following years. Ruby went on to graduate from a desegregated high school in the area. She worked as a travel agent and consistently advocated for racial equality in and out of the classroom. She stayed in touch with Dr. Robert Coles, a Harvard child psychiatrist who had begun counseling her in 1960. Inspired by their conversations, he published a children's book, *The Story of Ruby Bridges,* in 1995. Four years later, Ruby published her memoir, *Through My Eyes,* and, also in 1999, she started the Ruby Bridges Foundation, which works to eliminate racism in schools through community service. She and her husband still live in New Orleans, where they raised their four children, and where a statue of Ruby stands outside of William Frantz Elementary.

I first learned about Ruby Bridges at Horace Mann, the junior high school I attended in Little Rock. Horace Mann had previously been the all-black high school that Ernest Green and other members of the courageous Little Rock Nine attended before integrating Little Rock Central High School in 1957. Our teachers took the school's legacy seriously, and taught us about desegregation in Arkansas and across the country. What we didn't learn then — and I wish we had — was how segregated our schools still are, the result of many racist legacies, including white flight and redlining, a form of housing discrimination. Solving this injustice requires dedicated research and resources. It will take policies and action at the federal and local level to address everything from enrollment, curriculum, and discipline in schools to housing and transportation. Just as important, as many have pointed out, it requires the political will from our elected leaders to create good schools that are truly integrated.

In 2001, my father awarded Ruby the Presidential Citizens Medal. Her warmth and youth, even then (she was in her forties) were a reminder of just how much we asked of her at such a young age — to take a stand not just for her own right to an education but for the rights of millions of black Americans, with her head held high. Decades later, she remains a believer in the power of love and one person's ability to make a positive difference. "I now know that experience comes to us for a purpose," she has said, "and if we follow the guidance of the spirit within us, we will probably find that the purpose is a good one."

MALALA YOUSAFZAI

HILLARY AND CHELSEA

One of the women whose story has stuck with us since we first heard her name is Malala Yousafzai, the young Pakistani woman who was shot in the head in 2012 by Taliban fighters for her conviction that girls deserved to go to school. After surviving the shooting, she went on to finish high school and attend university, and continues to speak out about the difference that education can make in the lives of girls everywhere.

Malala's father, Ziauddin Yousafzai, raised his daughter to be brave and determined. Ziauddin is an educated man who could have left Pakistan with his family. Instead, he used his education for the advancement of his community in the Swat Valley in Northwest Pakistan. He realized the greatest need was to educate women and girls, so he started a girls' school, despite the local Taliban banning girls from getting an education. One of his students was his daughter, Malala.

By the time she was two and a half years old, she was sitting in classrooms with ten-year-olds, following along, and loving every minute. From the moment she learned to read, she loved books. She carried a Harry Potter book bag and read biographies of Benazir Bhutto, the late prime minister of Pakistan and the first woman in modern history to lead a Muslim nation, and Barack Obama. She often quoted a line from her favorite book, *The Alchemist:* "When you want something, all the universe conspires in helping you to achieve it."

When the Taliban began shutting down

> *"They thought that the bullets would silence us. But they failed. And then, out of that silence came thousands of voices. Weakness, fear, and hopelessness died. Strength, power, and courage were born."*
> — MALALA YOUSAFZAI

the schools in Pakistan, as they had done years earlier in Afghanistan, Malala's father kept speaking out. His young daughter began speaking out as well, saying that she had a right to hold a pencil in her hand, to learn to express her views and dreams just like anybody else. She went to protests with her father, once running up to a local reporter and asking to be on his show. "All I want is an education, and I am afraid of no one," she told his audience. At eleven years old, she gave a speech in front of the national press called "How Dare the Taliban Take Away My Basic Right to an Education." She blogged anonymously for BBC Urdu about life under Taliban rule. Later, in a TED Talk, her father said: "Don't ask me what I did, ask me what I did not do. I did not clip her wings."

When the Taliban couldn't shut down the school because her father was so courageous, and when they couldn't shut up Malala because she had learned to speak for herself, they boarded her school bus and tried to kill her.

Nine months later, still recovering from her injuries, she was back in school and speaking at the UN. For strength and good luck, she wore a shawl that had belonged to Benazir Bhutto. It was Malala's sixteenth birthday; as she spoke, her family watched proudly from the audience.

Today the Malala Fund raises money to support girls' education around the world. Malala is a student at Oxford University, where she is learning to balance school and work, occasionally starting assignments the night before they're due after staying up too late talking with friends, and championing the rights of the 130 million girls around the world who are out of school. Malala believes there has never been a more opportune time to take up the cause. "Everywhere you go today," she wrote in an essay for *Vogue,* "you see feminist T-shirts and hashtags — 'The future is female,' 'Girl Power,' 'Who runs the world?' — but if we really believe this, we need to support girls on the front lines of this fight. . . . Whether you're a feminist or an economist — or just a person who wants to live in a better world — you should want to see all girls in school." She concluded with her trademark optimism and certainty: "If one girl with an education can change the world, just imagine what 130 million can do." If Malala can continue finding new ways to champion girls everywhere, so can we all.

EARTH DEFENDERS

MARJORY STONEMAN DOUGLAS

CHELSEA

Marjory Stoneman Douglas published her first piece at sixteen and never stopped writing. As a young woman, she helped care for her sick mother, a concert violinist, after her parents' divorce, while also pursuing her studies. Like my mom, she went to Wellesley College and was very active on campus, notably in the women's suffrage movement. Unlike my mom, she graduated with a perfect grade point average!

In 1915, in her midtwenties, after her mother passed away and after her own divorce, she followed her father to Florida. (Her ex-husband may or may not have been officially separated from his last wife and spent time in jail for writing bad checks shortly after marrying Marjory. "I left my marriage and all my past history in New England without a single regret," Marjory said later.) In the then small town of Miami, her father published what would become the *Miami Herald*. While Marjory's initial job was as a society columnist, she quickly began to cover other topics, including women's rights, civil rights, and nature — notably, the Florida Everglades, the only subtropical preserve in North America. The conventional wisdom at the time, in the 1910s, was that the Everglades weren't particularly special. Marjory set out to convince people otherwise.

Marjory loved her job, and she cared deeply about her country. The following year, she joined the Naval Reserve and then the Red Cross to help care for World War I refugees. After the war, Marjory wrote for the paper and for other publications as a freelancer. She tackled issues related to public health, urban planning, women's suffrage, civil rights, and Prohibition, and also wrote essays, plays, and books. In the early 1940s, she found what would be the work of the second half of her life: celebrating and preserving the Everglades. She was even more determined that Floridians would recognize how special the Everglades are. She worried that Floridians didn't understand what was at stake: a vital, unique ecosystem and their own health. Today, one out of every three people in Florida depends on the Everglades for their drinking water.

In the summer of 2018, I read her seminal work, *The Everglades: River of Grass*. Published in 1947, the same year the Everglades opened as a national park, Marjory argued that the Everglades is not a swamp but a river. She made a forceful case that its exceptional environment of plants and animals merits protection. Her beautifully written and illustrated book grew out of extensive study and reporting on the Everglades. It took her five years to research and write.

HILLARY

I first heard about Marjory through our alma mater, Wellesley College. She had graduated with the title of class orator, which turned out to be very apt! I wanted to meet her, so on a trip to Miami in January 1992, I visited her at her home in the Coconut Grove neighborhood. I arrived late in the afternoon to see the "Grandmother of the Glades." At the time, she was 101. As our visit started, she informed me that she always had a glass of scotch at five p.m. and asked me to join her, which I did.

In 1993, my husband awarded her the Presidential Medal of Freedom for her conservation work. She wanted to accept it in person despite how hard travel was for her, so we invited her to come a day early and stay at the White House to rest up and prepare for the ceremony. I'll never forget the night Marjory spent in the White House at 103 years old! It may well be that she was the oldest person to sleep in the White House. I've always thought it fitting that students at her namesake school are following her lead in doing their part to build a better, safer America. She and they are an inspiration.

Marjory didn't stop her advocacy after publishing *River of Grass* — far from it. She continued working to protect Florida's wetlands, taking on developers, industrial farms, and the U.S. Army Corps of Engineers. I think Marjory's straight-talking, no-nonsense approach would resonate today, as would her gutsiness. She once said in an interview that the tension between nature and humans' interactions with it "is an enormous battle between man's

> *"I am neither an optimist nor a pessimist. I say it's got to be done."*
> — MARJORY STONEMAN DOUGLAS

intelligence and his stupidity. And I'm not at all sure that stupidity isn't going to win out in the long run."

Still, Marjory clearly had faith in us to ultimately do the right thing for nature and ourselves. Otherwise, I don't think she would have worked as tirelessly as she did. We're hurtling toward a tipping point in being able to prevent catastrophic global warming and its consequences. Whether we succeed in mitigating the effects of our coming climate catastrophe or not will hinge on how we treat our natural resources, something Marjory understood throughout her remarkable 108 years.

Rachel Carson

Hillary

Some trace the rise of the modern American environmental movement to 1966, when toxic smog descended on New York City over Thanksgiving, killing more than 150 people.

Others point to 1969, when the Santa Barbara oil spill — the third largest in U.S. history — turned Southern California's beaches black. Still others reference the day that same year when the Cuyahoga River in Cleveland, choked with pollution and slick with oily industrial waste, caught on fire. But before these catastrophes hit the headlines, there was a book, and there was the woman who wrote it.

Rachel Carson was born in 1907 and grew up on her family's small Pennsylvania farm. She knew from the start that she wanted to be a writer, and she published her first short story when she was eleven years old. She spent her childhood exploring the meadows, orchards, and woods around the farm, and although she lived hundreds of miles from the ocean, she began to daydream about the sea, imagining it in her mind's eye.

She was a voracious reader and graduated at the top of her high school class before attending the Pennsylvania College for Women (now Chatham University) in Pittsburgh. She first studied English but soon changed to biology. On a summer research trip to Woods Hole, Massachusetts, she saw the ocean at last.

Rachel earned a master's degree in zoology from Johns Hopkins but stopped short of getting her doctorate when her father died unexpectedly in the middle of the Great Depression. Rachel had already been

> "We stand now where two roads diverge. But unlike the roads in Robert Frost's familiar poem, they are not equally fair. The road we have long been traveling is deceptively easy, a smooth superhighway on which we progress with great speed, but at its end lies disaster. The other fork of the road—the one less traveled by—offers our last, our only chance to reach a destination that assures the preservation of the earth."
>
> — RACHEL CARSON,
> FROM *SILENT SPRING*

supporting her parents, her older sister, and her sister's two daughters on a lab assistant's salary; now, as the family's sole wage earner, she went to work for the federal Bureau of Fisheries, writing radio scripts and educational pamphlets.

For the next decade and a half, Rachel worked for the federal government by day and wrote about the ocean by night. An eleven-page essay she wrote for a Bureau of Fisheries assignment turned into a long piece in *The Atlantic* after her boss told her it was too good to end up in a government pamphlet; that essay turned into her first book. A few years after her father died, Rachel's sister did, too; Rachel adopted and raised her two nieces into adulthood. Her second book was serialized in the *New Yorker* and went on to spend eighty-six weeks on the *New York Times* bestseller list. She used the earnings to buy a house on the Maine coast, where she wrote a third book, this one about the sea. When one of her two nieces died suddenly, Rachel adopted her four-year-old grandnephew and raised him.

Rachel introduced her readers to scientific terms we take for granted today, like "ecology," and brought to life the many interactions of species and landscapes, weather and water, sky and sea. Her books were poetic and profound, scientifically rigorous and utterly accessible. She called the ocean "mother sea" and gently urged her readers to orient themselves in the wider circle of nature, and to understand, as she did, that this planet is wild and wonderful, precious and delicate, and urgently in need of protection.

After the end of World War II, the pesticides and chemicals developed for use in warfare began flooding into the U.S. consumer market without regard for their potential harm to people and the environment. The U.S. Department of Agriculture began using one chemical in particular, DDT, to try to stop an invasive species of insects in their tracks; the chemical didn't kill the bugs, but it seemed to kill just about everything else that flew, ran, or swam. Rachel had pitched an essay on DDT to *Reader's Digest,* but they turned her down. In the late 1950s, a citizen's committee filed a lawsuit against the chemical companies in New York State court. Rachel wrote about it for the *New Yorker.*

That assignment became *Silent Spring,* which was published in 1962. At the time, some five hundred new chemicals a year made their way into the consumer market, many for pest control, with little or no oversight. Rachel opened the book by imagining an American town in the near future where almost everything — the bees in the apple trees, the frogs in the ponds, the birds whose songs tell people that winter is over — has been destroyed by the unfettered use of dangerous chemicals. "These sprays, dusts, and aerosols are now applied almost universally to farms, gardens, forests, and homes — nonselective chemicals that have the power to kill every insect, the 'good' and the 'bad,'" she wrote. "Can anyone believe it is possible to lay down such a barrage of poisons on the surface of the earth without making it unfit for all life?"

The chemical companies tried to cast doubt on the scientific conclusions Rachel had drawn;

"Those who contemplate the beauty of the earth find reserves of strength that will endure as long as life lasts."

— RACHEL CARSON,
FROM *THE SENSE OF WONDER*

John F. Kennedy's administration went to work investigating the problem, and the president himself acknowledged the role that *Silent Spring* played in focusing the government's attention on the dangers of pesticides.

Eight months after *Silent Spring,* the president's Science Advisory Committee issued a report that backed most of Rachel's claims. She had testified before that committee as well as in the Senate, appeared on television programs, and spoken to dozens of reporters, despite her own failing health. While *Silent Spring* was galvanizing a nation to action, Rachel Carson was dying of breast cancer. After she died in 1964, her ashes were scattered at sea, near her home in Maine.

It's hard not to wish that Rachel Carson had lived longer than her fifty-six years, not only to see the results of her hard work — DDT was banned for agricultural uses nationwide in 1972, two years after the creation of the Environmental Protection Agency — but to turn her incisive pen and generous heart to today's environmental crises.

"Now in our own lifetime we are witnessing a startling alteration of climate," Rachel wrote in her second book, *The Sea Around Us,* in 1951. It is up to us today to save the planet and ourselves from the destruction of climate change — because as Rachel knew well, and as all her books and writing make clear, there is no "planet B."

JANE JACOBS AND PEGGY SHEPARD

JANE JACOBS

PEGGY SHEPARD

CHELSEA

As a girl from Scranton, Pennsylvania, Jane Jacobs's first glimpse of New York City came on a school trip in 1928. As her class emerged from the Holland Tunnel into Lower Manhattan, she recalled being "flabbergasted by the number of people in the streets . . . the city was just jumping." That amazement and curiosity would shape her work on urban planning, which would define much of her life.

After high school and a stint working an unpaid job at the local paper in Scranton, Jane left for New York, this time for more than a field trip. In her new hometown, she rode the subway, getting off at different stops to apply for jobs and explore neighborhoods. In Greenwich Village, she found both a secretarial job and a community.

During World War II, Jane worked for the Office of War Information. Following the war she started writing for *Amerika,* a pro-America Russian-language magazine. She was hounded by McCarthyism and investigated by the FBI because of her beliefs. In response, she wrote: "I do not agree with the extremists of either the left or the right, but I think they should be allowed to speak and to publish, both because they themselves have, and ought to have, rights, and once their rights are gone, the rights of the rest of us are hardly safe."

After leaving *Amerika,* Jane went to work for another, albeit quite different, magazine, *Architectural Forum.* She would later recount how, upon learning she was intended to be the publication's new expert on schools and hospitals, she became immediately suspicious of experts given how little she knew about both. Still, she was determined to learn all she could — first about architecture, then about urban planning and design. She began to question what made a city healthy — or not — and spent years researching what would become her seminal 1961 book, *The Death and Life of Great American Cities*. Putting "death" before "life" in the title was clearly purposeful. Many saw it as an attack on the status quo in city planning — probably because, in the book's introduction, she declared it "an attack on current city planning and rebuilding."

In her book, Jane criticized urban planning as "pseudoscience," with no real basis in facts, and she outlined the real destruction such planners were wreaking on communities where they themselves rarely lived. She popularized and may even have coined the terms "social capital," to articulate what provides cohesion for communities and other social groups, and "mixed primary uses," to explain why neighborhoods where people lived and worked were healthier than those where people do only one or the other. She gave us the beautiful phrase "eyes on the street," to talk about how in mixed primary use neighborhoods there were always people around — off early to work, walking kids to school, going about their day, going out at night, closing the bar, heading home after the late shift. And she wrote about how those neighborhoods, like her own in Greenwich Village, that engaged in a "sidewalk ballet" of consistent movement were more vibrant and protective. Those are the kinds of neighborhoods for living and working she wanted for everyone in urban environments.

Students in urban planning, architecture, economics, public health, history, and more study Jane's work today; I certainly did while pursuing my master's in public health at Columbia University's Mailman School of Public Health. Her reputation now is a contrast to the reaction she received from the male professional class in the 1950s and '60s. When her first articles came out criticizing contemporary urban renewal practices, she was called a "crazy dame." After she published her first book, the criticism was even fiercer and more sexist. Her lack of credentials was derided (she never graduated from college), and she was dismissed as "just a mother." She must have had moments of discouragement. But chauvinism couldn't stop the power of Jane's ideas, her voice, or her example.

Jane was not only a hugely important thinker and writer; she was also a powerful activist. In the 1950s and '60s, she spoke out against the efforts to develop East Harlem without including the East Harlem community; organized to stop slum clearance in her beloved Greenwich Village and a plan to run Fifth Avenue through Washington Square Park; helped stop the proposed Lower Manhattan

Expressway, which would have cut through neighborhoods; and trained countless citizens, particularly women, to be powerful advocates for the city they wanted. In 1968, while protesting the latest Lower Manhattan Expressway plans, she was arrested, spent a night in jail, and was later convicted of disorderly conduct.

Jane commuted to her court appointments from Toronto, where she had moved in 1968 partly in protest of the Vietnam War. There she again helped stop proposed expressways that would have cut up and disjointed neighborhoods, and again fought for urban planning that included, rather than excluded, community voices. She passed away in 2006, at eighty-nine, her life defined by her ceaseless work for the cities she thought everyone, whether in New York, Toronto, or anywhere else, deserved.

Like Jane, Peggy Shepard refused to be deterred by powerful corporations or leaders who would have preferred she sit down and shut up. After she was elected the Democratic Assembly district leader for West Harlem, she faced a serious question from her constituents — what could she do about a new sewage-treatment facility that had opened on the Hudson River and was emitting noxious fumes that families were convinced were making them sick? It also smelled like rotten eggs. Peggy drew on her skills as a former journalist and speechwriter for the New York State Division of Housing and Community Renewal and started investigating what was happening in her neighborhood. She learned that the new North River Sewage Treatment Plant had first been planned for a different part of Manhattan, well south of Harlem, and questioned why it had been moved. Was it because her neighborhood had among the lowest incomes in New York City? Because it was majority black? Because the city didn't think her neighborhood would notice that people were getting sick? All of the above?

Peggy kept asking these tough, important questions about racism, class, equity, and public health. She discovered that the City Planning Commission had never asked her community what it thought about a proposed waste treatment facility. Under pressure from Peggy and other local political and civic leaders, including filing a lawsuit, the city upgraded the facility to remove harmful fumes from the air and much, though not all, of the bad smell. And New York State's long-delayed promise to build a park on top of the plant finally began to take shape. After being approved in 1970, it finally opened in 1993.

The fight for city accountability and action on the North River Sewage Treatment Plant led Peggy to cofound WE ACT for Environmental Justice, to fight environmental racism in West Harlem and for meaningful participation by communities in the policies and plans that impact their neighborhoods and lives. Its record shows it has done just that, repeatedly, from the local to the national levels.

WE ACT's efforts led to the creation of West Harlem Piers Park, after the city had neglected to include Harlem in its new parks planning effort. The group pushed for new bus emission standards that required New York City buses to move from diesel to hybrid, leading to a 95 percent drop in tailpipe emissions. They worked to pass legislation to get lead out of New York City public housing and schools, and now are working to have those standards enforced. At the national level, they're working on setting robust environmental standards and ensuring that urban low-income communities are not forgotten, and are included in national legislation, like the annual farm bill.

Peggy has worked with the National Institutes of Health, served as the chair of the Environmental Protection Agency's National Environmental Justice Advisory Council, and cochaired its Research and Science Workgroup, a powerful statement about how vital it is to have community leaders be part of designing research standards and selecting research programs. WE ACT works with researchers at the local level in New York and also trains and supports local activists and advocates, continually building a multidisciplinary movement to fight environmental racism. It makes perfect sense that Peggy Shepard received the 2008 Jane Jacobs Lifetime Achievement Award, among countless other accolades. Both women understood that fighting for the change they knew was necessary was more likely to draw criticism than acclaim, but they never let that stop them from doing what needed to be done. They continue to inspire the next generation of environmental activists, including Majora Carter and Adrianna Quintero, who work for environmental justice to protect the health of black and Latino communities, including in New York City. The work they and other women are doing to build greener, more sustainable futures and fight the rollback of regulations that have safeguarded and improved our air, water, and land is critical. I like to imagine Jane agitating, advocating, and working alongside Peggy and others, and cheering them on.

Jane Goodall and "The Trimates"

CHELSEA

As a little girl in England in the 1930s, Jane Goodall loved animals. When she was just a year old, her father gave her a stuffed chimpanzee named Jubilee in honor of the baby chimp born at the London Zoo. The stuffed toy was nearly the same size as Jane. Friends cautioned her parents that a toy like that would give her nightmares, but Jane loved it. When she was five years old, she was so desperate to know how an egg came out of a hen that she hid inside the henhouse for several hours, waiting. She was oblivious to the fact that her family had been frantically searching for her, and had reported her missing to the police.

Even as a child, Jane dreamed of traveling to Africa to live and work alongside the animals she had only seen in zoos and read about in books. In 1957, on a trip to visit a family friend in Kenya, Jane sought out Dr. Louis Leakey, a paleoanthropologist and archaeologist, who was working to prove his hypothesis that humans first emerged in Africa, not Europe or Asia, as was then the widely accepted view by Western scientists. For his research team, Leakey recruited young scientists and aspiring scientists to study the evolutionary connection between *Homo sapiens* and primates. Leakey believed that directly observing primates in their native habitats, rather than in captivity, would help prove that an evolutionary link existed between primates and humans.

Leakey first hired Jane as a secretary to record his findings. He quickly recognized her talent and encouraged her to study primatology so she could do her own fieldwork. While she was studying and working for Leakey, her mentor raised the necessary funds to help launch Jane's work studying chimpanzees. (Chimpanzees, gorillas, and orangutans, are "great apes," which have larger brains than monkeys, larger bodies, and, as Jane judiciously continues to point out, no tail.) In 1960, Jane embarked on her pathbreaking work at Gombe Stream National Park, in Tanzania. Establishing her own research camp was already a remarkable achievement for someone with no undergraduate or advanced degree in her field of study. She would more than prove Leakey's faith in her, later pursuing a PhD in ethology (the study of animal behavior) from Cambridge University based on her research. She has the distinction of being one of that school's few doctoral graduates who didn't first earn an undergraduate degree.

When Jane began observing chimpanzees, we understood little about chimpanzees' behavior or our common ancestry. Her decision to live and work among them, as well as her commitment to observing and imitating them, was not then common research practice. She also insisted on naming the chimpanzees she watched for years, rather than giving them simple letter or numerical designations. This was controversial; researchers at the time were expected to remain removed from their animal subjects and certainly not to see them as humanlike. Yet the importance of Jane's work is indisputable. Early on, she made several discoveries: that chimpanzees have a highly complex social system governing their interactions; that they are omnivorous, not vegetarian; and that they make and use tools. Jane watched as chimpanzees turned a twig into a spoon to help eat termites — contradicting the idea that the making and use of tools were uniquely human characteristics. Today scientists have identified a number of tools used by chimpanzees. In her early work, Jane further showed that chimpanzees communicate using touches, gestures, and more than a hundred different unique sounds, but they do not have their own language. It is humans' ability to talk to one another that Jane is convinced drove our greater intellectual development.

While Jane watched chimpanzees commit acts of horrific violence toward one another, she observed great love in chimpanzees, too. She found common traits among good chimpanzee mothers, including being supportive, affectionate, playful, protective but not overly so, and able to use discipline. Jane saw the generational effects of this loving parenting when she noticed that females who had good chimpanzee mothers were more likely themselves to raise healthy, secure, happy offpsring. All of this influenced how Jane parented her own son, Hugo.

At a fundamental level, Jane changed what we understand not only about chimpanzees but also about ourselves. Scientists now believe, in part because of Jane's work, that humans and chimpanzees share a common ancestor. We know we share 98 percent of our DNA. It's not surprising, then, that Stephen Jay Gould, the acclaimed paleontologist and author, once called Jane's discovery of chimpanzees as tool-makers "one of the great achievements of 20th-century scholarship." The glowing praise from experts in the field may have come as a surprise to Jane, who has repeatedly said while she wanted to study chimpanzees, she never cared about being a scientist.

In the early 1960s, Jane fell in love with Hugo van Lawick, a photographer who had been sent by *National Geographic* to document her work. ("Jane disliked being photographed, but tolerated it for the sake of her research," wrote Lori Cuthbert in the same publication decades later. "She may have also tolerated it because Hugo was the one behind the camera; they were married a few years later.") They had a son together, and though they eventually divorced, they stayed close.

In the 1980s, Jane started to spend more time advocating for broader conservation efforts across Africa and around the world, sometimes working with her second husband, Derek Bryceson, the then director of

Tanzania's national parks. She highlighted the increase in mining, logging, slash-and-burn agriculture, illegal hunting, poaching, and the connection of all those activities to poverty, corruption, and underinvestment in local communities. For decades, Jane has advocated for and worked to put communities affected by environmental degradation at the center of shaping the solutions to this crisis. She has also shifted her writing away from purely reporting on her chimpanzee observations to trying to save chimpanzees, their environments, and the livelihoods of the people who live near them. Her concerns are well placed. In 1900, there were about a million chimpanzees in the wild. Today there are between 170,000 and 300,000. If current trends of deforestation, hunting, and disease continue, chimpanzees in the wild could disappear within two generations. Such a stark forecast, along with growing environmental devastation in the regions where she works, helps explain why, even well into her eighties, Jane shows no sign of slowing down in her work.

Following in Jane's footsteps, primatologists Dian Fossey and Biruté Galdikas also found their way to Dr. Leakey, who eventually nicknamed the three young women scientists the "Trimates." With Leakey's support, in the mid-1960s, Dian moved from Kentucky to the Virunga Mountains to set up her first research station, based in the present-day Democratic Republic of the Congo, then Zaire. Unlike Jane, she focused on gorillas — a great ape that is typically larger and less social than the chimpanzee. To prove she wasn't a threat to the gorillas she was studying, Dian began by observing gorillas from a distance and imitating their movements and sounds. She meticulously recorded the gorillas' individual and communal behaviors. Less than a year after she began her work, during a period of instability in the region where Dian was working, the Zairian military forced her to leave her research station. Determined to continue her work, Dian moved her work to the Rwandan side of the Virungas, set up the Karisoke Research Center, ingratiated herself with new groups of gorillas, and again began carefully recording what she observed. From her early days at Karisoke, Dian practiced what she called "active conservation," which meant fighting poachers as well as cattle herders she believed were infringing on gorilla territory. She also opposed wildlife tourism. Her controversial tactics and positions inspired both greater support for anti-poaching efforts and hostility for what many local community members around Karisoke believed was infringing on hunting and grazing practices. She received intense criticism for discouraging communities from even engaging in responsible wildlife tourism. In 1985, she was found murdered in her home. The crime has never been solved. Dian's work continues through the Dian Fossey Gorilla Fund in the Virunga Mountains of both Rwanda and the Democratic Republic of the Congo. The fund supports research and gorilla protection at Karisoke, and recent data shows that after years of decline, the Virunga mountain gorilla population is growing.

Biruté Galdikas's fascination with primates started at age six, when she checked out her first library book: *Curious George*. By second grade, she had decided she would be an explorer — a passion that would inform the rest of her life. While a graduate student in anthropology at UCLA, she met Dr. Louis Leakey and told him she dreamed of studying orangutans — a daunting task given that orangutans were notoriously solitary animals who often lived in deep, hard-to-reach swamps. Studying them in the wild, she had been told, would be impossible. But Biruté, inspired by Jane's and Dian's work, eventually convinced Dr. Leakey to send her to Borneo to do just that. She traveled to the remote Tanjung Puting National Park in 1971. There were no telephones, no roads, no electricity, and no mail service. In the reserve, she set up "Camp Leakey," where she studied orangutan behavior and ecology. In 1975, she wrote the cover article for *National Geographic,* bringing global attention to orangutans for the first time. She went on to create a safe haven for orangutans on the Borneo island park Pangkalan Bun, where she continues her research and efforts to rehabilitate orangutans and release them back into the wild.

As a little girl in Arkansas, I was captivated first by Jane and then by Dian and Biruté. Thirty years later, I still am. Now, reading the children's books based on Jane's life and the *National Geographic* articles about the Trimates with my children, I see that the lessons of their lives resonate through generations. For their courage and commitment to helping expand what we know about our world — even when it meant surrounding themselves with the unknown — their examples are ones I deeply admire.

Wangari Maathai

Chelsea

As a teenager in the 1990s, I watched in awe, from afar, as Wangari Maathai's Green Belt Movement planted trees in Kenya in an effort to fight environmental degradation and poverty. They planted one tree after another, eventually planting millions — all because of one young woman's dream.

Born in Nyeri, Kenya, in 1940, Wangari Maathai knew even as a little girl that she wanted to be a scientist. Pursuing that ambition took her from rural Kenya around the world. In the early 1960s, she moved to Kansas to study biology, then to Pittsburgh for her master's degree. Decades later, Wangari shared that while her student years were positive, even sheltered, she was deeply aware of the burgeoning civil rights movement in the United States. That experience would help her understand the connection between protecting the environment and advancing civil rights in Kenya.

After Wangari earned her master's in science from the University of Pittsburgh, she returned to Kenya to further her studies. She completed her PhD in veterinary anatomy at the University of Nairobi in 1971. This was a time when few women in the United States or in much of the world were studying science at a post-college level — in 1966, only about 15 percent of PhDs in biological and agricultural sciences in the U.S. were awarded to women. Wangari was the first woman in eastern and central Africa to earn a doctorate degree in any subject. If she had continued her studies in the United States, she would have been a pioneer here, too. But Wangari always knew she wanted to go home, to teach and to serve.

Later, as a professor and then a department chair at the University of Nairobi — the first woman to hold both positions — Wangari grew increasingly concerned about the deforestation of Kenya. Ninety percent of Kenya's forests had been cut down since 1950. Wangari initially recruited family and friends to help her plant trees. Then she broadened her recruitment to students, colleagues, and strangers. Her grassroots community-based tree planting efforts became the Green Belt Movement, her fight against environmental degradation and poverty through planting trees. She credited Dr. Martin Luther King Jr. with helping her understand the links between human rights and environmental protection, and the women she met with crystalizing her mission. "When we started the Green Belt Movement, I was partly responding to needs identified by rural women, namely lack of firewood, clean drinking water, balanced diets, shelter, and income," she said years later. "Throughout Africa, women are the primary caretakers, holding significant responsibility for tilling the land and feeding their families. As a result, they are the first to become aware of environmental damage as resources become scarce and incapable of sustaining their families."

Wangari's work was not without opposition.

Periodically, her efforts were met with significant, even violent resistance. In January 1992, she learned that her name was on a list of pro-democracy activists being targeted by the government for assassination. The next month, she joined mothers of political prisoners being held by Daniel arap Moi, Kenya's autocratic leader. Wangari and the others took part in a hunger strike at a local park. The police broke up the demonstration and beat Wangari so brutally that she was knocked unconscious. President Moi denounced her publicly, calling her a "madwoman" and "a threat to the order and security of the country." Still, she refused to give up on her mission.

Over time, the Green Belt Movement grew to encompass protecting disability rights, minority rights, women's rights, and democracy, along with an ambition to fight poverty and protect the human rights of everyone in Kenya. Yet Wangari never lost her focus on planting trees. In 2004, Wangari became

---

"In the course of history, there comes a time when humanity is called to shift to a new level of consciousness, to reach a higher moral ground. A time when we have to shed our fear and give hope to each other. That time is now."

— WANGARI MAATHAI

---

the first African woman to be awarded the Nobel Peace Prize; at the time, she was also an assistant minister for environment and natural resources. She moved between activism, science, teaching, running a nonprofit, and government work. She went wherever she thought she could make the maximum impact on saving Kenya's environment and advancing the human rights of its people. She took her passion into different areas, to work with different communities, in order to make Kenya more sustainable and respectful of all people.

When President Barack Obama nominated my mom as secretary of state in 2009, the *New York Times* asked experts around the world to share questions they hoped my mom would answer in her confirmation hearing. One of the experts was Wangari. Her questions covered human rights violations in Darfur, the need to protect forests in Africa — particularly in the Congo Basin — and how the United States would respond to African leaders' growing willingness to partner with China despite that country's disregard for human rights.

HILLARY

I had met and been impressed by Wangari, so I appreciated her questions; they broadened the scope of what issues the secretary of state should consider important for our country and the world. As I learned early on, ignoring or belittling a problem doesn't cause it to disappear.

I sat behind my mom during the hearing, so proud of her, and also determined to look calm throughout, in part because I knew my grandmother would be watching at home. (When my mom was a senator, my grandmother would keep C-SPAN on in the background while she was exercising, knitting, eating, even reading, because she never wanted to miss a moment of my mom speaking on the Senate floor, or even, I think, walking by.)

During the hearing, my mom mentioned the importance of trying to stop what she called the human devastation in Darfur, and clearly

---

"My mother's legacy is multifaceted, but the one thing that unites the various elements and life and work is the power of one person to be such a potent agent of change. It doesn't take a lot of people for real change to happen. At a time when so much seems to be going wrong, it is very easy to get overwhelmed. You don't need an 'army' of people. Each of us can be agents of change."

— WANJIRA MATHAI,
WANGARI MAATHAI'S DAUGHTER

---

called out climate change as a security threat. When she visited Kenya later in 2009, during her first year as secretary of state, she met with Wangari and then praised her at a forum at the University of Nairobi. At our family Thanksgiving dinner that year, I remember my mom reflecting that a favorite moment of her trip to Africa was meeting with Wangari.

HILLARY

Wangari was a pioneer and a true visionary. She knew better than anyone that women hold the key to the future. The Green Belt Movement was led by women, first in Africa, then around the world. And, even after she had been persecuted and threatened by leaders in her country, she continued to see government as a tool for positive change. She served in a successor government to the one that had overseen attacks on her life. She was a truly incredible person, and I was honored to call her a friend.

I was always struck by Wangari's recognition of herself as a role model. She once said in an interview, shortly after she won the Nobel Prize, that young women would come up to her with tears in their eyes to congratulate her, and that she "knew that what they were really saying was, 'if you can do it, then maybe I too can do it.'" At the time of her death in 2011, the Green Belt Movement had planted more than fifty million trees. Today it has planted more than fifty-three million trees across critical watersheds in Kenya, and the total only grows. Her daughter, Wanjira Mathai, continues her work.

Wangari wasn't afraid to be the first person to take up a worthwhile cause, or the loudest voice advocating for what she believed. But she knew that, as with the forests she planted, the greatest impact she could have would come from being one of many. That's why I think of Wangari when I learn about her kindred spirits, like G. Devaki Amma in India. Nearly four decades ago, inspired by a love of farming, she planted a single sapling in her backyard — then another, then another. Today she has cultivated her own forest, spread over four and a half acres in Kerala. She is passionate about helping her family and others neutralize their carbon footprint. At eighty-five years old she still walks the land every morning. By planting trees, she and others are making clear that forest health is integral to our health and to women's rights and human rights.

ALICE MIN SOO CHUN

HILLARY

Alice Min Soo Chun and her parents moved to the U.S. in 1968 when she was three years old, leaving behind poverty in South Korea and hoping for a different, brighter future in the United States. Growing up in a low-income neighborhood in Syracuse, New York, where none of the other kids looked like her, Alice focused on tuning out the bullying in order to simply survive. But she was always creative — a trait encouraged by her father, an architect; and her mother, a painter. Alice remembers helping to load a massive pile of wood onto the roof of the family car so her mother could bring it home and use it to build a fireplace mantel. "We were always doing things like that," she said, laughing.

Her parents moved back to South Korea when Alice was a teenager, and for a while, she stayed with them. But she wanted to go to school in the United States, and that's exactly what she did, putting herself through college at Penn State and graduate school at the University of Pennsylvania. Balancing school and work was grueling, and she didn't see her parents for nearly nine years. Through hard work and laser focus, she built a career for herself in New York City, eventually becoming a professor of architecture and material technology at Columbia University and at the New School's Parsons School for Design.

When Alice's son, Quinn, developed asthma, her life changed forever. On one of their frequent trips to the doctor, she looked up to see that the waiting room was crowded with worried mothers, looking on as their children puffed on inhalers or waited to be hooked up to a nebulizer. More than once, Alice and Quinn wound up in the emergency room. "When your child can't breathe, and their lips are turning blue, you would do anything to help them," Alice said. "I kept saying: Why is this happening to our kids?"

She had once heard a saying: "A worried mom does better research than the FBI." Alice delved into books and mined reports, searching for statistics and confirming soaring childhood asthma rates due to air pollution, especially in places like New York City. The more she learned, the more outraged she became. Her concern shifted from her son, who at least had access to quality medical care, to children around the world, particularly in places where families relied on dangerous, outdated technologies like kerosene lamps and solid-fuel cookstoves. They were breathing polluted air not only outside but inside of their homes. She learned that each year nearly 3.8 million people, mainly women and children, die prematurely from illnesses related to household air pollution. While electric lights and stoves could offer a safer solution, 1.6 billion people around the globe have no access to electricity, and Alice knew the urgency of climate change would require alternative energy sources. "I wasn't sure what to do, but I knew the risk of doing nothing was greater than the risk of being wrong," said Alice.

At work, she turned her focus to sustainable design and began looking for ways to incorporate solar energy into everyday life. As a materials lab director at the Parsons School of Design, Alice knew the material technology trends were becoming thinner, lighter, faster, and smarter. Why not literally weave solar energy into the fabric of her work? In 2008, she started sewing flexible solar panels to fabric and thin plastics, creating a canvas that was both beautiful and useful.

Alice began developing a prototype inflatable solar light in 2008. In 2010, after the earthquake in Haiti, Alice offered a challenge to her design students: Come up with a solution for disaster relief that could be used immediately by an individual. She and some of her students built the prototype for the solar light as a detail unit for a class project.

In 2011, Alice realized she could use origami techniques to create a cube shape that filled with air on its own, eliminating the germs that came from inflating by mouth. She named it the SolarPuff. Alice started a nonprofit called Studio Unite, trying to get the SolarPuff mass-produced. She soon realized that unfortunately the charity model was not sustainable for what she was attempting to do at a much larger scale. In 2015, she established Solight Design and launched the SolarPuff via a crowdfunding campaign that raised almost half a million dollars in thirty days. Alice set aside her teaching to be a full-time social entrepreneur.

Alice couldn't stop thinking about how to bring relief, safety, and security to disaster areas, along with hope, wonder, and awe. Her company sent SolarPuffs to volunteers who climbed Nepal's hillsides with Sherpas, bringing light to small villages. In the central plateaus of Haiti, farmers saw the lights and started to sing and dance and cry. Children laughed with delight when they saw how the SolarPuff popped up into a cube. Around the world, where SolarPuffs are, children can see at home to study in the evenings without a fire or a kerosene lamp, and mothers can cook food more safely. In a refugee camp in Greece, a wedding was lit by SolarPuffs. At that same camp, Alice and her "light warriors" put a SolarPuff by the bedside of a teenager who had been badly burned and faced a long recovery. After Alice left, she always wondered what happened to the girl. One day her team received a photograph: It showed the SolarPuff on a dining room table in Germany, where the young woman now lived.

After Hurricane Maria in Puerto Rico, Alice sent three thousand SolarPuffs to Carmen Yulín Cruz, the mayor of San Juan. The mayor began handing them out everywhere she went. People on the streets started calling the SolarPuff the "cube of hope." The next year at Christmas, disturbed to hear how many

> *"In order to survive a terrible situation, you have to have hope."*
>
> — ALICE MIN SOO CHUN

neighborhoods were still without power, Alice packed a suitcase with SolarPuffs and got on a plane. She had seen pictures of Puerto Rico and the island of Dominica showing fields of houses with the roofs ripped off from heavy winds. So she went to those places herself. She knew from her time in Haiti that children are often the most vulnerable after a disaster. She distributed hundreds of SolarPuffs at local schools for children to bring home so they could do their homework at night and light their families' homes. "What I realized was that children are the best teachers in the world," she said. "I would tell them: Even more powerful than the sun is the light in your mind, your imagination."

"It wasn't easy, starting a company and becoming a social entrepreneur," Alice said. "At times, it was extremely difficult. There were people who told me I wasn't good enough, I wasn't smart enough. Many times, I wanted to give up, but I didn't, because I kept thinking about my son — the life his children and grandchildren would have in an environment where pollution is compromising their health. I just kept going, and I didn't give up."

At the 2019 Clinton Global Initiative (CGI) conference in San Juan, I met Alice. She told me that the SolarPuff was available in twenty countries around the world and sold in the United States at camping stores like REI. Alice took the stage at the conference carrying her newest innovation, the QWNN solar lantern, named after her now-fourteen-year-old son. "It's individualized infrastructure," she said. "Every person has the power to harness energy and use it for their life, their livelihood. And together, we can bring light to the darkest corners of the world, one person at a time." By turning her outrage on behalf of her son and children everywhere into hope for millions, that's exactly what Alice has done.

GRETA THUNBERG

HILLARY

In August 2018, when it came time to return to classes at her high school in Stockholm, then fifteen-year-old Greta Thunberg decided to go on strike instead. Like many countries, Sweden had seen record-breaking heat that summer. The news out of the scientific community was bad, and Greta had had enough. She wrote "SKOLSTREJK FÖR KLIMATET" — "School Strike for Climate" — in black letters on a piece of wood. Then she put a few snacks in her backpack, put on her sneakers, and headed down to the Swedish national legislature, the Riksdag, to set up camp on the sidewalk out front. Her goal was to protest her government's inaction on what she sees as the greatest threat facing her generation: climate change.

Greta is part of a generation that has grown up seeing increasingly alarming news about the state of our planet. She has talked openly about her falling into a depression after learning about climate change at a young age. "I stopped talking. I stopped eating," she has said. She couldn't understand why everyone around her — from classmates to world leaders — wasn't similarly fixated on confronting

---

"I know so many people who feel hopeless, and they ask me, 'What should I do?' And I say: 'Act. Do something.' Because that is the best medicine against sadness and depression."

— GRETA THUNBERG

---

this global emergency. Then she decided to do something. She would later attribute her ability to focus so intensely on the issue in part to her Asperger's syndrome. "I see the world a bit different, from another perspective," she told *New Yorker* reporter Masha Gessen. "I have a special interest. It's very common that people on the autism spectrum have a special interest." Through activism, she found a purpose.

Greta's urgency is justified. Just a few months after she first went on strike, the Intergovernmental Panel on Climate Change issued a report warning the world that we need to cut our greenhouse gas emissions in half before 2030 to avoid passing the 1.5-degree Celsius threshold that would be catastrophic. Ancient glaciers are breaking up, leading to an anticipated sea-level rise that has forced nations like Indonesia to explore relocating cities on the coasts because they'll be underwater in fifty years. Villages in Alaska have already been moved. Scientists warn of thawing permafrost in Siberia leading to the release of more methane into the atmosphere and more warming from there, initiating devastating feedback loops. Destructive "hundred-year" floods, wildfires, and hurricanes have become regular events.

We often talk about tackling climate change as something we're doing "for the planet." Activists like Greta know that the planet will survive, but humans and life as we know it may not. That's what we have to worry about, and urgently. As Greta has said: "I want you to behave like our house is on fire. Because it is."

Greta was inspired to go down to the parliament building that day by the students of Marjory Stoneman Douglas High School in Parkland, Florida, and their activism around gun violence. She saw the Parkland students challenging adults to take long-awaited action on an issue that threatened their very lives, and she saw a parallel in her own growing anxiety about climate change. At first, she worried that the actions of one young girl couldn't make a difference. She didn't let her own doubts, or the ridicule she encountered from others, dissuade her. She was supported by her parents — actor Svante Thunberg and celebrated opera singer Malena Ernman, who travels to her performances by train and bicycle instead of flying in order to reduce her carbon footprint.

Just as the Parkland students inspired Greta, Greta has inspired young people all over the world to strike for climate action. That first day Greta packed her backpack, she was on her own. "I tried to bring people along to join me," she said, "but no one was really interested, and so I had to do it by myself." She went back to school after a few weeks but kept striking on Fridays in an ongoing protest she called #FridaysForFuture. Students across Europe and the world started joining — first

> *"We do need hope—of course we do. But the one thing we need more than hope is action. Once we start to act, hope is everywhere."*
>
> — GRETA THUNBERG

just a few, then dozens, then hundreds, and now thousands. On March 15, 2019 — a Friday, of course — 1.6 million young people all over the world joined protest marches from Sydney to San Francisco and Kampala to Seoul. "The most common criticism I get is that I'm being manipulated and you shouldn't use children in political ways," Greta has said. "And I think that is so annoying! I'm also allowed to have a say — why shouldn't I be able to form my own opinion and try to change people's minds?"

CHELSEA

So many of the leaders in the global movement to confront climate change are gutsy women — from activists like Greta to women at the UN like Christiana Figueres and Patricia Espinosa, each of whom has served as executive secretary of the United Nations Framework Convention on Climate Change. Christiana assumed the position in 2010, just six months after global climate talks in Copenhagen failed to produce a consensus. Five years later, thanks in no small part to what she called her "stubborn optimism," 195 countries came together in Paris and decided unanimously to "intentionally change the course of the global economy in order to protect the most vulnerable and improve people's lives." When Patricia took the helm in 2016, she helped widen the global conversation, including by launching an online effort that invites countries and nongovernmental organizations of all kinds to submit their own policy proposals to help achieve the Paris Agreement's targets. I am also grateful that Greta is talking about a climate crisis, not climate change. Every day we don't meet the commitments that Christiana helped negotiate and that Patricia is working to enforce, we are a day further from tackling our crisis and ensuring our planet is healthy and habitable for our children.

We face an immense challenge in making sure future generations can live and thrive on our planet. As a grandmother, mother, and human being, I'm personally invested in seeing climate action succeed. I'm grateful to Greta and all the young people who see a world in need of saving and have decided to act, individually and collectively, to save it. Talk about guts.

"Change is on the horizon," Greta has said. "But to see that change we also have to change ourselves." Let's do it.

■ ■ ■ ■

EXPLORERS AND INVENTORS

■ ■ ■ ■

Caroline Herschel and Vera Rubin

CAROLINE HERSCHEL

VERA RUBIN

Chelsea

Caroline Herschel grew up in Hanover in present-day Germany, the eighth child of Isaac, an oboist, and his wife, Anna Ilse. When she was ten years old, in 1760, Caroline contracted typhus, a bacterial disease that can cause a terrible fever and rash and even be fatal. She made a full recovery, but she

231

stopped growing. Her father had previously educated Caroline along with her brothers; that stopped after her illness. Her parents thought she would never marry because of her height — she was just over four feet tall, and they assumed that her small stature would inevitably lead her to a life of servitude.

But Caroline didn't believe her parents' predictions. When she was twenty-two, she left her native Germany to follow her older brother William to Bath, England. At the time, William was a composer, musician, and choral director. Caroline performed in his choir and kept house for her brother. In addition to music, William was also interested in astronomy and telescope design. Caroline assisted by experimenting with different types of lenses and optical tube lengths. When William discovered the planet Uranus, he was knighted and appointed court astronomer to King George III (yes, *that* King George III, from American history books and of *Hamilton* fame). William was the first person to discover a new planet in more than two thousand years. Suddenly, music became his hobby and astronomy his profession.

Caroline continued to help her brother with his experiments while pursuing her own studies in math and astronomy. William built larger, longer, and more powerful telescopes, often using lenses that Caroline had helped make in their laboratory next to the kitchen and the mirrors she had helped polish. In 1789, with Caroline's help, William finished building what was then the largest telescope ever; it had a focal length of forty feet. It took four years to construct and stood intact for more than fifty.

While William got most of the credit for their joint efforts, ten years after moving to England, Caroline became her brother's official apprentice. King George, recognizing her talent, began to support her career and work directly — likely the first time a woman was formally acknowledged by the British monarch for her scientific acumen. She proved herself to be more than deserving of such recognition.

On August 1, 1786, Caroline was looking through one of their telescopes when she noticed something moving across the sky: a never-before-identified comet. She saw it again the next night and alerted her brother and other fellow astronomers to its presence. Her brother deemed it, appropriately, "My Sister's Comet." Caroline is now known as the first woman ever to discover a comet. She would go on to discover eight in total.

Caroline was seventy-two years old when her brother died. After his death, she continued to record every observation she and her brother had made and noted the discrepancies between their work and the prevailing star catalogue of the time. Her "Catalogue of the Stars" was published in 1798. In 1828, the Royal Astronomical Society awarded her their Gold Medal for her work. No woman would be so honored again until 1996, almost 170 years later.

Caroline lived to be ninety-eight years old in an era when the average life expectancy for women was just fifty-five. Her astronomical maps are still in use today. When I learned that more than two decades ago, it astounded me — that someone could have so much clarity and vision that her work would help provide insight to scientists over two hundred years later.

More than eighty years after Caroline's death and on a different continent, Vera Rubin fell in love with the night sky outside her childhood bedroom window. Her father helped her build her own telescope, and he accompanied her to amateur astronomers' meetings. At her Vassar College graduation in 1948, she was the only graduating student who had majored in astronomy. After college, she hoped to enroll in graduate school at Princeton to continue her studies. She was told that Princeton didn't admit women in the astronomy program, without exception — a policy that wouldn't change until 1975.

Whenever I think of Vera and all the women who were kept out of higher education over the centuries because of the false conceit that only men belonged there, I hope those same

> *"We have peered into a new world, and have seen that it is more mysterious and more complex than we had imagined. Still more mysteries of the universe remain hidden. Their discovery awaits the adventurous scientists of the future. I like it this way."*
>
> — VERA RUBIN

colleges now realize what massive mistakes they made. Vera went on to Cornell and then Georgetown, completing her PhD in 1954 and providing research that proved the existence of galactic superclusters. These groups of smaller galaxy clusters are now believed to be some of the largest features of the known universe. At the time, her work was dismissed and derided; it would be decades before her findings were widely accepted.

When Vera started her doctoral work, she was pregnant with her second child. She encountered people, notably men, in her studies who openly doubted that a woman could take on such important scientific work and questioned whether a mother could possibly be committed to her studies at such a high level. The sexism didn't stop when she moved into her own full-time teaching and then onto a more research-oriented career. In the 1960s, one observatory where Vera hoped to work had no women researchers and no facilities for women. So Vera stuck a paper skirt to the sign outside a men's room, turning it into a women's restroom. With one of their main objections to her presence now removed, they had no choice but to let her become the first woman to work there; her work had earned her that right. Still, as Vera acknowledged, it took her "a long time to believe I was a real astronomer."

Vera continued to work on galaxy clusters and observed that their rotation curves defied predictions made according to contemporary theory. Narrowing her focus to single galaxies, she detected the same disconnect. The rotations of the galaxies were so swift, Vera hypothesized that gravity alone wasn't sufficient to explain why they didn't splinter apart. It was the first real evidence for dark matter, which scientist Fritz Zwicky had originally suggested after observing that galaxies seemed to be held together by something more than their own mass. Vera surmised that galaxies contain many times more dark matter than ordinary matter. Subsequent research would confirm her conclusions. We now know that dark matter accounts for 85 percent of the mass in the universe.

Vera didn't just help us understand the cosmos; her work led to new fields of study and research and inspired generations of scientists. In 1996, she became the second woman, after Caroline Herschel, to receive the Gold

Medal of the Royal Astronomical Society. Vera is considered by many in her field to be one of the Nobel Prize's most inexplicable misses. But that specific lack of affirmation for her work didn't seem to bother her. The same force she had felt as a little girl observing the stars from her bedroom motivated her throughout her career: an insatiable desire to know more about the universe we live in. We know more about our universe today thanks to Vera and Caroline.

ADA LOVELACE AND GRACE HOPPER

ADA LOVELACE

GRACE HOPPER

CHELSEA

In 1987, Santa Claus gave me my first computer for Christmas. At that time, women made up more than a third of computer scientists in the United States. Today, it's close to a quarter. That's far from parity, especially in a field that women helped invent.

In the nineteenth century, Ada Lovelace did

work that still echoes in the computers we use today. Ada's parents, the poet Lord Byron, and his wife, Annabella, separated when she was a baby; she never saw her father again. Her mother supported her daughter's interest in math, an unusual pursuit for women in the early 1800s, even those from families as privileged as Ada's.

Starting as a teenager, Ada worked alongside Charles Babbage, the inventor of an automatic calculator known as the difference machine. She posited that a machine could follow rules, and that numbers could represent other concepts — like music notes or letters of the alphabet. She became the first person — man or woman — to imagine, or at least articulate, that a machine could generate music, not just perform calculations. Ada was also the first to publish an algorithm, or set of steps for solving a mathematical problem, intended for a machine's use. For these reasons, she is often aptly described as the world's first computer programmer and the "Prophet of the Computer Age." It took guts to bring such unheard-of ideas into existence.

Ada died of cancer at thirty-six. Who knows what else she might have imagined or invented had she lived longer. I learned about Ada in college, when I read Tom Stoppard's play *Arcadia* (a gift from Marc — then my friend, now my husband). Ada was the inspiration for Thomasina, the play's most interesting

> *"I never am really satisfied that I understand anything; because, understand it well as I may, my comprehension can only be an infinitesimal fraction of all I want to understand about the many connections and relations which occur to me."*
>
> — ADA LOVELACE

character. I had always loved science — so how did I not know about the woman who helped lay the mathematical groundwork for computers? I should have learned about her in math class, or in my early computer classes. I hope students today learn about the remarkable woman who envisioned a computer's possibilities long before the first one was invented.

When Grace Hopper was born almost one hundred years after Ada in New York City, mathematics continued to be dominated by men (as math and computer science still are today). Before she turned thirty, Grace had earned a PhD in mathematics, a rare achievement for anyone in 1934. First a professor of math at Vassar College, her alma mater, Grace joined the U.S. Naval Reserve during World War II. She began working with the Mark I computer, becoming only the third person ever to program it. After the war, she continued working with computers in the private sector and in the navy, moving in and out of military service throughout her career.

HILLARY

I thought of Ada, Grace, and the many pioneering women in STEM when, in March 2019, U.S.-based mathematician Karen Keskulla Uhlenbeck became the first woman to receive the prestigious Abel Prize. Among other things, she has explored the mathematics behind the formation of soap bubbles. She described the experience of being one of a small handful of women earning her PhD in math at Brandeis in 1968, writing: "We were told that we couldn't do math because we were women. I liked doing what I wasn't supposed to do, it was a sort of legitimate rebellion." I love that phrase!

Like Ada, Grace imagined that computers could do more than the complicated arithmetic they performed at the time. She used math to help create the first computer compiler, a program that translates words into numerical code, as Ada had once imagined. Her work led to the invention of programming languages. When she began working on proving that computers had more potential than anyone had conceived, she encountered significant cynicism and resistance, particularly from her male colleagues. She didn't give up in the face of sexism; she pushed forward, tackling new frontiers in math. Grace once said, "If you do something once, people will call it an accident. If you do it twice, they call it a coincidence. But do it a third time and you've just proven a natural law!" For her contributions, propelled by her persistence and genius, she's known today as the Mother of Computing.

I learned about Grace in 1996, when the navy named a new ship the U.S.S. *Hopper* in her honor, a rare instance of recognizing a woman in such a way. I learned even more about her when I spoke many years later at the Grace Hopper Celebration, the largest gathering of women technologists in the world. It still bothers me that, as with Ada, I never learned about Grace in school, particularly when we started working on computers in high school. We should have known that our work was made possible by Grace's efforts during and after the war.

Both Ada and Grace deserve to be celebrated every time we sit down at a computer. In recent years, Ada Lovelace Day has become an international holiday dedicated to recognizing the achievements of women in science, technology, engineering, and math. That's a step in the right direction, but it's still not enough.

MARGARET KNIGHT AND MADAM C. J. WALKER

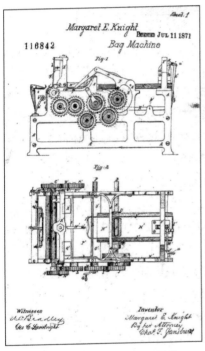

MARGARET KNIGHT'S
INVENTION

MADAM C. J. WALKER

CHELSEA

In 1850, when she was twelve years old, Margaret Knight left school in Manchester, New Hampshire, to support her widowed mother by working in a local cotton mill. There, she witnessed a terrible accident. A young boy was impaled by a steel-tipped shuttle carrying thread that had become disconnected from its spool. Child labor was common in the mills of the nineteenth century and the machinery dangerous; it was cheaper to employ children and more expensive to fence the machinery. Fingers, limbs, and lives were lost.

Margaret wanted to prevent more accidents like the one she had seen. A self-taught inventor from a young age, she had grown up building toys for her brothers and tools to make life easier for her mother around the house. This seemed like another problem she could solve. By the time her thirteenth birthday rolled around, she had invented a safety device for textile looms that automatically turned off a machine's power if it was malfunctioning. Although it would become common at mills throughout the United States, and Margaret's work helped prevent untold accidents, she received no credit for or income from her invention. Still, she kept inventing.

After the Civil War, Margaret went to work at the Columbia Paper Bag Company in Springfield, Massachusetts. Her job was folding every paper bag by hand — an inefficient and time-consuming task. In under a year, Margaret designed a machine that could cut, fold, and glue flat-bottomed bags together. While that might sound simple enough today, at the time, flat-bottomed bags were considered luxury items; most families carried groceries home in paper cones or large envelopes.

When she filed for a patent, her application was rejected. It turned out that a man she had shown her work to in its early phase had stolen her idea, copied it, and successfully applied for a patent, taking credit for her invention. Angry at the injustice of having her idea stolen, Margaret took him to court. When the man who had purloined her idea argued that no woman could possibly be capable of designing a machine like Margaret's, she presented page after page of hand-drawn blueprints. She won the case. In 1871, Margaret received the patent for her flat-bottomed paper bag–making machine. Although Mary Kies was the first American woman to receive a patent, in 1809 (for a novel approach of weaving straw and silk together), it was still rare for women to be awarded patents. By the end of her career, Margaret had obtained more than twenty. Newer versions of Margaret's paper bag–making machine are still in use today — so the next time you use a paper bag, or a cloth one modeled after her original design, thank Margaret!

Margaret Knight wasn't the only woman inventor in the late nineteenth and early twentieth centuries. Born in 1867 near Delta, Louisiana, Sarah Breedlove lost both her parents by the time she was seven. As a young, poor black girl in post-Emancipation Louisiana, her only source of education was her church, where she learned to read. Most of her young life was spent working in other people's homes to support herself, even after she moved in with an older sister in Mississippi. She married her first husband at fourteen and had her only child a few years later. After her husband died, she and her daughter, A'Lelia, moved to St. Louis. When Sarah began to lose her hair in her thirties, she tested lots of different remedies, some of which had been recommended to her by her four brothers, all barbers. She also tried the products of Annie Malone, a black woman hair-care entrepreneur. Sarah wasn't wholly satisfied with anything she tried that someone else had made or suggested, so she began working on her own formula to fight hair loss. A combination of infrequent hair washing (because of a lack of indoor plumbing and central heating), nutrient-poor diets, and scalp diseases helps explain why hair loss was a fairly common challenge for women, especially black women, in the late nineteenth century. When Sarah's third husband, Charles Joseph Walker, who had a vibrant career in advertising, encouraged her to start her own hair care line, and to do so under the name Madam C. J. Walker because it sounded catchier, Sarah — now Madam C. J. — began to do just that.

Madam Walker's Wonderful Hair Grower

was a line of hair care products and treatments that Madam C. J. developed for herself and then began marketing to other black women, initially in Denver, Colorado, where she worked as a sales distributor for Annie Malone. Annie would later accuse Madam C. J. of stealing her formula; while the ingredients were the same, the formula was slightly different, and Madam C. J.'s marketing effort was wholly her own (with some help from her husband). While she traveled across the country to demonstrate how to use her first signature product and treatment, a scalp conditioning and healing formula, A'Lelia managed the mail-order branch of the business. Sales numbers grew so quickly that she opened her first factory the next year. She moved her business to Pittsburgh and then to Indianapolis to be closer to new markets and railway lines. In 1910, she opened her first factory. She expanded into makeup and other beauty products. She then opened beauty schools to train beauticians on how to use her growing product line. In under a decade, she expanded internationally, eventually building a workforce of forty thousand predominantly black women and men.

Madam C. J. became one of the wealthiest black women of her time and is known as the first self-made black female millionaire (though some historians doubt the veracity of that moniker). "I got my start by giving myself a start," she would say. She used her resources and considerable platform to support the YMCA and the NAACP, investing in education and speaking out against racism and lynching. She died of kidney failure in New York City in 1919. Eighty-two years later, A'Lelia Bundles published a biography of her great-great-grandmother, *On Her Own Ground: The Life and Times of Madam C. J. Walker.*

I was lucky to learn about Margaret Knight and Madam C. J. Walker thanks to my American history teacher in my junior year of high school, Mr. Ellis Turner. He staunchly believed American history was too often populated by just men, and particularly white men, and he worked hard to introduce us to American women inventors, reformers, artists, advocates, authors, journalists, and leaders who helped push our country forward. If they were alive today, I would hope Margaret Knight and Madam C. J. Walker would be heralded and recognized by all as the innovators they clearly were.

MARIE CURIE AND IRÈNE JOLIOT-CURIE

IRÈNE JOLIOT-CURIE AND
MARIE CURIE

CHELSEA

In 1863, a few years before Marie Curie was born in Warsaw (in what is today Poland but was then a part of the Russian Empire), the country's Ministry of Education formally banned women from enrolling in universities. But Marie, born Maria Skłodowska, was consistently the first in her class at school and was determined to pursue a university education.

Marie excelled in the face of tragedy. During her childhood, her oldest sister died of typhus, her mother died of tuberculosis, and her father lost his job because of his pro-Polish beliefs. After she graduated from high school, Marie attended "The Flying University," a series of women-only underground classes and lectures, including in math and science, which moved from private home to private home to evade the authorities. While pursuing her studies in secret, Marie worked as a teacher and governess to support herself and to help her older sister afford medical school in Paris.

In 1891, at the age of twenty-four, Marie moved to Paris and began studying physical sciences (physics) and math at the Sorbonne, one of France's most prestigious universities. While she received some support from her sister and, later, a scholarship, she largely supported herself, living without heat in the winters, eating a sparse diet, and tutoring in the evenings, all while going to school and studying during the day. Her diligence paid off. She placed first in her class for physical sciences and second in math and began working in a laboratory while still a student.

> *"Unknown in Paris, I was lost in the great city, but the feeling of living there alone, taking care of myself without any aid, did not depress me. If sometimes I felt lonesome, my usual state of mind was one of calm and great moral satisfaction."*
> — MARIE CURIE

In 1894, while looking for lab space for her experiments on the magnetic properties of different types of steel, Marie met Professor Pierre Curie. Despite a promising early working relationship, Marie returned to Poland that summer to visit her family and apply for a job at Kraków University. Her application was rejected because of her gender. The ban on women students in Poland apparently extended to women faculty, too.

Back in Paris, Marie began exploring a series of research questions with Pierre and on her own that would define — and ultimately end — her life. Those experiments would also bring her and Pierre closer together. Pierre wrote letters to Marie, overflowing not with romantic prose but with his aspirations for all the scientific work he hoped the two of them could accomplish together. That didn't bother Marie: "[F]or Pierre Curie there was only one way of looking at the future," she wrote later. "He had dedicated his life to his dream of science: he felt the need of a companion who could live his dream with him." They would marry in 1895, with Marie wearing her only dress: the lab dress she wore every day. I've always loved that they met thanks to her work on magnetism.

In 1897, after analyzing her experiments' results, Marie theorized that uranium emits particle rays that come not from an external energy source but from the element's atomic structure. She named this phenomenon "radioactivity." It would later form the basis of atomic physics and lead to Pierre working full-time to support Marie's research. Marie and Pierre later isolated a new radioactive element, which they named polonium, after Poland. They then discovered another new radioactive element, radium, which they recognized destroyed tumor-producing cells more quickly than other healthy cells. All of this work, the dozens of published scientific papers that emerged from it, and Marie's first Nobel Prize (in physics), shared with Pierre and scientist Henri Becquerel for their work on radioactivity, occurred within a decade.

"Nothing in life is to be feared; it is only to be understood."

— MARIE CURIE

Marie was the first woman to receive a Nobel. I first learned about Marie when, as a kid, I asked my mom which women had won a Nobel, then promptly looked her up in the *Encyclopaedia Britannica* I'd gotten for Christmas a couple of years earlier.

While engaged in the research that the Nobel Committee cited in her award, Marie had her two daughters, Irène and Ève. "It became a serious problem how to take care of our little Irène and of our home without giving up my scientific work," she wrote later. "Such a renunciation would have been very painful to me, and my husband would not even think of it; he used to say that he got a wife made expressly for him to share all his preoccupations. Neither of us would contemplate abandoning what was so precious to both." Like many other women of privilege throughout the ages, she got some relief by hiring a housekeeper.

Marie took on more work to support her family. She began teaching at the prestigious École Normale Supérieure de Jeunes Filles and pioneered a new method of teaching based on experimental demonstrations. In case working multiple jobs wasn't enough, she oversaw her daughters' education, home-schooling them as part of a cooperative and also arranging sessions with her students and fellow faculty members. Her daughters were taught by university professors at a young age, at a time when girls were still not permitted to study at universities in many countries around the world. Later, Marie and Irène would collaborate to write the entry on radium for the thirteenth edition of the *Encyclopaedia Britannica*. Reading the letters between Marie and her daughters throughout their lives, I am struck by how much joy her daughters brought her. "Dear Irène," began one response, "I've just received your sweet letter of Saturday and I wanted so much to hug you that I almost cried."

Unlike some historical figures who become famous only after death, Pierre and Marie captured international attention after they won the Nobel for the discovery of radium. For Pierre especially, fame had its highs and lows. "We have been pursued by journalists and photographers from all countries of the world; they have gone even so far as to report the conversation between my daughter and her nurse," he wrote to a friend.

Marie and Pierre appreciated the "quiet living, organized according to our desires," which made it possible for them to pursue their work. "It can be easily understood that there was no place in our life for worldly relations," Marie wrote. "We saw but a few friends, scientific workers, like ourselves, with whom we talked in our home or in our garden, while I did some sewing for my little girl." When Pierre died in an accident in

> *"It is impossible for me to express the profoundness and importance of the crisis brought into my life by the loss of the one who had been my closest companion and best friend. Crushed by the blow, I did not feel able to face the future. I could not forget, however, what my husband used to sometimes say, that, even deprived of him, I ought to continue my work."*
>
> — MARIE CURIE

1906, Marie was shocked and devastated. She further immersed herself in the work that she and her husband had started together. "I am working in the laboratory all day long, it is all I can do," she wrote in her journal. That same year, she was appointed to fill Pierre's professorship, becoming the first woman to teach at the Sorbonne.

In 1910, Marie finally isolated pure radium, after years of work, and she defined the unit used to measure radioactive emissions, appropriately called the "curie." For this work, the Nobel Committee awarded Marie her second Nobel Prize, making her the first person ever to receive a Nobel in two separate disciplines: first physics, then chemistry.

Marie's unprecedented scientific achievements were still insufficient for the all-male membership of the French Académie des Sciences to elect her to their ranks. It wouldn't be until 1962 that the first woman was elected: a scientist named Marguerite Perey, who had studied under Marie. Marie's Nobel Prizes also didn't protect her from xenophobia, sexism, or from the anti-Semitic rumors that claimed she was secretly Jewish. In 1911, Albert Einstein wrote her an encouraging letter that began: "Do not laugh at me for writing you without having anything sensible to say. But I am so enraged by the base manner in which the public is presently daring to concern itself with you that I absolutely must give vent to this feeling." He concluded by urging her: "If the rabble continues to occupy itself with you, then simply don't read that hogwash, but rather leave it to the reptile for whom it has been fabricated."

Marie seemed to take his advice. She didn't let the critics shake her loyalty to her adopted country of France, where she opened the Radium Institute at the University of Paris, or her home country of Poland, where she would open the Radium Institute in Warsaw in 1932.

After World War I broke out, Marie turned her talents to inventing the first "radiological cars," or cars containing portable X-ray machines. She hoped her new radiological cars could help battlefield medics and doctors more accurately diagnose injuries and conduct surgeries. After she raised the money

> *"That one must do some work seriously and must be independent and not merely amuse oneself in life—this our mother has told us always, but never that science was the only career worth following."*
> — IRÈNE JOLIOT-CURIE

needed to produce her new fleet of traveling X-ray machines, called "little Curies," she and Irène trained woman volunteers to operate them. Marie also learned, in her late forties, to drive a car and be a mechanic so she could operate a little Curie herself. Marie's traveling X-ray cars inspired similar efforts by different countries' militaries.

Although they were already worried about the long-term health effects of X-ray exposure, Marie and Irène clearly determined that their military service was worth the risk. (I hope they informed the more than 150 women they trained throughout the war of these risks so that those women, too, could make a decision about whether or not to drive and operate little Curies.)

After the war, Marie continued her work with radium (and rescued the valuable stash that she had hidden away in a bank vault in Bordeaux in case of German occupation of Paris) and raised money to support her work and that of the radium institutes she had created. Irène returned to her studies, interrupted by the war, focusing on alpha rays emitted by polonium. Her later work with her husband, Frédéric Joliot-Curie (the couple made the decision to hyphenate their last names, an uncommon practice at the time), examined how polonium affected other elements. Like her parents, Irène and her husband worked side by side on their research. Eventually, they artificially created radioactive versions of usually stable elements. In 1935, Irène followed in her parents' footsteps when the Nobel Committee jointly awarded her and Frédéric the Nobel Prize in chemistry.

Their work helped drive progress in multiple fields, including in cancer research. But as had been true for her mother, despite her Nobel Prize and many other prestigious recognitions, the Academy of Sciences never admitted Irène. In addition to her contributions to science, she was involved in politics throughout her life — standing up for adequate funding for scientific research, for human rights, and against fascism.

While Marie always believed in the importance of X-rays and the healing properties of radium, both she and Pierre suffered radium burns during their experiments; indeed, sometimes the burns were purposeful parts of the experiments. Marie also often carried test tubes of radium in her pockets for convenience. Marie died in 1934 of aplastic anemia,

> *"The farther the experiment is from theory,*
> *the closer it is to the Nobel Prize."*
> — IRÈNE JOLIOT-CURIE

a blood disease associated with radiation exposure. In 1956, Irène died of leukemia, likely from her decades of work with polonium. Frédéric died two years later of liver disease, also likely caused or exacerbated by his long work in radioactivity. The radiation experiments Marie conducted were so intense, and done without protective equipment (because no one yet knew how necessary it would be), that Marie's notebooks and papers can still be viewed only by people wearing specially purposed protective gear.

Six decades after her death, Marie's ashes were enshrined in the Panthéon in Paris; she was the first woman to receive this honor for her own achievements. In her life, Marie was single-minded. She sacrificed much in service of her work: friends, living near her family, her health. In the end, she wrote, "I appreciated the privilege of realizing that our discovery had become a benefit to mankind, not only through its great scientific importance, but also by its power of efficient action against human suffering and terrible disease. This was indeed a splendid reward for our years of hard toil."

HEDY LAMARR

When I was growing up, my Grandma Dorothy didn't share my interest in peering into space and trying to understand the world above us. She always said there was so much to learn about here on Earth and inside us. Next to reading good history and fiction, she loved gardening, flowers, plants, trees — really anything that grew. She also loved movies from the 1930s and '40s. Her favorite actresses were always those who were great at their craft and lived useful — or at least interesting — lives off-screen. When she told me about the many lives of Hedy Lamarr, our shared interests found a fascinating common ground. My grandma could never understand why more people didn't know Hedy for more than her beauty or acting.

Hedy was born in Austria in 1914 into a well-off Jewish family. When she was little, her father would take her for long walks, pointing out the inner workings of streetcars and other machines around them. At five years old, she already loved to take apart her music box and put it back together, trying to understand how it worked.

Hedy was "discovered" at age sixteen and began acting in smaller European films. One of her early fans became her first husband, though the marriage didn't last. He was in the arms industry and did business with the Mussolini government in Italy and had ties to the Nazis in Germany. She hated having to play the doting host to her husband's business partners and eventually fled to London. There, she was introduced to Louis B.

Mayer of MGM Studios, gaining her entrée to Hollywood.

In the United States, she would work on her designs and inventions while in between movies and even in her trailer between takes. She pioneered new technology, inventing new wing designs for planes, creating a new kind of stoplight, and developing a tablet that dissolved in water, turning it fizzy. When my grandma and I were watching *The Golden Girls,* nature documentaries, *60 Minutes,* or any of her favorite shows and saw an Alka-Seltzer commercial, she'd mention Hedy! (Even though Hedy didn't invent the actual pill known as Alka-Seltzer; Maurice Treneer did in 1931.)

During World War II, Hedy didn't want to just continue to make money in the movies (this was always what most impressed my grandma). She wanted to do something to help the war effort. She wanted to put to good use her own talents as well as the things she'd overheard in her home, absorbed at dinner parties with Nazis, and learned at scientific meetings she had attended in Austria. She hoped to join the National Inventors Council but was rejected and told to use her star power to sell war bonds. She did — but she didn't stop there.

Hedy began working with George Antheil, a composer friend on a frequency-hopping system that could prevent military radio signals from being bugged or interrupted. She knew that would be important for general communications, and to ensure that the Germans and other Axis powers could not interfere with American and Allied radio-controlled torpedoes. When she first approached the U.S. Navy, they ignored her. Maybe it was because she was a woman, or because she was a beautiful woman (my grandma's theory). Maybe it was the fact that she wasn't yet a naturalized American citizen, or wasn't in the navy. Or maybe it was because Hedy and George's system was challenging to use consistently and effectively. While the patent on their invention expired before their invention was used, Hedy never lost faith in what she knew was groundbreaking technology.

It wasn't until much later in her life that Hedy's talent was recognized. Eventually, her work *was* used by the U.S. Navy, first in the early 1960s. She was finally honored in 1997 with the Electronic Frontier Foundation Pioneer Award and posthumously inducted into the National Inventors Hall of Fame. As for the frequency-hopping technology she developed, its impact is all around us today: Hedy and George's invention paved the way for modern-day cell phones, Wi-Fi, and GPS.

SYLVIA EARLE

HILLARY

On September 19, 1979, oceanographer Sylvia Earle, wearing an armored diving suit, descended 1,250 feet with the help of a research submersible to the seafloor, where she spent over two hours exploring. (Talk about pressure — Sylvia withstood six hundred pounds per square inch!) No human being had done that before or since.

As a little girl growing up on a small farm in 1930s New Jersey, Sylvia noticed the way her parents treated all living things with respect and empathy. She was fascinated by wildlife, and later, when her family moved to Florida, she loved investigating the creatures living in salt marshes and seagrass beds. Learning how to scuba dive in college at Florida State University, where she majored in botany, opened up a new frontier for her. As America entered the "space race" with Russia, Sylvia cast her sights downward, into the still-mysterious depths of the oceans. For her PhD, she collected more than twenty thousand samples of algae. In 1968, she discovered a landscape of undersea dunes off the coast of the Bahamas. The more she saw, the more she felt the inextricable connection between life on land and marine ecosystems, which were essential and needed to be protected. As she would later put it: "No ocean, no us."

Sylvia made national headlines in the 1970s, when she led the Tektite II experiment off the U.S. Virgin Islands. The first all-women's team of aquanauts lived and worked fifty feet underwater for two weeks, exploring both the marine world and the possibility of future habitats at sea or even in space, with

> *"I think if others had the opportunity to witness what I have seen in my lifetime . . . from thousands of hours underwater, I would not seem like a radical at all."*
> — SYLVIA EARLE

its similar environment. Their predecessors, the Tektite I team, had been all men. Sylvia and her crew did the same work as their male counterparts, with the same rigor and expectations. The all-women's team of accomplished scientist-divers was seen as a novelty — one local paper kept referring to them insultingly as the "aqua-naughties." Sylvia wasn't losing sleep over the misogyny; she was too busy exploring the deep. The experiment led to important discoveries about aquatic life and human behavior: Crews living in the undersea habitat developed fierce bonds and became unusually cooperative with one another, while sometimes finding the "topside crew" extremely irritating.

During the experiment, Sylvia was struck by the fragility of the marine life she observed, including the impact of pollution on coral reefs. Afterward, she made it her life's mission to sound the alarm and help everyone else understand the urgency of preserving and protecting the ocean. Over the years, her fellow scientists would often refer to

Sylvia as "Her Deepness" or "The Sturgeon General."

In 1990, Sylvia became the first woman to serve as chief scientist at the National Oceanic and Atmospheric Administration, and in 1998 was named by *Time* magazine as its first hero for the planet. She was also a National Geographic explorer in residence — which has to be one of the best job titles ever. I met her at the National Ocean Conference in 1998 and was impressed by her passion for sharing what she had seen with the rest of the world. To this day, she remains dedicated to making the case for mapping and exploring the oceans before they are damaged further, and she has committed her prodigious skills and talents toward that end.

When I think about Sylvia's work, I am reminded how important it is for all of us to pause and consider what we want to leave to the generations who come after us — how we'll honor the past, imagine the future, and give gifts to those who will live out their lives long after we're gone. That's exactly what Sylvia's life as a scientist, an engineer, a teacher, and an explorer should inspire all of us to do: we must preserve our oceans for the future.

SALLY RIDE

HILLARY AND CHELSEA

Hillary

I was in sixth grade when, in 1958, President Eisenhower signed the National Aeronautics and Space Act, establishing NASA. I had watched the "space race" unfold as a little girl, with the United States and the Soviet Union competing to be the first to send a satellite into space. After the Soviets launched Sputnik 1 in 1957, it set off a flurry of activity in our own country and inspired new investments in science, technology, and research. When NASA announced a little less than a year later that they were exploring the possibility of sending human beings into space, I was fascinated. In eighth grade, I wrote them a letter saying that I dreamed of becoming an astronaut, and asking what I had to do to prepare. Someone wrote back thanking me for my interest but explaining that they weren't taking girls into the program.

Of course, had my gender not stopped me from becoming an astronaut, my nearsightedness probably would have, but still I was outraged. It was one of the first times I can remember being told I couldn't do something, not because of my personal inadequacies or any lack of skill but simply because I was a girl. I was upset on behalf of girls everywhere.

Meanwhile, a few thousand miles away, a little girl named Sally Ride in Encino, California, was also intrigued by space travel. "At the time I grew up, the space program was on the front page of the newspaper almost every day," she recalled. "It was the coolest thing around. I idolized the astronauts, but I never thought really seriously about becoming one."

She was an excellent student with a passion for science, and a star tennis player. After high school, she enrolled at Swarthmore College in Pennsylvania but couldn't help but wonder whether she might have been missing out on the chance to have a successful career in tennis. After a year at Swarthmore, Sally dropped out to pursue the sport, then eventually decided to return to college. (According to her *New York Times* obituary: "Years later, when a child asked her what made her decide to be a scientist instead of a tennis player, she laughed and said, 'A bad forehand.'")

Chelsea

She then went to Stanford, where she studied English and physics. I'm pretty sure the first time I ever heard of Stanford was because of Sally Ride.

She stayed to earn a master's and a PhD in physics. One day, she read an advertisement in the Stanford University newspaper: NASA was recruiting scientists — men and women — for the space shuttle program. "The women's movement had already paved the way, I think, for my coming," she said later. She was one of more than eight thousand applicants for thirty-five positions in the first class of astronauts open to women, and to men of color. Sally was one of six women accepted; Guion "Guy" Bluford was one of three black men accepted.

Her astronaut class of 1978 was referred to as the "Thirty-Five New Guys," or "TFNG." Each of the six women who had been accepted had met rigid standards and were adamant that the bar for them be as high as it was for their male classmates. She and her fellow would-be astronauts practiced jumping out of planes with parachutes and surviving in open water. They underwent gravity and weightlessness training and learned how to fly a jet plane.

Meanwhile, the development of NASA's first space shuttle was changing the landscape for future generations of women astronauts. It was bigger than a "capsule" and could fit a larger crew, opening opportunities for more people to join a mission in different roles. Six years earlier, NASA had begun to design spacesuits, seats, and crew equipment for a larger range of sizes, as well as modifying waste management systems for women.

After five years of training, Sally was selected as a mission specialist for a flight. She was chosen in part for her reputation as being unflappable and her experience with helping to build a robotic arm for the shuttle. Along with four crewmates, she launched aboard the Space Shuttle *Challenger* on mission STS-7. On June 18, 1983, she became the first American woman in space. (Almost twenty years earlier to the day, Soviet cosmonaut Valentina Tereshkova had become the first woman in space. Between Valentina and Sally, there was only one other woman, cosmonaut Svetlana Savitskaya. So, while it took NASA two decades after the first woman in orbit, there certainly wasn't a rush anywhere in the world to support women pursuing celestial aspirations.)

Sally helped deploy and retrieve a satellite, the first time the shuttle was used to return a spacecraft to Earth. They landed six days after launch at Edwards Air Force Base in California. She grinned and told reporters: "I'm sure it was the most fun that I'll ever have in my life."

Hillary

I followed the launch from Arkansas with then three-year-old Chelsea by my side, poring over headlines and photos of the crowd of 250,000 at Cape Canaveral, which included people in T-shirts quoting the song "Ride Sally Ride." I was struck by how much had changed in the two decades since I had written to NASA. Not only were women being accepted into the program, they were being actively recruited and sent into space. For the first time, the sky was quite literally the limit.

But it wasn't easy. "The only bad moments in our training involved the press," she later said in an interview with Gloria Steinem. "Whereas NASA appeared to be very enlightened about flying women astronauts, the press didn't appear to be. The things they were concerned with were not the same things that I was concerned with. . . . Everybody wanted to know what kind of makeup I was taking up. They didn't care about how well prepared I was to operate the arm, or deploy communications satellites." (Even today, it's hard to think of a woman in the public eye who couldn't relate.) She endured questions about whether space flight would damage her reproductive organs and how she would go to the bathroom. Johnny Carson cracked that the shuttle flight might be delayed because Ride was looking for a purse to match her shoes.

Chelsea

After the 1986 *Challenger* tragedy, when the space shuttle broke apart shortly after launch,

---

"I never went into physics or the astronaut corps to become a role model. But after my first flight, it became clear to me that I was one. And I began to understand the importance of that to people. Young girls need to see role models in whatever careers they may choose, just so they can picture themselves doing those jobs someday. You can't be what you can't see."
— SALLY RIDE

---

killing all seven crew members, Sally's astronaut career came to an end. Though she had been slated to go on the *Challenger*'s next flight, NASA temporarily suspended the shuttle program. By the time Sally left NASA, she had logged a total of 343 hours in space.

Her work for NASA and to support women in space continued. Sally served on the *Challenger* accident investigation board and was part of the team that articulated NASA's long-term spaceflight goals. She devoted her life to closing the distance between Earth and space for everyone. Bonnie Dunbar, a fellow astronaut, described befriending Sally on the Flight Crew Operations coed softball team and remembered conversations about how lucky they had been to have "teachers and parents and other mentors who encouraged us to study math and science in school — the enabling subjects for becoming an astronaut." Sally championed STEM education for young people from all backgrounds, especially young girls. She founded a company, Sally Ride Science, that provided science curriculums for schools. She started an online project through NASA in which middle school students could both shoot and download images of the Earth from space. Close to my heart as a mom and children's book author, she also wrote wonderful space books for kids, delving into such topics as how to make a sandwich in space. (Quickly, before it floats away!)

Hillary

In March 2009, when I was secretary of state, I went to Israel and crossed over to the West Bank to Ramallah, to the headquarters of the Palestinian Authority. I visited a classroom where Palestinian students were learning English through a U.S.-sponsored program. They were studying women's history month, and their lesson was about Sally Ride. The students — especially the girls — were captivated by her story. When I asked for a single word to describe Sally and her accomplishments, a student responded: "Hopeful."

Chelsea

Even after her death in 2012, Sally Ride kept breaking barriers. She came out as a lesbian quietly, without fanfare, in an obituary written by Dr. Tam O'Shaughnessy, her partner of twenty-seven years. At various chapters in her life, she worried that being open about who she was would hurt NASA, would hurt her company with corporate sponsors, would hurt her career. They didn't hide their relationship from family and friends, but, heartbreakingly, they felt they had to wait until after Sally's death to reveal it publicly. Not long after her death, Tam received a call that surprised her, from Ray Mabus, then secretary of the navy. The navy hoped to honor Sally by naming a research vessel after her. Secretary Mabus was calling to ask whether Tam would be the ship's sponsor — a role that had, up until that point, been filled by the wife of the man for whom the ship was named. "I think it is fitting that the celebration of Sally's legacy as a pioneering space explorer and a role model includes an acknowledgment of who she really was and what she cared about," said Tam. The R/V *Sally Ride,* commissioned in 2016, is the first navy research ship named for a woman. Her legacy lives on in the scientific curiosity sparked in the girls and boys she continues to inspire, the ship that bears her name, and a spot on the moon named after her by NASA.

MAE JEMISON

CHELSEA

A few years after Sally Ride first went into orbit, Mae Jemison was accepted into NASA's astronaut program. As a girl growing up in Chicago in the 1950s and '60s, Mae had dreamed of going into space. She adored science, and was constantly looking for patterns in stars, watching ants, and even learning all she could about pus after she got a splinter in her finger. Like Sally, she also had interests that stretched beyond science. Mae loved to dance and, in high school, had to make the decision whether to pursue dancing professionally or go to college. She chose the latter and went to Stanford.

After college, Mae went to medical school, then served as a doctor with the Peace Corps, based in Liberia. Later, she worked as a vaccine researcher with the Centers for Disease Control. Even across the world and in a lab, she never gave up on her dream of going into space. As part of the NASA astronaut program starting in 1987, Mae initially worked on launch support activities, including during the period of the 1988 *Discovery* flight. That was NASA's first space mission after the

"Never be limited by other people's limited imaginations. If you adopt their attitudes, then the possibility won't exist because you'll have already shut it out. . . . You can hear other people's wisdom, but you've got to reevaluate the world for yourself."

— MAE JEMISON

Challenger tragedy more than two years before. In 1992, Mae finally realized her childhood goal of journeying into space. While thousands of miles above Earth, Mae investigated how weightlessness and motion sickness affected the shuttle crew, including herself, and conducted bone cell research. As a fellow dance lover, I've always appreciated that Mae took not only her medical training into space but also an Alvin Ailey poster (along with a Michael Jordan jersey).

While she left NASA soon after her space flight, Mae remained engaged in the sciences in a variety of ways, from teaching environmental studies at Dartmouth, to working on a satellite company aiming to improve health care delivery in Africa, to becoming the first actual astronaut to appear on the television show *Star Trek.* She later led NASA's 100 Year Starship effort to advance the necessary research to bring interstellar travel out of the realm of *Star Trek* and science fiction and into reality. In 2017, Mae and Sally were two of the women featured in the inaugural Women of NASA LEGO set. My kids aren't old enough to play with it yet, as some of the pieces are very small, but we have it high on a shelf, ready to go as soon as they are.

Today, more than sixty women have been to space, including fifty Americans who have flown with NASA. While that number is much higher than it was thirty years ago,

> *"It's by pursuing things that [are] extraordinary that we build a better world today. We didn't get to where we are now by being timid. . . . Let's push bigger."*
> — MAE JEMISON

women still comprise less than 20 percent of the number of Americans who have traveled to space and barely break 10 percent worldwide.

Sally and Mae are among the women who helped make it possible for American girls to imagine themselves in a space suit, on a spaceship, in outer space. Those women include Ellen Ochoa, the first Latina astronaut, who flew on four shuttle flights, logged more than a thousand hours in space, and went on to lead NASA's Johnson Space Center, otherwise known as Mission Control. They include Sunita Williams, an American astronaut who ran the first marathon in space. (Really! She ran 26.2 miles on the space station treadmill while the Boston Marathon was taking place on Earth.) And they include Peggy Whitson, the first female space station commander and the woman and American who has spent the most time in space: 665 days. Their stories are proof that when one barrier is broken, it can set off a domino effect.

■■■■

HEALERS

■■■■

FLORENCE NIGHTINGALE

CHELSEA

Between Sunday school and the church service at First United Methodist in Little Rock, I would go to our church library. It was there that I discovered Florence Nightingale and

283

embarked on a now-lifelong fascination with the woman who helped invent modern nursing, dramatically improved hospitals, and pioneered data visualization.

Florence was named for her birthplace in Italy in 1820. (Though her parents were British, she was born during their extended honeymoon.) Her parents, especially her father, were committed to her education. She studied math, history, philosophy, and literature, and from a young age, she could read and write in French, German, Italian, Greek, and Latin. At the time, it was seen as imperative for a young woman of her social standing to learn "domestic pursuits," such as cleaning, cooking, and sewing — and she did. But Florence's interests lay elsewhere; she was much more interested in having spirited political debates with her father. (A woman after my own heart!)

From the time she was a teenager, Florence believed she had been called to help alleviate human suffering. She dreamed of being a nurse and persevered despite her family's initial — and staunch — opposition. She defied her parents and signed up for training, becoming first a nurse, and then a superintendent of the Institution for the Care of Sick Gentlewomen in Distressed Circumstances, a hospital in London. She confronted outbreaks of cholera and other diseases while honing her administrative skills and working to improve hygiene throughout the hospital. She had just come to the realization that her passion was training others to become nurses when war broke out on the Crimean Peninsula in 1853.

British newspaper reports from the time depicted horrifying conditions for British soldiers being cared for at hospitals away from the front lines: Supplies were inadequate, conditions were unsanitary, staff was untrained, and patients were crowded into too-small facilities. At the British government's request, Florence brought a delegation of thirty-eight nurses to try to improve conditions at a hospital in Scutari, the British base hospital in what was then Constantinople.

Florence and her fellow nurses were not welcomed by the military hospital staff, who resented the idea that they should have to answer to a group of civilian women. The hostility of the doctors and the conditions of the hospital led Florence to refer to the facility as the "Kingdom of Hell." Others might have given up, but Florence was determined to do anything and everything she could to help the soldiers in the hospital whose health was getting worse, not better.

Through tenacity and sheer force of will, Florence and her colleagues implemented basic standards of care at the hospital. Under her leadership, practices like applying clean dressings to wounds, bathing patients, and providing healthy meals became commonplace. She believed that psychological well-being was an important component of recovery — an uncommon view in the 1850s — and spent time helping soldiers write letters home and reading the responses from their loved ones. Her habit of walking the wards at night, tending to patients by a small light she carried with her, led to her being nicknamed "the Lady with the Lamp."

When the war ended, Florence, suffering from exhaustion and illness, was welcomed home to England as a hero. But she was more interested in continuing her work than being celebrated. She used the money the British government gave her in recognition of her efforts during the Crimean War to establish a hospital and nurse training school in London. She met with government authorities and lobbied for a special commission to further investigate how to improve hospital conditions for soldiers and civilian patients alike. She had kept meticulous records during her time in Turkey. Her careful plotting and colorful visualizations of data, along with her statistical analyses, helped make the case for the importance of hygiene in all medical care. Florence also developed the "coxcomb," a new type of graph to show how causes of mortality fluctuate over a twelve-month period; it is still in use today. Teaching about Florence Nightingale makes for some of my favorite moments every year at Columbia's Mailman School of Public Health. My students are often surprised by

> *"How very little can be done*
> *under the spirit of fear."*
> — FLORENCE NIGHTINGALE

how much of what we take for granted today can be linked to Florence.

Throughout her life, even after she herself was bedridden and homebound with chronic illness, Florence kept up her work to make handwashing, good ventilation, good food, and clean sheets and bandages in hospitals all part of the standard of care — an effort that reduced the mortality rate at the British base hospital in Scutari from 40 percent to 2 percent. She elevated the profession of nursing, and women from across Britain and across different social classes came to her school, hoping to follow her example. Her most popular book, *Notes on Nursing: What It Is, and What It Is Not,* is still in publication today. Clara Barton, who lived in the same era and founded the American Red Cross, cited Florence as one of her inspirations. When Florence died in 1910, her family respected her wishes and refused a national funeral. "Her life was devoted to the relief of suffering at first," reported the *Times,* "while her strength remained, by the tenderness of her own ministrations, and then by the great system of trained nursing which was one of the glories of this age."

CLARA BARTON

HILLARY

When the Civil War started in 1861, thirty-nine-year-old Clarissa Harlowe Barton, better known to her friends as Clara, was working in the United States Patent Office in Washington, D.C., as a copyist. Before that, she had spent more than a decade as a teacher, during an era when most teachers were men. (She even ran a free school for poor children in New Jersey, though when a male principal was hired at twice her salary to take over, she resigned in protest. "I may sometimes be willing to teach for nothing," she said, "but if paid at all, I shall never do a man's work for less than a man's pay.") She was forceful, independent, and focused. All her life, she would struggle with bouts of depression; the best thing to help her bounce back was usually a problem in need of solving.

When the war broke out and troops poured into D.C., Clara quickly realized many of the soldiers were hurt and hungry. She gathered clothing, food, and bandages and brought them to the troops being housed in the not yet completed U.S. Capitol Building. To Clara, they were "her boys." In addition to gathering medical supplies, she read to the men, cooked for them, wrote letters for them, listened to their problems, and prayed with them. Soon, though, she realized that the place she was needed most was the battlefield itself.

Clara lobbied the army to give her the credentials she needed to bring supplies and support to the front lines and volunteer. She convinced them to let her go. One night in 1862, after a particularly brutal battle in northern Virginia, she showed up at a field hospital around midnight with a wagonload of supplies. A surgeon working at the camp wrote: "I thought that night if heaven ever sent out a[n] . . . angel, she must be one — for her assistance was so timely." She became known as the Angel of the Battlefield.

Danger didn't bother Clara; being stuck with the medical units at the back of the military procession, sometimes days behind the action, did. During a winter-imposed break in Civil War battles, she wrote in her diaries: "I am depressed and feel dissatisfied with myself." She struggled with the "thin black snakes" of sadness that threatened to close in around her until the fighting started up again and she could throw herself into another task. She even contemplated killing herself. More than once she raced ahead so she could be there for soldiers on the battlefields until the official aid got there. "I could run the risk," she explained. "It made no difference to anyone if I were shot or taken prisoner." It clearly did make a difference to the soldiers whose lives she saved through her daring.

As the war ended, Clara searched for another

problem to solve. In 1865, she found one. That year, President Lincoln wrote in a letter: "To the Friends of Missing Persons: Miss Clara Barton has kindly offered to search for the missing prisoners of war. Please address her . . . giving her the name, regiment, and company of any missing prisoner." She helped start the Office of Correspondence with Friends of the Missing Men of the United States Army, and she and her team answered 63,000 letters and identified over 22,000 missing men. Clara went on to help establish a national cemetery for the Union soldiers who died at Andersonville Prison in Georgia, the largest Confederate prison camp.

In 1869, while traveling in Europe, Clara heard about the global Red Cross network, headquartered in Geneva, Switzerland. Its members had called for international agreements to provide voluntary aid, and Clara took up the cause when she came home, helping to wage a successful fight alongside famous friends like Frederick Douglass to argue for the creation of an American chapter of the organization.

In 1881, at sixty years old, she founded the American Red Cross, which she led for the next twenty-three years. During her time, the American Red Cross helped victims of a forest fire in Michigan and a dam break in Pennsylvania. It shipped cornmeal and flour to Russia, where famine was rampant, and provided disaster relief to residents of the Sea Islands in South Carolina after a flood and survivors of a hurricane in Texas.

After she stepped down as president of the American Red Cross, Clara helped found the National First Aid Association of America and served as its honorary president. The organization focused on first aid instruction and emergency preparedness, both of which would later become key activities of the American Red Cross. She took up other causes, from prison reform to public education, suffrage to civil rights. She was recognized around the world for spearheading relief efforts during periods of immense suffering. Her firm, uncompromising personality sometimes rubbed people the wrong way, if you can believe it.

Clara was ahead of her time, and she refused to wait for society to catch up. She had bold ideas about our country's obligation to help not only our own citizens but people around the world in times of crisis. She charged bravely forward. Because she did, she helped more people than we will ever know find relief, comfort, and peace — even when she had a hard time finding it herself.

ELIZABETH BLACKWELL, REBECCA LEE CRUMPLER, AND MARY EDWARDS WALKER

ELIZABETH BLACKWELL

REBECCA LEE CRUMPLER

MARY EDWARDS WALKER

293

Elizabeth Blackwell was an unlikely candidate to become the first woman in America to receive a medical degree. She wrote in her autobiography, *Pioneer Work in Opening the Medical Profession to Women,* that as a young woman, she initially "hated everything connected with the body." But she found herself called to medicine by a dying friend who Elizabeth believed suffered unnecessarily because she didn't have access to a well-qualified woman physician. Elizabeth understood before most that the life experiences of doctors matter to the quality of care that patients receive, particularly when prejudice and bigotry abound.

In the 1840s, a decision to become a doctor didn't mean Elizabeth could immediately start studying medicine. Although she had been tutored alongside her brothers and been a teacher, she was still a woman. She moved to Philadelphia in 1847, hoping friends there could help her apply to medical school. All but one school rejected her: Geneva Medical College in rural New York. Though it turned out her admission had been intended as a "joke" by the school, Elizabeth took them seriously and enrolled.

In 1849, she received her medical degree, having earned the grudging respect of her professors and classmates. She traveled abroad to gain more experience, working in London and Paris, where she contracted an infection that cost her the vision in one eye. Although she knew it would prohibit her from becoming a surgeon, as she had once dreamed, she refused to give up her medical career. She opened a small women's health clinic in New York that grew into the New York Infirmary for Women and Children.

In time, she became more and more convinced that women doctors were an important part of ensuring that women patients received good care. In the late 1860s, she opened one of the first medical colleges for women in the United States, with a focus on training new doctors to care for poor women and children. A few years later, she helped establish the first medical school in Britain to train women as physicians.

I first learned about Elizabeth from Sara Auld, my senior-year roommate at Stanford. Sara's thesis focused on Charlotte Blake Brown, one of the first woman doctors in California. Like Elizabeth, Charlotte left home to study medicine and then opened a hospital focused on women and children in San Francisco. Listening to Sara talk about her research into this remarkable nineteenth-century American is one of my favorite memories from college.

Sara's interest in Charlotte and Elizabeth prompted us to look for other women medical pioneers and heroes, leading us to Dr. Rebecca Lee Crumpler, the first black woman doctor in the United States. Born in Delaware in 1831, she grew up in Pennsylvania watching her aunt care for sick people in their community. Rebecca worked as a nurse until she was accepted to medical school. After she graduated in 1864 from the New England Female Medical College, she started her career as a physician caring for low-income women and children in Boston. When the Civil War ended, she moved to Virginia, where she worked for the Freedman's Bureau to care for freed slaves.

Rebecca faced intense racism and sexism from her colleagues in the South. Her fellow physicians snubbed her, and pharmacists ignored her. She couldn't fully take care of her patients if prescriptions went unfilled. She moved back to Boston and continued her career while also working on a book about good medical care for mothers and children. When, in 1883, she published *A Book of Medical Discourses: In Two Parts,* Rebecca may have been the first black American to have a medical textbook in print. It was notable for its focus on children at a time when most medical tracts focused solely on adults. Her book is dedicated to "mothers, nurses, and all who may desire to mitigate the afflictions of the human race." Her legacy lives on in the Rebecca Lee Society, one of the first medical societies for black women.

Through our explorations, Sara and I also

found Dr. Mary Edwards Walker, the only woman in her medical school class at Syracuse Medical College in 1855. She was a practicing physician when the Civil War broke out. She desperately wanted to enlist in the Union Army as a surgeon but wasn't allowed to because she was a woman. Initially, she was called a nurse, since women generally weren't considered doctors. Because women were not allowed to enlist, Mary had to volunteer, working for free at a temporary hospital, first in Washington and then in Virginia, where she traveled to Union field hospitals across the commonwealth. Mary watched other surgeons routinely perform dangerous, unnecessary amputations on soldiers suffering from fractures and other injuries. She began discreetly advising soldiers against the procedures when she thought they were not warranted. After the war, she would receive thank you letters from patients whose limbs had healed. When her medical credentials were finally accepted, she moved to Tennessee and became a War Department surgeon — a paid position that was the equivalent of a lieutenant in status.

"Let the generations know that women in uniform also guaranteed their freedom."
— DR. MARY EDWARDS WALKER

During the war, she crossed enemy lines to treat the wounded and was arrested by Confederate forces as a spy. She was held for several months before she and some of her colleagues were exchanged "man for man" for Confederate medical officers. After her release, she was contracted as a surgeon — the first female surgeon ever commissioned in the army — and served through the end of the war.

Mary was not only a surgeon; she was also an activist. One of the causes close to her heart was for women to be able to wear clothes that actually allowed them to move freely. Born in 1832, in Oswego, New York, Mary worked on her family's farm from a young age, wearing boys' clothing, which was much better suited to physical labor than the tight corsets and full skirts that women were expected to wear. Years later, when she married one of her medical school classmates, she wore trousers and a dress coat. (She also struck "to obey" from the marriage vows, and she kept her own name.) Throughout the Civil War, she famously sported "bloomers," or a combination of a dress and pants. During her time in Virginia, though she was not yet officially credentialed by the military, she designed her own uniform: blue with a green sash, similar to the clothing worn by male physicians on the battlefield. The *New York Tribune* described her in an article: "Dressed in male habiliments . . . she carries herself amid the camp with a jaunty air of dignity well calculated to receive the sincere respect of the soldiers. . . . She can amputate a limb with the skill of an old surgeon, and administer medicine equally as well. Strange to say that, although she has frequently applied for a permanent position in the medical corps, she has never been formally assigned to any particular duty."

After the war Mary traveled the country, lecturing on dress reform, and was even elected president of the National Dress Reform Association. She sported men's pants, a top hat, and a bow tie and was arrested several times for "impersonating" a man. (Keith Negley's wonderfully titled children's book, *Mary Wears What She Wants,* tells her story and is a favorite in our house!) She used her public platform to campaign for equal rights for women for the rest of her life, including advocating for a woman's right to vote. In 1865, Mary was awarded the Congressional Medal of Honor, the first woman to be so recognized. As hard as it is to believe, she is still the only woman ever to be deemed worthy of this honor. In 1917, Congress rescinded her medal — along with hundreds of others — citing a lack of combat experience. Dr. Walker refused to return the medal. Instead, she wore it every day until her death. Decades later, President Jimmy Carter posthumously reinstated the award.

These are just a few of the many women who felt called to be physicians before most medical schools admitted women. They are part of a global sisterhood of women whose impact continues to this day — women like Kadambini Ganguly, who in 1886 became the first Indian-educated woman doctor; and Yoshioka Yayoi, who in 1892 became the first woman physician in Japan and later founded the Tokyo Women's Medical School. All of them fought not just to break down barriers for themselves but to advocate for their peers and the women who would come after them.

BETTY FORD

HILLARY AND CHELSEA

Hillary

Betty Ford was not only an influential first lady in the last half of the twentieth century, she was also a transformational American.

Aside from being gracious, humble, and welcoming, she was fierce. She advocated passionately for the Equal Rights Amendment, which would guarantee all Americans equal rights regardless of sex — and which still hasn't passed. She never shied away from expressing her views. "I believe the Equal Rights Amendment is a necessity of life for all citizens," she said. "The Cabinet sometimes felt that I shouldn't be so outspoken."

Chelsea

Betty was born in Chicago in 1918 and spent her childhood in Grand Rapids, Michigan. She took dance lessons from the time she was eight years old and, after graduating from high school, briefly pursued a dance career. As a student at Bennington College in Vermont, she studied with modern dancer and choreographer Martha Graham — someone who, Betty later said, shaped her life "more than anyone else." After college, she moved to New York City to dance as part of Graham's company. She then moved back to Grand Rapids where she worked in fashion and taught dance to children with disabilities. She married a childhood friend and cared for him as he struggled with alcoholism and poor health; after five years, they divorced. Betty later met and married a World War II veteran and lawyer named Gerald Ford.

Hillary

I felt Betty's influence throughout my life, especially her work around breast cancer. It was very personal to me; my mother's best friend, who lived across the street from us in the 1960s, was diagnosed with breast cancer, and at the time no one talked about it. I knew my mother was over there every afternoon, but I had no idea what was wrong with her friend. It was only after she died that I learned what she had been going through. But then along came Betty Ford. She talked about her ordeal, even sharing a photo of herself in her hospital room after surgery in 1974. It was reassuring and invigorating to have an important person, let alone our first lady, be so open and honest and personal about her cancer. She explained that "maybe if I as First Lady could talk about it candidly and without embarrassment, many other people would be able to as well." She also campaigned for early detection and screening, research, and better access to treatment, and

"I do not believe that being First Lady should prevent me from expressing my ideas. . . . Why should my husband's job or yours prevent us from being ourselves? Being ladylike does not require silence."
— BETTY FORD

blew away the stigma that had kept countless women from even getting examinations. We'll never know how many lives she saved, both directly and indirectly, because of her courage in facing up to her own illness.

After she left the White House Betty was equally open about her successful battle against substance use disorders and addiction. I visited the Betty Ford Center with her years ago, and was stunned by the dignity with which patients were treated; there was no place for stigma at the Betty Ford Center. She could have just given her name to the facility and left it at that; but of course she didn't. She knew the names of every staff member and every patient. (When I expressed my awe, she brushed it off, explaining that she only knew their *first* names. Still!) To me, Betty has always embodied grit and guts.

Chelsea

In addition to her campaign to destigmatize breast cancer and addiction, and expand treatment for both, Betty also championed the Equal Rights Amendment and gender pay equity. She was vocally pro-choice; while her husband suggested *Roe v. Wade* went too far, Betty publicly celebrated the landmark Supreme Court decision that legalized abortion. *Time* magazine named her the "Fighting First Lady" for her unapologetic political, social, and public health stances.

That steeliness continued throughout her life. Her support for full equality under the Constitution and a woman's right to make her own reproductive health decisions never wavered, even as the party her husband had led moved further away from them both.

MATHILDE KRIM

CHELSEA

In high school, I read *And the Band Played On,* Randy Shilts's extraordinary book about the early days of the AIDS (acquired immune deficiency syndrome, caused by HIV

306

or human immunodeficiency virus) epidemic. Shilts detailed the painful toll of AIDS on the gay community in San Francisco and New York in the early 1980s, exacerbated by those in the medical world and government at all levels who ignored the suffering because AIDS was seen as a "gay disease." Shilts also wrote movingly about the heroic doctors and researchers who did the opposite, throwing themselves into caring for AIDS patients and diving into research to find the cause of the disease and how to stop it. One of those doctors was Mathilde Krim.

As a young scientist in the 1950s, Mathilde studied cancer-causing viruses in Israel. She also studied cytogenetics and was part of the team that developed prenatal testing to determine the sex of a fetus. After she moved to New York, she was a researcher at Cornell Medical College and Memorial Sloan Kettering Cancer Center. Throughout the 1960s and her life, Mathilde supported the civil rights movement, the gay rights movement, and the women's movement in the United States, as well as the independence movement in Zimbabwe and anti-apartheid movement in South Africa. She was also a strong supporter of Israel, then a relatively new country. Mathilde was clearly not one to shy away from controversial issues or scientific challenges; her character was shaped as a child growing up in Switzerland during World War II. In an interview, she described the experience of watching the liberation of the Nazi death camps: "I confronted the reality that racism is murderous." She would later realize that bigotry in any form can kill.

Early in the AIDS epidemic, Mathilde was one of the first scientists to recognize that AIDS was a new disease with possible catastrophic consequences. In 1983, she and others started the AIDS Medical Foundation to raise money to fund research. Her efforts were particularly important at the time because the American government was largely ignoring AIDS, with the exception of a few notable heroes at the Centers for Disease Control and the National Institutes of Health.

In addition to raising research dollars, Mathilde pushed New York City and the federal government alike to invest more in AIDS; to name AIDS; and most important, to treat AIDS patients with dignity. She pushed her medical colleagues to do the same. When asked by a *New York Times* reporter why she

---

"Most people start with this idea that they can't do anything because 'I'm only a little guy and I can't have an effect on public policy.' It's not so. Everybody can do something."

— MATHILDE KRIM

---

had gotten involved, she answered, "Because I was incensed! So many young men were dying. . . . And many would be dying abandoned or alone because they were afraid to contact their families." She made it her personal mission to provide compassion, good medical care, and hope.

Her work and advocacy, along with the work of other researchers and health care providers, yielded real results. In 1985, Congress significantly increased AIDS research funding. In 1987, the American Medical Association declared that doctors have an obligation to care for people with AIDS, including asymptomatic patients. Throughout the 1980s, Congress allocated more and more funding for AIDS research. In 1990, Congress passed the Ryan White Comprehensive AIDS Resources Emergency Act, which was then and remains the largest federal program for people living with HIV/AIDS.

Alongside the doctors who were waging a research battle were advocates like Elizabeth Glaser, who contracted HIV in 1981 from a blood transfusion while giving birth to her daughter, Ariel. Elizabeth later passed on HIV unknowingly to Ariel through breastfeeding, and to Jacob, her son, in utero. The Glaser family raced against time to fight for access to treatment. Tragically, it was too late for Ariel. Galvanized by Ariel's loss, the Glasers started a foundation to raise funds for pediatric AIDS research. Elizabeth's work, like Mathilde's, helped save other lives, including her son's. A few years before Elizabeth's death in 1994, she wrote about her family's struggles with HIV/AIDS in *In the Absence of Angels*. As my Grandma Ginger would have said, both Elizabeth and Mathilde were engaged in God's work — and, I think she would say, closer to angels than most people would ever be.

Larry Kramer, the great playwright and LGBTQ rights activist, once said of Mathilde: "One can only be filled with overpowering awe and gratitude that such a person has lived among us." I agree. I was proud to honor her in 2011 at an event for amfAR, the Foundation for AIDS Research, a successor organization to the one she started in the early 1980s. I talked that night about how grateful I am to live in a world with real heroes like Mathilde, who saved countless lives through her resolve, adaptability, curiosity, intelligence, and heart. I believe Mathilde would be appalled, but not surprised, by current efforts to diminish HIV/ AIDS research, prevention, and treatment funding in the United States and around the world. We must protect the progress she, Elizabeth, and many others fought so hard for and keep fighting until every patient with HIV/AIDS is treated with dignity and receives the treatment they need, while continuing the search for a vaccine and cure.

DR. GAO YAOJIE

HILLARY

Back in 1996, in the midst of the exploding global AIDS crisis, a retired Chinese gynecologist, Dr. Gao Yaojie, consulted on the case of a forty-two-year-old woman who was not improving after ovarian surgery. After examining her, Gao demanded an HIV test because, based on her own practice, she knew that AIDS was present where she lived, in Henan Province. Her colleagues could not imagine how a peasant farmer could have contracted HIV, a "foreign disease" they perceived to only affect drug addicts and sex workers. The test came back positive, sending Gao on a hunt to find out what had happened. She discovered that the woman had contracted AIDS from a transfusion that used blood from a government blood bank. Gao immediately understood that if the government was supplying the blood, much of the supply could be tainted, and many more people could be infected both from transfusions and from selling their own blood and plasma.

Gao traveled across rural China, finding high rates of infection and little understanding by the people affected about how they had become infected and why they were sick and dying. She also discovered that corrupt local government officials were complicit in turning a blind eye to poor farmers selling their blood, creating the "plasma economy" between 1991 and 1995.

Gao and other doctors urged the government to warn people about the risk of contracting AIDS from blood donations and transfusions, and to stop the system. When that didn't happen, Gao began making speeches and distributing written warnings. She even began speaking to the press, an especially courageous move given how closely the Chinese government monitored the media. After a few years, the story about the Chinese government's complicity in the blood scandal started being covered in both the Chinese and the international media. The negative global press finally forced China to ban unlicensed plasma and blood collection centers, but it was too late for the thousands of people already infected.

Gao burned with righteous anger at the deadly injustice done to vulnerable people, and kept pushing the government for legal rights and compensation for victims. She gave financial help to children orphaned because of AIDS. She was nicknamed "AIDS Granny" and "Grandmother Courage." Her relentless campaign to raise the profile of victims and hold the government accountable enraged local officials, many of whom had profited from the blood centers. They threatened her and her family but failed to stop her.

It was not the first time she suffered under the Communist Party regime. As an educated doctor, she was accused of being an elite counterrevolutionary and spent a year in a forced labor camp. She and her family were finally reunited in 1973, and she returned to her medical practice.

The first time I heard of Dr. Gao Yaojie

was early in 2007. She had been invited to the United States to receive an award for her AIDS advocacy from Vital Voices, an organization that I helped start as first lady. When the local authorities in China learned about the award, they put her under house arrest. When I heard that she wasn't being allowed to travel, I wrote a letter to President Hu Jintao and Vice Premier Wu Yi asking that they permit her to come. Vice Premier Wu Yi, the highest-ranking woman in the Chinese government at the time, also Health Minister and a politburo member, played an instrumental role in getting Gao released and granting her permission to come to the United States.

I met Dr. Gao at my senate office for a long talk in March 2007 and saw for myself how formidable this diminutive woman was. Her walk was hobbled from her feet having been bound as a child, but she was an unstoppable energy force.

I saw her again on my very first trip as secretary of state to China in February 2009, where I said: "Change really does come from individual decisions, many millions of individual decisions, where someone stands up like Dr. Gao and says 'No, I am not going to be quiet.' That's what we have to encourage." We were together again on November 30, 2009, in my office at the State Department on the eve of World AIDS Day. I pointed out then that "Dr. Gao Yaojie has been harassed for speaking out about AIDS in China. She should instead be applauded by her government for helping to confront the crisis."

Later, Gao told me that I reminded her of her mother (even though I was much younger than she!). She and I connected despite our different life experiences. Of our connection, she said: "I didn't need to explain too much. I could tell how much she wanted to understand what I, an eightysomething-year-old lady, went through in China — the Cultural Revolution, uncovering the largest tainted blood scandal in China, house arrest, forced family separation. I talked about it like nothing, and I joked about it, but she understood me as a person, a mother, a doctor. She knew what I really went through." I recently visited her apartment in New York City, where she has lived since May of 2010. Although confined to her bed, she proudly told me she was working on her thirty-first book. Her resilience in the face of almost unimaginable difficulties, and her insistence on speaking the truth no matter who tries to silence her, are a powerful reminder of what one determined woman can overcome.

DR. HAWA ABDI

HILLARY AND CHELSEA

Hillary

Imagine you're an obstetrician-gynecologist responsible for ninety thousand people living as displaced persons on your family property in war-torn Somalia. And then, in May 2010, your office is overrun by hundreds of Islamist militants. "Women can't do things like this," they say. The militants hold you under house arrest, and take over the camp. Many people would be paralyzed by fear, or would try to escape in order to save themselves. Dr. Hawa Abdi was not, and she did not. Instead, she confronted the militants.

"I'm not leaving my hospital," she told them. "If I die, I will die with my people and my dignity." Then she went a step further: "You are young and you are a man, but what have you done for your society?" Her captors stayed for a week, ultimately leaving after the UN intervened. Hawa promptly went back to work.

Chelsea

Hawa's answer to the question she posed stretches back to her childhood. Her mother died when she was pregnant with her seventh child, leaving twelve-year-old Hawa to care for her younger siblings. She has said that

---

"[Women] are not just the helpless and the victims of the civil war. We can reconcile. We can do everything."

— DR. HAWA ABDI

---

because she couldn't prevent her mother's death, she decided to become a doctor.

In 1983, she opened her first clinic on her family farm. As violence in Somalia increased, many people, mostly women and children, sought refuge on her property. She organized a camp to house and care for everyone she could. Hawa prohibited domestic violence and made it clear from its inception that the camp would care for all Somalis, regardless of clan, religion, or politics. She named the camp, appropriately, Hope Village.

Years of violence drove many families off their land, and the drought made farming impossible for many others, leading to a catastrophic famine and causing widespread starvation that killed first the cattle, then children and the elderly. Hawa opened her heart and her doors. She took in more people and provided food, medical supplies, and other necessities. She was determined to save not only those in her care but her entire country. She kept going through every danger and obstacle — including threats on her life and removal of a benign brain tumor for which she had to leave Somalia. As soon as she recovered, she returned home.

Hillary

The threats against Hawa continued. Her brave refusal to give in prompted hundreds of women from the camp to protest against the militants and demand that they leave. This display of courage prompted Somalis around the world to condemn the militants, who eventually backed down. Hawa then insisted that the young militants apologize in writing. And they did. She writes about her experiences in her book, *Keeping Hope Alive: One Woman, 90,000 Lives Changed*.

Chelsea

When I met Hawa in 2010, one of the things that stood out most strongly was her pride at being joined in her work by two of her daughters. Dr. Amina Mohamed and Dr. Deqo Mohamed help run the Dr. Hawa Abdi Foundation, which raises money to sustain the hospital and camp on their family's land. "I'm thankful for my daughters," Hawa has said. "When they come to me, they [help] me to treat the people . . . They have done what I desire to do for them." Alongside the hospital, Dr. Hawa Abdi Hope Village — as it is known today — now has a primary school, a high school, a women's education center, and free fresh water, available to the 10,000 people who live there and others who come from outside the village. Hawa's courage has proven that hope is so much more than a word — it is untold lives saved, babies born safely, children educated, and a different, more peaceful future beginning to be realized.

FLOSSIE WONG-STAAL

CHELSEA

While Yee Ching Wong was growing up in the 1950s in Guangzhou, China, and later in Hong Kong, none of the women in her family worked outside the home. Still, her parents

320

and her teachers encouraged her interest in learning, especially when it came to the sciences. She excelled in school and decided to go to college in the United States. In preparation, her teachers urged her to change her name to fit in with her new classmates. She became known as Flossie, after a typhoon that had struck the area a week before. When I first learned that detail, it struck me as an extraordinary metaphor, given that Flossie would help us understand the greatest and most threatening public health "storm" in my lifetime.

Her academic journey in science started at age eighteen, when Flossie moved to California to study bacteriology at UCLA. Her natural talent combined with hard work led to her earning a BS in just three years. In 1972, before she had turned twenty-five, she earned a PhD in molecular biology.

Flossie's postdoctoral work took her to the National Cancer Institute, where she began a lifelong study of retroviruses, a group of viruses that insert their viral DNA into the DNA of a host cell. In 1983, she was a core part of the team that identified a retrovirus known as human immunodeficiency virus (HIV) as the cause of acquired immunodeficiency syndrome (AIDS). A French team at the Pasteur Institute had simultaneously identified the virus, and both teams published their findings in *Science* a year apart.

After years of disputing who had made the discovery first, the lead scientists agreed to share the credit and work together to fight a scourge that was already infecting tens of thousands around the world and tens of millions today. Now it's generally agreed that the French team first isolated the HIV virus, and Flossie's team first recognized it as the cause of AIDS. What is not disputed is that in 1985, Flossie became the first person in the world to clone HIV. That breakthrough enabled Flossie and her team to map the virus, paving the way for the development of blood tests to detect the presence of HIV.

After almost two decades at the National Cancer Institute, in 1990, Flossie continued her research on HIV/AIDS at the University of California at San Diego. She focused on the then emerging field of gene therapy, moving genes or parts of genes into cells that have missing or defective genes in order to help treat or prevent diseases. Flossie explored the use of gene therapy to repress HIV in stem cells. In particular, she focused on trying to better understand the relationship between a type of protein and the Kaposi's sarcoma lesions found on some patients with HIV/AIDS. Her work was about more than science for science's sake; it led to better treatments.

Not content to make one major discovery, Flossie eventually moved on to another challenge. Later in her career, she began applying

> *"It adds to the joy of discovery to know that your work may make a difference in people's lives."*
> — FLOSSIE WONG-STAAL

her work in HIV/AIDS to hepatitis C, a virus that also spreads through transfusions, dirty needles, and sex (though sexual transmission is rare, unlike with HIV/AIDS). Left untreated, hepatitis C can cause liver damage, liver cancer, and liver failure, all of which can lead to death. Flossie founded a company focused solely on discovering and developing drugs to treat this deadly disease. More than seventy million people worldwide are believed to be infected with hepatitis C, and hundreds of thousands of people each year die because they don't receive early diagnosis or the treatment that exists. More troubling still, hepatitis C rates are currently on the rise in the United States. Now in her seventies, Flossie is still hard at work confronting the virus. I hope she will have the same impact on hepatitis that she had on HIV/AIDS. She is remarkable not only for her talent but for her tenacity and unwillingness to let any virus go unchallenged.

MOLLY MELCHING

HILLARY

In March 1997, Chelsea and I visited a number of African countries, meeting with political and civic leaders in cities and villages to emphasize a message of respect and friendship on behalf of the United States. Our first stop was Senegal, the ancestral home of millions of black Americans who had been sold into slavery through Gorée Island off the coast of Dakar, the capital. At the small fort where slaves were held, leg irons and chains were still attached to the walls of musty cells. Innocent people, ripped from home and family and reduced to chattel, were herded through the Door of No Return at the back of the fort, dropped onto the beach, and loaded into boats to be rowed out to the anchored slave ships — all reminders of the human capacity for evil and of the original sin of the United States.

In the village of Saam Njaay, an hour and a half from Dakar, I saw a revolution in women's lives and health in the making. Molly Melching, an American from Illinois, was our guide and teacher. Molly had come to Senegal to study French at the University of Dakar in 1974. After completing her studies, she stayed in Senegal and served in the Peace Corps, working with children. She published books, started a center to serve children who lived on the streets, and used songs and plays to educate young people about health.

In 1991, Molly created Tostan, a nonprofit organization committed to promoting democracy, community empowerment, and child development. Three years later, UNESCO chose Tostan as one of the world's most innovative education programs. When Molly took Chelsea and me to Saam Njaay, we saw the organization in action. The word "tostan" translates from the Wolof language as "breakthrough," and that's exactly what started happening as women in Saam Njaay talked with each other and with Molly about their own power to fix injustices in their community.

Molly did not initially plan to take on the controversial practice of female genital cutting, but, as she recounts in the book written by Aimee Molloy about her work, *However Long the Night: Molly Melching's Journey to Help Millions of African Women and Girls Triumph,* she changed her mind because of what she heard from girls — and because of her own daughter, Zoe. Molly was stunned when nine-year-old Zoe, who had been brought up in Senegal, asked her mother if she could be cut in the same way her Senegalese friends were going to be. Molly saw the powerful pull of tradition and peer pressure, explaining, "It was a very decisive moment in my own understanding of the power of female genital cutting, and I knew now what I had to do." She added women's rights and human rights to Tostan's empowerment programs, including the sensitive issues of female genital cutting and child marriage.

As a result of Tostan's work and, crucially, the local leaders who made its mission their own, women in Senegal began speaking up

> *"If I feel we are moving forward respectfully and peacefully, I am never afraid, and will continue on with confidence and patience. But that for me is not courage— just determination and perseverance."*
>
> — MOLLY MELCHING

about the pain and terrible health effects — including death — they had seen or experienced because of female genital cutting. Tostan organized village-wide discussions, and one by one, villages started voting to end the practice. Imams and other male leaders joined the effort, traveling to neighboring villages, which followed suit. The movement's leaders petitioned Senegal's then president, Abdou Diouf, to outlaw the practice throughout the country. When I met the president and his wife, Elisabeth, I praised the grassroots movement and endorsed the call for legislation. Due to popular demand, Senegal passed a law banning female genital cutting, and more than eight thousand villages across eight nations in West Africa soon decided to stop practicing not only female genital cutting but also child marriage and forced marriage.

Making good on those pledges has been difficult, since deeply engrained cultural traditions die hard. But the determination of imams, community leaders, elected officials, and models like Tostan's that empower communities to drive the changes they want to see, has helped to free hundreds of thousands of girls from female genital cutting, as well as both boys and girls from forced marriages.

DR. MONA HANNA-ATTISHA

CHELSEA

By now, most people know the beginning of the story: In April 2014, the town of Flint, Michigan, switched its drinking water source from Lake Huron to the Flint River to save money. But the river water was more corrosive than the water from the lake, and the city did not add the right chemicals to the water to ensure the water was safe to drink by the time people turned on their taps.

Soon after the switch, the people of Flint started to worry. Their new water smelled bad, and it was the wrong color. They complained to the city, but their concerns were largely dismissed. A few months later, the city advised residents to boil their water to eliminate fecal and total coliform bacteria. They began adding more chlorine to the water to kill the bacteria and assured the people of Flint that the problem had been fixed.

Pediatrician Dr. Mona Hanna-Attisha saw hundreds of Flint kids at her clinic. When worried parents asked whether the tap water was safe to drink, wash in, and cook with, she said yes. She had faith in the city and state public health authorities to protect Flint's families. She didn't yet know how wrong she was. "My naïve trust in the government — local, state, and national — had made a liar out of me," she wrote later in the *New York Times*.

Then, one evening in the summer of 2015, over a glass of wine, a friend of Mona's who had worked for the Environmental Protection Agency in Washington mentioned that because the city hadn't treated the water with corrosion control, it probably contained lead.

Mona hadn't seen any symptoms of lead poisoning among her patients, but she knew that didn't mean this dangerous neurotoxin wasn't affecting Flint's kids. The effect of lead on brain development could be devastating for children, leading to lower IQ rates and behavior problems. There is no safe level of lead in drinking water.

Her friend urged her to do her own studies on the blood lead levels of the children she saw in her clinic. When Mona looked at her patients' blood lead numbers, her stomach dropped. Afraid to put them in an email, she asked her friend to meet her at the soccer field where her daughter was practicing that evening. She printed out the results and stuck them in her bag, and with her friend, she pored over the findings. The percentage of kids with elevated lead had increased dramatically after the water supply switch. Flint kids were being poisoned. In that moment, everything changed. "I was becoming something new — an activist, and a detective. Huddled there on Field 3 with Elin, I felt that my life was beginning to resemble an episode of 'Scandal.'"

Mona reached out to the state health department, asking for their data. They refused. What she didn't know until later was that they had already noticed a spike. Michigan authorities knew lead levels were surging in kids. And they did nothing.

Determined to advocate for her patients, she held a press conference to warn families to not drink or use the water, particularly for kids. She hoped that her findings would sound the alarm within every level of government, and that her willingness to share the raw data rather than waiting for it to be published in a peer-reviewed journal (a risky decision for a researcher) would underscore the urgency of her results. Instead, the state denied her claims and conclusions. Though it was painful, she pushed back, never doubting her methodology or her conviction that Flint's kids had to come first. She knew all too well that she was witnessing not only a public health disaster but a failure of the democratic institutions that were supposed to protect the people of Flint.

Born in 1976, Mona grew up in Michigan, in the proverbial shadow of General Motors. She is the daughter of Iraqi immigrants who were afraid to return home after Saddam Hussein took power. She has always held fast to the principles of social justice and democracy that she believed were rooted in her family's adopted country.

Yet she knew that racism and generations of neglect had helped create the situation in Flint, a city that went from high per capita incomes, low unemployment rates, strong unions, good schools, and good public health indicators to the exact opposite in a matter of decades. By

> *"What happened in Flint could happen elsewhere, as the push for austerity and a disdain for science are combined with antidemocratic measures like voter disenfranchisement, gerrymandering and state-appointed emergency managers. One of the lessons of Flint is that science and public health won't save us without a functioning democracy."*
>
> — DR. MONA HANNA-ATTISHA

2013, half of all black citizens in Michigan were living under emergency management control, compared to just 2 percent of the white population. The pattern was clear: Predominantly white state government officials had turned a blind eye to what was happening to Flint's lower-income black residents. In 2011, the state-appointed emergency manager had taken control of the city away from the locally elected mayor, with a mandate of austerity to avoid bankruptcy. That mandate had led to the decision to switch water sources in the first place. In other words, without the state's push for austerity measures, the Flint lead-poisoning crisis may never have happened.

A few weeks after Mona's press conference, the state capitulated, switching Flint back to Great Lakes water, but the pipes had been corroded and new pipes were needed to ensure no lead found its way into the water. Flint was an unnecessary man-made disaster born out of greed and negligence. Without Mona's activism and audacity, it could have taken even longer for the crisis to be discovered and for parents to be informed.

Today Mona is focused on raising funds for programs that mitigate the effects of lead and getting as many kids into those programs as possible. She shares her platform, lifting up the voices of others who embody hope and resilience in Flint — including Mari Copeny, "Little Miss Flint," who has been working to address this crisis since she was eight years old.

I was honored to meet Mona in 2016, and am grateful to my friend Sarah Lewis, associate professor at Harvard of Art History and African American Studies, for including our conversation about Mona's book and work in the Spring 2019 Vision & Justice convening. The issue of lead, painfully invisible to the naked eye and more painfully visible in its effects on kids' brains, is an issue of justice.

I'm proud to call Mona a friend and role model; the lesson of her story resonates today as much as ever: When leaders deny science, disregard facts, and ignore the people they represent, the consequences are disastrous. In this moment when thousands of communities in the United States still have unsafe lead levels due to paint, plumbing, and industrial waste, none of us can be complacent.

VACCINATORS

CHELSEA

I don't remember my first vaccine shots, but I definitely remember my kids': They each got a hepatitis B vaccine at birth and have stayed on the vaccine schedule recommended by the

Centers for Disease Control. Over the last couple of years, Charlotte and I have gotten our flu shots together while Marc and Aidan have gotten theirs at the same time. It's a tradition we plan on continuing, with the support of the wonderful doctors and nurses at our pediatrician's office — and one we don't take for granted.

Around the world, doctors, nurses, and dedicated vaccine workers do the lifesaving but often dangerous work of vaccinating kids and adults alike. In many countries, that work is done primarily by women, often in dangerous circumstances. Vaccine workers have been prevented from entering communities and even murdered on the job. Nine polio vaccine workers, all women, were executed in Nigeria in 2013. More than a hundred vaccine workers, almost all women, were killed around the world from 2013 to 2017. A mother-and-daughter polio vaccination team was killed in Pakistan in 2018. And amid an ongoing Ebola outbreak in the Democratic Republic of Congo, eighty-five health workers, many racing to give the new Ebola vaccine, were killed or wounded in the first five months of 2019.

In much of the world, "routine vaccinations" are anything but. While most kids have been vaccinated against at least one disease, many others still go without vaccinations for deadly but preventable diseases, like pneumonia, which kills hundreds of thousands of kids

> *"Denying children lifesaving vaccinations violates the most fundamental principles of morality, disregards the core tenets of human decency, and breaks the contract of ethical responsibility between generations. Everyone has the chance to do the right thing."*
>
> — DR. CLAIRE POMEROY, PRESIDENT OF THE ALBERT AND MARY LASKER FOUNDATION

under two every year. In some areas, people are afraid that vaccines cause sterilization (they don't). In others, people are concerned about outsiders coming into their community, including health workers. In many places, there simply aren't enough shots, enough health workers, or sufficient systems to vaccinate every person. In Pakistan, which has had seventeen cases of polio paralysis in the first five months of 2019, vaccinators are confronting rumors as well as fake fear-mongering videos that have been covered on national television, and public suspicion. One worker trying to persuade a family to vaccinate was shot and killed by an eighteen-year-old family member.

In the U.S., as well as much of Europe and Australia, we face growing challenges of our own. Some parents don't think the benefits of vaccinations outweigh concerns about vaccine safety; some don't believe in or know the benefits of vaccinations; some have religious or cultural concerns; some worry about the pain of the shots; some believe pharmaceutical companies push vaccines only to make a profit and not for their kids' health. For some parents, it's probably a mix of all of the above. In countries with high levels of vaccine skepticism, many of the nurses, doctors, and public health workers debunking misinformation and talking about the benefits of vaccines are women.

Women have also been in the vanguard of vaccine research. In the 1940s, the work of Drs. Pearl Kendrick and Grace Eldering led to the first vaccine for pertussis, or whooping cough. Later, they combined that vaccine with diphtheria and tetanus, creating the DTP shot that's still administered today. In the 1970s, Dr. Ruth Bishop led the research team that first identified rotavirus, the leading cause of severe diarrhea in infants and young kids, which can be deadly because of the severe dehydration it can trigger. It's also very common: Most kids around the world will be infected with rotavirus before they're old enough to go to kindergarten. I wasn't vaccinated against rotavirus, since the first vaccine against it wasn't approved for use in the U.S. until I was already in college. I'm grateful my kids have been vaccinated against rotavirus — and even more grateful that millions of kids who live in places without reliable access to clean, safe water have been vaccinated.

From local to global efforts, women have also led public campaigns in favor of vaccines. Former First Lady Rosalynn Carter has been a strong advocate on behalf of immunizations for more than thirty-five years, going back to her time as first lady of the state of Georgia. She still serves on the board of Vaccinate Your Family.

We know that it's possible to eliminate diseases because it's happened in the last few decades. In 1980, the World Health Organization declared smallpox officially defeated. We are closer than ever to beating polio, thanks to the extraordinary efforts coordinated by the Global Polio Eradication Initiative over the last three decades: More than 20 million vaccine workers have immunized more than 2.5 billion children. A growing body of research shows that the human papillomavirus (HPV) vaccine is reducing rates of cervical cancer — a promising step forward in a disease that affects more than half a million women worldwide every year.

These gains are possible only when people actually take advantage of the vaccines available to them. In 2000, the CDC declared the U.S. on track to be measles-free. As of early June 2019, more than a thousand recent cases prove that prediction to have been optimistic. Many parents continue to refuse the measles, mumps, and rubella (MMR) vaccine specifically because of concerns that it can cause autism, even though multiple studies have shown that vaccines are safe and don't cause autism — rather, as one of my favorite sayings goes, "Vaccines cause adults." Vaccines are important because they help protect on an individual level, and because they create "herd" immunity, the level of vaccination coverage required to help prevent a disease from spreading, and to protect those who can't be fully vaccinated or aren't yet — including babies who are too young to receive most vaccines or patients who are immunocompromised. Again, many of the people in the United States who patiently demystify vaccines to parents and explain concepts like herd immunity are women — from pediatricians to nurses to public health workers who are working to put us back on track to eliminate measles and other diseases.

Despite the challenges and even deadly threats, polio eradication campaigns, pneumococcal vaccine campaigns, rotavirus vaccine campaigns, and other inoculation efforts haven't stopped. Every year, more and more children are vaccinated against more and more diseases. None of that would be possible without the heroism of the women who work tirelessly around the world to protect kids from getting sick, even when that means putting their own health and lives at risk.

■ ■ ■ ■

ATHLETES

■ ■ ■ ■

Alice Coachman and Wilma Rudolph

ALICE COACHMAN

WILMA RUDOLPH

Chelsea

In the segregated South of the 1920s and '30s, few opportunities existed to support black male athletes and even fewer for black girls and women. Born in 1923, in the small town of Albany, Georgia, Alice Coachman discovered her love of sports early. At first, she pursued her passion by running and jumping on her own, using old equipment that others had thrown away. She couldn't practice at official tracks because of segregation, so she trained by running barefoot on dirt roads. When she got to high school, the boys' track coach spotted Alice's innate talent and drive and began training her. Soon after her formal training began, Alice broke the American high school and college high jump records — barefoot. That was all before she graduated from high school at Tuskegee Preparatory School. As a student at Albany State College, she ran even faster and jumped even higher, becoming the national champion in the 50- and 100-meter races and the high jump, as well as a member of the winning 400-meter relay team.

Though the Olympic Games were suspended during World War II, it's fair to think that Alice would have been a core member of the team in 1944, maybe even in 1940. Sportswriter Eric Williams wrote, "Had she competed in those canceled Olympics, we would probably be talking about her as the number one female athlete of all time." When the Olympics resumed in 1948, Alice joined the American team in London. She became the first black woman ever to win Olympic gold, and she set a new Olympic record. Forty years earlier, John Taylor had become the first black athlete to win gold; twenty years after that milestone women were allowed to compete in track and field events for the first time. As Alice walked to the podium to collect her medal, the weight of what she had just accomplished started to sink in. "I saw it on the board, 'A. Coachman, U.S.A., Number One,'" she said. "I went on, stood up there, and they started playing the national anthem. It was wonderful to hear."

What should have been heralded as a major milestone was barely mentioned in the American news reporting from the Olympics. President Harry S. Truman congratulated her at the White House, but Alice ultimately returned home to little fanfare. It was a notable difference from the parades and celebrations often greeting athletes when they returned — especially those who had set records and won gold medals and who also were white and male. When Alice returned to Albany, the town held a parade and a celebration in her honor; but because it was still segregated, black attendees were relegated to one side of the auditorium. The mayor sat on the stage with Alice but refused to shake her hand. When the event was over, she left through a side door. Alice later reflected, "We had segregation, but it wasn't any problem for me because I had won. . . . That was up to them, whether they accepted it or not."

After the Games, Alice retired from the track and finished her college degree. Although newspapers had largely ignored her and her hometown had given her a segregated reception, Coca-Cola asked Alice in 1952 to be a national spokesperson — the first time they had ever asked a black American. Throughout her life, Alice would support young athletes and retired Olympians, and inspire countless aspiring track and field stars.

It's not hard to imagine Alice cheering on Wilma Rudolph when, twelve years after Alice's Olympic feat, Wilma became the first black woman to win gold in the television era. Like Alice's, Wilma's story started in the segregated South. Born prematurely in Saint Bethlehem, Tennessee, now Clarksville, in 1940, Wilma contracted polio at the age of four. She had to wear cumbersome leg braces and was prescribed intense therapy to help her recover. The local hospital refused to treat Wilma because she was black. So every week, twice a week, Wilma's mother brought her to Nashville for therapy. Every day at home, her parents or siblings helped her repeat her exercises and massaged her legs.

Wilma worked hard to strengthen her legs: She walked, hopped, and even played basketball with her siblings. By the time her braces came off when she was around twelve, she had also survived scarlet fever, whooping cough, and measles. After she said goodbye to the braces for good, Wilma wanted to do more than walk or hop; she wanted to run, and she wanted to compete. She started accompanying her sister to basketball practice and joined a local girls' track team. In 1956, Wilma earned a spot on the U.S. Olympic track and field team. She was sixteen, still in high school and just a few years out of the braces. At the Melbourne Games that year, Wilma won a bronze in the 4x100-meter relay.

When she was seventeen, Wilma got pregnant with her first child. She missed competing during her senior year in high school, but her sister helped take care of the new baby so Wilma could resume her training in college. At Tennessee State, Wilma got faster. At the 1960 Rome Olympics, she became the first American woman to win three gold medals in a single Olympics: the 100-meter, the 200-meter, and the 4x100-meter relay, which she anchored. She broke three world records. It was the first time the Olympic summer games were televised. A dozen years after the media had ignored Alice Coachman, Wilma was recognized as the star she was.

Back from the Olympics, her hometown wanted to throw a parade in Wilma's honor. At first, she refused the offer; the town of Clarksville and the state of Tennessee were still segregated. Finally, Tennessee's segregationist governor agreed to have an integrated parade and celebration. Wilma took part, and they were the first integrated events Clarksville had ever held.

Wilma returned to college, finishing her degree and ultimately her track career. After graduation, she taught at her old elementary school and later coached track at her high school. She mentored and inspired countless athletes, including Florence "FloJo" Griffith Joyner, the fastest woman of all time (at least as of 2019!) and Jackie Joyner-Kersee, considered one of the greatest female athletes of all time. I remember watching the 1988 Seoul Olympics with my Grandma Dorothy when FloJo set her 100- and 200-meter records. My grandmother told me about watching Wilma smash barriers and how she hadn't known women could do that. Even before anyone else did, Alice and Wilma knew it was possible — and they made it happen.

Junko Tabei

CHELSEA

As a girl growing up in Japan in the 1950s, Junko Tabei was small and fragile for her age. But she developed an interest in a physically and mentally challenging pursuit: mountain climbing. When she was ten years old, her elementary school class took a trip to Mount Nasu, a volcanic mountain in Nikkō National Park. She would later reflect that when she was on top of the mountain, she realized not only how much fun she was having but how much of the world she had never encountered. That was the day she decided to climb whenever she could. Throughout high school, she hiked and climbed. While she was a student at Showa Women's University, she joined a mountaineering club. But when she started to look for a climbing group to join after graduation, she had an unpleasant surprise: Every group was made up almost entirely of men. She struggled to convince her male teammates to take her seriously — they thought she was there to look for a husband.

Still, Junko kept climbing. She supported her hobby by working constantly, editing a scientific journal and giving English and piano lessons. Within a few years, she had climbed all of Japan's highest mountains. That was when Junko's dream of going to the Himalayas with an all-female team first took root. In 1969, she helped found the Joshi-Tohan, or the Ladies' Climbing Club. Their excellent — and straightforward — motto was: "Let's go on an overseas expedition by ourselves." At a time when women in Japan were expected to stay home with their families, or at least stick to secretarial work, their efforts raised more than a few eyebrows.

In 1960s Japan, for any club to be permitted to climb in the Himalayas, it had to be registered as part of the Japan Mountaineering Association and receive the group's endorsement. Initially, Junko's Ladies' Climbing Club was refused membership. They kept applying and eventually became the first women's club accepted. The Ladies' Climbing Club's inaugural trip to the Himalayas was the 1970 expedition to Annapurna, in Nepal. The climb had been completed only once before and never by a group of women. Tabei and her team made it, forging a new path up the mountain's south side.

When Junko and the other club members decided to try Everest next, the overwhelming view of men in the climbing community in Japan, and likely outside it, was that an all-women's expedition would never make it to the top of the world. When Junko's team received a permit for Everest in 1972, they were determined to prove the naysayers wrong. Translating that determination into financing for the Everest expedition proved challenging. Sponsorship from a Japanese newspaper and television station provided only part of the needed funding. Junko financed her portion of the expedition by once again teaching piano lessons. She saved money by making climbing pants from old curtains. Many years later, a reporter from *Outside* magazine asked her: "Was there a moment before you went to Everest that you wondered if you should quit?" Tabei didn't beat around the bush: "No," she answered. "I never thought of giving up once. We had worked so hard to obtain the climbing permit."

In 1975, Junko and her party set out for the world's most famous summit. Adding to the already grueling climb was an avalanche that came after midnight, when Junko and her fellow climbers were asleep in a tent at camp. "Without any sign, we were hit by an avalanche, and buried under snow," she recounted later. "I began to suffocate, and thought about how our accident would be reported. Then suddenly, I was pulled up by Sherpas and revived. It was very lucky that none of us had been injured, but it still took three days until I could walk and move normally." The doctor at base camp tried to persuade her to return to the bottom of the mountain. Her answer was clear: Absolutely not.

On May 16, 1975, Junko, accompanied by her Sherpa guide, Ang Tsering, became the first woman to reach the summit of Mount Everest. When she reached the top, her first thought was simply: "Oh, I don't have to climb anymore." The simple observation about finally ending this particular journey fit Junko's often repeated approach to climbing:

to put one foot in front of the other. She took photos and 8mm movies, made radio calls to base camp, and buried a thermos of coffee at Everest's peak to mark her ascent.

HILLARY

Since Junko's triumph, women around the world have followed in her footsteps. One of the most thrilling examples is Ascend Afghanistan, an all-girls' climbing group. In 2018, Hanifa Yousoufi, a twenty-four-year-old member of the group, became the first Afghan woman to climb Mount Noshaq. She confronted freezing temperatures, gender expectations, and even Taliban attacks. After she made it to the top of the mountain, she explained: "I did this for every single girl. The girls of Afghanistan are strong and will continue to be strong."

After Everest, Junko did what she always did: She kept putting one foot in front of the other, making her way up mountains. She found that she was just as thrilled at thirty-five years old as she had been at ten by the prospect of seeing things she'd never seen before. The way she saw it, it was straightforward: She loved climbing, and she was still having fun. In 1992, she became the first woman to complete the storied Seven Summits, reaching the peak of the tallest mountain on each continent. At seventy-six, Junko had climbed the highest peaks in seventy-six countries. She didn't stop climbing until the cancer that finally took her life made it impossible, and that was just a few months before she died.

Junko's dedication to her sport didn't end when she was at lower elevation. She advocated for climbers to respect their natural environments and to clean up after themselves. She was a vocal supporter of limiting climbing permits on Everest so that the mountain didn't take more stress than it could reasonably endure. She worried — rightly — about mounting trash, water quality issues, and growing deforestation as more climbers tried to make it to the top or even to Everest base camp without the ecologically minded ethos of not leaving a trace. She told an interviewer toward the end of her life that she would tell her younger self, "Do not give up. Keep on your quest." She never gave up — not on climbing, and not on her faith that humanity could find a way to conquer the natural world's challenges without harming it.

BILLIE JEAN KING

HILLARY

The date was September 20, 1973. My friends
and I were crowded around a television set,
and I was nervous. We were a handful of
the ninety million people around the world

tuned in to "The Battle of the Sexes," the most watched tennis match in history. On the screen, Billie Jean King was carried by burly-looking men into Houston's Astrodome like Cleopatra on her throne. Her opponent, Bobby Riggs, rolled in on a rickshaw, accompanied by a pack of scantily clad women he called "Bobby's bosom buddies." Riggs, ever the showman, seemed to revel in the circus-like atmosphere. But from the steely glint in Billie Jean's eyes, it was clear: She had come to play tennis.

We were rooting for her as though she were a friend we had known all our lives. I was on the edge of my seat, reminding myself to breathe in and out. I knew, and Billie Jean *definitely* knew, that she had a lot riding on her shoulders. Riggs was a self-described male chauvinist who said: "The male is supreme. The male is king." If she lost to him, Billie Jean worried, she would undermine the newly passed Title IX, bring shame to women's tennis, and set the women's movement back fifty years. But if she won, she would send a resounding message to women and men everywhere that everyone deserved a level playing field. We really, really, *really* wanted her to win.

And win she did, trouncing Riggs decisively: 6–4, 6–3, 6–3. The audience in Houston rushed onto the court. Riggs leaped over the net to shake her hand and admitted: "I underestimated you." As in so many other hard-fought victories in her life, Billie Jean didn't win this one just for herself — she won it for all of us. It may have been a symbolic match, but it had a very real effect on how people saw themselves, women in particular.

Billie Jean King first captured my attention over a decade earlier, in the early 1960s. As an aspiring (and mediocre) tennis player myself, I thought: "Here is an American woman, not that much older than I am, and she's doing something I know is really hard, and doing it well." Most of all, she really seemed to love what she did.

She grew up in a family of athletes. One day, a friend brought her along to play tennis at the country club. She loved the physical aspect of the sport — jumping, running, hitting the ball. But she knew playing a country club sport was out of the question for a kid like her, who came from the "wrong side of the tracks." It wasn't until someone told her there were free lessons at her local public park that she thought: "That's more like it." She worked odd jobs for her neighbors until she finally managed to save up the eight or nine dollars a racket cost. She had high standards for herself from the beginning. One day, she calmly told her mother: "I am going to be number one in the world."

Growing up, Billie Jean always knew things were different for her than they were for her brother. "Girls didn't have the power," she said. "People wouldn't listen to us the way they listened to boys. I couldn't articulate it then. I felt all these things bubbling up inside me." Her first experience with outright gender discrimination came at age eleven, when she was barred from a group photo of junior tennis players because she had decided to wear a shirt and tennis shorts that day rather than a skirt.

Before long, the tennis world started to take notice of Billie Jean. By 1966, she was ranked number one in the world. Between 1961 and 1979, she won twenty Wimbledon titles, thirteen United States titles, four French titles, and two Australian titles — a total of thirty-nine Grand Slam titles. She was sure-footed and fast, with a strong backhand and a competitive spirit. The sport had never seen anyone quite like Billie Jean, on the court or off.

Billie Jean's ascent in tennis coincided with social upheaval in America. President John F. Kennedy had signed the Equal Pay Act into law in 1963, but that didn't change the glaring disparities in tennis. When Billie Jean King won the Italian Open in 1970, she was awarded six hundred dollars. The male winner took home nearly six times as much. The discrepancy in prize money was sometimes as much as eight to one. Along with eight other brave women players, "The Original Nine" broke away from the tennis establishment and launched their own tour in 1970, signing

> *"Everyone thinks women should be thrilled when we get crumbs, and I want women to have the cake, the icing, and the cherry on top, too."*
> — BILLIE JEAN KING

contracts for one dollar with publisher Gladys Heldman. They were risking their careers and their standing in the sport by taking this stand. But they did it anyway, because they knew how much it mattered. Three years later, the newly created Women's Tennis Association would absorb the tour.

The Battle of the Sexes was one of the most visible wins in the struggle for equality, but it was far from Billie Jean's only one. After she threatened to boycott the 1973 U.S. Open, it became the first major tournament to award equal prize money to men and women. She became the first woman to be chosen *Sports Illustrated*'s "Sportsperson of the Year." Meanwhile, she founded World TeamTennis, a coed league, and started the Women's Sports Foundation.

After she was publicly outed as a lesbian in the 1980s, Billie Jean lost her endorsement deals. Even this unwelcome invasion into her private life she took in stride. She squared her shoulders, kept her head high, and decided she wasn't going to back away from who she was. "This is important to me, to tell the truth," she later said. True to form, she not only came out, she became a fierce advocate for LGBTQ equality. Once again, when it would have been far easier to stay quiet, Billie Jean spoke out.

For Billie Jean, it was never enough to fight for herself; she was in it for the generations of athletes who have come after her. When a group of champion soccer players was struggling with the low pay and lack of attention for women players, they looked to Billie Jean. Soccer star Julie Foudy remembered going up to the icon and asking her what could be done. Billie Jean immediately turned the question back on the questioner, demanding: "What are you doing, Foudy? Like you, as players — what are you doing? . . . You have the leverage! You change it!" Thanks in part to her encouragement, Julie and her teammates took up the fight for equal pay for women's soccer — a fight that continues to this day despite the fact, in 2019, U.S. women's soccer games have for the past three years generated more revenue than U.S. men's games.

Billie Jean King is even more inspiring to me today than she was the day of the Battle of the Sexes in September 1973 — because of the life she's lived, the fights she's waged, and the integrity she brings to everything she does. She is a constant reminder that none of us can rest for very long. In the fight for equality — on the court and off — there is always more to do.

Diana Nyad

Hillary

There have been plenty of times, as a woman lawyer and politician, when I felt like I was swimming with sharks. Diana Nyad actually did. In 2013, she became the first person to swim from Havana, Cuba, to Key West, Florida, without a protective cage. Along the way, she braved the treacherous currents of the Gulf Stream, the lethal box jellyfish, and the infamous oceanic whitetip shark — not to mention the exhaustion of swimming for nearly fifty-three hours straight.

Born in 1949 in New York City, Diana grew up in Florida, leaving the house before dawn to put in a few hours at the pool before school. She survived sexual abuse as a teenager, at the hands of the beloved swimming coach she regarded as a father figure. Despite her shame and hurt, she threw herself into swimming. When she was in high school, a teammate urged her to finish a race knowing she couldn't have done it even a fingernail faster. Diana wrote in her autobiography, *Find a Way,* "I walked out of that locker room determined to tackle my future just that way, each day not a fingernail better. No regrets."

Her extraordinary willpower led her to marathon swimming, which opened up the world. She swam in lakes, rivers, and oceans. She was the first person to swim from north to south across Lake Ontario, and in 1975, at twenty-five, she swam around Manhattan. And then, at twenty-eight years old, she made her first attempt to swim from Cuba to Florida, shore to shore. With a boatload of friends to help navigate, cheer her on, and keep watch for sharks, she headed out into eight-foot waves. Eventually, the wind and currents took her so far off course, she had to stop. Two years later, she retired from swimming.

Yet for the next three decades, she couldn't shake the nagging idea of trying again. So, try again she did, at the age of sixty-one. And again later that year. And again. And again. She set out for her fifth try in 2013, at the age of sixty-four, with the help of a world-renowned jellyfish expert, a determined navigator, a team of shark divers, and a group of friends and family. She spent long hours fighting seasickness and the cumbersome suit designed to keep the jellyfish away, staying focused by counting strokes and going through a mental playlist of her favorite songs. And then, finally, she made it. When she staggered onto the beach, overcome with emotion and exhaustion, she managed to offer a few words of wisdom to the gathered spectators: "One: Never, ever give up. Two: You're never too old to chase your dreams. Three: It looks like a solitary sport, but it's a Team."

There are lessons in Diana's story for any woman — any person, really — who is navigating uncharted waters. Lessons about the power of taking risks and refusing to be defined by failure. Lessons about the incredible strength each of us possesses, even those of us who aren't world-class athletes. Lessons not just about sports but about life — about the importance of not simply trying to reach the finish line but learning to enjoy the journey, with all its disappointments, setbacks, and suffering. I have always felt a kinship with Diana and her team because of their mantra, which they repeated before, during, and after each swim: "Onward!"

ABBY WAMBACH

HILLARY AND CHELSEA

Hillary

Abby Wambach shattered records as a soccer player and cocaptain of Team U.S.A.: the most goals scored for the U.S. Women's

National Team and the most goals scored in international matches by anyone, man or woman — records she still holds today. But what makes Abby so remarkable is this: She's powerful, and she knows it. She doesn't apologize for it the way women are so often taught to do. She uses it — to level the playing field for women athletes and to change the story that we tell young girls about their own worth and potential.

If you haven't watched Abby's 2018 commencement speech at Barnard College, it is not to be missed. She referenced her childhood in Rochester, New York, which she spent playing on boys' teams before making her U.S. Women's National Team debut in 2001. I read her speech after the fact and couldn't stop thinking about it. I still can't. It's full of advice I wish someone had told me when I was in college: words of encouragement mixed with some tough truths. It made me realize that the locker room pep talks Abby gave her team as cocaptain must have been legendary. I even

---

"If I could go back and tell my younger self one thing, it would be this: 'Abby, you were never Little Red Riding Hood; you were always the wolf.'"

— ABBY WAMBACH

---

wrote Abby a letter thanking her for inspiring not only the "badass" (her words) Barnard graduates but everyone who has come across her words — myself included.

Chelsea

Abby understands the power of leading by example, which she does even when it might make some people uncomfortable. "Dissent is the highest form of patriotism," she tweeted after Megan Rapinoe said that she would not be visiting the Trump White House. Two days later, Megan scored both of Team U.S.A.'s goals in the Women's World Cup quarterfinals, beating France 2–1. After Megan and her teammates won the World Cup, Abby said, "This team showed America what's possible — no, they showed us what is inevitable: Women will lead us. And will win. And we won't keep our mouths shut about inequality any longer. Now pay them."

Abby is honest on and off the field, including about her complex feelings around coming out ("[I]t didn't matter to the way that I played the game," she once said, "but it does matter to who I am as a person"), as well as the joy her marriage and family bring her. Along with her wife, Glennon Doyle, she talks about important, sometimes thorny issues, like systemic racism and how white women can be better allies. "If you don't like me, that's not my problem. Not my worry, either,"

Abby once said in *Time*. She doesn't bend over backward to make people comfortable; she's too busy for that, and life's too short.

Just like she owns her wins, Abby Wambach owns her failures: the losing games, the time she didn't make the starting lineup for her last-ever World Cup, even an arrest for drunk driving that she said humiliated her into getting clean. "Failure is not something to be ashamed of — nor is it proof of unworthiness," she said. "Failure is something to be powered by. When we live afraid to fail, we don't take risks. We don't bring our entire selves to the table — so we wind up failing before we even begin. Let's stop worrying: What if I fail? Instead, let's promise ourselves: When I fail, I'll stick around."

After the U.S. team won the World Cup in 2015, Abby immediately ran to the stands and kissed her then wife, Sarah Huffman. It became an iconic moment because of how revolutionary it felt to see same-sex couples celebrate their love and each other's achievements in such a public forum. The following

---

"Women have learned that we can be grateful for what we have while also demanding what we deserve."

— ABBY WAMBACH

---

year, Abby got divorced, and talked publicly about the toll her struggles with substance abuse took on her relationship. After her second marriage, to Glennon, she has been just as candid about the challenges and rewards of parenting.

Hillary

In 2015, Abby retired from professional soccer. Retirement can be a terrifying moment in any athlete's life, and that was certainly true for Abby. "Without soccer who would I be?" she asked herself.

Then one day, her sponsor Gatorade surprised her by unveiling a plan for her send-off commercial. The message was simple: "Forget me." "They knew I wanted my legacy to be ensuring the future success of the sport I'd dedicated my life to," Abby said. "If my name were forgotten, that would mean that the women who came behind me were breaking records, winning championships, and pushing the game to new heights. When I shot the commercial, I cried."

Those words still ring in my head: "Forget me." I look forward to voting for the first woman president as surely as Abby looks forward to cheering on future championship teams. It's nice to be remembered. But Abby is right: Sometimes it's more powerful to pave the way for others.

MICHELLE KWAN

HILLARY

In the fall of 1992, Michelle Kwan's figure skating coach went out of town. When he came back a week later, he got some surprising news. While he was gone, his quiet, rule-following twelve-year-old student had taken the test to move up to the senior competition level — without his permission. Frank Carroll had wanted Michelle to wait, to spend the year winning at the junior level instead of moving up to compete against older, more experienced skaters.

"I was supposed to stay in juniors," she admitted with a smile to a *Los Angeles Times* reporter a few months later. "But I had a little urge to go into seniors." Michelle had taken matters into her own hands, and even her coach couldn't help but admire her guts. "It shows a little bit that she has strength inside," he conceded.

At that year's U.S. National Figure Skating Championships, Michelle became the youngest senior competitor in two decades. She would go on to become the most decorated figure skater in U.S. history, winning five World Championships, nine U.S. National Championships, and two Olympic medals. She dominated her sport for over a decade, landing one triple jump after another and captivating audiences with her moving performances. On the ice and off, Michelle Kwan has come to embody grace and grit.

Michelle was born in Los Angeles, the daughter of immigrants from China who came to the U.S. in the 1970s. Her father, Danny, worked for the phone company, and

> *"My parents didn't have the means to provide brand-new skates, flashy costumes, or ice time. They were barely juggling multiple jobs, providing a roof over our heads, feeding us, working at the restaurant . . . and then they gave me this crazy opportunity to ice skate! It seemed foolish at the time, but it was my dream to compete at the Olympic Games."*
>
> — MICHELLE KWAN

her mother, Estella, ran the Chinese restaurant that her family owned in a California suburb. When Michelle was just five years old, she and her sister, Karen, started taking skating lessons at a local ice rink. Both girls were talented and determined; before long, their lessons had gone from weekly to daily.

Figure skating is an expensive sport. There are the costumes, the skates, the ice time, the coaching. The Kwans sold their house in Rancho Palos Verdes and moved into one that Danny's parents owned in Torrance to support their daughters' skating. When Michelle and Karen earned scholarships to train at an elite rink a hundred miles away from home, Danny moved with them. Estella stayed back with their brother, Ron.

"I made it to the national championships in used skates that were custom-made for another girl," Michelle said later. "I still have those skates. Underneath the arch, there was a name crossed out and my dad had 'Michelle Kwan' written in. . . . But I didn't feel disadvantaged. I felt empowered because I had these opportunities. I was going to try to make the most of it."

At sixteen, Michelle won her first U.S. National Championship and World Championship titles with programs that were both technically difficult and artistically beautiful. The next year, she didn't fare as well, coming in second to an up-and-coming skater named Tara Lipinski. The year after that, despite months of struggling with injuries, a growth spurt, and her own self-confidence, Michelle, competing with a stress fracture in her foot, became the first woman in history to receive a perfect score for her short program at nationals.

Heading into the 1998 Olympics in Nagano, Japan, Michelle was the clear favorite to win. Comparing her to fifteen-year-old Lipinski, her biggest rival, reporters wrote and talked about Michelle as a mature, seasoned veteran — never mind the fact that she was just eighteen years old herself, incredibly young to carry the burden of such immense pressure. The unique expectations of the sport made it even harder: Figure skaters are expected to be beautiful, polite, and poised. Commentators loved that Lipinski broke into a delighted smile each time she landed a jump; Michelle skated with a more serious expression.

When it was her turn on the ice in Nagano, Michelle managed to shut it all out. She skated beautifully. But Lipinski also skated flawlessly and earned higher marks for the technical difficulty of her program. That night, the world saw two skaters, both at the top of their game, compete on the Olympic stage. When the results came in after the final competition, Michelle didn't win gold, as so many people had predicted; she finished second to Lipinski.

Despite what must have been profound disappointment, Michelle rose to the occasion yet again. She was gracious as she congratulated her rival. As she said, "I didn't lose the gold. I won the silver." And then, true to form, Michelle got back to work. She kept pushing herself, kept training, and won a second gold medal at the World Championships a few months later. In 2002, she again made the Olympics, where she won the bronze medal.

After she retired from competitive skating, Michelle didn't lose her focus; she simply shifted it. She went to college, then graduate school, earning a master's degree in international relations. Then she put her degrees to good use, serving as a U.S. public envoy pursuing diplomacy through sports, and on the President's Council on Sports, Fitness, and Nutrition under President Obama. She came to work as a senior adviser at the State Department when I was secretary of state, and I was impressed by her bright mind, incredible work ethic, and unfailingly cheerful personality. I was delighted when, a few years later, she came to work on my 2016 presidential campaign.

Today Michelle serves on the board of Special Olympics International, where she travels the world, talking about the difference this important organization, founded by Eunice Shriver, has made in bringing hope to so many people with intellectual disabilities and their families. To the delight of her Instagram followers, she has even gotten back on the ice. She is still involved in politics, having recently gone to work on her second presidential campaign.

Michelle is a role model not simply because of her talent, or her grace under pressure, or her composure after losing an important competition on the international stage. Her significance comes from something even more extraordinary: In a world where women, especially those in the public eye, are pigeonholed into being just one thing, Michelle has embraced complexity and seeming contradiction. She is proof that you can be more than one thing: powerful and graceful, fiercely competitive and a good sport, a student and an athlete, an Olympian and a public servant, pragmatic and an optimist.

"When I look back, I wouldn't have changed anything," she said when asked how it felt to not have won Olympic gold. "I couldn't have worked harder. There was the dedication to the sport. The amazing family and team that I had. The mind-set, the drive, the motivation, the grit, it was all there. There was just that one thing. You can't always be perfect." Too true!

Venus and Serena Williams

VENUS WILLIAMS

SERENA WILLIAMS

Hillary and Chelsea

Venus and Serena Williams have a particular talent for shutting out the noise and nonsense and focusing on what really matters — whether it's smashing records, winning titles, or advocating for people who will never have the kind of platform they do.

Over the years, they've had far too much

practice honing this talent. For decades, the two world-class athletes who helped redefine the sport of tennis have dealt with sexism, racism, and body shaming. Reporters and commentators have tried to undermine their athletic abilities (as they have with so many other women athletes — especially black women athletes) by suggesting that they're not women at all, or that they're using performance-enhancing drugs. After Serena pushed back against an umpire's suggestion that she was cheating in the 2018 U.S. Open final against Naomi Osaka ("I don't cheat to win," she protested, "I'd rather lose") and became visibly frustrated on the court, an Australian newspaper published a racist cartoon depicting the events. ("Well done on reducing one of the greatest sportswomen alive to racist and sexist tropes and turning a second great sportswoman into a faceless prop," tweeted *Harry Potter* author J. K. Rowling.)

Contrary to what their performance on the court might suggest, Venus and Serena aren't superhuman. They have both spoken publicly about how painful it is to be on the receiving end of ugliness and hostility — and about their determination not to let it distract them from doing what they do best. "I felt defeated and disrespected by a sport that I love," Serena wrote in *Harper's Bazaar* of her experience at the 2018 U.S. Open. "One that I had dedicated my life to and that my family truly

> *"We work hard and we learn from our losses. Because just like on the court, your losses teach you how to win."*
> — VENUS WILLIAMS

changed, not because we were welcomed, but because we wouldn't stop winning."

From the time they were toddlers in the early 1980s, Venus and Serena, with their parents' support, were logging hours practicing on the public courts of Los Angeles. "Venus was older and playing tournaments," recounted their sister Isha. "Venus was enrolled in this particular tournament, and Serena wasn't. Unbeknownst to my dad and mom, Serena sent in the application and signed herself up for the tournament. Who does that? . . . Even then, she wanted to compete." After a few years, the family moved to Florida so that the girls could get the elite-level coaching their talent and determination deserved. It paid off; both turned professional in the mid-1990s, before they graduated from high school. Venus led by example, pushing her little sister to work harder, never letting her win a friendly game. "My first job is big sister and I take that very seriously," she said later.

Venus and Serena played with tenacity and heart, chasing after every ball, delivering powerful serves and ground strokes. In 1997,

> *"What others marked as flaws or disadvantages about myself—my race, my gender—I embraced as fuel for my success. I never let anything or anyone define me or my potential. I controlled my future."*
> — SERENA WILLIAMS

Venus defied expectations when she became the first unseeded U.S. Open women's finalist, meaning she had not been ranked among the seeded players deemed most likely to win. In 2000, Venus won two Olympic gold medals in Sydney: one in singles and one in doubles, with Serena. That same year, Venus won the U.S. Open and Wimbledon. The next year, she did it again. In 2002, Serena followed suit.

CHELSEA

I was lucky enough to cheer for the Williams sisters in person during the 2000 Olympics and at multiple Grand Slam matches in the years since. I'm always inspired by their focus on the court and their support for each other there and everywhere else.

The years that followed weren't easy for the Williams sisters. Their half sister Yetunde Price was murdered in a shooting in Compton, California, in 2003. Venus and Serena were distraught. "She was a wonderful person," Serena said. "We're dealing with it however we can. Some days are better than others." More than a decade later, the two opened the Yetunde Price Resource Center in Compton, to honor their sister's memory and help people who don't have the same support network the Williams family did.

In 2008, Venus and Serena returned to the Olympics, this time in Beijing. Once again, they took home the gold in women's doubles. Four years later, in London, they won again. During the 2017 Australian Open, Serena, who had once again been rising steadily through the ranks, beat Venus to win her twenty-third Grand Slam title, and earned the ranking of number one in the world. (She has spent more than three hundred weeks, spread over fifteen years, ranked number one.) As she often has, Serena credited her sister for her success. "There is no way I would be at twenty-three without her. There is no way I would be at one without her. She

---

"The women in Billie Jean King's day supported each other even though they competed fiercely. We've got to do that. That's the kind of mark I want to leave. Play each other hard, but keep growing the sport."

— SERENA WILLIAMS

---

is my inspiration. She is the only reason I am standing here today and the only reason that the Williams sisters exist."

That same year, mid-tour, Serena announced she was pregnant. She gave birth to her daughter, Alexis Olympia, in September 2017 — meaning she won the Australian Open while pregnant. Afterward, she courageously shared the nightmarish complications she had experienced after delivering her daughter by C-section. Because she had a history of blood clots, she was hypervigilant in watching for the signs of clotting after the surgery. When she felt a familiar sensation, she spoke up. The nurse suggested that the pain medication had left her confused, but Serena knew exactly what was happening. She insisted on getting scans, which confirmed her fears. She wound up having two more surgeries.

"I was terrified," she said later. "It was a whole new kind of fear." She has since helped bring attention to maternal mortality in America, where seven hundred women die every year as a result of complications from

---

"Some people say that I have an attitude. Maybe I do. But I think that you have to. You have to believe in yourself when no one else does. That makes you a winner right there."

— VENUS WILLIAMS

---

pregnancy or childbirth. Even though maternal mortality around the world has been steadily decreasing over the last several years, it's actually rising in the U.S. As she has done all her life, Serena is turning a crisis into an opportunity to raise visibility around an important issue that affects too many women, especially women of color.

Serena is also continuing to speak out, with her typical candor, about the challenges women face on the court and off. Every woman who has felt that she was trying to play by ever-changing rules empathized when, after Serena wore a black catsuit during a match, the French Tennis Federation president decided to change the dress code at the French Open. Serena explained that, in addition to making her feel like a superhero, the catsuit's compression helped to prevent blood clots. He stuck by his decision: "It will no longer be accepted. One must respect the game and the place." Why is it that nothing seems to make some people more uncomfortable than a woman in pants? Serena laughed off the controversy and continued to not only accept but also celebrate herself. After her daughter was born, she posted a picture on Instagram, proudly declaring: "She has my arms and legs! My exact same strong, muscular, powerful, sensational arms and body." At the 2018 U.S. Open, she showed up in a tennis tutu. When she came back to the French

Open, she was wearing a bold outfit covered in the French words for "Mother, Champion, Queen, Goddess."

CHELSEA

I have loved watching Serena champion equal pay for women, athletes and nonathletes alike. I shared her fabulous open letter in November 2016 with friends and on social media. She wrote: "[W]hen the subject of equal pay comes up, it frustrates me because I know firsthand that I, like you, have done the same work and made the same sacrifices as our male counterparts. I would never want my daughter to be paid less than my son for the same work. Nor would you." She is a role model, for all of us and for our daughters and sons.

As for Venus, in addition to continuing to compete at the highest levels of tennis, she continues to build on her creative talents. She founded her own women's activewear brand, and she directs her own interior design firm. Though she has talked about the challenges of building a new career, as she says, "I don't focus on what I'm up against. I focus on my goals and try to ignore the rest." In the end, it's that ability to tune out the distractions and zero in on chasing their dreams that has made the Williams sisters two of the greatest athletes in the world.

Ibtihaj Muhammad

Chelsea

When she was growing up in New Jersey in the 1990s, Ibtihaj Muhammad's parents wanted all their children to be able to compete and win in sports. They also wanted to ensure that their daughters remain fully covered and wear hijab to cover their heads, in keeping with their family's religious beliefs. Ibtihaj experimented with different sports but always had to modify the uniforms. Fencing, however, seemed like a perfect option: Since fencers wear full-body suits and masks, the uniforms wouldn't need to be altered.

When she started fencing at thirteen, Ibtihaj didn't fall in love with the sport right away. At her mother's encouragement, she continued with fencing because she hoped it would be a good way to bolster her future college applications. She confronted racism and Islamophobia early on. Her teammates wondered whether a black woman could succeed in a generally white sport. Ibtihaj was told her legs were too muscular and that no one who wore hijab could ever be a champion. "When most people picture an Olympic fencer, they probably do not imagine a person like me," she said in her USA Fencing bio. "Fortunately, I am not most people."

Over time, Ibtihaj repeatedly overcame the bigotry directed at her and proved her detractors wrong. As a college student at Duke, she was a three-time all-American athlete and the 2005 Junior Olympic champion. During her junior year, she took time off from the sport, deciding to focus on completing her double major in African studies and international relations. "Being a student athlete is so difficult, and I would argue even more so at a school like Duke," she said. "It was the right decision to make." But she never gave up on her fencing dreams.

After college, she turned her attention to fencing full-time. "I saw there was a lack of minorities in the sport," she said. "There were barriers that needed to be broken in women's saber." She was determined to win an Olympic medal and believed that if she worked hard enough, she could do it. In 2010, she qualified for the World Fencing Championships in France. While there, Ibtihaj was asked for her autograph for the first time. Paris has long been the center of the competitive fencing world; it's also the capital of a country that passed legislation the same year Ibtihaj competed at the World Fencing Championships banning full-face covering in public, known as a niqab or burqa. The European Court of Human Rights upheld the ban four years later. When she was later interviewed about the competition, Ibtihaj said, "In France, a place that has struggled with the idea of hijab and with the Muslim community, I feel like it was a moment for even French citizens to see a Muslim woman on television."

After the World Championships, Ibtihaj made history when she secured a spot on the 2016 United States National Fencing Team for that year's Summer Olympics in Rio de Janeiro, Brazil, a first for an American Muslim woman. The more she succeeded, the more people criticized her. "People told me that my goals weren't attainable for whatever reason — especially when I was trying to achieve a feat that has never been done before — and that was discouraging," she said. Still, she refused to be deterred by the ignorance, bigotry, and hate she received, even when they came from people who should have been supporting her. Her teammates asked her whether she used a "magic carpet" to pray and deliberately didn't tell her about team practices. "Then it became very clear, 'We don't want you here,'" she said. She also would later say that both the U.S. Fencing Association and Olympic Committee didn't take the death threats against her as seriously as they should have. "If anything, as a national governing body, I would hope that USA Fencing would want to protect me, and I never felt that from them," she said.

Ibtihaj has always recognized her importance as a role model to other young Muslim women and women of color, particularly those drawn to fencing. Rather than feeling weighed down by that responsibility, she is spurred on by it. As she has often said, "Never allow anyone to dictate your journey." At the Rio Games, she became the first hijab-wearing Muslim American to win an Olympic medal, taking the bronze as part of the team sabre event. I remember watching Ibtihaj and

> *"I wanted to challenge the narrative that Muslim women are meek and docile and oppressed. Being unapologetically Muslim, black, a woman . . . Either you like it or you don't, and I don't really care either way."*
>
> — IBTIHAJ MUHAMMAD

her team win while breastfeeding Aidan, my then almost two-month-old son. The triumph and joy Ibtihaj felt was palpable through the television screen, thousands of miles away. I later learned that her mantra is "I'm ready. I'm prepared. I'm strong. I'm capable. I'm a champion." That conviction was visible on her medal-winning day in August 2016, and it still is today.

After the Olympics, Ibtihaj kept fencing, kept pushing herself into new territory, and kept shattering stereotypes, including through her frank discussions about her battles with anxiety and depression. In her 2018 memoir, *Proud: My Fight for an Unlikely American Dream,* Ibtihaj wrote about how, in 2014, after she qualified for the U.S. National Fencing Team, she would wake up on the mornings of competitions exhausted, even after a good night's sleep. During competitions, she often felt lethargic, like she couldn't move her arms and legs. She knew something more than nerves was happening, and she sought out her team's sports psychologist, who explained that her physical fatigue was the result of performance anxiety. She conquered this hurdle the way she overcame others in her path, with hard work and focus. Every morning, she did thought exercises and spent time meditating and in prayer. I have no doubt that her candor and courage in sharing this part of her Olympic journey will help others — athletes and nonathletes alike — feel more comfortable with discussing their challenges and with seeking the help they need.

In 2017, Ibtihaj hit a new milestone when she got her own Barbie doll as part of their Shero series. She helped design the Barbie, the first ever to wear hijab, and when it went on sale in 2018, it quickly joined Charlotte and Aidan's toy box. Our family is eagerly awaiting her first children's book, *The Proudest Blue: A Story of Hijab and Family,* which is due to be published in 2019. After years of not being able to find clothing that was both modest and fashion-forward, she started her own clothing line in 2014. She remains a marquee member of the U.S. National Fencing team and a vocal supporter of human rights and democracy. When asked whether she would ever consider running for office, she answered, "Honestly, I had never thought of it before. But I'm also one of those people who thinks they can do anything." And we do, too.

Tatyana McFadden

Chelsea

Tatyana McFadden spent the first six years of her life in an orphanage in St. Petersburg, Russia. Born with spina bifida, she was paralyzed from the waist down, and her birth parents couldn't afford to take care of her. Tatyana recalls that the staff at the orphanage did their best to encourage her independence

("I must have been a handful!" she said later, laughing), and though there was no wheelchair for her, she learned to walk on her hands in order to keep up with the other children.

When Deborah McFadden was in graduate school, an autoimmune disease called Guillain-Barré syndrome left her temporarily paralyzed from the neck down. She used an electric wheelchair for four years, then crutches for eight more while she continued to recover. The discrimination she faced at school and work because of her disability made her into an advocate for others with disabilities. In 1989, the year Tatyana was born, Deborah had helped write the Americans with Disabilities Act.

Five years later, on a visit to distribute U.S. aid, Deborah met Tatyana at the orphanage where she lived. Deborah came back to see Tatyana several times over the next year, and when she learned that Tatyana was going to be transferred to a different orphanage, she couldn't bring herself to say goodbye. "It had never been on my mind to adopt, but the moment they said they were going to transfer her to this place that, frankly, in your worst nightmare you can't imagine, I said, 'You can't do this,'" Deborah said. Twelve months later, Tatyana came to live with Deborah and her partner, Bridget O'Shaughnessy, in Clarksville, Maryland.

> *"I knew I could do anything if I just set my mind to it. I always figure out ways to do things, even if they're a bit different."*
>
> — TATYANA MCFADDEN

When doctors told Deborah and Bridget that Tatyana was unlikely to have a long life because she hadn't had the medical care she'd needed while in Russia, they refused to accept the grim prognosis. Instead, they decided to sign their daughter up for sports to help her build strength. When they tried to sign Tatyana up for swimming lessons, every instructor except one turned them away. The first time Tatyana submerged herself in the water and popped back up to the surface, she shouted, *"Ya sama!"* ("I can do this!") That was only the beginning of what would become a life-long love of sports. "I tried a lot of sports, and I really fell in love with wheelchair racing," Tatyana remembered later. "It made me feel so fast and free." After years of building the muscles in her arms, shoulders, and back, she excelled at the sport. She would eventually earn the nickname "The Beast" from her coach because of the way she charged up even the steepest hills.

As a teenager, Tatyana set her sights on the Paralympics. She qualified for the U.S. Track and Field Team at fifteen years old, becoming the youngest athlete on the 2004 team. In that year's Paralympic Games in Athens, Greece, she won a silver medal in the 100-meter and a bronze medal in the 200-meter. The next year, she tried to join her high school track team and got an unpleasant surprise. The school refused to let her race alongside other students, claiming that her wheelchair was a safety hazard for other athletes. Deborah went back and forth with the school before finally making a demand: "You give her a uniform and you let her run around the track." As Deborah remembers, the school responded, "Sue us," so that's what they did.

Tatyana and her mother filed a lawsuit against her school with the help of attorneys from the Maryland Disabilities Law Center. Tatyana's standing up for her fundamental right to compete alongside everyone else didn't always make her popular with the other athletes. "[T]hey were always booing," Tatyana said. "But on the inside, I just knew this was the right thing to do." The day she testified, the courtroom was full of her friends. Before she took the stand, Tatyana turned to her ten-year-old sister, who has a prosthetic leg, and promised, "Hannah, you'll never have to fight to run." They won their case, and Tatyana was granted the right to continue competing. As the presiding U.S. District Court judge told the courtroom before deciding in Tatyana's favor, "She's not suing for blue ribbons,

> *"I wanted to get the same thrill and the same experience as all the other high school students. There's no competition by myself. It was lonely and embarrassing, and I just didn't like it. Other competitors would come up to me and they would say, 'Good race,' but it wasn't really a good race because I was running by myself."*
>
> — TATYANA MCFADDEN

gold ribbons or money — she just wants to be out there when everyone else is out there."

Still, the Maryland Public Secondary Schools Athletic Association continued to throw up roadblocks. They determined that they would allow Tatyana and other wheelchair athletes to compete but refused to allow their victories to earn points for their schools' teams. With her mother by her side, Tatyana advocated for the Fitness and Athletics Equity for Students with Disabilities Act, which passed the Maryland legislature in 2008. The new law required schools in Maryland to give students with disabilities a chance to participate in school sports, without being treated differently.

After high school, Tatyana attended the University of Illinois, in part because of its exceptional wheelchair athletic program. In

2008 she competed in the Beijing Paralympic Games, where she won four medals: silver in the 200-meter, 400-meter, and 800-meter, and bronze in the 4x100-meter. Four years later, she won three gold medals in London. That year, she and her sister Hannah became the first siblings to compete against each other at the Paralympic Games. In 2014, Tatyana returned to the country of her birth for the Sochi Paralympic Games, her first time competing in a Winter Olympics; she won a silver medal in cross-country skiing. She said, "I was really nervous because I've only been skiing less than a year. I just had to ski with my heart, and having my family here has been absolutely wonderful. I went up against people who have been doing cross-country for years, so I'm absolutely proud of myself." She made the top of the podium again in 2016 in Rio — four times — and is currently training for her sixth Paralympics in 2020. Tatyana has also broken records as a marathoner, becoming the first person to win four major marathons in a year — Boston, London, Chicago, and New York — and then doing it three more times. Every time I see Tatyana race, whether in person from the sidelines of the New York City Marathon or through the screen during the Olympics, I am in awe of her focus, grit, and athleticism.

In addition to excelling across multiple wheelchair racing distances from the 100-meter to the marathon, Tatyana is also a passionate advocate for athletes with disabilities. She has lobbied Congress for equal access, treatment, and pay — some marathons award seven times as much prize money to medalists outside the wheelchair division, and it wasn't until 2018 that the U.S. Olympic Committee voted to start giving Paralympians the same medal bonuses as Olympians. She started a foundation "to create a world where people with disabilities can achieve their dreams, live healthy lives, and be equal participants in a global society." She isn't shy about the hard work and courage it has taken to achieve her own success and clear a path for others. "It's taken me a long time to get where I am," she has said. "I didn't just wake up, and this all happened."

CASTER SEMENYA

CHELSEA

Caster Semenya grew up running barefoot on a grassy track in Limpopo, South Africa. Her natural talent was evident early on to her family, her coaches, and her fellow athletes. In

2008, the same year she graduated from high school, she finished seventh in the 800-meter at the World Junior Championships. During the 2009 World Championships in Berlin, she exploded onto the international stage, winning gold in the 800-meter race and clocking her then personal best of 1:55.45.

As journalist Ariel Levy wrote in her *New Yorker* profile of Caster in November of that year: "She has a powerful stride and remarkable efficiency of movement: in footage of the World Championships, you can see other runners thrashing behind her, but her trunk stays still, even as she is pumping her muscle-bound arms up and down. Her win looks effortless, inevitable." Even watching the video and knowing the result, I was rooting for Caster as she emerged from the middle of the pack, made her way to the front, and pulled far ahead of her competitors, with just one quick look over her shoulder to make sure no one was gaining on her. (No one was.)

Caster's exceptional talent, her dramatic improvement from the previous year's competition, and her muscular build drew intense scrutiny — an all-too-common development, especially for women athletes of color. So did her confident, unapologetic post-race interviews and on-the-track celebrations. (Why are women's celebrations of hard-fought victory so often treated as unseemly when there is absolutely nothing wrong with them and so much that is right?) The International Association of Athletics Federations (IAAF) forced Caster to undergo invasive "gender testing," ostensibly to assess her hormones and physiology, to determine whether they would allow her to compete against other women athletes. She wasn't allowed to compete for eleven months, until the IAAF finally cleared her — but the fight wasn't over.

Two years later, in 2012, I remember watching from home as Caster carried the South African flag during the opening ceremony for the Summer Olympics in London. She won a silver medal in the 800-meter, which was later upgraded to gold when the winner was found guilty of doping; Caster passed all her drug tests. In 2016, she became the first person ever to win a gold medal in the 400-, 800-, and 1500-meter races at the South African championships. That year, she also won gold in the 800-meter in Rio at the Olympics.

In 2018, the IAAF put forward new regulations targeting athletes with differences in sex development. Under their proposed rules, women athletes with higher levels of testosterone who compete in events between 400 meters and a mile would have to take drugs or undergo invasive surgery to reduce their testosterone in order to continue to compete against women. It is not a coincidence that their new rules apply specifically to several of the races Caster has won. Caster, along with South Africa's track and field federation, challenged the rule. She called it "discriminatory, irrational, unjustifiable," and she's right. Unfortunately, in May 2019, the Swiss-based Court of Arbitration in Sports officially gave the IAAF permission to move forward with the rule, effectively denying Caster the ability to compete in the body she was born with.

The South African government has already said they plan to appeal, pointing to a stunning lack of scientific evidence that higher testosterone levels actually give an unfair advantage at any distance. In fact, the research that the IAAF cited to make their case has been repeatedly called into question by the scientific community. Additionally, the World Medical Association, which represents more than a hundred physician associations and millions of doctors around the globe, has called on its members not to follow the IAAF recommendations, because these new rules contradict their core ethical standards.

"I just want to run naturally, the way I was born. It is not fair that I am told I must change. It is not fair that people question who I am. I am Mokgadi Caster Semenya. I am a woman and I am fast."

— CASTER SEMENYA

Members of the public health community have also expressed alarm that sports governing bodies now seem to be in the position of defining gender — a disturbing trend that should be stopped. Caster has repeatedly said she will not take the testosterone-suppressing drugs mandated by the IAAF should she wish to compete. She's following science and doctors' medical advice; the IAAF isn't.

Caster has been treated unfairly not only by the governing bodies of her sport but often by the media. One thoughtful analysis by writer Parker Molloy pointed out, "Whether journalists knew it or not, they were priming their readers to think Semenya's win was unjust. Making matters worse, these stories included quotes from other athletes saying things like 'She's not a woman. She's a man,' and a dismissive 'Just look at her.' . . . [Y]ou'd be hard-pressed to find a story about Semenya that didn't make mention of her eligibility or include a quote about 'fairness' from a competitor upset about not finding a spot on the podium." The sexism and bigotry aren't even subtle.

In the meantime, Caster is still running, competing, and living her life. She married her wife, Violet, in 2015, and credits her with encouraging Caster to finish her college degree. She started the Caster Semenya Foundation to coach and support young athletes. "We as women need to come together and

> *"I am 97 percent sure you don't like me.*
> *But I'm 100 percent sure I don't care."*
> — CASTER SEMENYA, IN RESPONSE TO NEW
> IAAF RULES

support each other," she has said. "Without that, you will still feel discriminated, you still feel oppressed, you still feel criticized in everything that you do, and you will still feel like you are not recognized."

The debate Caster has been pulled into has raised big questions: Who gets to define gender? And isn't the idea of a level playing field in sports a myth, anyway? After all, no two bodies are the same. Some people are naturally taller, others shorter; some more muscular, others less so. As Ariel Levy asked: "Is Caster Semenya's alleged extra testosterone really so different?" The answer — clearly — is no.

Through it all, Caster has made an impressive and deliberate effort not to let anyone undermine her success, her self-confidence, or her commitment to championing younger athletes. She remembers Nelson Mandela telling her: "People can talk, people can do whatever they want to do, but it's up to you to live for yourself first before others." She sums it up this way: "Be fearless, be brave, be bold, love yourself." In the end, that may just be the gutsiest thing any of us can do.

ALY RAISMAN

CHELSEA

It's not the pomp and circumstance that get me most about the Olympics, Paralympics, and Special Olympics. It's not even the moving backstories that sometimes make me cry. It's watching athletes brush up against the limits of human persistence, over and over again, just to see what they can do with their artistry, unimaginable strength, speed, focus, and years of training. Sometimes those years start before the athletes even remember. Born in Needham, Massachusetts, in 1994, Aly Raisman was just two years old when she began training as a gymnast. By fourteen, she was already considered an elite athlete. It was to the surprise of no one in her close-knit family that she qualified for the 2012 U.S. Women's Gymnastics Olympic team the same year she finished high school. In London for the Olympics, Aly helped lead a team known as "the Fierce Five," which included Gabby Douglas and McKayla Maroney, to a gold medal. And then she and her teammates cheered Gabby on to victory for the all-around gold.

Aly once again led an all-star team to gold in Rio de Janeiro in 2016. She and her teammate Gabby Douglas are the only Americans who have won consecutive team gold medals in gymnastics. It was thrilling to watch them compete and create history. I'll also never forget watching Aly and her teammate Simone Biles perform their floor routines; I was mesmerized. When Aly finished her routine, she immediately began to cry, in a mix of exhaustion, relief, and pride. Simone won the gold, and Aly, the silver.

Some athletes fade from public consciousness after their Olympic careers end, but Aly

> *"I have both power and voice, and I am
> only beginning to just use them."*
> — ALY RAISMAN

made history once more, in January 2018. Two months after telling a reporter at *Time* that former U.S.A. Gymnastics team doctor Larry Nassar had sexually abused her throughout her childhood and career, Aly was one of more than 150 women to testify against him at his trial. Aly courageously used her recent fame as a multiple medal-winning Olympian as a platform from which to decry her abuser and the system that had enabled him for decades. She also launched a campaign, Flip the Switch, to train adults to notice signs of sexual abuse and the ways in which trauma manifests in child victims. Thanks to the brave testimony from so many gymnasts, including Aly, Nassar was sentenced to over forty years in prison after he pled guilty to charges involving more than three hundred athletes. Also in 2018, Aly filed a lawsuit against U.S.A. Gymnastics and the U.S. Olympic Committee over their failure to protect her and other athletes from Nassar. U.S.A. Gymnastics has filed for bankruptcy and is facing decertification efforts as the sport's national governing body. Its past practices are also being scrutinized by the U.S. Senate.

Aly continues to speak out about all that went wrong for so many years in the training of elite American gymnasts, and about what needs to be done to ensure that all gymnasts are treated with care and respect and given the protection they deserve. "There are so many people out there that are survivors, but there are few that have a voice," she told ESPN's Mina Kimes. "I know that I'm one of the few that are being heard, so I just want to do right by people."

■ ■ ■ ■

ADVOCATES AND ACTIVISTS

■ ■ ■ ■

Dorothy Height and Sojourner Truth

DOROTHY HEIGHT

SOJOURNER TRUTH

Hillary

In her memoir, *Open Wide the Freedom Gates,* Dr. Dorothy Irene Height, a legend of the civil rights movement, declared: "I am the product of many whose lives have touched mine, from the famous, distinguished, and powerful to the little known and the poor."

If you live in America and vote, whether you

know it or not, Dorothy Height has touched your life. I first met Miss Height — that's what we always called her — back when I was just out of law school and working for another fiercely courageous woman, Marian Wright Edelman, at the Children's Defense Fund. Miss Height was elegant but with no airs; brilliant without a trace of arrogance; passionate, but never overheated. And though she spent much of her later years sitting down, she was never sitting still. Because when Dorothy Height set her mind to something, there was no stopping her.

Miss Height grew up outside Pittsburgh and attended integrated schools. She won a national oratory contest in high school that provided a college scholarship, but when she arrived at Barnard College in 1929, she was turned away and informed that the college had already admitted two black students — apparently its yearly quota. So she headed downtown and enrolled at New York University, where she received her bachelor's degree and a master's in educational psychology.

After college, she went to work for the YWCA and joined the National Council of Negro Women, beginning a career of fighting for civil rights and equality for black Americans and women. She served as the Council's president for forty years, from 1957 to 1997. Alongside the "Big Six" of the civil rights movement, which included legends like Dr.

Martin Luther King Jr. and John Lewis, Miss Height was called "the unheralded seventh." She was the only woman given that distinction. Her activism attracted the notice of Eleanor Roosevelt, Dwight Eisenhower, Lyndon Johnson, and many others who sought her out for advice. She was a nonpartisan adviser to presidents of both parties. She received the Presidential Medal of Freedom from my husband in 1994, and the Congressional Gold Medal from President George W. Bush in 2004.

When I was in the Senate, Miss Height and a group of other civil rights leaders — including Dr. C. Delores Tucker and E. Faye Williams of the National Congress of Black Women — came to me and Congresswoman Sheila Jackson Lee of Texas. They argued that it was past time for the U.S. Capitol Building to have a statue of the pioneering black suffragist Sojourner Truth, right alongside other national heroes.

Sojourner Truth, then named Isabella Baumfree, was born into slavery in New York around 1797. She escaped with her infant daughter, Sophia, in 1827 — a year before New York's emancipation law went into effect. She later used the new law to sue for the return of her five-year-old son, Peter, who had been illegally sold to a slaveholder in Alabama. She is considered the first black woman to win such a case.

In 1843, she became a Methodist and took the name Sojourner Truth, explaining to her friends: "The Spirit calls me, and I must go." She never learned to read or write, but she traveled the country, preaching in favor of the abolition of slavery. Her memoir, *The Narrative of Sojourner Truth: A Northern Slave,* was published in 1850, the same year she spoke at the first National Women's Rights Convention in Worcester, Massachusetts. In 1851, she attended the Ohio Women's Rights Convention in Akron. In a crowded church, she delivered her famous extemporaneous speech on women's rights, "Ain't I a Woman." From her towering height (she was nearly six feet tall), she responded to the male speakers who had argued that women were inferior to men and too weak to be entrusted with the vote. "If the first woman God ever made was strong enough to turn the world upside down all alone, these women together ought to be able to turn it back and get it right side up again!" she declared in her deep, booming voice. "And now they is asking to do it, the men better let them."

Her speech became an immediate sensation, prompting competing stories about how she presented herself and even what she had said. When a heckler at a speech in 1858 questioned whether she was, in fact, a woman, she answered by opening her blouse to reveal her breasts.

> *"That man over there says that women need to be helped into carriages, and lifted over ditches, and to have the best place everywhere. Nobody ever helps me into carriages, or over mud-puddles, or gives me any best place! And ain't I a woman? Look at me! Look at my arm! I have ploughed and planted, and gathered into barns, and no man could head me! And ain't I a woman? I could work as much and eat as much as a man—when I could get it—and bear the lash as well! And ain't I a woman? I have borne five children, and seen most all sold off to slavery, and when I cried out with my mother's grief, none but Jesus heard me! And ain't I a woman?"*
>
> — SOJOURNER TRUTH

During the Civil War, she helped recruit black soldiers for the Union Army and worked with the National Freedman's Relief Association in Washington, D.C. In 1864, she met with President Lincoln at the White House. While in Washington, she helped force desegregation of local streetcars by riding them. When a conductor tried to stop her from boarding, she had him arrested, took him to court, and won her case, nearly a century before Claudette Colvin and Rosa Parks refused to give up their seats on the bus.

After the war, she met with President Ulysses S. Grant. She gathered thousands of signatures on a petition to provide land grants to help former slaves escape poverty and build new lives. She campaigned for Grant's reelection, and in 1872, she even tried to vote, though she was turned away. Sojourner kept speaking out about abolition, women's rights, prison reform, and capital punishment until her death in 1883.

With a record like this, you might not think it would be controversial to add Sojourner Truth to the U.S. Capitol's Emancipation Hall. But, as it turns out, it's hard to get Congress to do just about anything. We faced one delay after another. Lesser women would have gotten discouraged, settled for less, or just given up. That wasn't Miss Height's way. She just kept pushing, calling, and writing.

It took us years, but we finally got Sojourner's statue put up. And on April 28, 2009, we gathered in the Capitol Visitor Center for the unveiling. The celebrated actress Cicely Tyson recited "Ain't I a Woman."

With her very presence, Cicely, like Sojourner, embodied the indivisibility of women's rights and civil rights. You couldn't be for one and not the other. You couldn't give the vote to just some women. Or just some black Americans. Our democracy belongs to all of us, and it needs to protect and serve every citizen. We all are freer when every one of us is free. We all have more opportunity when everyone has opportunity. That was Sojourner Truth's mission. It was Dorothy Height's mission. And today it must remain our mission.

Ida B. Wells

Hillary and Chelsea

Over a century before the 2017 Women's March, there was the 1913 Women's Suffrage Parade. The day before the inauguration of President Woodrow Wilson, more than five thousand women converged on Washington,

D.C., to march for the right to vote. At the front of the procession was white suffragist and lawyer Inez Milholland, dressed in white, astride a white horse. At the back of the parade was a group of black women, including the twenty-two founders of the Delta Sigma Theta sorority. But Ida B. Wells, a sorority member who had brought several members of the Alpha Suffrage Club of Chicago to march that day, was not with them.

Over the weeks prior, the parade's organizers, including twenty-eight-year-old Alice Paul from New Jersey, had been quietly discouraging black women from marching in the parade at all, worrying that their inclusion would alienate Southern politicians who might otherwise support the cause of suffrage. Understandably, that did not sit well with Ida. When she was told that the members of the Delta Sigma Theta sorority should march at the back of the parade, she made it very clear: She would not take part unless her group could march with the rest of the Illinois delegation near the front. On the day of the parade, defying the white suffragist leaders, that's exactly what Ida did. "When white suffragists told her to march at the back of the line, she went straight to the front," recounted historian Alexis Coe on the podcast No Man's Land. "And she organized one of the first black women's clubs to fight for enfranchisement."

Ida B. Wells did not bear injustice quietly; instead, she fought against it with all her might. At barely five feet tall, she is among the most courageous women the United States has ever seen. She was born into slavery in Holly Springs, Mississippi, three years before the end of the Civil War. At sixteen, she lost both parents and her brother to a yellow fever epidemic. To support the rest of her siblings, she dropped out of high school, moved to Memphis, and became a teacher by lying about her age. She finished school herself at night and on weekends.

When she was twenty-one years old, Ida bought a first-class train ticket to get from Memphis to her teaching job in nearby Woodstock, Tennessee. When the train conductor came to punch tickets, he told her she was in the wrong car. She knew exactly which car she was in; it was not the wrong one. He insisted that she move to the blacks-only carriage. And when he "tried to drag me out of the seat," Wells wrote in her autobiography, "I fastened my teeth in the back of his hand."

That incident sparked the beginning of Ida's career as a journalist. She took the railroad company to court and won five hundred dollars in damages, which would be a little over twelve thousand dollars today. Three years later, the Tennessee Supreme Court reversed the decision and charged the court costs to Ida. Furious at the court's verdict, she wrote about the incident in a local newspaper, the *Living Way*. Her account gained national attention, and in 1887, the National Afro-American Press Convention heralded her as the most prominent reporter of the American black press.

In 1891, she was fired from her teaching job for publishing editorials exposing the poor conditions of segregated black schools. The next year, Ida's life again changed forever after the lynching of three of her close friends — Calvin McDowell, Thomas Moss, and Will Stewart — who owned a grocery store that competed for customers and profits with a white grocery store in the same community. By the late 1880s, after over twenty years of black men voting in elections, winning elections, and joining the police force, some white Memphians were determined to reassert white supremacy and rule.

Her horror and anger following her friends' murders inspired Ida to write about lynching. Her reporting took her to some of the most dangerous parts of the country for a black woman, where she told the stories of victims of racial violence and published their names so they would not be forgotten. She wrote her stories for the newspaper she co-owned, the *Memphis Free Speech and Headlight.*

When eight black men were lynched in one week across the South in 1892, Ida published — under a pseudonym to protect herself — an

> *"If this work can . . . arouse the conscience of the American people to a demand for justice to every citizen, and punishment by law for the lawless, I shall feel I have done my race a service. Other considerations are of minor importance."*
>
> — IDA B. WELLS,
> AFTER FLEEING MEMPHIS

editorial challenging the old, offensive canard that whites were justified in lynching black men because white women were attracted to them. The white papers responded by attacking the editorial's author. One paper ominously warned: "There are some things the Southern white man will not tolerate."

Ida's anti-lynching editorials were met with death threats against her across the South, and a white mob destroyed her newspaper office. Even after that, she published, under her own name, *Southern Horrors* and *The Red Record,* pamphlets that called out lynching for what it was: racial violence intended to suppress the economic and political progress of black Americans.

She moved to Chicago in 1894 and married Ferdinand Barnett, Illinois's first black assistant state's attorney and the editor of the city's first black paper, the *Chicago Conservator.* Throughout their life together, Ferdinand cooked dinner for the family most nights, and cared for the children, though his own job was demanding. It's clear that he recognized the importance of Ida's voice in speaking out against racism and other injustices.

While in Chicago, Ida helped create the National Association for the Advancement of Colored People (NAACP), founded the first black women's suffrage association in the United States, and started the first kindergarten for black children in Chicago. She continued to call out white suffragists and politicians for their racism and exclusionist views about blacks and immigrants. And she fought for equal education for black children and young people, a free press, women's rights, civil rights, and against lynching.

Ida knew lynching wasn't only a Southern crime. After years of intense activism by Ida and others, the governor of Illinois signed anti-lynching legislation in 1905. But in 1909, a mob in Cairo, Illinois, lynched William James after he had been charged with the rape and murder of a white woman. The mob then stormed a local jail and lynched Henry Salzner, a white man accused of murdering his wife. Under pressure from Ida as well as the recently formed NAACP and other civil rights leaders — and likely with new urgency in reaction to the white victim — the Illinois governor enforced a provision in the 1905 anti-lynching law that any officers who didn't protect their prisoners would lose their jobs.

In December 2018, nearly ninety years after Ida died, the United States Senate unanimously — and finally — passed legislation making lynching a federal crime. Before that point, Congress had considered more than two hundred anti-lynching bills and passed none. It is certainly progress — long overdue — and, as of mid-2019, the House of Representatives is expected to pass their own equally strong version of the bill.

Ida probably would have agreed with nineteenth-century German sociologist Max Weber's description of politics as "a strong and slow boring of hard boards." Despite all she had seen and experienced, however, she refused to become cynical or give up on the possibility of progress. Near the end of her life, in 1930, she ran for the Illinois state senate — before black women were permitted to vote in most states.

In her lifetime, Ida fought tirelessly against white supremacy and for freedom of the press. She began a legacy carried on by journalists and advocates who are holding the powerful accountable just as she did and proving that, in Ida's words, "The way to right wrongs is to turn the light of truth upon them." And after a ten-year crowdfunding effort, Ida's great-granddaughter Michelle Duster recently announced that she had successfully raised enough money to commission a statue honoring Ida near her former home in Chicago. "You can't just gloss over history," Michelle said. "She was called fearless. I don't believe that she had no fear. I believe she had fear and she decided to keep going forward."

ELEANOR ROOSEVELT

HILLARY

Eleanor Roosevelt is a continuing inspiration to me. Throughout her life, she overcame personal, political, and public challenges that would have flattened most of us. When I think of women I admire, she's at the top of my list.

My admiration starts with her resilience during her childhood. She was rejected as unattractive and too serious by her beautiful socialite mother, who called her young daughter "Granny"; neglected by the handsome and charming alcoholic father she adored; and told to care for her brothers. She was orphaned and, by the age of ten, had lost one of her brothers to illness.

Raised in the home of her maternal grandmother, Eleanor craved affection and considered herself an "ugly duckling." She received limited private tutoring until she left for a "finishing" school outside London, where she thrived under the direction of the headmistress, Marie Souvestre, who encouraged independent thinking among her students. Souvestre mentored Eleanor, who flourished at the school until she was ordered home in 1902 at the age of eighteen to make her social debut.

Back home, Eleanor began a courting relationship with her fifth cousin Franklin Delano Roosevelt, and they became engaged the following year. Franklin's formidable mother, Sara Ann Delano, opposed the marriage. But her son was determined, and on March 17, 1905, Eleanor and Franklin were married, with Eleanor's uncle, President Theodore Roosevelt, giving the bride away.

Eleanor had six children, but one tragically died in infancy. Having lost her own mother when she was eight, Eleanor hoped Sara would be the mother she never had; instead, her marriage was complicated by her mother-in-law's constant interference and demands. Sara paid all the bills and controlled their lives. She even gave them a home connected to hers — without any locks on the connecting doors.

Sara also fought to control the raising of Eleanor's children, telling them: "Your mother only bore you, I am more your mother than your mother is." It was another blow to the still-insecure Eleanor, who later wrote that she did not consider herself suited for motherhood. With no space of her own, either to relax or parent as she wished, Eleanor reached the breaking point and told her husband that Sara's dominance made her feel like a stranger in her own home.

In 1918, Eleanor discovered her husband's affair with her social secretary. She was devastated. Franklin rejected her offer of divorce, which in those days was very difficult to obtain for a woman. She decided to stay in the marriage (which can be, as I know well, a "gutsy" decision). She found her voice and redoubled her commitment to alleviating poverty, pursuing peace, and helping veterans.

And then, once again, adversity struck.

When Franklin was stricken with polio in

1921, Eleanor took over his care, probably saving his life. The doctor treating Franklin praised her as a "rare wife" who bore "your heavy burden most bravely," and proclaimed her "one of my heroines." That might have been the first recorded time anyone really spoke about the depth of Eleanor's strength and determination. She took charge of Franklin's recovery and stood up to her mother-in-law by championing Franklin's potential for a future political career, even though his mother wanted him to retire from public life. Eleanor entered politics in New York on behalf of her husband and other Democrats in the 1920s, and advocated for a progressive agenda. When Franklin was elected governor in 1928 and then president in 1932, Eleanor emerged not only as an activist first lady but as an effective — and controversial — public leader for the rest of her life.

Allida Black, the American historian and

"Courage is more exhilarating than fear and in the long run it is easier. We do not have to become heroes overnight. Just a step at a time, meeting each thing that comes up, seeing it is not as dreadful as it appeared, discovering we have the strength to stare it down."

— ELEANOR ROOSEVELT

---

founding editor of *The Eleanor Roosevelt Papers,* described this period of Eleanor's life: "In the twenties, Eleanor Roosevelt found her voice, and Franklin and Eleanor found new ways to complement, support, and care for one another. They had battled betrayal and polio, loneliness and despair in ways that made them both courageous, more hopeful, more skilled, and more independent. They forged a compromise that allowed them to grow into the leaders they wanted to be and the nation needed them to be."

Through her time as first lady, she encountered controversy, backlash, vicious personal attacks, and even assassination plots against her. After FDR's death in 1945, Eleanor continued her activism into the next chapter of her life. President Harry Truman invited her to join the first U.S. delegation to the newly created United Nations. She accepted but was unsure of her role and aware that she was the only woman and the only member without a college degree. By the time she left the UN seven years later, she was regarded as a skilled debater, smart negotiator, and stalwart supporter. She took up the cause of the sixty million displaced persons in Europe and toured the camps where they were held, seeing and hearing firsthand the horrors of the war and the Holocaust. She used her writing and speaking to urge Americans to learn that "you cannot live for yourselves alone. You depend on the rest of the world and the rest of the world depends on you."

Her greatest public achievement was as the chair of the UN Human Rights Committee. She oversaw thousands of hours of contentious debate and traveled thousands of miles to discuss the idea of a universal declaration of human rights (UDHR) to guide the world forward after the horrors of two world wars in fifty years. She worked relentlessly to convince the member countries to accept the UDHR, which embodied the most far-reaching and advanced definition of social, economic, cultural, civil, and political rights in human history. "Where, after all, do universal human rights begin?" she asked. "In small places, close to home — so close and so small that they cannot be seen on any maps of the world. Yet they are the world of the individual person; the neighborhood he lives in; the school or college he attends; the factory, farm, or office where he works. Such are the places where every man, woman, and child seeks equal justice, equal opportunity, equal dignity without discrimination. Unless these rights have meaning there, they have little meaning anywhere. Without concerned citizen action to uphold them close to home, we shall look in vain for progress in the larger world."

Eleanor continued to use her visibility throughout the 1950s and until her death in

1962 to speak out for racial justice and in favor of school desegregation and voting rights for black Americans. Her outspokenness brought death threats from the Ku Klux Klan, but she persisted, pushing politicians of both parties to live up to our nation's founding ideals. "Do what you feel in your heart to be right — for you'll be criticized anyway," she once said. "You'll be damned if you do, and damned if you don't."

There's no easy way to describe Eleanor's impact on our country. She was born into privilege but became a teacher, journalist, party leader, citizen activist, lecturer, writer, and diplomat. She stood up against racism, advocated for the trade union movement, worked to alleviate poverty and create jobs during the Great Depression, advised her husband on New Deal programs (whether he wanted her advice or not!), and held her own press conferences in the White House. She advised against the internment of Japanese Americans, urged women to join civil defense work and enlist in the military, and became FDR's emissary during World War II, traveling to visit American troops on battlefields across the Pacific theater. At the same time, she published a weekly column and answered thousands of letters. She wrote 28 books, 580 articles, and 8,000 columns describing her life and views.

In her last book, *Tomorrow Is Now,* she

stressed that America's greatness sprang from the power of its ideas, not its economic or military power. She worried about our country, and she described her purpose for writing this last book in its introduction as what she wanted to tell her fellow Americans: "One woman's attempt to analyze what problems there are to be met, one citizen's approach to ways in which they may be met, and one human being's bold affirmation that, with imagination, with courage, with faith in ourselves and our cause — the fundamental dignity of all mankind — they will be met."

During my time as first lady, I used to kid people that I'd have imaginary conversations with Eleanor Roosevelt. In reality, however, those interior dialogues were helpful. I often asked myself: "What would Eleanor do?" Many times, I'd arrive somewhere to do something only to discover Eleanor had been there first. There was finally one thing I did as first lady that Eleanor Roosevelt had not done before me: winning a Grammy in 1997 in the spoken word category for my book *It Takes a Village*. I was surprised and delighted. But I quickly realized that, had Eleanor ever recorded one of her books, she probably would have beaten me to the Grammy stage as well.

I still often think of Eleanor. Her words, and her example of a courageous life well lived, are as important and relevant today as they always have been.

ELIZABETH PERATROVICH

CHELSEA

Thanks to Mr. Ellis Turner, the same excellent history teacher who introduced me to Margaret Knight and Madam C. J. Walker, I learned about several American heroes I likely wouldn't have otherwise encountered in a high school class, particularly in the mid-1990s. One of those heroes was Elizabeth Peratrovich.

A member of the Tlingit tribe in Alaska, growing up in the 1920s, Elizabeth experienced the brutal reality of segregation and racism from a young age. Some of her first memories of education involved a school with no Alaska Native teachers, where students who spoke Tlingit were sometimes punished for having the audacity to speak in their native language. (The Indian Citizenship Act of 1924 granted citizenship to American Indian and Alaska Native people born in U.S. territories, but it didn't guarantee them the same rights — far from it.)

When Elizabeth moved to Juneau with her husband, Roy, to raise their three young children, discrimination greeted her everywhere. A sign at a local general store read "No Natives Allowed." Restaurants boasted "All-White Help." As they made the rounds looking for a house, they met one landlord after another who refused to rent to them. Though they were American citizens, Alaska Natives were often subject to attempts to prevent them from exercising their right to vote, including by forcing them to take literacy tests and not providing voting information in native languages.

The last straw for Elizabeth came when,

having finally found a place to live, she discovered that her children couldn't go to the school a block away: It was reserved for white children only. Elizabeth decided to take matters into her own hands and went to meet with the superintendent. By the time she left his office, she had persuaded him that her children should be able to attend the school of their choice. Her son Roy Jr. became the first Alaska Native child to attend an all-white school in Juneau.

The years surrounding World War II saw even more hostility toward Alaska's Native people — including the forced relocation to camps of thousands of men, women, children, and elders from villages in the Aleutian Islands. Elizabeth and her husband, by now leaders in their community, helped draft an anti-discrimination bill. With the support of the governor, it was presented to the legislature in 1943, but failed. Because the legislature met every other year, they had two years to prepare for their next attempt. Elizabeth, then in her early thirties, hit the road, traveling by plane and dog team to remote villages, to explain why the anti-discrimination bill was necessary and to implore Alaska Natives to vote and even run for office.

In 1945, the anti-discrimination bill passed the Alaska House. This time, it came down to a vote in the Alaska Senate. The legislative gallery was packed. Elizabeth sat in the back, knitting and watching, her young daughter at her knee. The debate was heated, with members of the legislature lobbing racist slurs and offensive comments. At one point, State Senator Allen Shattuck demanded: "Who are these people, barely out of savagery, who want to associate with us whites, with five thousand years of recorded civilization behind us?" He said this despite the fact that Native people had lived in Alaska for thousands of years before white fur traders arrived around the time of the American Revolution. White supremacy was front and center.

At the end of the discussion, per tradition, the floor was opened for anyone else who wanted to speak. One person stepped forward: Elizabeth. Her head held high, she began to speak calmly and deliberately. "I would not have expected that I, who am barely out of 'savagery,' would have to remind gentlemen with five thousand years of recorded civilization behind them, of our Bill of Rights." The gallery burst into raucous applause. (When Mr. Turner read us this exchange in history, our entire class applauded, too. I love that the boys applauded this strong woman.)

The bill passed. Nearly twenty years before the Civil Rights Act of 1964, Alaska became the first state in the country to pass nondiscrimination legislation, providing for "full and equal accommodations, facilities, and privileges to all citizens in places of public

> *"Rich and poor, strong and weak gave their help in this difficult fight. All this without hate, notoriety, or malice. Finally, Alaska pulled herself out of her deep unnecessary sleep and the laws began to change. Why? Because people were awakened to their obligation to their fellow men."*
>
> — ELIZABETH PERATROVICH

accommodations within the jurisdiction of the territory of Alaska." Decades later, the day it was signed into law, February 16, was recognized by the Alaska Legislature as Elizabeth Peratrovich Day.

As for Elizabeth, she kept going. She confronted the editor of the local newspaper over biased reporting, helped to revise the Alaska juvenile code, and fought for access to health care for Native communities. The Tlingit people treasure public speaking and storytelling, and Elizabeth drew on her talent and rich cultural traditions to argue against injustice. She believed the greatest barrier to equality was ignorance, and she dedicated her life to speaking the truth, no matter how vocal her opposition. Elizabeth's work is far from done. As recently as 2014, it took litigation to force Alaska to provide voting information in Yup'ik, Inupiaq, and Gwich'in languages. Her son Roy Jr. has taken up the mantle of telling his mother's story, including in a book for young readers written with Annie Boochever, the wonderfully titled *Fighter in Velvet Gloves: Alaska Civil Rights Hero Elizabeth Peratrovich*. I can't wait to read it with our kids when they're a little older.

Rosa Parks and Claudette Colvin

ROSA PARKS

CLAUDETTE COLVIN

Hillary and Chelsea

We've all heard — we hope — about that moment on the bus on December 1, 1955: Rosa Parks finished her shift at the Montgomery Fair Department Store, where she worked as an assistant tailor. Her shoulder was bothering her, so she stopped at the drugstore and considered buying a heating pad before deciding it was too expensive. When the bus pulled up, she climbed aboard, set down the packages she was carrying, and took a seat in the middle of the bus, where she and other black passengers were allowed to sit. Soon the white section filled up; a white passenger was left standing. The driver ordered Rosa to move, and she calmly said, "No."

What happened that day was not just an isolated moment to be honored and put on a shelf in the history books. It was the result of countless acts of courage and sacrifice by people from many walks of life, including a community of organizers in Montgomery. It was also the tip of the iceberg, just the most prominent action of Rosa Parks's lifetime of activism.

Born in 1913 in Tuskegee, Rosa Parks grew up in segregated Alabama. Her grandparents had been enslaved; at night, the KKK rode through her town. After her father left, her mother raised her on her own, teaching her about black heroes like Booker T. Washington and George Washington Carver. As a little

---

"I got on first and paid the same fare, and I didn't think it was right for me to have to stand so someone else who got on later could sit down."

— ROSA PARKS

---

girl, Rosa read voraciously. She loved Sunday services at the AME Church, especially the songs. When Rosa was eleven years old, her mother enrolled her in Miss White's School for Girls, where teachers encouraged her and her classmates to dream big and stand up for themselves. In eleventh grade, she dropped out of Alabama State Teachers College's High School to help take care of her grandmother. After she met her husband, Raymond, he encouraged her to go back and finish her degree — which she did.

Raymond was Rosa's partner in everything she did and the love of her life. She called him "the first real activist I ever met." With his support, she went to workshops at the famous Highlander Folk School, studied black history, and learned the principles of grassroots organizing and nonviolent social action. In 1943, she went to a meeting of the Montgomery NAACP. She was the only woman in the room; the men asked her to take notes and, eventually, to serve as branch secretary. Rosa later admitted that she was "too timid to say no."

Despite being private and reserved by nature, Rosa was outraged by the injustice she saw all around her. The 1940s were a daunting time to be a civil rights activist. *Brown v. Board of Education* was years away. Rosa and her fellow NAACP members wrote letters to Congress in support of an anti-lynching bill they knew was unlikely to pass. Over two decades before the Voting Rights Act, she tried several times to vote in Montgomery and was turned away each time. Twice, she "failed" the literacy test required of black voters, with no explanation as to what she had gotten wrong. On her third try, the test administrator saw her taking notes on the questions and her answers to reference later; she suddenly passed. Before she could vote, however, she had to pay years of back poll taxes.

In addition to voting rights, Rosa's major passion was engaging young people. The NAACP's Youth Council met most Sundays at her apartment. She encouraged them to be civically engaged and to challenge segregation. One of the most painfully visible frontiers of segregation in Montgomery was the bus, where black people made up the majority of riders but were frequently mistreated, humiliated, and forced to give up their seats to make room for white passengers.

Chelsea

One of the participants in the Youth Council meetings was fifteen-year-old Claudette Colvin. On March 2, 1955, she and her classmates climbed on a city bus to go home from school. When a white passenger boarded, all the seats were taken, and the driver ordered Claudette and her classmates to move to the back and stand. Three of her classmates complied; she

> *"Whenever people ask me: 'Why didn't you get up when the bus driver asked you?' I say it felt as though Harriet Tubman's hands were pushing me down on one shoulder and Sojourner Truth's hands were pushing me down on the other shoulder. I felt inspired by these women because my teacher taught us about them in so much detail."*
>
> — CLAUDETTE COLVIN

refused. Because of the segregation laws, the white woman still couldn't sit down, since it would mean sharing a row with Claudette.

Technically, Claudette wasn't breaking the law, and she knew it: Black passengers were not required to move if there were no other seats. She had just written a paper for school on the problems of segregation in Montgomery. She told the driver she had paid her fare and intended to stay where she was. "We had been studying the Constitution in Miss Nesbitt's class," she explained later. "I knew I had rights." As she told me in a radio interview we did together in 2017, "I didn't move because history, Chelsea, had me glued to the seat."

The bus driver called the police; two officers boarded the bus. They forcefully handcuffed Claudette and threw her into the squad car. The officers mocked her and made lewd comments; she was terrified. They brought her to an adult jail and left her for hours in a small cell. By the time her mother came with her pastor to post bail, she was shaken and angry. Her father stayed up all night with a shotgun, ready to defend Claudette if the KKK showed up.

Rosa Parks leaped into action, fund-raising to support Claudette's impending court case. Ultimately, the court dropped two of the three charges against her, including the charge of breaking Montgomery's segregation law, which meant she couldn't challenge it.

Hillary

On December 1, 1955, nine months after Claudette's stand, Rosa decided that she, too, had been pushed far enough. Just four days before refusing to give up her seat on the bus, she had attended a meeting about the murder of Emmett Till and lynchings across the South. A seasoned activist, she carefully considered her options when the bus driver demanded she move that day. "I didn't even know if I would get off the bus alive," she reflected. In the end, she made up her mind: "I felt that, if I did stand up, it meant that I approved of the way I was being treated, and I did not approve." She kept her seat and was arrested for civil disobedience.

The night Rosa was arrested, the Women's Political Council swung into action, passing out flyers that called for a bus boycott on

> *"People always say that I didn't give up my seat because I was tired, but that isn't true. I was not tired physically, no more tired than I usually was at the end of a working day. . . . No, the only tired I was, was tired of giving in."*
>
> — ROSA PARKS

December 5, the date Rosa was due in court. That day, tens of thousands of black passengers walked or carpooled to work. Many buses were completely empty. As Rosa walked into the courthouse, she said, "I was not especially nervous. I knew what I had to do." She was found guilty and fined fourteen dollars.

In the days to come, black leaders in the community formed the Montgomery Improvement Association (MIA) and elected a young reverend, Martin Luther King Jr., as their president. Rosa not only sparked the 382-day boycott; she was instrumental in sustaining it. She raised money, organized support, and even served for a month as a dispatcher in the citywide carpool effort to help participants get to work and school. When rumors spread that arrests would be made in an effort to stop the boycott, Rosa and her fellow organizers decided not to wait. She presented herself, along with many members of MIA, to the sheriff. The famous photos of Rosa, impeccably dressed and looking absolutely unflappable as she had her mug shot and fingerprints taken, are from that day.

That year Rosa met Eleanor Roosevelt, who noted her "very quiet, gentle" personality. Still, Eleanor wrote in her regular newspaper column of the bus boycott, "These things do not happen all of a sudden. They grow out of feelings that have been developing over many years. Human beings reach a point. . . . 'This is as far as I can go,' and from then on it may be passive resistance, but it will be resistance."

Chelsea

In 1956, a district court ruled that public bus segregation laws in Montgomery and throughout Alabama were unconstitutional. The Supreme Court upheld the ruling later that year. Claudette was one of the four plaintiffs in the case, all women. Claudette had won, and so had Rosa and everyone else who had the courage to challenge bus segregation in Alabama.

Claudette was glad for the victory. At the same time, she felt abandoned by leaders in the community. They had decided she was a less than ideal public face for the issue: she was too outspoken, too uncontrollable, and too young, not to mention the fact that she came from a low-income family. When they found out she was pregnant it seemed to confirm their own worst biases.

One of the few adult leaders who stayed

in touch with her was Rosa. "She was very kind and thoughtful," Claudette said. "She knew exactly how I liked my coffee and fixed me peanut butter and Ritz crackers, but she didn't say much at all. Then when the meetings started, I'd think, 'Is that the same lady?' She would come across very strong about rights. She would pass out leaflets saying things like 'We are going to break down the walls of segregation.'"

After the Supreme Court ruling, Claudette struggled with college and finding work in Montgomery. She eventually moved to New York, where she worked as a nursing aide for more than thirty years. She has maintained, even after decades of hardship and a lack of recognition, that she would never change her decision to remain seated on the bus that day in 1955. While it's Rosa's name we remember, it's Claudette's name in the Supreme Court ruling; she, too, is an important figure in American history.

Hillary

Like Claudette, Rosa Parks paid a price for her stand. Strangers called her at home to make death threats. The FBI monitored the activities of the local NAACP. Her coworkers shunned her, and five weeks after she refused to give up her seat, she was "dismissed" from her job. Not long after, Raymond was forced to give up his job, leaving the Parkses without

> *"Mine was the first cry for justice, and a loud one."*
> — CLAUDETTE COLVIN

a source of income. She developed insomnia, and painful ulcers that landed her in the hospital, leaving her with a bill she struggled to pay.

In 1957, Rosa and Raymond moved to Detroit to be near family and, they hoped, to find jobs. Still, they continued to face financial hardships, even as Rosa traveled the country speaking out on behalf of civil rights. She took part in the 1963 March on Washington, though no women were permitted to speak from the podium, and went back to Alabama to march from Selma to Montgomery, though because she was not an "official" participant, she was repeatedly pulled out of the procession by police.

Rosa continued her activism in Detroit and, in 1964, volunteered on the long-shot congressional campaign of John Conyers for "jobs, justice, and peace." When he was elected, he hired Rosa to work in his Detroit office doing administrative duties. She traveled all over the city, meeting with constituents at hospitals, schools, and senior citizen homes. She was dedicated to criminal justice reform, spoke out against the war in Vietnam and the confirmation of Clarence Thomas, and demonstrated against segregation. She took up issues even closer to home, attending meetings on curbing the heroin epidemic in Detroit, marched in support of affordable public housing, and championed the movement to eat locally grown produce.

Decades after her place in history was secured, Rosa came to Washington to sit with me at the 1999 State of the Union. She looked beautiful in a jewel-colored dress with her head crowned in a long braid, just like in her booking photos from the day she was arrested. The entire Congress rose to give her a lengthy standing ovation.

Hillary and Chelsea

Too often, the story of Rosa Parks is told as a single inevitable act. It was not. She spent years studying the principles of nonviolent resistance, informing her political beliefs, and helping to shore up a community of activists. Like Claudette's before her, Rosa's refusal to give up her seat on the bus was an act of astounding courage and clear-eyed conviction.

"I'd like people to say I'm a person who always wanted to be free, and wanted it not only for myself."

— ROSA PARKS

It was also an act that led to Rosa's tireless organizing to keep the bus boycott going, and a lifetime of taking action around causes she cared about, often with no recognition and at enormous personal risk. She understood better than anyone that progress takes decades of hard work, persistence, and the courage to keep going.

CORETTA SCOTT KING

HILLARY AND CHELSEA

When the two of us think of Coretta Scott
King, we think of a woman who lived out her
calling — who answered the call by saying
"Send me." She lived her life as an extension
of her faith, conviction, and hope.

Growing up in segregated Alabama in the 1930s and '40s, she didn't just understand the intersection of racism and poverty — she lived it. Her great-grandfather was enslaved, her great-uncle lynched. At ten years old, she picked cotton to pay for her schooling. When she was fifteen, her house was set on fire. Her father refused to sell his newly opened sawmill to a white man; it was burned to the ground. The racial violence she witnessed firsthand planted the seeds for what would become her life's work, fighting for justice, opportunity, and peace.

Chelsea

It was also during this time that she encountered her first love: music. Coretta grew up listening to the trailblazing and talented Marian Anderson. She sang spirituals at church on Sundays, solos in the school choir, and Handel's *Messiah* every Christmas. After graduating as valedictorian of her high school, she studied music and education at Antioch College in Yellow Springs, Ohio, where she joined the local chapter of the NAACP. From Antioch, she went on to earn a degree in voice and violin at Boston's New England Conservatory of Music. "This is where I knew I was supposed to be," she said later.

Hillary

In Boston, she met a young divinity student named Martin Luther King Jr. through a mutual friend. In her posthumous autobiography, *My Life, My Love, My Legacy,* she described the sight that greeted her when Martin came to pick her up for their first date in his green Chevy. "My first thoughts reaffirmed what I had anticipated: He was too short and he didn't look that impressive." But by the end of their date, she was singing a different tune. "I felt he was a man of substance, not like I had envisioned. In fact, the longer we talked, the taller he grew in stature and the more mature he became in my eyes." On the drive home, Martin cut to the chase, telling Coretta she had the character, intelligence, personality, and beauty that were everything he ever wanted in a wife.

I can imagine that she thought for a minute, "What am I getting myself into?" In fact, she waited six months to give him an answer, because she had to have known in her heart that she wasn't just marrying a young man but was bringing her calling to be joined with his. She was a fiercely independent person, true to herself. On their wedding day, they promised to love, honor, and cherish each other — but not to obey. "I had made up my mind that I wanted the traditional language about 'obeying' and submitting to my husband deleted from our marriage vows. The language made me feel too much like an indentured servant," she wrote.

As Martin and Coretta began their marriage

and their partnership, it could not have been easy. There they were: young, becoming parents, starting their ministry at a moment in history when they were called to lead. Leadership is something that many who are called refuse to accept. But they made their choice, and they made it together. Now living in Montgomery, Alabama, Coretta took up her duties as a pastor's wife and continued her own activism every chance she got. She spoke at churches, schools, and civic groups, and while she had set aside her dreams of being a classical singer, she put her musical talents to work organizing a series of "Freedom Concerts" to raise money for the Southern Christian Leadership Conference (SCLC), an organization dedicated to ensuring civil rights and eradicating racism.

Chelsea

Coretta did not approach this work blindly. During the 1955–56 Montgomery bus boycott, their house was bombed, with Coretta and baby Yolanda inside. Her family urged her to leave the city, but she refused. In the midst of the boycott, when strangers called late at night to deliver a hate-filled rant, Coretta started telling the person on the other end of the line: "My husband is asleep. . . . He told me to write the name and number of anyone who called to threaten his life so that he could return the call and receive the threat in the

> *"I am not a ceremonial symbol. I am an activist."*
> — CORETTA SCOTT KING

morning when he wakes up and is fresh." She was heartbroken and disturbed by the assassinations of President Kennedy and Malcolm X. She would later become close friends with Myrlie Evers-Williams, whose husband, Medgar, had been shot and killed in their driveway by white supremacists on June 12, 1963, in Jackson, Mississippi. The photos from Medgar's funeral, with Myrlie comforting her crying son, are a portrait of a woman who embodies strength and resilience in the face of horrific violence. I think of those nights when Coretta was putting the children to bed and worrying about the violence, worrying about the threats, and determined not to show any of the natural fear that any of us would feel and to protect her children and her husband. She was courageous every single day.

Hillary

As was evident on their wedding day, Coretta came to her marriage with her own fully formed political views and passionate opinions. She urged her husband to oppose the Vietnam War and took part in the Women's Strike for Peace during the 1962 Disarmament

Conference in Geneva, Switzerland. When Martin canceled a scheduled appearance at a peace rally in Washington, Coretta still went. When someone asked Martin whether he had educated Coretta on matters of politics and social justice, he answered, "She educated me."

Four days after her husband was assassinated, Coretta went to Memphis to support the sanitation workers and lead the march he was supposed to have led. I remember listening in amazement, as a college student, to the news reports of this woman, three of her children in tow, taking up her husband's struggle on behalf of the dispossessed. She told the fifty thousand people gathered in the drizzling rain at Memphis City Hall that she was there to continue his work to make all people truly free. Not just free from the obvious shackles, not just free from the legal segregation, not just free from the oppression that one can see, but truly free inside, knowing that each of us has a personal relationship with God that can take us through any darkness.

I'll never forget the photos of Bernice King curled up in Coretta's lap during Dr. King's funeral, wearing a white dress and pigtails. She is so young and so small, and the expression on her face breaks my heart. Decades later, Bernice King is a minister and a leader in her own right on issues of human rights, civil rights, peace, and justice. When her niece Yolanda Renee, the granddaughter of Coretta and Dr. King, joined Bernice at the March for Our Lives rally against gun violence in 2018, Bernice said she was a "very proud aunt."

Throughout her life, Coretta traveled the world, speaking out for the causes of nonviolence, peace, poverty, civil rights, human rights, and women's rights. She trained tens of thousands of people in the principles of nonviolent resistance, and she consulted with world leaders. In 1985, she was arrested with three of her children at the South African Embassy in Washington, D.C., protesting apartheid in South Africa. Despite warnings from some of the people closest to her, she spoke out for LGBTQ equality in the 1990s.

Chelsea

In 1986, Coretta wrote to Senator Strom Thurmond to "express [her] sincere opposition" to the nomination of Jeff Sessions as a federal judge in Alabama. "Mr. Sessions has used the awesome powers of his office in a shabby attempt to intimidate and frighten elderly black voters," she wrote in a nine-page letter. "For this reprehensible conduct, he should not be rewarded with a federal judgeship." His nomination ultimately failed — the first time a Reagan nominee was rejected by the Senate Judiciary Committee. But that

458

wasn't the end of the story — not for Jeff Sessions, and not for Coretta's letter.

A little over a decade later, Jeff Sessions was elected to the United States Senate; in 2017, he was nominated by the Trump administration to become attorney general. When Senator Elizabeth Warren went to the floor to read Coretta's 1986 letter, Majority Leader Mitch McConnell cut her off; she was told to "take her seat" and McConnell prohibited her from speaking until after the vote. Later that night he famously tried to justify his actions, saying, "She was warned. She was given an explanation. Nevertheless, she persisted." In other words: She should have known her place and sat down.

My mom was in the Senate for eight years and never saw this happen to any other senator. This unprecedented display of power and sexism against Senator Warren and disrespect toward Coretta Scott King infuriated us both. Senator Warren's refusal to be silent, and Coretta's decades of doing the same, inspired the title of my book, *She Persisted*. I doubt it was Senator McConnell's intent to create a rallying cry for women around the world, but that's what he did!

Hillary and Chelsea

Throughout her life, Coretta was determined to remain fiercely true to herself. "Often, I am made to sound like an attachment to a vacuum cleaner: the wife of Martin, then the widow of Martin, all of which I was proud to be. But I was never just a wife, nor a widow. I was always more than a label," Coretta said.

Each time we are called, let's remember Coretta. Let's channel her drive and commitment and answer, as she did: Send me.

DOLORES HUERTA

HILLARY

I first learned about Dolores Huerta — labor leader, organizer, feminist, and activist for women's rights, civil rights, and environmental justice — in 1965 because of the

461

grape boycott, started by Filipino workers in California, that spread across the United States. I had babysat the children of migrant farmworkers through my church while their parents and older siblings worked Saturdays in the fields outside Chicago. Because of that experience, I had become interested in their lives, and I paid attention to news about farmworkers. Farmworkers, mostly Asian and Latino, lived in migrant camp housing. Their lives were full of economic hardship, physical and sexual abuse, and exposure to dangerous pesticides and contamination. They often had little power to demand better working and living conditions or fairer wages from their employers.

Dolores cofounded the United Farm Workers Union (UFW) with Cesar Chavez in 1962 to help the laborers who planted, tended, and picked the vegetables and fruits grown on American farms. By organizing together as a union, the workers could build the collective power they needed to bargain with the corporations that employed them. The UFW supported the California grape boycott and helped take it national. In 1966, Dolores negotiated a contract between the UFW and the Schenley wine company, which was the first time that farmworkers anywhere in the United States were able to shape a contract with an agricultural company. In 1975, thanks in large part to Dolores's work at the helm of grape, lettuce, and wine boycotts, California passed the state's first law recognizing the right of farmworkers to bargain collectively.

CHELSEA

Dolores was one of the first activists I remember hearing about. My mom would talk about her experiences babysitting the children of migrant farmworkers, and she told me then about the great Dolores Huerta and her fight for farmworkers' rights, labor rights, civil rights, and women's rights.

Dolores has spent her life fighting prejudice and injustice. Her father was a farmworker, miner, union activist, and state legislator in New Mexico, where she was born in 1930. After her parents' divorce, she and her two brothers moved with their mother to Stockton, California. Dolores saw how hard her mother worked, between running a small hotel and being active in civic organizations and her church. Following in her mother's footsteps, Dolores also became active in school and community affairs. Unlike many women in the 1940s, she went to college and eventually became a teacher. Within months, she discovered her life's calling. "I couldn't tolerate seeing kids come to class hungry and needing shoes," she said. "I thought I could do more by organizing farmworkers than by trying to teach their hungry children."

Dolores was among the first voices to speak out against the use of toxic pesticides that threatened workers, consumers, and the environment. She was also on the front lines of protests and would be arrested twenty-two times over the course of her career for nonviolent acts of civil disobedience. During a 1972 protest, she coined the UFW's motto, *"Sí, se puede,"* which means "Yes, we can," a mantra borrowed and made famous by Barack Obama in his 2008 campaign. When President Obama awarded Dolores the Medal of Freedom in 2012, he acknowledged that she had originated the phrase and thanked her for letting him borrow it.

Dolores's organizing activities also included voter registration drives to convince eligible citizens to register and vote. Her efforts caught the attention of political candidates who sought her support. On June 5, 1968, she stood on the platform beside Senator Robert F. Kennedy at the Ambassador Hotel in Los Angeles as he delivered his victory speech after winning the California primary in that year's presidential election. Dolores had a big smile on her face and a red UFW flag in her hair. Only minutes later, Kennedy and five other people were shot walking through the hotel kitchen. Kennedy died the next day. In the documentary about her work and life,

Dolores, she says that Kennedy's assassination felt like the "death of the future."

Although Dolores and Chavez were co-founders of the UFW, he was often the public face of their struggle to obtain justice for farmworkers. Behind the scenes, Dolores was an experienced organizer and lobbied for legislative changes to achieve fair wages, medical coverage, pension benefits, and improved living conditions for workers. In one television interview they did together about their work, Chavez was asked about his leadership of the organization and protecting Dolores during protests. Dolores was asked about motherhood and whether she ever wanted to take a day off and go to a spa!

In September 1988, at the age of fifty-eight, Dolores was in San Francisco, peacefully protesting Vice President George H. W. Bush, who was then running for president. She was severely beaten by a baton-wielding police officer and suffered significant internal injuries, resulting in broken ribs and a damaged spleen that had to be removed in an emergency surgery. A film of the brutal beating was broadcast widely. Dolores later won a large financial settlement against San Francisco and its police department, which she used to benefit farmworkers and to structure a modest monthly payment that she relies on still for income. She also helped spur changes in police policies governing crowd control and officer discipline.

After a lengthy recovery from the beating, Dolores took a leave from the UFW to focus on women's rights and to encourage Latinas to run for office. She became an ally of Gloria Steinem, advocating together for the cause of women's rights. Dolores called herself "a born-again feminist" because of the sexism she witnessed in the labor movement. "When my epiphany came is when I started seeing that within the movement, once everything kind of got settled down, and all the women who had been on the front lines and on strike — all of a sudden you look around, and where are the women?" she said. Gloria Steinem has said that Dolores shaped her thinking and actions and helped bring the voices of women of color and farmworkers to the feminist movement.

"I think that's a problem with us as women— we don't think we need to be in the power structure, that we need to be on those boards where decisions are being made. Sometimes we think, Well, I'm not really prepared to take that position or that role. But I say [to women out there]: Just do it like the guys do it—pretend that you know. And then you learn on the job."

— DOLORES HUERTA

Today, at eighty-nine years old, Dolores is as passionate, energetic, and determined as ever. Running into my friend Dolores on the campaign trail in 2016 always gave me (and everyone else around her) a boost of energy. She was always at the center of the crowd, chanting into a bullhorn and dancing at the same time, or sharing stories with a group of rapt young people.

In recent years, she has knocked on doors for candidates in every corner of the country, joined teachers in Los Angeles who were striking for better public schools, and spoken out to protect access to safe and legal abortion in New Mexico. "When it came to the abortion issue, I had to struggle with that, given my Catholicism, my traditional beliefs," she said. "And I'm glad I went through that, because I think it helps me to be able to talk to Latina women, to be able to say why this is an important issue."

Through the Dolores Huerta Foundation, she trains leaders and community organizers. She raised her eleven children (yes, that's right, eleven!) while building a movement, and even if they didn't always understand why their mother was gone for long periods of time when they were children, many of them are now part of that movement as lawyers and civil rights activists themselves. "When we think of the kind of inheritance that we want to leave to our children or our grandchildren, think of leaving them a legacy of justice," she has said, and that's just what she has done throughout her life. Her famous call to action — *"Sí, se puede"* — is a reminder that each of us has a voice and that we are more powerful than we realize.

THE PEACEMAKERS

JOYCE McCARTAN

LEYMAH GBOWEE

MONICA McWILLIAMS

TAWAKKOL KARMAN

Increasingly we know that the security and peace of countries is related to the involvement of women in their societies and in peacemaking itself. Women, however, have traditionally been excluded from the work of ending conflicts, but there are examples where gutsy women have made a profound difference.

In the midst of the Troubles, a decades-long period of sectarian violence between Catholics and Protestants in Northern Ireland, women played critical roles — starting in 1976 when Máiread Maguire and Betty Williams won the Nobel Peace Prize for their efforts to encourage a peaceful resolution, through the signing of the Good Friday Agreement twenty-two years later in 1998.

When Bill and I first went to Belfast in 1995, I met a group of women who had come together at a time of violence and bitter conflict. One of them was sixty-five-year-old Joyce McCartan, a Catholic mother whose seventeen-year-old son had been shot dead by a Protestant gunman. All told, she had lost more than a dozen family members during the Troubles. Joyce refused to retreat into anger and grief, and instead brought together Protestant and Catholic women to set up a safe place where women of both communities could talk over a cup of tea, and Joyce invited me to join them.

Nine women sat around a small table at the Lamplighter Traditional Fish and Chips restaurant, drinking tea and talking about their hopes that the current cease-fire would continue and the violence would end once and for all. They told me how, after they had reached across their divide, they found that they had more in common than not. They may have attended different churches on Sunday, but they all said a prayer when their husbands and sons went off to work or out for the night. They all worried when their children left for school each morning. The deep-rooted causes of the violence — the terrors of sectarianism, the burdens of poverty, the despair of unemployment — touched all their lives. And in the end, for them and for so many other women across Northern Ireland, love of family ran deeper than calls to hatred.

These women didn't stop being Catholic and Protestant. They didn't believe in their faiths any less deeply. But they learned that they could understand one another and work together. Those kitchen-table conversations played an important role in the peace process, and as Joyce put it: "It takes women to bring men to their senses." And these women simply would not take no for an answer.

Monica McWilliams, a Catholic, and Pearl Sagar, a Protestant, cofounded the Northern Ireland Women's Coalition, which was granted two seats at the multiparty negotiations that led to the Good Friday Agreement. Mo Mowlam, the British secretary of state for Northern Ireland, urged that women be included in the negotiations.

Inez McCormack, a trade unionist and the first female president of the Irish Congress of Trade Unions, campaigned successfully for strong equality and human rights provisions in the agreement, stayed active in working for their implementation, and pushed for greater shared economic advantages so that people felt the benefits of peace. In 2011, *Newsweek* named her as one of its 150 women "who shake the world."

Also back in 1995, Bill and I met a fourteen-year-old girl named Sharon Haughey, from Armagh, a town in Northern Ireland. She had written a letter expressing her hopes for peace: "Both sides have been hurt. Both sides will be hard to forgive." Bill read part of that letter to the crowd at Belfast City Hall before we lit the Christmas tree. I stayed in touch with Sharon, and as she got older, she came to work for me as an intern in my Senate office. She learned a lot in Washington, and when she went home she got involved in local politics. At just twenty-four years old she was elected to the district council of her town. She worked hard and eventually became lord mayor of Armagh.

In 2012, I visited Belfast, and Sharon met me for lunch, wearing her ceremonial chain of office. She told me she was about to be married and hoped to start a family. When I saw her again in Dublin a few years later, she came with her three boys: sons who are growing up only learning about the Troubles in history books.

A world away, other women raised their voices for peace and justice. When the First Liberian Civil War started in 1989, Leymah Gbowee was just seventeen years old. She went, in her words, "from a child to an adult in a matter of hours." As the conflict dragged on, she raised her children, became a social worker, and counseled survivors of trauma. What she saw convinced her that women have an essential role to play in promoting peace, and she set out to build a network of women across Liberia and West Africa who shared her conviction.

In 2003, Liberian women started saying to one another, "Enough is enough." Leymah helped turn this discontent into a movement, organizing women in nonviolent protests. That spring, thousands of women from all walks of life — Christians and Muslims together — flooded the streets, marching, singing, and praying. Dressed all in white, they sat in a fish market in the hot sun under a banner: "The women of Liberia want peace now."

First the warlords tried to ignore them. Then the warlords tried to force them to disperse.

But the women wouldn't leave. Finally, the warlords agreed to begin peace negotiations. But as the talks dragged on, the women became justifiably impatient. So Leymah led a delegation of women to the peace conference in neighboring Ghana and held a sit-in. They linked arms and blocked the doors and windows until the men inside reached an agreement. When security forces tried to arrest Leymah, she threatened to disrobe, which, according to traditional beliefs, would have brought a curse upon the men. Her threat worked, and it turned out to be an important turning point in the peace process. The story is captured in a documentary by Abigail Disney, *Pray the Devil Back to Hell,* and Leymah's 2011 book, *Mighty Be Our Powers.*

I met Tawakkol Karman for the first time during my visit to Yemen in 2011 as secretary of state. Born seven years after Leymah in the city of Taiz, she, too, grew up against a backdrop of political upheaval. When she was eleven years old she witnessed first the unification of North and South Yemen then a civil war between the two sides that led to a repressive government.

When she got older, Tawakkol became a journalist, reporting on the human rights abuses she saw. In 2005, she founded an organization, Women Journalists Without Chains, to provide training to up-and-coming journalists and to stand up for freedom of the press.

"Because of women like us, I believe that in the end, tyranny will never succeed, and goodness will always vanquish evil. Although I may not see it in my lifetime, peace will overcome. I believe, I know, that if you have unshakable faith in yourself, in your sisters, and in the possibility of change, you can do almost anything."

— LEYMAH GBOWEE

All around her, Tawakkol saw violence, authoritarianism, poverty, and relentless attempts to silence dissenting voices, including her own. As with Leymah, the more she saw, the more she felt she needed to do. In 2007, she started organizing weekly protests in Sana'a, the capital of Yemen, demanding the corrupt government be investigated. Even in the midst of chaos, Tawakkol kept her movement together and advocated for a nonviolent approach. ("We will not turn to violence, no matter what the government does," she vowed to a reporter in 2011.) Even when the country's president threatened Tawakkol's brother that his sister would be killed for disobeying him, she didn't retreat. She kept protesting until 2011, when she called on her fellow activists to channel their efforts into supporting the Arab Spring. They called her "Mother of the Revolution" and "the Iron Woman." The conflict in Yemen eventually became a proxy war between Arab states and Iran, leading to a horrific humanitarian crisis. Tawakkol has persistently advocated that the UN Security Council pass a resolution demanding an end to the war and sponsor the political process to achieve that.

In 2011, Leymah and Tawakkol were awarded the Nobel Peace Prize, along with Liberian president Ellen Johnson Sirleaf, "for their nonviolent struggle for the safety of women and for women's rights to full participation in peace-building work." Their dedication to building peace, advancing reconciliation, and defending the rights of fellow citizens in their own countries is remarkable but not unique. Leymah and Tawakkol are shining examples of the difference women can make and the progress they can drive when given the opportunity to make decisions about the future of their societies and countries. In her book, Leymah reflected on what keeps her going: "The work is hard. The immensity of what needs to be done is discouraging. But you look at the communities that are struggling on a daily basis. They keep on — and in the eyes of the people there, you are a symbol of hope. And so you, too, must keep on. You are not at liberty to give up."

As America's first woman secretary of state, Madeleine Albright stood firm against the barbarism of the Bosnian War and the ethnic cleansing in Kosovo, including advocating the use of military force to end both conflicts. She famously said: "There's a special place in hell for women who don't help each other." She and the other peacemakers I've met were determined to help women, children, and men by ending war. Some succeeded, some did not; but their bravery encouraged others to keep trying. In her most recent book, *Fascism: A Warning,* Madeleine poses a question that should be on all our minds, asking, "Who has the responsibility to uphold human rights? The answer to that is: everyone."

VICTORIA MXENGE

HILLARY

In 1997, Chelsea and I visited South Africa. Three years earlier, I had attended President Nelson Mandela's inauguration as part of a big, exuberant American delegation. This time, we had more time and saw more of the country. Mandela showed us his own cell on Robben Island where he spent eighteen years. We met with Bishop Desmond Tutu and observed the work of the Truth and Reconciliation Commission as they sought to heal South Africa after apartheid. We visited classrooms where children were learning English and met with students attending the University of Cape Town. One of the most unforgettable moments of our trip was meeting with women on a dusty patch of land on the edge of Cape Town.

Under apartheid, the women we met had been homeless squatters on this desolate piece of land off the highway; they had nowhere else to go with their children. Together, they started to build a community. They formed their own housing and credit association, modeled on the Self Employed Women's Association started by Ela Bhatt in India. Pooling their savings and microloans, they bought shovels, paint, and cement, and learned how to lay foundations and put in a sewer line. When Chelsea and I visited, they had built eighteen homes. When I came back with Bill on a state visit a year later, there were 104. I loved a line from one of the songs they sang as they worked: "Strength, money, and knowledge — we cannot do anything without them." Good advice for women everywhere!

The women decided to name the settlement

after Victoria Mxenge, a South African anti-apartheid activist. She was working as a nurse in 1964 when she married civil rights lawyer Griffiths Mxenge, who was well known for defending victims of apartheid. While working and raising her family, Victoria also got her law degree. After she finished her studies, she joined her husband's practice in 1981.

That year, her husband was abducted near their home and murdered, his body mutilated by the apartheid government. Victoria took over his law practice, continuing the struggle for liberation and vowing to discover the truth about her husband's murder. She represented youth who were mistreated in detention facilities, defended anti-apartheid activists being tried for treason, and became a member of the Release Nelson Mandela Committee.

In 1985, she spoke at the funeral of the Cradock Four, young activists who had been murdered by the security police. ". . . when people have declared war on you, you cannot afford to be crying," she said. "You have to fight back. As long as I live, I will never rest until I see to it that justice is done, until Griffiths Mxenge's killers are brought to book."

Just a few days after that funeral, she was murdered in the driveway of her home in front of her children. It is believed that she was killed by the government's security forces. Thousands of people attended her funeral; mourners took to the streets and clashed with the police, leaving several people dead and more injured. In 2006, she was posthumously awarded the Order of Luthuli in Silver for her contribution to the field of law and her role in the fight against apartheid's oppression.

When I returned to Cape Town as secretary of state in August 2009, I visited the Victoria Mxenge community once again. I even helped do a little landscaping (and there was also some dancing involved!). Patricia Matolengwe, the head of the Victoria Mxenge community, told me how much progress they had made — in part because they were driven by the enduring example of Victoria's bravery. They had gone from eighteen homes in one place to more than fifty thousand across South Africa, and had taken over more land to keep building. I was honored to learn that they named a street after me, and I have the souvenir street sign they gave me. But the real story of that visit was how these poor, landless women had been empowered by another woman's life and death, and used her example to chart a better story for themselves. It reminds me of the words that tens of thousands of women chanted as they protested back in 1956 to demand an end to apartheid: "You strike a woman, you strike a rock."

AI-JEN POO

CHELSEA

Ai-jen Poo is a self-described futurist. Her understanding of the changing demographics of America and its workforce are at the heart of everything she does — from her earliest activism to her work with the National Domestic Workers Alliance, which she cofounded in 2007. She has a sense of where our country is headed (or at least should be headed) and what we need to do to build a more hopeful and equitable future for everyone.

The daughter of immigrants from Taiwan, Ai-jen was born in Pittsburgh in 1974. Her mother had moved to the United States to study chemistry and later became a doctor. Ai-jen remembers that her mother was the only woman in her medical school class who was also raising two young children. She spent her career treating patients with melanoma, and Ai-jen grew up hearing about the stories and struggles of cancer patients and their families, and surrounded by her mother's commitment to do all she could for every patient.

Ai-jen became an activist while a college student at Columbia University. "I started volunteering at a domestic violence shelter for Asian immigrant women, which then led me to organizing," she remembers. "In general, I was hungry to understand how to have an impact on the world. I signed up for every class on social change, feminism, and movements for justice I could find." One night in April 1996, she and some of her fellow students occupied Columbia's Low Library to demand that the university hire more ethnic studies faculty and design a curriculum that reflected the diversity of New York City and America.

> *"When you listen to women, especially to those who have been the least visible in society, you will hear some of the most extraordinary stories that represent the best of who we are as a nation."*
>
> — AI-JEN POO

She stayed in the building all night and was arrested the next morning. Calm and undeterred, Ai-jen kept advocating for what she knew was right — and necessary. She soon took part in another student-led occupation: This time, they took over the school's main administrative buildings for five days, teaching their own classes. The protests helped put pressure on the campus to create the Center for the Study of Ethnicity and Race, which still exists today.

After graduation, Ai-jen went to work for the Committee Against Anti-Asian Violence. The experience opened her eyes to the fact that domestic workers — including housekeepers, nannies, and home care workers — were some of the most underpaid and exploited people in New York City. Despite the essential work they did, including caring for children and the elderly and making it possible for people with disabilities to live independently, they frequently labored in the shadows, excluded from the basic protections that should be afforded to everyone working in America. Ai-jen believed it was past time to start valuing and empowering these "invisible" workers. She started a new organization called Domestic Workers United to help lobby for long-overdue policy changes in New York City.

In 2007, Ai-jen, together with fifty domestic workers and organizers from around the country, founded the National Domestic Workers Alliance. It was an effort to take her local work national, to recognize and support "the work that makes all other work possible." She helped pass a Domestic Workers' Bill of Rights in New York State in 2010. It granted rights like overtime pay, paid family leave, and protection from harassment and discrimination to domestic workers. It

---

"The work itself is associated with work that women have historically done, work that's been made incredibly invisible and taken for granted in our culture. But it's so fundamental to everything else in our world. It makes it possible for all of us to go out and do what we do in the world every single day, knowing that the most precious aspects of our life are in good hands."

— AI-JEN POO

---

was the first time that some of America's 2.5 million domestic workers had guaranteed access to these protections. I remember thinking about my Grandma Dorothy after it had passed. As a young teenager, she worked as a maid and "mother's helper," and while she was always grateful for what she saw as her employer's kindness, she worked hours each day before and after school; her working conditions nearly ninety years ago are not too different from what many domestic workers face today.

Since New York's breakthrough law, seven more states — and counting — have passed similar legislation. In 2011, inspired by her family's experience caring for her grandfather in a nursing home, Ai-jen launched a new initiative called Caring Across Generations, which aims to address the need to better care for the elderly with respect and dignity.

Three years later, she was awarded a MacArthur Fellowship in recognition of her game-changing work. Even though the recognition was exciting, it felt complicated to Ai-jen. "Representing a workforce of unrecognized and undervalued women, I'm very conscious about the politics of visibility. I work with so many women who deserve recognition and never receive it," she said later. Following the advice of a mentor who encouraged her not to shrink from her "moment in the sun," she decided she needed to own her contributions and successes — and share them. Especially since receiving the prestigious award, she has gone out of her way to create "moments in the sun" for more of the women she works with — whether they're domestic workers or her colleagues at the office.

HILLARY

In addition to being a tireless organizer, Ai-jen radiates compassion and empathy — two things we urgently need more of in our country's policy discussions. She is a beautiful speaker and writer and has a unique ability to bring moral clarity to any issue. Today she is organizing women — and men who believe in gender equity — through a new group, Supermajority, that has brought together leaders from reproductive rights, racial justice, and economic opportunity to work together toward a common agenda.

The principles of Ai-jen's work are expansive; she doesn't limit herself to one cause or issue. She has advocated for a path to citizenship for undocumented people in America, many of whom work as caregivers. Ai-jen and her colleagues have helped launch a campaign to keep families together at the border, and she has argued that what we are facing is a national moral emergency; I couldn't agree more. She has urged Americans to "think like a domestic worker who shows up and cares no matter what. [Choose] love and compassion, no matter what. Show up like a domestic worker, because our children are counting on us." Her words rang true the day she uttered them and every day since.

Sarah Brady, Gabby Giffords, Nelba Márquez-Greene, Shannon Watts, and Lucy McBath

SARAH BRADY

GABBY GIFFORDS

SHANNON WATTS

NELBA MÁRQUEZ-GREENE

LUCY McBATH

Many of the people I admire are not lifelong activists but reluctant advocates who find themselves wholeheartedly taking on a cause. That is certainly true of Sarah Brady, Gabby Giffords, Nelba Márquez-Greene, Shannon Watts, and Lucy McBath. None of these women dreamed of becoming a national leader in the fight for gun violence prevention. But when the issue forced its way into their lives, they took it on — knowing what they were up against, knowing the resistance they would face, but also knowing that the pain of doing nothing would be far greater than the pain of doing something so hard. Each of their stories is different, but they share a common dedication to preventing more families from having to live through the pain of losing a loved one to preventable gun violence.

On March 30, 1981, Ronald Reagan's press secretary, James Brady, was shot in the head during an assassination attempt on the president's life. He was left partially paralyzed and with brain damage. His wife, Sarah Brady, became a gun control activist. Her mission was simple: to keep guns out of the hands of criminals, children, and the mentally ill. She tirelessly lobbied legislators and made speeches and television appearances in support of the Brady Handgun Violence Prevention Bill. When that bill was finally signed into law by my husband in 1993, Sarah and James were there.

The Brady Bill required a five-day waiting period before the purchase of a handgun, and a background check on individuals seeking to purchase firearms from a federally licensed dealer. And it worked: Around 2.1 million ineligible people were stopped from buying a gun between 1994 and 2014.

Sarah didn't stop after the Brady Bill was signed. She served as chair of the Brady Campaign to Prevent Gun Violence and the Brady Center to Prevent Gun Violence. She spent the rest of her life speaking out about loopholes in our gun laws that allowed, as she pointed out, "deadly consequences."

Thirty years after James Brady was shot, on January 8, 2011, Gabrielle "Gabby" Giffords, a third-term Congress member from Arizona, was holding a public meeting with constituents in the parking lot of a Safeway supermarket in Tucson. Gabby had served in the state legislature from 2000 through 2005 and

---

"The gun lobby finds waiting periods inconvenient. You have only to ask my husband how inconvenient he finds his wheelchair from time to time."

— SARAH BRADY

---

was elected to Congress in 2006, where she made her mark standing up for America's security and standing with the men and women who serve in our nation's military. She was a rising star in the Democratic Party, often considered a future candidate for the Senate and even the presidency. I admired her for her quick wit, bold ideas, and ability to hold a rational conversation with anyone — no matter the political views.

On that morning, as she greeted the people who had come to see her, a gunman shot her in the head and killed six and wounded thirteen others. Despite the national news incorrectly reporting otherwise — a painful reminder of the importance of fact-checking — Gabby survived. She spent months in a rehabilitation facility working to recover her strength. She did it all with her trademark humor, kindness, and relentless optimism. (On January 8, 2014, she marked the three-year anniversary of the shooting by going skydiving. She told the *Today* show that it was "a lot of fun" and "peaceful, so peaceful.")

On August 1, 2011, Gabby returned to the House to vote and received a standing ovation before resigning the following January to focus on her physical and speech therapy. I'll never forget the sight of her standing there on the House floor, surrounded by friends and colleagues, as resolute and brave as ever. From that moment forward, with the support

> *"Even in our grief, we must summon the courage to fight against this fear. Americans must find the courage to imagine a country where these massacres do not occur. Our leaders must find the courage to accept the confines of their politics and pursue the moral necessity of peace and safety."*
>
> — GABBY GIFFORDS,
> AFTER THE 2018 SHOOTING IN
> PARKLAND, FLORIDA

and partnership of her remarkable husband, former astronaut Mark Kelly, she has dedicated her life to helping save the lives of others by advocating for gun violence prevention. "We need politicians to show the same courage demonstrated by survivors of gun violence: challenge the NRA, and pass safer gun laws," she has said. "But we also need to be tough. That's why we hold politicians accountable when they take NRA money and vote against the safety of our kids and communities."

In 2017, I attended a ceremony for the commissioning of a United States Navy ship, the USS *Gabrielle Giffords*. The ship's motto is "I Am Ready." That's Gabby. She came out of a tragic experience with grace and faith that are hard to imagine. Instead of asking the question many of us would ask — "Why me?"

— she asked herself how she could make the most out of the miracle of her survival.

Less than two years after Gabby was shot, twenty schoolchildren and six educators were murdered on December 14, 2012, at Sandy Hook Elementary School in Newtown, Connecticut. One of those children was six-year-old Ana Grace Márquez-Greene — a singing, dancing, joyful little girl. Her mother, Nelba Márquez-Greene; her father, Jimmy Greene; and her brother, Isaiah, were plunged into unfathomable shock, sadness, and anger, just like every other family struck by death that day.

A marriage and family therapist, Nelba understood the grief she was experiencing, but that didn't make it any easier. In the months and years since, she has been open about her struggles with depression, even her thoughts of suicide. She gets through the pain in part by working to build a country where no other family has to suffer the way hers has.

CHELSEA

In 2013, Nelba started the Ana Grace Project, which aims to confront isolation in schools by promoting community, professional development, and music and arts opportunities. I've been honored to support this wonderful organization and am grateful to call Nelba a friend. She speaks openly and bravely about her grief, the additional pain brought by those who deny the Sandy Hook tragedy, and her eternal love for both of her children. "I would say that the only difference between the early days and now is that the shock has worn off," she said. "When you have lost a child, a beloved, prayed-for child, to gun violence, I will only say for us, it doesn't get better."

When I met Nelba, she gave me the book that she and her daughter had been reading the night before Ana Grace went to school for the last time: *Junie B. Jones and the Mushy Gushy Valentime* [sic]. She asked me to read that book to my granddaughter. It was an extraordinarily powerful gesture from someone with a gift for helping others to understand the depth of sadness she and too many other families have had to endure. She recently posted on social media a picture of a pink bicycle, hanging up in her garage, unused. "Some survivors do not want to be visible," she reflected. "It doesn't mean they're not courageous. Some do want to be. There is no right or wrong way. Either case requires care, as long as we have to look at hand-me-down bikes hanging from garage ceilings and empty seats where children should be."

Nelba also described to me an experience that is all too common for anyone who takes a stand against gun violence: being subjected to vile harassment on the Internet in

> *"I feel the weight of a million grief-struck mothers in my soul. I can't outrun or ignore it. I have decided to make it a seat and whisper, 'I am not afraid of you. Teach me how to use what I hear and understand—to be helpful.'"*
> — NELBA MÁRQUEZ-GREENE

an organized effort to intimidate and silence. ("You look like you should be deported," someone tweeted at her on her birthday.) Nelba and everyone else who withstands that kind of viciousness — like the Sandy Hook family that has been forced to move seven times because of it — deserves our support for their tenacity and resilience.

The day after the Sandy Hook shooting, Shannon Watts, a mother of five children, stay-at-home mom, and former communications executive, started a Facebook group in which she urged Americans to do more to reduce gun violence. That group eventually led to her founding Moms Demand Action for Gun Sense in America, which she has built into a nonpartisan grassroots movement with five million members and chapters in all fifty states. Moms Demand Action has helped elect candidates who believe in commonsense gun reform and worked with responsible gun owners to help change the culture around gun safety.

CHELSEA

Shannon is fearless on social media and off. In the face of sexist slurs and violent threats toward her family, she is always there, calmly repeating the facts on gun violence prevention, calling out disinformation, and generally infuriating the gun lobby. She is incredible, and so is her book, *Fight Like a Mother: How a Grassroots Movement Took on the Gun Lobby and Why Women Will Change the World.*

She has been called "the NRA's worst nightmare" more than once, a title she wears with pride. She receives death threats and harassment on an almost daily basis. But Shannon isn't deterred. "I hope your 5 kids all get shot dead," one person messaged her on Instagram. "It's going to be real funny when someone comes to your house in the middle of the night, uninvited," said another. Shannon replied: "Despite the death threats I'm receiving, the NRA is still posting to encourage additional threats on my life on Instagram. I couldn't be more thrilled that they're terrified of a middle-aged mom."

Just a few weeks before the Sandy Hook shooting, Jordan Davis was shot and killed at a gas station in Jacksonville, Florida. The white man who killed him thought the music Jordan was listening to in his car was too loud and too "thug." Jordan was just seventeen years old.

I met his mother, Lucy McBath, on the campaign trail in 2016. She and Trayvon Martin's mom, Sybrina Fulton, were sitting at the same table with other mothers who had lost children to gun violence or as unarmed young black men and women in encounters with the police. Lucy told me she remembered comforting Jordan after they had heard about Trayvon Martin's murder on the news. Jordan didn't know Trayvon. They lived in different parts of Florida. But the news hit him hard. "Mom, how did this happen to Trayvon?" he asked. "He wasn't doing anything wrong." Nine months later, Jordan was dead, too. Lucy and Sybrina would go on to

---

"The power of mothers to effect change is not a new phenomenon: Women have been the secret sauce in the progress we've made on many social issues throughout history. . . . Women never looked back and continued fighting political battles in America to end child labor, expand voting rights and civil rights, stop drunk driving—all the way up to exposing the water crisis in Flint, Michigan. It's almost always women who are leading the charge for social change, and gun violence prevention is no different."

— SHANNON WATTS

---

form the Mothers of the Movement, a group of extraordinary women who travel the country speaking about their experiences losing their children and advocating for necessary change in gun laws and police actions.

Like too many others, Lucy experienced every parent's worst nightmare. Then, she turned her private pain into public activism, and brought others along with her. After the heartbreak of the 2016 election, learning that Lucy had decided to run for office filled me with hope. She had been considering a run for the statehouse, but after the Parkland school shooting in February 2018, she chose to run for Congress. She had a significant public role as an advocate, yet she wanted to do more. She started out without much name recognition in her district, taking on an incumbent. And then, to the surprise of no one who knew her, she shattered expectations and won.

CHELSEA

The gun lobby, predictably, has gone after Lucy at every turn. She has faced ugly, racist attacks. The head of the NRA claimed she had won her election because she is "a minority female," despite the fact that every other person who has held her seat, going back to 1827, has been a white man, with the exception of one white woman. Her opponents harassed her elderly mother-in-law, then lied about it. A radio host in Atlanta said Lucy should get "back into the kitchen" and go back to "sewing stuff." ("I don't even know how to do those things," Lucy pointed out.) But none of that has stopped Lucy from helping shepherd the passage of the first major gun legislation since the Brady Bill through the U.S. House of Representatives. Lucy's success in Congress is a testament to her courage and conviction that no other parent should ever lose a child to gun violence.

Over the last several years, there has been a concerted effort to try to undermine and marginalize the experiences of brave women like Sarah Brady, Gabby Giffords, Nelba Márquez-Greene, Shannon Watts, and Lucy McBath, and anyone who speaks out on the issue of gun violence. We've seen people try to blame the victim, or the family, or the neighborhood, or even promote the cruel lie that a mass shooting like Sandy Hook was a hoax. It's past time to follow the lead of

---

"I was just a Marietta mom. I loved my son, Jordan, more than anything else in this world. After Jordan was murdered, I realized that nobody was going to change our laws for us, so I had to do it myself."

— CONGRESSWOMAN LUCY MCBATH

Sarah, Gabby, Nelba, Shannon, Lucy, and so many others, and admit what's true: We have too many guns in this country in the wrong hands, and we have a responsibility to all our children and families to do something about it. If women whose lives have been touched by gun violence can find the courage to act, there is no excuse for the rest of us.

Nza-Ari Khepra, Emma González, Naomi Wadler, Edna Chavez, Jazmine Wildcat, and Julia Spoor

NZA-ARI KHEPRA

EMMA GONZÁLEZ

NAOMI WADLER

EDNA CHAVEZ

JAZMINE WILDCAT

JULIA SPOOR

CHELSEA

According to the Giffords Law Center — named in honor of Gabby Giffords — three million children are exposed to gun violence each year. More than 215,000 students in America have experienced a shooting at their school since the tragedy at Columbine High School in 1999. Sixty percent of teenagers in America say they're worried about one happening at their school. And two-thirds of gun deaths are deaths by suicide: Gun suicides claim the lives of nearly 22,000 Americans every year, including more than 950 children and teens. In fact, guns are now the second leading cause of death for kids and teens in America, after car accidents.

HILLARY

It's chilling to see children as young as elementary schoolers marching with signs that read "Am I Next?" And it broke my heart when a high school student who had just survived a shooting in Santa Fe, Texas, told a reporter she wasn't surprised because "it's been happening everywhere" and she "always kind of felt like eventually it was going to happen here, too." We are failing young people every single day that we do not act.

All of these statistics are tragic; none is inevitable. We know that commonsense gun safety laws lead to fewer gun deaths, including fewer suicides and fewer mass shootings. That's the future that a new generation of activists is working toward, spurred on by their own experiences with gun violence.

Nza-Ari Khepra was sixteen years old when her friend Hadiya Pendleton was killed on a playground near their high school in Chicago. A week before she was killed, Hadiya had performed as a majorette with her school band at President Obama's second inauguration. "Hadiya was like a magnet to everyone she met," Nza-Ari told the website The Trace. "Once she knew you, she made sure to go out of her way to make you feel special."

A month after the shooting, Nza-Ari and her friends started an organization, Project Orange Tree, dedicated to educating young people about violence and confronting its root causes. "One of our small goals at the beginning stages of Project Orange Tree was to host food drives because neighborhoods affected by the city's gun violence were also food deserts," she said. "That may seem like an unimportant thing to do when you're fighting against gun violence, but it was one small thing that we could accomplish."

Today Nza-Ari is a twenty-two-year-old graduate of Columbia University. She returned to Chicago for her job, and to continue her activism with Project Orange Tree to prevent more tragedies in her city and

> *"Gun violence is such a complex issue. We need to recognize every portion of it—mass shootings, inner-city violence, domestic violence. It hurts that such dreadful situations ignite people into action, but at the same time, that's exactly how I got started."*
>
> — NZA-ARI KHEPRA

our country. When I met her at the Clinton Global Initiative University meeting in 2018, she talked about how racism, poverty, and gun violence intersect. Her courage and candor in tackling such enormous and important issues makes her a role model to younger students — and those of us who aren't as young. "Maybe you care more about domestic violence than you do urban violence, or gun suicides, or accidental shootings," she tells anyone who will listen. "Do whatever you're most passionate about."

Days after the shooting at Marjory Stoneman Douglas High School in Parkland, Florida, that killed seventeen of her classmates, Emma González stood behind a podium at a rally. "Every single person up here today, all these people should be home grieving," she started. "But instead we are up here standing together, because if all our government and president can do is send thoughts and prayers, then it's time for victims to be the change that we need to see." She kept going, wiping tears from her face. By the time she finished her speech, she had given millions of people a new sense that maybe this time would be different, that gun laws might change. "They say no laws could have prevented the hundreds of senseless tragedies that have occurred," she said. "We call BS. That us kids don't know what we're talking about, that we're too young to understand how the government works. We call BS." She was absolutely right.

Emma spent her whole life in Parkland, raised by her mother, a math tutor, and her father, an attorney who came to the U.S. from Cuba. She built her skills as an activist while serving as president of her school's Gay-Straight Alliance. In the days after the shooting, she, along with her fellow Parkland students and students across the country who had been speaking out about gun violence for years, started organizing. The Parkland students set up a makeshift headquarters in one of their living rooms, met with young activists in other cities, and got to work putting together the March for Our Lives. I took my then three-year-old daughter, Charlotte, to the march in New York City. I wanted her to see young people leading the efforts to save other young people from gun violence — a fight that never should have come to them, just like bullets never should have taken those students' lives in Parkland or in any school, mall, park, movie theater, sidewalk, or anywhere in our country.

During the March for Our Lives rally in Washington, D.C., six weeks after the shooting in Parkland, Emma listed the names of students who were killed, then stood on the stage in silence until she had been there for six minutes and twenty seconds, the amount of time the shooting lasted. Emma is remarkable for her skills as an organizer, her gifts as an orator, and her ability to channel her sadness, her grief, and her passion into action. After the shooting in Parkland, she and her fellow students organized the largest single day of protest against gun violence in history. Inspired by the Freedom Riders of the 1960s, they spent the summer touring the country talking about gun violence prevention; along the way, they registered more than fifty thousand new voters. All of this helped fuel a historic youth turnout in the 2018 midterm elections, which saw a record number of thirty-three NRA-backed candidates lose their seats in Congress.

"We are grieving, we are furious, and we are using our words fiercely and desperately because that's the only thing standing between us and this happening again."

— EMMA GONZÁLEZ

> *"My friends and I might still be eleven, and we might still be in elementary school, but we know. We know life isn't equal for everyone and we know what is right and wrong. . . . We know that we have seven short years until we, too, have the right to vote."*
> — NAOMI WADLER

Another student who captured attention at the March for Our Lives was eleven-year-old Naomi Wadler from Alexandria, Virginia. After the Parkland shooting, her mother, Julie, talked to her about what had happened and explained that one of her own friends from high school, Fred Guttenberg, had lost his fourteen-year-old daughter Jaime that day. When Naomi learned that high school students across the country were planning to walk out of class on March 14, the one-month anniversary of the shooting, she organized a walkout of her own at her elementary school.

When she took the stage at the March for Our Lives rally in Washington, Naomi was confident, poised, and determined. And when she spoke, she brought a critical perspective, and one too often ignored in national conversations about gun violence. "I am here to acknowledge and represent the African American girls whose stories don't make the front page of every national newspaper, whose stories don't lead on the evening news," she said. "I represent the African American women who are victims of gun violence, who are simply statistics instead of vibrant, beautiful girls full of potential." I admired her bravery as one of the youngest speakers that day. She raised her voice and said something that so urgently needed to be heard.

Seventeen-year-old Edna Chavez was already politically engaged before the March for Our Lives. As a student in South Los Angeles, she'd knocked on her neighbors' doors before the 2016 election and asked to talk with them about issues, including immigration reform. When her father was incarcerated for being an undocumented immigrant, and later deported, it inspired her to pass out flyers in her community with information about immigrants' legal rights, and to hold "Know Your Rights" workshops to help people safely manage interactions with law enforcement.

Edna spoke at the March for Our Lives as a sister whose brother, Ricardo, had been killed in a shooting outside their home. "That moment onstage, it was not just me," she told

---

"This is normal, normal to the point that I learned to duck from bullets before I learned how to read."

— EDNA CHAVEZ

Teen Vogue later. "It was people from Chicago, from Baltimore, from so many different areas that we were talking about everyday gun violence. We made sure it was engraved into people's minds that shootings happen every day in low-income communities." As she ended her speech at the march, she said: "Remember my name. Remember these faces. Remember us and how we're making a change. *La lucha sigue.*" The fight continues.

Jazmine Wildcat's family owns guns, like a lot of people in Riverton, Wyoming, where she lives. But Jazmine, who is a member of the Northern Arapaho Tribe, isn't afraid to confront deep-seated cultural ideas, even if she's doing it alone. When Jazmine, then a fourteen-year-old student, organized a walkout at her school in 2018, "We only had about fifty people out of about three hundred take part," she said. "People came and mocked us."

For Jazmine, this fight is personal. She remembers having to help her family members collect her grandfather's guns after he had threatened to take his own life. Her

---

"I have my work cut out for me. . . . We cannot just sit here and wait for the next violent event to happen."

— JAZMINE WILDCAT

---

grandfather had PTSD from the Vietnam War; she believes that he never should have had access to a gun in the first place.

Being from a conservative town, Jazmine is used to dealing with people who don't agree with her. She has also had a lot of practice dealing with online trolls. They have called her ignorant, weak, and worthless because of her activism. But Jazmine remains steadfast. She continues to write letters to lawmakers, calling on them to pass sensible gun laws. When she grows up, she says, she might become a politician, fighting for the same issues that are on her mind right now. I hope she does.

September 25, 2009, is a day Julia Spoor will never forget. Ten days before her eighth birthday, her father died by suicide. Her father, Scott, was a forty-three-year-old engineer and had struggled with depression; he had previously attempted to take his own life a year earlier. A few years after his death, Julia finally learned how her dad had died. "With other methods of suicide there's still a chance," she pointed out later. "There is more time between the act and death for the possibility of a reversal. But not with a gun."

Julia wanted to use her loss to help other families protect loved ones struggling with depression and other mental health issues, and to stand up to gun violence broadly. When she was thirteen, she started marching

> *"I feel passionate about a lot of things and I feel angry about a lot of things and the ability that I have to change it is not something I ever want to overlook."*
>
> — JULIA SPOOR

with her mother and volunteering with Moms Demand Action. Two days after the shooting at Marjory Stoneman Douglas, she co-founded Students Demand Action, a national group led by high school and college students. They are currently forty thousand strong and growing.

These young leaders and so many others who are working on the issue of gun violence prevention come from different places of experience and pain. They are unified by their courage to stand up to anyone who values a gun more than their lives or the lives of their friends. They are fiercely imagining a different future. I look forward to the day when the movement they're building out of their anger, grief, and sadness succeeds, and future generations no longer have to be angry, go to school in fear, or mourn the loss of family and friends to gun violence.

BECCA HELLER

Before she was an internationally recognized human rights lawyer, Becca Heller was already good at arguing. Even when she was a little girl growing up in California in the

1980s, her parents could never get away with a simple "Because I said so" — they had to provide compelling reasons why she should listen to them. In high school, Becca skipped the classes that bored her. When her school dropped the debate team, she signed up to compete for another school. Years later, one of her friends would tell a *New York Times* reporter that in high school, she was voted "most likely to debate with a teacher." Now, the friend said, "she's most likely to argue with the president."

What makes Becca such an excellent advocate is the same thing that has driven her all her life: She refuses to accept the status quo, especially when it's arbitrary or unfair. In college at Dartmouth, she created a program to turn extra food from local farms into frozen meals for a nearby homeless shelter. After she graduated, she received a Fulbright Scholarship to work in Malawi on nutrition policy. Then, to the surprise of few people who knew her, she went to law school.

During her time at Yale Law School, she interned for a human rights organization in Israel. On a trip to Jordan, she met six Iraqi refugee families who changed her life. "I met with these families, and every single one said their biggest problem was legal assistance," she said later. "They were being processed by the United Nations and the United States, and they didn't understand the process. It was

> *"What I like about working with refugees is that they are fighting so hard. In other public service work you can spend a lot of time trying to convince people they are worth fighting for. It's really refreshing to advocate alongside people who are advocating for themselves."*
> — BECCA HELLER

totally opaque to them." When she came back to campus, she teamed up with a classmate, Jonathan Finer, to launch the Iraq Refugee Assistance Project (IRAP), dedicated to providing legal aid to Iraqi refugees. Soon after they introduced the program at a student activity fair, a hundred of their classmates signed up to help.

While still in law school, Becca traveled back and forth from New Haven to the Middle East and Washington, D.C. After she graduated, she moved to New York City to focus full-time on her organization, which she expanded and renamed the International Refugee Assistance Project (IRAP). By 2014, there were chapters at dozens of law schools, partnerships with more than fifty law firms, and offices in Amman, Jordan, and Beirut, Lebanon. The program focuses on helping the most vulnerable refugees, from children with medical emergencies to people being persecuted because of their sexual orientation.

Within three years, Becca and her team had worked on more than two hundred cases and had a 90 percent success rate; they had resettled as many as a thousand Iraqi refugees in seven countries around the world.

After the 2016 election, Becca knew that her work had become exponentially more important. When the administration announced its cruel and discriminatory travel ban on Muslims entering the United States in January 2017, Becca was ready. She sent out an email with the subject line "URGENT — protect refugees arriving at airports." When the order took effect two days later, thousands of lawyers were already standing by. Becca and her supporters headed to John F. Kennedy International Airport in New York, where she helped lead a team of lawyers offering legal help to travelers trying to enter the country. As the *New York Times* observed, "The public saw not so much a spontaneous reaction as the meticulous preparation of a loud, pugnacious thirty-five-year-old lawyer who is now in the middle of one of Mr. Trump's biggest policy fights." One of IRAP's clients became the first to win a ruling against the ban, which led to a nationwide stay the next day. The pressure against President Trump's Muslim ban intensified over the next weeks, with protests around the country. Marc and I went with friends to the first #NoBanNoWall protest in New York, and brought our kids with us to the next one. They won't remember it, but when they're older, they'll know they were there.

In March 2017, I met Becca for the first time when friends asked if I would take part in a conversation at their home with Becca and Farah Marcolla, a former IRAP client and an Iraqi refugee. I was honored to be there with these two brave women to help raise funds to support IRAP's vital work. Hearing from Farah, who was able to live safely in America thanks to IRAP's efforts, left me with an even greater sense of urgency around championing this lifesaving organization and opposing the discriminatory policies of the Trump administration.

In 2018, Becca was recognized for her work with a MacArthur Fellowship. She is still working to support the rapidly growing number of forcibly displaced people around the world, while educating younger lawyers on the importance of this work, especially now. At a time when our government is turning its back on refugees and vulnerable people around the world, it's good to know that Becca and others are questioning unjust laws and rules — and, even more than that, working to change them.

■ ■ ■ ■

STORYTELLERS

■ ■ ■ ■

Maya Angelou

Hillary

I read *I Know Why the Caged Bird Sings* right around the time it was published in 1969. It was a chaotic time for America. Dr. Maya Angelou's book seemed like a fitting capstone to a decade of assassinations, riots, war, and social change.

Maya's book recounts the cruel racism and backbreaking poverty she grew up surrounded by in Stamps, Arkansas, and the horrific rape she experienced in St. Louis at the age of eight, after which she stopped speaking for five years. Yet despite the tragedy and tumult of her own life, she came to embody unconquerable resilience. While I was reading that book, I had no idea at the time that I would one day live in Arkansas, be married to its governor, meet Maya, and become friends with her.

After Bill was elected president in 1992, I recommended that he invite her to speak at his inauguration. He enthusiastically agreed, and on January 20, 1993, Maya's voice rang out over the large crowd stretching down the Mall. She recited the poem "On the Pulse of Morning," which she had written for the occasion: "Lift up your hearts," she said, "each new hour holds new chances for new beginnings."

Maya was an expert on new beginnings and a champion of the human spirit. During the years she didn't speak, she read every book in the black school library and as many as she could get from the white school's. She memorized Shakespeare and Langston Hughes, Longfellow and James Weldon Johnson. Plays, poems, sonnets, passages — all of it fed her imagination. Out of the evil of the rape she suffered, she re-created herself: "I think that the courage to confront evil and turn it by dint of will into something applicable to the development of our evolution, individually and collectively, is exciting, honorable," she explained.

Maya wrote books of essays, volumes of poetry, and six autobiographies. One of her signature pieces was "Phenomenal Woman: Four Poems Celebrating Women," which she recited and performed all over the world. The words became an anthem of liberation and empowerment. "Pretty women wonder where my secret lies. I'm not cute, or built to suit a fashion model's size," she began.

When I ran for president in 2008, Maya hosted me at Wake Forest University, where she first lectured in 1973. There's a section in a poem she wrote about my campaign that stuck with me: "There is a world of difference between being a woman, and being an old female. If you're born a girl, grow up and live long enough, you can become an old female. But to become a woman is a serious matter. A woman takes responsibility for the time she takes up and the space she occupies."

Dr. Maya Angelou was not only a wonderful poet — she was a wonderful friend to so many who knew her. Hard times were made easier, joyful times sweeter, because she was on your side. She was a walking, talking work of art. Being in a room with her was a bit like being in a room with the *Mona Lisa*. She was elegant, arresting, and six feet tall, but she seemed taller to me. And that voice! When she opened her mouth, that extraordinary voice would pour forth: rich, enthralling, making her seem even larger than life. She chose her words with care. She did not suffer fools, and never hesitated to tell you when she thought you were wrong. When she said that she believed in you, you actually believed her and began believing in yourself. Her sage advice has resonated throughout the years: "When someone shows you who they are, believe them the first time."

Part of Maya's magic was the fact that there wasn't anyone else like her in the world, but somehow everyone could see something of themselves in her story, her aspirations, and the sheer scope of her life. You're Italian? Maya spoke Italian. You're a dancer? So was she. You're from San Francisco? She conducted a streetcar there. She knew everyone, lived everywhere, read everything, and felt it all. The whole world was her home. All people were her people.

There's a scene in Thornton Wilder's play *Our Town* that almost could have been describing Maya. Emily Webb is saying goodbye to the world one last time, and she asks the stage manager: "Do any human beings ever realize life while they live it? — every, every minute?" And he says, "No. The saints and poets, maybe — they do some." That was Maya. She realized her life while she lived it. And not only that, she savored it — every single second.

Throughout her life, she was often slotted into subcategories as writers wrote about her: A black writer. A civil rights activist. A women's leader. Maybe that was the only way people could wrap their heads around who she was. In truth, she transcended all labels. There is, however, one that does stick. She could have been born anywhere in the world, but only in America could she have become who she did. Our country's triumphs and progress over the past century are written all over her life. More than that — she helped write them. We're a better country today because of her. She urged, demanded, and inspired millions of Americans to live kinder, braver, more honorable lives.

It's hard to imagine a better example to follow.

Mary Beard

Hillary

In 2012, a well-known British television critic took author and renowned Cambridge classics professor Mary Beard to task — not for her arguments, or for the content of the documentary series on Ancient Rome that she hosted on the BBC, but for being too unattractive to appear on television. As she later paraphrased it to me, his message was, in effect: "You look like the back end of a bus. How dare you come into our living room with those teeth?" After listening patiently to her friends' well-intentioned advice not to take the bait, Mary came to a different conclusion: She took the bait.

Her response began: "As a classicist, I know a lot about revenge: the Ancient Greeks and Romans were horribly good at it. But not the crude, getting-your-own-back sort; they always ensured their retribution was absolutely appropriate to the crime." She countered the critic's ludicrous argument (as well as his time-worn caveat that he was, of course, being neither sexist nor beside the point) line by brilliantly written line. She didn't shy away from the fact that his nasty comments were hurtful — to her, and to the vast numbers of women around the world who looked like her.

"I'm every inch the 57-year-old wife, mum and academic, half-proud of her wrinkles, her crow's feet, even her hunched shoulders from all those misspent years poring over a library desk," she wrote unapologetically. "The real point is not what I look like, but what I do." A cheer went up from women around the world who were all too familiar with the miserable feeling of being told, either explicitly or implicitly: "Go away. You have nothing to say."

Mary grew up in the 1950s in Shrewsbury, England, the daughter of a school headmistress and an architect. During her summers in high school, she would join archaeological excavations — which offered a thrilling learning experience. After graduating from Cambridge University, she began writing and teaching. She earned her PhD, studying state religion in the Roman republic, and wrote a pioneering work on the Vestal Virgins in 1980. After she and her husband, an art historian, had their two children, she struggled to carve out the time serious research demanded. In 1989, she published her first book written alone in her own name: *The Good Working Mother's Guide*. Sharing the practical tips she had learned from experience, she said later, "seemed a fun thing to do." She then returned to history, publishing books, teaching at Cambridge, and bringing classics to viewers on the BBC.

After Mary's spot-on column in 2012,

she received an outpouring of support from women. Queen Elizabeth II made her a Dame of the Order of the British Empire (not for the book, but for her contributions to public life). She kept appearing on television. In one of my favorite appearances of hers, in 2016, she debated politician Boris Johnson for charity on the subject of Greece versus Rome. She explained that, going into the debate, she knew her only chance of winning was to be "fantastically prepared." That's something women everywhere can relate to. In the end, her preparation paid off, and she won resoundingly.

Along the way, Mary has built an appropriately large and appreciative Twitter following. She routinely uses the platform to stand up for facts and stand up to her trolls not with anger but with what she calls "aggressive politeness." She even publicly shamed one particularly vicious tweeter into taking her out to lunch to apologize. (Dare to dream!) "You just start to care less when you're old," she has said. "It's a great pleasure that I can

"We have no template for what a powerful woman looks like, except that she looks rather like a man."

— MARY BEARD

show younger women that you can stand up to these guys. You can call them out. And life goes on." (Yes it does!)

In 2017, Mary published a book that made me want to stand up once again and applaud. *Women & Power: A Manifesto* chronicles centuries of silencing women who dared to speak their minds, from *The Odyssey* to the 2016 presidential election. In it, she takes on years of criticism of women's oratorical style, the complicated dynamics of speaking up in a meeting as a woman, the "first recorded example of a man telling a woman to 'shut up,'" and more. When I had the opportunity to sit down with her on a visit to London in 2017, I refrained from reading back at her every line that had resonated with me, since we would have been there all day. In her manifesto, she concluded: "If women are not perceived to be fully within the structures of power, surely it is power that we need to redefine rather than women?" At every step of her career, Mary has been doing her part.

JINETH BEDOYA LIMA

HILLARY

"On the first day that Jineth Bedoya Lima arrived for work at the offices of Colombia National Radio in Bogotá," begins an article in the *Guardian,* "she was assigned to cover a story that would become her life. That day, in December 1996, her task was to report on what is probably the most dangerous prison in the world, La Modelo, infamous as a focal point for trafficking in drugs and arms between the forces of state, cartels, and rival militias."

Born in 1974, Jineth grew up in the aftermath of Colombia's long civil war, with Pablo Escobar and his cartel on the rise. After Escobar was killed, the empire he had built broke into factions, and the country descended into violent chaos. At La Modelo, Jineth saw "complicity by the army in many of the massacres carried out by the paramilitaries, and ways in which the military were arming the paramilitaries," she told the *Guardian*. "Some members of the military were even selling weapons to FARC," a violent rebel group. Her commitment to truth-telling and shining a light on the corruption within the government made powerful people uncomfortable. "I can see now," she said, "that as well as being furious at what I was writing, they were offended by the fact that I was a woman — young, pretty, petite, but sticking my nose into their affairs." In 1999, she was the victim of an attempted assassination. Still, she continued her investigative reporting.

In May 2000, she landed an interview with a paramilitary leader who was imprisoned in La Modelo. When she arrived at the prison,

> *"How did I overcome my fear, when it looked like my life was over? How did I continue as a woman and a journalist when faced with this black wall? I needed to know what happened. When I leave this world, I need to have known what happened to Jineth Bedoya, to my colleagues and so many other women."*
>
> — JINETH BEDOYA LIMA

she was kidnapped at gunpoint as a "message to the press in Colombia." She was raped, tortured, and left on the side of the road. "My body was destroyed. I was covered in wounds. They had cut my hair as well," she said. "I knew that the only way to continue living was to continue being a journalist."

Within weeks, she had returned to work. She started reaching out to other women who had been kidnapped and sexually assaulted — not for an article, but for herself. "There's a distinction between what happened to you as a journalist and what happened to you as a woman," she has said. In 2003, she traveled to the town of Puerto Alvira, which had been taken over by the FARC. She was kidnapped and again held hostage. After her release, despite the constant threats to her safety, she kept working to investigate violence, conflict, drug trafficking, organized crime, and sexual violence.

Six years later, Jineth launched a public advocacy campaign to raise awareness about the violence against women within the Colombian conflict. She called the campaign No Es Hora De Callar (Now Is Not the Time to Be Silent). In 2012, when I was secretary of state, First Lady Michelle Obama and I honored Jineth with the International Women of Courage Award. In 2017, she received the Hillary Clinton Award at Georgetown, along with several others who were doing essential work in bringing women to the table during the peace process in Colombia. I celebrated her that day as "a journalist who continued her pursuit of the truth and her advocacy for victims of sexual violence in the face of her own horrors."

Jineth still works as a journalist. She lives with her mother, under the protection of bodyguards. She receives near-constant threats of kidnapping and violence, wearing a bulletproof vest and traveling to work in an armored car. Despite everything, she refuses to be dissuaded. "The worst that can happen to me has already happened," she has said. At a time when too many politicians and government officials around the world lash out at the press and punish individual journalists, I am in awe of her courage and her determination to tell the truth, no matter what.

CHIMAMANDA NGOZI ADICHIE

HILLARY

When Chimamanda Ngozi Adichie was nine years old, in school in Nigeria in the 1980s, her teacher made a proposition to the class: She would give them a test, and the student who got the highest score would be the class monitor. At this, Chimamanda's ears perked up. Being class monitor meant getting to patrol the classroom, a long cane in hand, taking down the names of any troublemakers you noticed. She very much wanted the job.

Sure enough, she got the highest score on the test. But then, to her surprise, the teacher clarified that the monitor couldn't be a girl — it had to be a boy. She had neglected to mention that earlier, because she assumed it was obvious. The boy who had earned the second-highest score was made class monitor, and the incident opened Chimamanda's eyes to the way gender affects who gets ahead and who is held back. "Now, what was even more interesting about this," she added later in a TED Talk, "is that the boy was a sweet gentle soul who had no interest in patrolling the class with the cane, while I was full of ambition to do so. But I was female, and he was male, and so he became the class monitor."

From her childhood through the present day, Chimamanda has deliberately noticed and named insidious dynamics of racism and sexism. An early reader and writer, she loved British and American novels and copied their style in the pencil stories with crayon illustrations that she wrote for her mother. When she discovered African writers like Chinua Achebe and Camara Laye, her perception of the world shifted. "I realized that people like me, girls with skin the color of chocolate,

> *"Stories matter. Many stories matter. Stories have been used to dispossess and to malign, but stories can also be used to empower and to humanize. Stories can break the dignity of a people, but stories can also repair that broken dignity."*
> — CHIMAMANDA NGOZI ADICHIE

whose kinky hair could not form ponytails, could also exist in literature. I started to write about things I recognized."

Chimamanda grew up in Nsukka, a college town in Nigeria, raised by a college professor father and university registrar mother — the first woman to hold the job. Her parents hoped Chimamanda would become a doctor, and she spent a year studying medicine before admitting to herself and her family that what she really wanted to do was write. She would go on to earn a master's in creative writing from Johns Hopkins, then study African history at Yale. Her first play, *For Love of Biafra,* was published in Nigeria in 1998. In her typically funny, frank style, she has shrugged it off as "an awfully melodramatic play." She was twenty-six years old when she published her first book, *Purple Hibiscus,* a coming-of-age story. Three years later, she followed up with *Half of a Yellow Sun,* a historical novel based on the Biafran War in Nigeria. After that came a collection of short stories, *The Thing Around Your Neck,* and the novel *Americanah,* about a Nigerian blogging on the topic of race in the U.S.

In 2008, Chimamanda won a MacArthur Fellowship. Five years later, she received a jaw-dropping recognition of a different kind when none other than Beyoncé, another gutsy woman, sampled her TED Talk, "We Should All Be Feminists," in her song "Flawless." Chimamanda's book by the same title is filled with wry and wise observations about feminism.

During the 2016 presidential election, Chimamanda was frustrated with the way many of my supporters, especially women, were silenced online and in the press — so she wrote an essay speaking up for those who could not do it for themselves. When I saw her in 2018, she had recently published *Dear Ijeawele, or A Feminist Manifesto in Fifteen Suggestions,* and was full of insights about the connection between free speech, democracy, and feminism. She also wanted to talk about my Twitter bio. "The first word that describes you is 'wife,'" she pointed out. "And then I think it's 'mom' and then it's 'grandmother.' And when I saw that, I have to confess that I felt just a little bit upset. And then I went to look at your husband's Twitter account, and the first word was not 'husband.'" She was right. I promised

> *"We teach girls to shrink themselves, to make themselves smaller. We say to girls, 'You can have ambition, but not too much. You should aim to be successful, but not too successful, otherwise you will threaten the man.'"*
>
> — CHIMAMANDA NGOZI ADICHIE

her I would change it when I got home, and that's what I did.

When I told Chelsea, she said, "Chimamanda's right! And I love that she just came right out and told you what she thought — and what you needed to hear."

In addition to her smart, deliberate voice — on the page and off — I admire another gift of Chimamanda's. She has the rare ability to sum up even the biggest societal problem swiftly and incisively and, in the next breath, offer a solution. In her 2009 TED Talk, she illustrated what she called "the danger of a single story," and immediately proposed a new approach to inform and shape the way we perceive others. I can't wait to see how she continues to do just that.

AMERICA FERRERA

CHELSEA

The first thing I noticed when I met America Ferrera was how warm, funny, and honest she is. We were in Nevada at a campaign event for my mom. It was 2008, six years after her powerful role in the independent film *Real Women Have Curves,* three years after *The Sisterhood of the Traveling Pants,* and one year after she had won her first Emmy for starring in the TV show *Ugly Betty.* She told her story — the story of a first-generation American whose parents had moved to the United States from Honduras to give her opportunities that changed her life. She talked candidly about how hard it was at times being one of six kids to an immigrant mother and relying on free lunch at school to eat. She spoke about her certainty that she — as a woman of color, as the daughter of immigrants — needed to use her platform to help other people build a more just, more inclusive, and kinder world. The way she saw it, there was no better way to build that world than by participating in politics. We were on the road together a lot during that campaign, and before long, we had formed what I knew would be a lifelong friendship.

HILLARY

I also met America during that campaign as she traveled around the country for me. She's always struck me as a well-named, vibrant example of our country.

America started acting when she was just seven years old. She starred in her school productions of *Hamlet* — what I wouldn't give to go back in time and see that! — and *Oliver!* Her mother worried about America and tried as hard as she could to steer her daughter away from acting. But America knew where her passion and talents were. "My dream was to be an actress," America said later. "And it's true that I never saw anyone who looked like me in television or in films, and sure, my family and friends and teachers all constantly warned me that people like me didn't make it in Hollywood. But I was an American. I had been taught to believe that anyone could achieve anything — regardless of the color of their skin, the fact that my parents immigrated from Honduras, the fact that I had no money. I didn't need my dream to be easy, I just needed it to be possible."

After high school, America enrolled at the University of Southern California, where she studied theater and international relations. Before long, she dropped out to focus on acting (though she would come back to finish her bachelor's degree years later, in 2013, and I will never forget how proud she and her family were that day). In some ways, her mother was right to worry; America felt the racism and sexism of Hollywood constantly. Instead of conforming to someone else's idea of who she should be, she carved out her own path. She took on roles she could be proud of, and brought her whole, authentic self to every project.

That didn't mean it was easy, though. America once described the experience of standing onstage at the Emmys for *Ugly Betty:* "I'd imagined being in this room, clutching this statue ever since watching my first Emmy broadcast at seven years old. Now I was actually at the podium and accepting the award on national television. It was 2007, and I was twenty-three. . . . This should have been a moment of sublime celebration. But it wasn't. I can't remember the words that came out of my mouth, but I do remember, clear as day, the words that ran through my mind: 'Who do you think you are? You don't belong here. No one here thinks you deserve this. Hurry up and get off the stage.'" It took nearly a decade of hard work and therapy for her to finally beat her "nagging internal critic."

As America has worked to silence that critic, she has spoken openly about her struggles with self-doubt and how our politics has fed that doubt, leading her to question her place in her country. "Some of us don't have the privilege of living our lives outside of politics," she said later. "People make decisions every single day that impact my life — the air I breathe, my ability to walk down the street and be safe, how much money I make for the job I do, whether I can choose what happens to my body."

Politics is personal; America understands that deeply and feels a responsibility to share

> *"I am just one of millions of people who have been told that in order to fulfill my dreams, in order to contribute my talents to the world, I have to resist the truth of who I am. I for one am ready to stop resisting and to start existing as my full and authentic self. . . . My identity is not my obstacle. My identity is my superpower. Because the truth is, I am what the world looks like."*
>
> — AMERICA FERRERA

her story and her platform to help enfranchise and protect people — particularly immigrants, people of color, and women. She's partnered with Voto Latino and other organizations to expand civic engagement and participation, and campaigned for candidates she believes in. She refuses to apologize for her voice or her advocacy.

America is always looking toward the future, asking herself what she can do to help build the world she wants to live in while confronting injustices. After the 2016 election, she and her husband, filmmaker Ryan Williams, founded a group called Harness that works with other artists to encourage people to vote, and to tell untold and important stories. She also supports other activists, including our friend Elsa Collins who, since 2018, has led multiple bus trips to San Diego and Tijuana to bring desperately needed supplies to families on both sides of the border, including children separated from their parents.

In 2017, America courageously shared her story of being sexually assaulted at nine years old, and joined millions of women who were raising their hands to say "Me too." She became a founding member of TIME'S UP, an organization that emerged from the ongoing and long-overdue global reckoning around the abuse and misbehavior of powerful men. America and others from the entertainment industry came together to talk about what they could do to create change for women everywhere. Today, TIME'S UP and the TIME'S UP Legal Defense Fund are supporting women fighting for justice from the entertainment industry to the restaurant industry to the technology sector.

In politics and in her own life, America is constantly pushing herself to do things that scare her. In 2016, she decided to do a triathlon. She shut out the negative voices in her head that told her she was "the fat kid, the procrastinator, the quitter," and started training. "Sensing my own self-doubt, I doubled down, announcing my triathlon plan on every social media platform I have," she wrote later. By the time she got in the water for her first ocean swim, she had developed a mantra: "You are a warrior, you are strong, and sharks are not real." On the day of the race she achieved her two goals: Finish, and stay positive. True to form, as she passed other athletes she cheered them on, explaining that her only goal was to yell louder than the voices in their heads. When she finished, she said, "I finally got my answer to that question: Who do you think you are? I am whoever I say I am." As an actress, as an advocate, as a writer, as an athlete, and as a mother, America has proved again and again that it's a gutsy thing to own our own story.

ALI STROKER

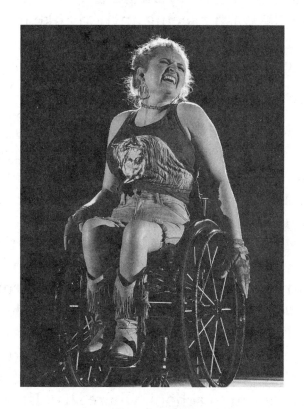

CHELSEA

When Ali Stroker accepted a Tony Award in 2019 for her performance as Ado Annie in *Oklahoma!,* she knew she was making history. No actor who uses a wheelchair had won the

547

prestigious theater award before. "This award is for every kid who is watching tonight who has a disability, who has a limitation or a challenge, who has been waiting to see themselves represented in this arena — you are," she said in her acceptance speech. As a little girl growing up in Ridgewood, New Jersey, she'd known all too well how it felt to have to be her own role model. "I'm very aware that when I was a little girl, I wasn't seeing anybody like me," she said, "and on days when I'm exhausted or discouraged about something, that lights a fire."

At age two, a car accident left Ali with a spinal cord injury, paralyzing her from the chest down. She has used a wheelchair ever since. From the very beginning, she says, her parents taught her to focus not on the things she couldn't do, but on the things she could. And one thing she could do was sing.

Her first experience with musical theater came when she was seven years old and took part in a neighbor's backyard performance of *Annie*. Ali played the starring role, and knew instantly that she belonged onstage. "It was a really special summer," she said later. "I remember my life beginning." She acted throughout high school, where she also served as class president, and later became the first actress in a wheelchair to earn a degree from New York University's Tisch School of the Arts. Her motto was "Make your limitations your opportunities."

> *"Who says that dance isn't turning on wheels? Who says dancing isn't throwing your arms in the air and grabbing someone else's arms to be propelled across the stage?"*
> — ALI STROKER

In 2012, Ali captured national attention when she competed in *The Glee Project,* a reality television competition to earn a role in the musical comedy TV show *Glee.* Three years later, she made her Broadway debut in Deaf West Theatre's revival of the musical *Spring Awakening.* The role gave her an opportunity to translate choreography, collaborating with the cast and crew to create a performance that was uniquely her own.

In addition to being a phenomenal performer, Ali is also a committed advocate. She traveled to South Africa to hold theater workshops and classes for women and children affected by HIV/AIDS, founded an anti-bullying campaign called Be More Heroic, and helped launch ATTENTIONTheatre to create more meaningful opportunities for performers with disabilities. "We will do so with no agenda to inspire, or to promote these artists as heroes among us," reads the group's mission statement. "We will represent all people as we all are: Human beings striving toward desire and identity."

The night she won her history-making Tony, Ali entered from backstage rather than from the audience; there was no ramp to the front of the stage. Afterward, she pointed out that "Broadway theaters [are] all made accessible to patrons, but the backstage areas are not. So I would ask theater owners and producers to really look at how they can begin to make the backstage accessible so that performers with disabilities can get around."

We still have a long way to go to make theater truly accessible — for audience members, production crews, creators, and performers alike. But through the power of her own example, her commitment to making space for others, and her willingness to ask hard and important questions, Ali is ensuring that aspiring performers with disabilities — maybe even a little girl in a wheelchair who dreams of starring in *Annie* or *Oklahoma!* — can see themselves represented and celebrated.

Amani Al-Khatahtbeh

Chelsea

Amani Al-Khatahtbeh was nine years old and living in New Jersey on September 11, 2001. Her parents had moved to the United States from Jordan and Palestine because they wanted to surround Amani and her brothers with opportunities to go as far as their dreams could take them. But after 9/11, Amani found herself scorched by racism and rampant Islamophobia, including in her own school and community.

At seventeen years old, she started an online magazine called MuslimGirl. "It was my personal refusal from having Muslim women's voices be exploitatively collected, hijacked, and sidelined by media corporations that claim and twist our narrative," she later wrote. "It began as a way for millennial Muslim girls to connect and communicate with each other, and evolved into a platform to defiantly carve out a space for ourselves in the middle of post-9/11 anti-Islam hatred, stereotypes, and misconceptions." When she started MuslimGirl in 2009, nothing like it existed in the United States. She knew it was important for her and for other young Muslim American women, and she wanted to help amplify voices like hers. Each time she checked, the site had more views.

Amani kept MuslimGirl going beyond high school. She worked on the site while a student at Rutgers, all while serving as the opinions editor of the student newspaper — the first Arab Muslim American to hold the position. After college, she worked for a nonprofit in D.C. She left when she landed her dream job working in media in New York City — but

> *"People always ask me, 'How did you start MuslimGirl?' . . . I bought a domain, got some hosting, and 'started.' But that was the easy part. The questions people should be asking me are, 'How did you stick with MuslimGirl throughout college when all you wanted to do was go to concerts and chill with friends in the dorms?' 'What did you respond to your father when he suggested that maybe you should "start considering something serious" after you graduated?' . . . that's where it gets a whole lot more difficult."*
>
> — AMANI AL-KHATAHTBEH

the company collapsed before she started. She moved to New York anyway and turned her focus to building MuslimGirl as a full-time job. The site saw a 90 percent increase in traffic that year alone. By 2017, it had 1.7 million page views a year.

Today MuslimGirl has a team of more than forty people and produces content "at the intersection of Islam and feminism," which Amani sees as complementary; she's trying to help others see it that way, too. The platform Amani built took on new relevance during and after the 2016 election, when Islamophobia spiked once again, this time stoked by (first candidate then) President Trump. She and her staff published a "Crisis Safety Manual for Muslim Women," and she spoke out against Donald Trump's attacks on Muslims. "His comments perpetuate the Islamophobic attitudes that compelled us to advise Muslim women at the time to carry their phones charged at all times, know which numbers to call or apps to use to record a hate crime, and consider less conspicuous hijab styles in areas of extreme threat," she said.

Even in this hostile environment, Amani has preserved MuslimGirl as a place that celebrates her community. Recent headlines range from "Stop What You're Doing and Bake These Bars for Your Next Iftar Party" to "How a Quote from the Qur'an Affected My PTSD" to "So What Does an Abnormal Period Actually Mean for Your Fast?" On March 27, 2017, she launched Muslim Women's Day, which has been celebrated every year since by elected officials, activists, artists, and more.

In 2016, I met Amani at the Clinton Global Initiative University. She took part in a discussion on having "The Courage to Create," which explored what it takes to move from having a great idea to making that idea a reality. As Amani spoke, her courage was evident — as was her passion to share why she believed anyone could create something meaningful, disruptive, and powerful, as she had with MuslimGirl.

That courage was again palpable when I read the autobiography she published later that year, *Muslim Girl: Coming of Age*. It chronicles her upbringing and her personal struggles with feelings of not being enough — struggles that were amplified by formative years spent experiencing acute Islamophobia and racism.

In May 2017, Amani and I were on a panel together in Washington, D.C., at the Cooperative for Assistance and Relief Everywhere (CARE) national conference. The conference's theme was "Now More Than Ever," and we spoke about the many challenges that girls and women face today. We discussed how those of us with a platform have the obligation to share it, to give a voice to the historically voiceless. I was impressed by Amani's continued willingness to take on difficult subjects, knowing that sometimes her job is to force everyone, including her own readers, to question their own views. "We published a conversation from a transgender Muslim woman convert about what her experience has been," she said in an interview. "She referred to God as 'She' in her article and everyone just went haywire."

As Amani's work has reached bigger and bigger audiences, and more and more people have wanted to feature her, she has stayed true to the values that led her to start Muslim-Girl in the first place. In her writing and on social media, she tackles the new challenges that come with being recognized, including tokenization. "There have been a lot of times where different outlets have wanted to use me as an ornament, to tick off that box where a Muslim woman is included without having to speak, and that's important for me to consider," she has said. She openly addresses the privilege that comes with being beautiful, Western-educated, and lighter-skinned. She lives her values, even when it means passing up a chance to be publicly celebrated: When Revlon wanted to give her an award for her advocacy in 2018, she turned it down because she objected to the views of another nominee.

Amani has never been the kind of person to wait for public opinion to shift or our political climate to get better. Instead, from the time she was a teenager, she has taken it upon herself to carve out a space where she can create the world she envisions — the world that Muslim girls, and all girls, deserve.

■ ■ ■ ■

ELECTED LEADERS

■ ■ ■ ■

BELLA ABZUG

HILLARY

Bella Abzug was always herself. Every day of her long, active life, she never tried to be anyone else — she stuck to her principles and brought her passion and fearlessness to everything she did. As a result, when the history is written about what women in America have done, what they have said, and how they have stood up for themselves, Bella's name and accomplishments will rank up there with the best of them.

The trailblazing politician was born in the Bronx in 1920, the year women won the right to vote. (I always have this image of her saying, "No, I'm not arriving on the scene until I can be part of this great moment.") She gave her first soapbox speech in a subway station at age eleven. After she graduated from Columbia Law School she became a lawyer, fighting for women, people of color, lesbians and gay men, and working people — those who were, in her words, "on the outside of power." She stood up for civil rights and represented people who were targeted by Senator Joseph McCarthy's witch hunt. In 1970, she was elected to the U.S. House of Representatives, where she served three terms. Her slogan was unforgettable: "This woman's place is in the House," she would declare. "The House of Representatives!"

I first heard about Bella in 1970, when she was elected to Congress. I would sit in the law library and read the newspapers, where she was constantly featured. She stood out for many reasons — not just her ever-present hats — and I especially admired her for her anti-war stance. Legend has it that she once accepted an invitation to the White House from President Nixon. She waited patiently in line, and when her turn came to shake hands with the president, she announced for all to hear that she was there on behalf of her constituents, to demand withdrawal from Vietnam. At the time, even though I was interested in politics, I never pictured myself running for office. Bella inspired me because she was one of the few women who was in the thick of political and policy decisions. In the midst of the crisis in our democracy with eerie parallels to our current moment, Bella was the first member of the U.S. House of Representatives to speak out in favor of impeaching Nixon.

In Washington, they called her "Battling Bella," a style that came naturally to her. As *Life* magazine said, "She arrived in Congress . . . and began shouting." It was true: She let you know exactly how she felt, to the point of yelling. But she was also a savvy behind-the-scenes politician. Publicly, she would be throwing off those great one-liners she became known for; meanwhile, she managed to become a favorite of some of the very members of Congress who epitomized the good-old-boy network. She had a strong, effective presence. She knew how to play the game. But she never lost sight of whom she was fighting for. She unapologetically delivered for her constituents and for anybody who needed a champion. Bella used her tenacity to coauthor historic pieces of legislation, including Title IX, the Freedom of Information Act, and the first law making it illegal to prevent women from opening a line of credit in their own name simply because of their gender. After Congress failed to pass the Equal Rights Amendment, Bella didn't sit around wringing her hands; she got together with Gloria Steinem, Shirley Chisholm, Fannie Lou Hamer, Mildred Jeffrey, and Betty Friedan to form the National Women's Political Caucus in 1971.

After her three terms in Congress, she became the first woman to run for the U.S. Senate from New York. She lost by less than 1 percent of the vote. Next, she became the first woman to run for New York City mayor. She loved politics, and she never apologized for that. "I'm a politician," she said simply. "I run for office. That's my profession."

As first lady, often when I walked into a room of non-governmental organizations (NGOs) or sat at an international conference, I could count on seeing Bella. She was usually the one who organized the women's caucuses at these conferences and fought to ensure that women had a seat at the table at all. ("First they gave us the year of the woman," she said. "Then they gave us the decade of the woman. Sooner or later, they'll give us the whole thing.") During her last years, her health started to fail. But Bella wasn't going to give

> *"I've been described as a tough and noisy woman, a prizefighter, a man hater, you name it. They call me Battling Bella, Mother Courage, and a Jewish mother with more complaints than Portnoy. There are those who say I'm impatient, impetuous, uppity, rude, profane, brash, and overbearing. Whether I'm any of these things or all of them, you can decide for yourself. But whatever I am—and this ought to be made very clear at the outset—I am a very serious woman."*
>
> — BELLA ABZUG

up; she kept moving. When I saw her at the Beijing Women's Conference in 1995, she was in a wheelchair but still battling away. The Chinese government had placed the NGO conference at Huairou, which was far from Beijing. It was raining cats and dogs, and there was a lot of mud. But that didn't stop Bella. She was there, proving that no sickness, no obstacle, nothing could ever dampen her fighting spirit.

She never stopped organizing; she never stopped demanding results. Near the end of her life, I saw her at a ceremony at the White House, where we were giving out awards for successful microcredit efforts — a commitment we had announced at the Beijing conference and something Bella cared deeply about. She came up to me afterward and didn't spend a moment celebrating the victory she had helped fight so hard for. Instead, she took a deep breath and began: "Okay. Now here's what we've got to do next." She never let anybody forget that no matter how much we thought we might have accomplished, there was so much more to be done.

Years later, I wound up running for the same Senate seat she had run for. As her daughter Liz recently pointed out to me, Bella was the first woman to try, and twenty-four years later, I was the first woman to succeed. I thought a lot about her and other women pioneers in New York. I thought about how tough it had been — and still was — to break into statewide politics. Mostly, I was sorry she wasn't around. Just about everywhere I went during that campaign, I met people who would say: "The first woman I ever voted for was Bella Abzug, and I'll vote for you, too." Whether it's Central Asia, Africa, or anywhere else, I still meet women who introduce themselves by saying, "I'm the Bella Abzug of Russia," or "I'm the Bella Abzug of Kazakhstan," or "I'm the Bella Abzug of Uganda." What they're really saying is that they, too, are pioneers; they, too, are willing to take on the establishment in their society to demand equal rights for women.

In 1998, I spoke at Bella's memorial service.

Nearly everyone there that day wore a fabulous wide-brimmed hat, just like the hats Bella famously wore. She had started wearing hats after being mistaken for a secretary at the beginning of her career. "When I was a young lawyer, I would go to people's offices and they would always say: 'Sit here. We'll wait for the lawyer.' Working women wore hats. It was the only way they would take you seriously," she explained. Later, when she came to Congress and realized her male colleagues wanted her to take off the hat, she made up her mind once and for all: The hat stayed.

Bella didn't just change laws and policies; she changed opportunities for women in public office. Men in politics have always come in all shapes, sizes, and rhetorical styles. Women, too often, are still expected to fit into a preexisting mold. Bella broke that mold. She carved out a place for herself and, in the process, made room for generations of women who have come after her.

Shirley Chisholm

HILLARY

Long before I ever dreamed of running for office myself, there was Shirley Chisholm.

She was a woman of tenacity, ingenuity, and pride. When she became the first woman to run for the Democratic Party's presidential nomination in 1972, her campaign slogan defiantly proclaimed: "Unbought and Unbossed." Born in Brooklyn, New York, in 1924, she stood tall at a time when women, and black women in particular, faced more shut doors than open ones in nearly every corner of American life.

I was in college when I first heard about Shirley, and I avidly followed her career. The daughter of immigrants, she started out in the 1950s as a nursery school teacher and rose in the ranks to become the director of two day care centers. Because of her expertise in education, she would go on to consult with the city of New York on day care programs. In 1968, when redistricting efforts added a new congressional district in her neighborhood of Bedford-Stuyvesant in Brooklyn, Shirley decided to throw her hat in the ring. She campaigned on her deep roots in the community. During her campaign, she would drive through the district in a sound truck, announcing: "Ladies and gentlemen, this is fighting Shirley Chisholm coming through." She beat three candidates in the primary. In the general election, she faced an opponent who argued that the district needed "a man's voice in Washington," not a "little schoolteacher."

If anything, we need *more* teachers and early childhood education specialists in Washington. That was true then and it's true today.

During her campaign, Shirley went door-to-door, meeting families in housing projects and speaking to people in fluent Spanish. She won the general election and became the first black woman ever elected to Congress.

Some suggested that breaking that barrier was enough — that once she was in Congress she should stay quiet, keep her head down, and not make waves. Shirley wasn't interested in that at all. Above all else, she was a legislator who got things done — an attribute that inspired me then and still does. If it meant saying the unpopular thing, well then, she'd say the unpopular thing. People called her brusque, pushy, impolitic — the kind of things people have always said about strong women. None of it stopped Shirley. "I have no intention of just sitting quietly and observing," she said. And she didn't.

From her first days in office, she fought for the rights of workers and immigrants, poor children and pregnant women. In 1971, she worked on legislation along with Congresswoman Bella Abzug of New York and Senator Walter Mondale of Minnesota to provide federal funds for child care for the first time. Though the bill was vetoed by President

Richard Nixon, it sent a resounding message. The next year, she was instrumental in creating the Special Supplemental Nutrition Program for Women, Infants, and Children (WIC) to make sure "poor babies have milk and poor children have food." The Children's Defense Fund, where I worked during law school, supported both bills and considered Shirley a champion for children. I did, too.

She fought successfully to extend unemployment insurance and minimum-wage protections for domestic workers because, growing up in Brooklyn, she saw how "domestics" worked themselves to the bone and were often exploited or left destitute if their job disappeared. She was a champion for Title IX because she knew from her own life how hard women had to fight for their education — and because, as a teacher, she believed education was the key to just about everything.

Shirley didn't just leave her mark on America; she left her mark on Congress. She cofounded the Congressional Black Caucus and the Congressional Women's Caucus, because

---

"At present, our country needs women's idealism and determination, perhaps more in politics than anywhere else."
— SHIRLEY CHISHOLM

---

she knew firsthand how hard it was to be both a black person and a woman in Congress. She wanted to make sure everyone who came up after her wouldn't have to struggle quite as hard as she did. She saw that as a sacred responsibility. And as one of those people who did come up after her, I will always be grateful for that.

CHELSEA

The first elected women I ever remember my mom telling me about as a very young girl were Shirley Chisholm and Geraldine Ferraro. She wanted to be absolutely sure I grew up knowing women could be and do anything, and so could I.

Shirley's run for president in 1972 was surprisingly effective given her meager fund-raising, the logistical difficulties of waging a national campaign, and the resistance she faced as a black American and a woman. She received 152 first-ballot votes at the Miami Beach Convention, coming in fourth behind George McGovern, the eventual nominee. Years later, Shirley said she ran for president "In spite of hopeless odds . . . to demonstrate the sheer will and refusal to accept the status quo." She was also very clear about the obstacles she faced as a woman in politics. "When I ran for president, I met more discrimination as a woman than for being black. Men are men."

I thought about Shirley often when I was out on the campaign trail. It's not easy running for president. But even my hardest days were nothing compared to hers. She ran in the face of unimaginable discouragement and hostility. But she kept going. It was as if all that hostility only fueled her fire. "If you can't support me and you can't endorse me, get out of my way," she'd say. A lot of people did end up supporting her. They knew no one would work harder.

At the end of her life, Shirley knew that she had made history. But she didn't want to be celebrated just for the barriers she crossed. That felt secondary to her. "I don't want to be remembered as the first black woman who went to Congress. And I don't even want to be remembered as the first woman who happened to be black to make the bid for the presidency. I want to be remembered as a woman who fought for change in the twentieth century. That's what I want."

Well, Madam Chisholm — you got it.

ANN RICHARDS

HILLARY

Ann Richards had already lived a full life by the time she came anywhere near the world of professional politics. She grew up in Waco,

Texas, during the Great Depression, raised by a tough-as-nails mother and a father who encouraged her to dream big. ("I have always had the feeling I could do anything, and my dad told me I could," she would say. "I was in college before I found out he might be wrong.") She stuck close to home, going to Baylor University to become a teacher, which she would later say was the hardest job she'd ever had. She later married her high school sweetheart — the two of them would stay up nights debating politics — and raised four children. Ann poured her energy, intelligence, and wicked sense of humor into going all-out for every holiday — baking recipes straight from the glossy pages of women's magazines — and throwing herself into every political cause that came through town.

Like a lot of women, she started out behind the scenes: stuffing envelopes, making phone calls, and doing the hard, unglamorous work it takes to win over voters block by block and door by door. "In those days," she liked to say, "men made the decisions and women made the coffee." Her big break came when she got the chance to manage the campaign of Sarah Weddington for the state House of Representatives. At twenty-six years old, Sarah had argued *Roe v. Wade* before the Supreme Court, legalizing abortion in America. Sarah won her election; Ann found her calling.

A few years later, local Democrats approached

Ann's husband, urging him to run for county commissioner. He turned them down and asked instead, "What about Ann?" She ran, won, and showed that not only could she do the job — she could do it better than anyone predicted. When she decided to run for state treasurer, it was the same story: People didn't give her much of a chance, but she believed she could do it, and she never wavered. Her election sent ripples across the country. Suddenly, this funny, smart, tough woman had won a statewide position in Texas. People started to think: If it could happen there, it could happen anywhere.

Ann used to tell people she got into politics because she didn't want her tombstone to read "She kept a clean house." Instead, she went into government and cleaned house. She burst onto the national consciousness in 1988 with her extraordinary keynote speech at the Democratic National Convention. I was there on the floor and can attest that she had the entire convention — and the millions of people watching on television — in the palm of her beautifully manicured hand as she laid out a hopeful vision for Texas and America. Near the end of the speech, with her voice full of tenderness, she talked about her "nearly perfect" granddaughter. When she described sitting on the floor and rolling a ball back and forth with Lily, it didn't matter who you were or where you were from; you were part of Ann

Richards's family. Decades later, and now a grandmother myself, that image is even more meaningful.

By the time she walked off the stage that night, people were calling for Ann to run for Congress or even the presidency. She launched a long-shot campaign for governor, tapping into a network of women, young people, and people of color across the state who had been shut out of the political process for too long. Her opponent was Clayton Williams, a good old boy businessman who joked about rape, who jabbed his finger in Ann's face to try to intimidate her, and who refused to release his taxes. More than once during the 2016 election I wished I could call her up to commiserate! On Election Day in 1990, she became the first woman elected in her own right as governor of Texas.

Ann ran for governor, she said, "to open up the doors of government and let the people in." And that's just what she did. She appointed more women, Latinos, African Americans, and LGBTQ people than all of the state's previous governors combined. I watched her governorship with great admiration because of her determination that everyone — no matter who you were or where you were from, no matter the color of your skin or your accent — could feel part of what she called "the new Texas." She sent that message far and wide.

Ann faced every challenge head-on. She

> *"The public does not . . . ask their public officials to be perfect. They just ask them to be smart, truthful, honest, and show a modicum of good sense."*
> — ANN RICHARDS

acknowledged something many of us, particularly in public life, are afraid to: that she was a human being, too. After her divorce, she knew her personal life would become the subject of public speculation. So she had a witty comeback for every insult and invasion of privacy. She talked openly about her struggle with alcoholism, and her hard-fought recovery. Because of her example, more people got sober, took charge of their lives, and even ran for office themselves. She made a difference not only in the lives of those who knew her, but countless others.

In 1994, Ann lost her reelection campaign. In all the time I spent with her in the years after, I never heard any what-ifs, no could-haves or should-haves. It was all about the future, about her next adventure. "I have very strong feelings about how you lead your life," she once said. "You always look ahead, you never look back." Whenever I had a loss or setback in my own life, I knew just what she'd say to me: "Precious, get over it, and get on with it."

Politics can be brutal. The partisan bickering, the gridlock, the mean-spirited attacks — they can take a toll. Ann laughed off the bad and embraced the good; she made public service a whole lot of fun. She was always there when you most needed her, a loyal friend in good times and hard times.

Ann was also a friend who could not resist giving you advice, whether you wanted it or not. In 1994, I went to South Texas for a rally to support her reelection. I gave a speech standing on the tarmac at an airport while the wind blew my papers all over the place. Afterward, Ann took me aside and said: "Hillary, this is called a speech box, and it keeps your papers from flying around. You need one of these. In fact, I am going to send you one, because I cannot bear to see how pathetic you look out there with those papers flying everywhere." Sure enough, within a few days she had mailed me my very own speech box. Every time I use one — which is quite often — I think of where my first one came from,

---

"If you give us a chance, women can perform. After all, Ginger Rogers did everything that Fred Astaire did. She just did it backwards and in high heels."

— ANN RICHARDS

---

and of all the wisdom Ann shared with me over the years: "Never wear patterns on television"; "If you can't remember somebody's name, just call them 'Honey'"; "If you're going to be a woman in the public eye, you'll save yourself a lot of trouble if you pick a hairstyle and stick with it." I could have saved myself a lot of heartache if I'd followed that advice!

When I was considering whether or not to run for the Senate, I called Ann. She spoke plainly and from the heart, as she so often did. "Do you want to run?" she asked. "It has to be from deep inside you, not from what anybody else says. Do you want to do it? Do you want the job? Do you want the responsibility? Make it because you want it."

When Ann died of cancer in 2006, it was hard to say goodbye. She still had so much good left to do. But the message she sent to so many other women still reverberates today: Set your own course, dream your own dreams, and go where you want to go, even if nobody has gone there before. That message lives on every day at the Ann Richards School for Young Women Leaders, an all-girls public school she started in Austin.

Ann paved the way for a new generation of public servants in Texas and across the country — including members of her own family. Her oldest daughter, Cecile Richards, embodies what it means to stand up and speak out.

As the president of Planned Parenthood, she defended the organization against false and malicious attacks and helped build a powerful movement for reproductive rights. I'll never forget watching her testify before Congress in 2015 after Planned Parenthood was the victim of a video smear campaign — a lot of "fake news." For five hours, male members of Congress talked down to her and talked over her, criticizing her for everything from her salary to her attitude. Even though the experience smacked of sexism, she kept her cool the whole time; I thought of her a few weeks later when I spent my own eleven hours in front of some of the same people. After twelve years of extraordinary leadership at the helm of Planned Parenthood, Cecile has now turned her focus to starting a new organization, Supermajority, dedicated to building women's power and civic participation. I know Ann would have loved that.

My friendship with Ann came full circle in 2015 when I launched my campaign for president. One of our very first hires was none other than the granddaughter she had talked about all those years ago, now a political powerhouse in her own right. I would come to learn that Lily Adams is every bit as funny, tough, and talented as her grandmother, with the same extraordinary gift for communicating a message that packs a punch.

Now more than ever, we could use Ann's

moral compass, her guts, and her boundless empathy. But if she were here, I know just what she'd tell us: Open up every door that is blocked, remember where you came from, and don't ever forget that others want to come along with you. She would tell you that not only can you break that barrier or reach that glass ceiling — you have to. There were no ifs, ands, or buts about it. You just had to get up, get going, and believe in yourself.

GERALDINE FERRARO

HILLARY

On July 19, 1984, Geraldine Ferraro stepped up to the microphone at the Democratic National Convention and made history. She couldn't get a word out for eight minutes —

the crowd wouldn't stop cheering. I was one of thousands of women on the floor of the Moscone Center in San Francisco that night. I beamed and clapped until my hands ached. Later I would explain to four-year-old Chelsea that Geraldine Ferraro was a congresswoman, she was a mom, and she had just been nominated to become vice president of the United States.

To the millions of women who saw their futures open up that night, Geraldine Ferraro was a pioneer. To the press who covered her 1984 campaign, she was a fresh face, an upstart, a surprise. To at least one old-school politician, she was "young lady" — even though she was a three-term congresswoman. But to herself, she was always "a housewife from Queens." It was a title that captured so many things she loved: her family, her community, New York City. And to her friends — of which she seemed to have thousands — she was simply, wonderfully, Gerry. When she made her electrifying debut in San Francisco, she told women everywhere, "If we can do this, we can do anything."

She traveled thousands of miles on the campaign trail, speaking to huge crowds full of parents with daughters on their shoulders. When she came through Little Rock, I brought Chelsea to meet her. The photo I have of the four of us — Gerry, Bill, Chelsea, and me — is something we cherish. To the women of my generation, Gerry meant so much for us and our futures — but even more for our daughters and theirs.

Gerry became famous for one thing — one great thing. But her campaign for vice president was only four months of a life that encompassed so much more. Gerry was a teacher; a prosecutor; an advocate for women, children, and the elderly; a Harvard fellow; a wife, mother, aunt, and grandmother. And to all her many friends, she was our best friend. She was down-to-earth, personal, and ferociously loyal to the people she loved. When Gerry had your back, you knew you were covered. Maybe it's because she grew up with a mother who always had *her* back — a mother who would say about their family name: "*Ferro* means iron. You can bend it, but you can't break it. Go on."

Gerry and I were often linked together in articles about women in politics. She is seen, correctly, as someone who paved the way for my career and the careers of so many women in Washington and statehouses across the country. At the end of my 2008 presidential campaign, I spoke about eighteen million

---

*"Some leaders are
born women."*

— GERALDINE FERRARO

---

cracks in the glass ceiling; she'd put one of the biggest chips in it twenty-four years earlier.

Still, parts of her legacy go unnoticed, such as her work on human rights. When Bill named her to lead the American delegation to the UN Commission on Human Rights, Gerry pushed to ensure that women's rights were viewed as human rights, as they should be. We were both in Beijing in 1995 for the Fourth World Conference on Women, where she raised hot-button issues, including violence against women in wartime. I couldn't help but think how fitting it was that she was born on Women's Equality Day — the anniversary of the passage of the Nineteenth Amendment, which enfranchised women across America (though in practice it only reliably applied to white women).

Something else was clear in Beijing: Gerry had a gift for making a global issue personal. When the conference took up the question of how to define a family, there were some who argued there was only one kind of family: a mother, a father, and their children. Gerry got out of her seat, pulled out a family photo from her pocketbook, and walked from table to table, waving a picture of herself, her widowed mother, and her brother. "Are you telling me that we were not a family?" she said. Gerry knew how to make a point.

When she was diagnosed with multiple myeloma, the doctors told her she could expect to live no more than three to five years. She lived for another twelve. And she handled the challenge of battling cancer like she did everything else. She could have said, "I've done quite a bit in my life. I've helped many people, I've served my country. I'm going to take it easy now." No one would have begrudged her that. Instead, she became a fierce advocate for people living with cancer. She was interviewed on the *Today* show at her doctor's office. She also went down to Washington and testified before the Senate.

I remember that day well. She was eloquent, courageous, funny, and so personal. She said, "I'm a lucky woman. I have great doctors, an early diagnosis, and . . . a family that is always there to boost me up." But what bothered her, she said, was that the treatment available to her wasn't available to every person in this country with cancer — and it should be. In 2001, the Hematological Cancer Research Investment and Education Act was passed. That was pure Gerry: turning her illness into another chance to help others, and showing that iron spirit — the "ferro" in Ferraro.

"If we can do this, we can do anything," Gerry said all those years ago. When the day comes when a woman is elected president or vice president of the United States — and that day will come — we will know that she helped make it possible. And we will say, "Gerry, we did this — we can do anything — thanks to you."

BARBARA JORDAN

HILLARY

In early 1974, I was living in Cambridge, Massachusetts, working for Marian Wright Edelman at the Children's Defense Fund, and Bill was teaching at the University of

Arkansas School of Law. I was visiting him in Fayetteville when he received a phone call from John Doar. Doar was an old-fashioned Republican lawyer who had worked for Bobby Kennedy in the Civil Rights Division of the Justice Department; he had been tasked with leading the impeachment inquiry staff of the House Judiciary Committee, investigating President Richard Nixon. He was calling that day to ask if Bill wanted to join him.

Bill declined — he was exploring getting into politics and wanted to stay in Arkansas — but asked who else Doar planned to call. He said Bill's name was at the top of his list, along with three other Yale classmates, including Hillary Rodham. Bill said he thought the others on the list might be available; Doar said he would call me next. I accepted the offer to move to Washington and join the staff as one of the junior lawyers. Doar was devoted to the Constitution and the rule of law, and he demanded the same from all of us who worked for him. He was also adamant that the serious work entrusted to us had to be pursued based solely on the facts — not conjecture, conspiracy theories, or partisanship. I felt privileged to work for him and the other experienced lead lawyers he attracted.

It was a profound moment in American history, and there was no more effective, eloquent inquisitor than Barbara Jordan, a congresswoman from Texas who served on the Judiciary Committee. As a twenty-six-year-old fresh out of law school, I was riveted by her and more than a little intimidated. I got to talk with her, which was thrilling. I got to hand her papers, which was equally exciting. But mostly, I got to watch and listen to this unstoppable woman.

Born in Houston in 1936, Barbara was a lawyer, educator, Democratic politician, and civil rights leader. She was also a collector of "firsts": the first black person elected to the Texas Senate since Reconstruction; the first southern black woman elected to the United States House, in 1972; and the first black person and woman to deliver a keynote address at a Democratic National Convention, in 1976. She defended and continued the civil rights legacy of Dr. Martin Luther King Jr., and her friend and mentor President Lyndon Johnson. In particular, she was a staunch advocate for the Voting Rights Act, which had helped make it possible for her to be elected. In the face of fierce opposition, Barbara led the fight to extend the special protections of the Voting Rights Act to Hispanic Americans, Native Americans, and Asian Americans. I had first heard about her when she was running in 1972, while I was in Texas registering voters for the DNC and George McGovern's presidential campaign.

Because she was on the Judiciary Committee,

I read up on her and the other members, like the new young member Elizabeth Holtzman from New York. I was asked to appear before them with John Doar and Joe Woods, the lawyer I was working under to research the meaning of "high crimes and misdemeanors" in the Constitution's reference to impeachment and the procedural rules to be followed. (I know, you can't make up my life! Years later, I reread the memo I had helped write and still agreed with its analysis.)

Even though Barbara had recently arrived in Congress, she stood out, not only because she was a black woman. From the moment I saw her sitting at the table during the hearing I attended, she seemed larger than life. The word "presence" to describe someone can be overused, but she sure had it.

Not only did she have gravitas; she had a one-of-a-kind sense of humor, which she used to break down even the most complicated political issues into simple terms, and to punctuate her points. She also had the most irresistible voice: deep and booming, imbued with significance and passion. Decades after my experience on the committee, I would find myself talking with her and Ann Richards — between the two of them, forget about trying to get a word in at all! They were telling me how they loved to go to the University of Texas Lady Longhorns basketball games. Barbara would be there, by then in her wheelchair, and Ann would be holding court, so to speak, right next to her. Barbara would yell directions as if she were the coach: "Why are you doing that? Jump higher! That's not a pass!" Ann recalled how she said, "Barbara, encourage these young women, don't just criticize them." And Barbara turned to her and said: "When they deserve it, I will!"

She cemented her place in American history when the Judiciary Committee convened to debate whether to recommend that the full House adopt articles of impeachment against President Richard Nixon. Those of us on Doar's team had put together the evidence that made a compelling case for impeachment. Based strictly on the facts and law, not politics, Doar presented proposed articles of impeachment that specified the charges against the president, citing abuse of power, obstruction of justice, and contempt of Congress. No one knew for sure how the committee vote would turn out, but no one was in doubt about how it should after Barbara Jordan spoke on July 25, 1974.

She had been a champion debater at Texas Southern University, regularly winning national contests over debaters from Ivy League schools, and she had studied the Constitution. She began her remarks by recognizing that "When that document was completed on the seventeenth of September in 1787, I was not included in 'We the people.' I felt somehow for many years that George Washington and Alexander Hamilton just left me out by mistake. But through the process of amendment, interpretation, and court decision, I have finally been included in 'We the people.'

"Today," she went on, "I am an inquisitor. I believe hyperbole would not be fictional and would not overstate the solemnness that I feel right now. My faith in the Constitution is whole; it is complete; it is total. And I am not going to sit here and be an idle spectator to the diminution, the subversion, the destruction of the Constitution." She went on to explain "the nature of impeachment" and how it fits into our system of checks and balances, rooting her argument in the history of the Constitutional Convention and the debates in the states about whether to ratify the Constitution. She reviewed the charges and evidence and then concluded: "If the impeachment provision of the Constitution of the United States will not reach the offenses charged here, then perhaps that eighteenth-century Constitution should be abandoned to a twentieth-century paper shredder!"

As I watched the committee debate, Barbara's commanding rhetoric, passion, and moral clarity brought me to tears. The nation reacted positively to her and the arguments she made. Little wonder that those remarks are considered among the best American speeches of the twentieth century. The committee passed the articles with six Republican votes, which led to President Nixon's resignation on August 9. Nixon was gone, but Barbara Jordan's powerful example persisted.

Barbara Mikulski

Hillary

As a little girl in 1930s Baltimore, Barbara Mikulski was not blessed with athletic abilities. So, the *Washington Post* recounted, "tired of skinning her knees trying to jump rope 'double dutch,' Barbara coaxed her little cousins and friends into taking part in plays and shows in her parents' garage, shows in which she served as a playwright, producer, and director." Though nobody could have guessed it at the time — least of all Barbara — those leadership skills would take her from her working-class neighborhood to the floor of the United States Senate.

The daughter of parents who owned a neighborhood grocery store, Barbara still remembers delivering groceries in a little red wagon, instructed by her father to never accept a tip. Her parents' greeting to their customers — "Good morning. Can I help you?" — introduced her early on to the concept of service. So did the nuns at the Catholic school she attended, who taught her about the Christopher Movement, which is built on the belief that "It is better to light one candle than to curse the darkness." Those teachings shaped Barbara's view of the world, and instilled a passion for social justice. "I even thought about being a Catholic nun," she said decades later, "but that vow of obedience kind of slowed me down a little bit."

Instead, she became a social worker, helping at-risk young people in Baltimore with her characteristic "tough love" approach. When she learned about a plan to build a sixteen-lane highway through several Baltimore neighborhoods without compensating homeowners, primarily immigrants and black Americans, she decided to do something about it. The fierce and unapologetic Barbara

594

helped found the Southeast Council Against the Road, a name she coined for its appropriately "militant" acronym: SCAR. They took on City Hall and won, saving Baltimore's Fells Point and Inner Harbor neighborhoods. Barbara was elected to the city council later that year.

Barbara got her start in politics at a time when women were expected to be neither seen nor heard. But three years after winning her city council seat, she announced that she planned to challenge Charles Mathias, the state's beloved Republican senator. To some people, running against a seemingly undefeatable member of the political establishment seemed like a foolish decision. Barbara was told over and over again: "No woman can win in an ethnic, hard-hat neighborhood. No woman can win who isn't part of the political machine." To her, that was even more reason to run: She had nothing to lose, so why not try? She didn't win, but she built name recognition and a following.

In 1976 she ran for Congress. This time, she won. The old boys' network never saw her coming. But the voters of Maryland not only saw her — they elected her. "I got started in public life because of volunteers and activists who, on their own time and on their own dime, volunteered themselves to not only help me get elected but to be involved in their communities, to be civically engaged, to make their community and their country a better place," she'd later say.

Ten years later, she again set her sights on the U.S. Senate. It was a brutal race, one that forced Barbara to hone her gift for deflecting criticism when her brash, take-no-prisoners style that might have been applauded in a male candidate was described by her opponents and the media as a liability. She was called "shrill," "abrasive," and an "anti-male feminist." If the criticism hurt, Barbara didn't let on, and she made no apologies. "Nobody would ever use the term mellow to describe me," she agreed. "I'm not caffeine-free, that's for sure."

Barbara wasn't interested in changing her personality, though over time she did decide to change her appearance. (Even though, Chelsea and I agree, she shouldn't have had to!) "A stocky, 4-foot-11, rough-edged East Baltimore politician once described as having 'the heft of a stevedore and a voice to match,'" was how the *Washington Post* characterized her. But once she made up her mind to run for the Senate, Barbara decided the time had come to change her image. She approached the challenge the same way she approached everything else: with a fighting spirit and a twinkle in her eye. She exercised vigorously, logging miles on a stationary bike, and joked on the campaign trail about her efforts to lose weight. When she later met President Ronald

Reagan, who had campaigned for her opponent, she introduced herself, saying, "I'm the one you said would go the way of the Edsel, the hula hoop and the asparagus diet. Mr. President, I'm on the asparagus diet." She could play the game when she chose to, but she did it with a healthy dose of self-awareness, acknowledging that "a lot of Americans, black or white or female, are always told that they don't look the part. It's one of the oldest code words."

With a little help from an up-and-coming organization called EMILY's List and a whole lot of Mikulski moxie, Barbara won that election, and became the first Democratic woman elected to the United States Senate in her own right without having first served in a relative's seat. From the very beginning, she worked on what she called "the macro issues and the macaroni-and-cheese issues." The big picture was important to her, but so was making sure people's day-to-day needs were met. Over her five terms in the Senate, she fought to improve public schools and take better care of seniors and veterans. She championed civil rights and women's rights, universal health care, and funding for science and research. As the first woman to chair the powerful Senate Appropriations Committee, she put her tenacity to work on behalf of the people of Maryland and the people of America. Even after tough legislative losses, she never gave up. When Republicans blocked the Paycheck Fairness Act in 2012, she declared: "I say to the women out there in America, let's keep this fight going. Put on your lipstick, square your shoulders, suit up, and let's fight for a new American revolution where women are paid equal pay for equal work, and let's end wage discrimination in this century once and for all."

Of Barbara's many accomplishments, I am personally grateful for a fight she waged within the Capitol in 1993. She'd noticed that on weekends male members of Congress would wear casual clothes to the office, but women were still required to wear skirts and

---

"I might be short, but I won't be overlooked."

— BARBARA MIKULSKI

---

pantyhose. That didn't sit well with Barbara, so she and Republican senator Nancy Kassebaum — the only other woman in the Senate — showed up one Saturday wearing pants and told all the women staffers to do the same. "I walk in that day and you would have thought I was walking on the moon," she recounted later. She won that fight, making her a founding member of the sisterhood of the traveling pantsuit!

Barbara's was one of the first calls I got when I was elected senator for New York. The conversation went something like this: "Congratulations. I followed it. That was a hard-fought race. Now you need to figure out how to be a Senator since you've been elected to serve as one." With her help, that's what I did. As the dean of the Senate women, she had immense expertise and was happy to share it. She's always known that it isn't enough to be "the first" if you're also "the only." She has dedicated her life to kicking down the door for other women at every level of politics. In the midst of chatter over whether the nominee — presumably a man — would put a woman on the ticket as his running mate in 1984, she commented, "We are being pursued like some kind of new fad, like a new kind of Lite Beer or something. . . . It can feel a little humiliating." (Some things never seem to change, even when there are multiple women running for president!) When she arrived in

Congress in 1977, there were eighteen women in Congress. Today there are more than one hundred.

Barbara was the one who officially nominated me at the 2016 Democratic National Convention, saying, "Our Founding Fathers gave us a great start. But it was the Founding Mothers who said, 'Do not forget the ladies, for we will foment our own revolution.'" That's a promise Barbara has spent her life working to keep.

ELLEN JOHNSON SIRLEAF

HILLARY

In 1985, in the midst of Liberia's long and bloody civil war and her campaign for a seat in its senate, Ellen Johnson Sirleaf criticized military leader Samuel Doe's regime. As a result, she was sentenced to ten years of hard labor. But against all odds, she would be released from prison after only a short time, go into exile, return, and be twice elected president, becoming the first woman elected to lead any African country.

As biographer Helene Cooper recounts in *Madame President: The Extraordinary Journey of Ellen Johnson Sirleaf,* perhaps her political ascent shouldn't have been such a surprise. Days after Ellen was born in Monrovia, the capital of Liberia, in 1938, an old prophet who wandered through the city making predictions visited the new baby. He took one look at her and is said to have announced: "This child will be great. This child will lead."

But, first she married and had four sons. She eventually got divorced from her husband, who beat her severely. She got an education, studying both at home and abroad, and then got to work. She landed at the Ministry of Finance of the Liberian government, eventually rising to finance minister. She later ran for a senate seat, criticizing the regime of dictator Samuel Doe. He imprisoned her and then she fled the country. During her twelve years of exile in Kenya and the United States, she worked at the World Bank and the United Nations.

After a tentative truce was reached in Liberia's civil war, she returned to run for president in 1997 against warlord Charles Taylor

> *"So I urge my sisters, and my brothers, not to be afraid. Be not afraid to denounce injustice, though you may be outnumbered. Be not afraid to seek peace, even if your voice may be small. Be not afraid to demand peace. If I might thus speak to girls and women everywhere, I would issue them this simple invitation: My sisters, my daughters, my friends, find your voices!"*
> — ELLEN JOHNSON SIRLEAF

— whom she originally had supported in his rebellion against Doe before turning against him once, as she would later put it, "the true nature of Mr. Taylor's intentions became known." She lost that race, but stayed committed to Liberia.

Ellen kept going. In 2005, she ran for president again. She campaigned on the promise that she would take on corruption, rebuild the country's crumbling infrastructure, and work toward a peaceful, democratic Liberia. As she said, "If your dreams do not scare you, they are not big enough." Liberian women understood that. Many rallied behind Ellen, some walking for days and standing in line for hours to vote for her. As she marched through the streets of Monrovia during the last days of her campaign, people shouted, cheered, and waved signs that read "Ellen — she's our man." When the first round of votes was counted, she finished second, securing her place in the runoff election. On November 8, 2005, she won the runoff, beating a popular Liberian soccer star.

In her inaugural address, she called out violence perpetrated against women and girls during the civil war and promised "to make the children smile again." Once she was president, Ellen closed Belle Yellah, the most notorious prison in Liberia. She appointed women to lead the police force and international security teams, and went out of her way to advocate for women's inclusion in the security sector.

In 2006, she created a Truth and Reconciliation Commission to eradicate corruption and heal a still-divided Liberia. She had

"My life was forever transformed when I was given the privilege to serve the people of Liberia—taking on the awesome responsibility of rebuilding a nation nearly destroyed by war and plunder. There was no roadmap for post-conflict transformation. But we knew that we could not let our country slip back into the past. We understood that our greatest responsibility was to keep the peace."

— ELLEN JOHNSON SIRLEAF

promised to make corruption "public enemy number one." That proved an impossible task in a country where bribes had become a way of life. She fired ministers who spent government funds as though they were their own salaries. Critics decried nepotism when she appointed her banker son to lead the national oil company of Liberia. He ultimately resigned, but her reputation undertstandably took a hit. She also publicly apologized for having supported Charles Taylor in the early years of the civil war, and sent him to The Hague to be tried for war crimes.

Despite having originally planned to serve only one term, Ellen ran for president again in 2011. The country had made progress recovering from its brutal civil war, but not nearly enough; she wanted to continue the work. Her courage in bringing peace to the war-scarred nation, and the courage of Liberian women like Leymah Gbowee, drew attention around the world. Four days before her reelection, Ellen and Leymah were awarded the 2011 Nobel Peace Prize. Ellen called the timing of the prize a coincidence; she never once mentioned it on the campaign trail.

By that time, I had known Ellen for a number of years. I traveled to Liberia as secretary of state in 2009. She asked me to address the Parliament while I was there and stress the need for unity in the face of ongoing problems. She told me I would be speaking to an assembly that included her political enemies and former warlords, including the ex-wife of now-convicted war criminal Charles Taylor. I returned to attend her second inauguration in 2012.

In her two terms in office, Ellen racked up a notable list of achievements: She orchestrated Liberia's first peaceful transition of power in seventy-four years when she left office in 2018, prioritized free and compulsory primary education, signed into law the first freedom of information law in West Africa, and reduced the country's national debt to international institutions and other countries through better budgets, debt relief, and debt cancellation. But Ellen has warned that corruption remains a problem that has to be constantly addressed by all countries, even as it seems evident that she herself should have tried to do more. (It's also true that for the first time in many years, we in the United States know only too well what she means.)

As someone who has followed Liberia's challenges for years, I respect Ellen for her service under very difficult conditions. Her rise is proof that an unapologetic economic-policy wonk can not only toil away behind the scenes but also win elections and lead a nation. As she has said: "I work hard, I work late, I have nothing on my conscience. When I go to bed, I sleep." That's a pretty good summary for any life in public service.

WILMA MANKILLER

HILLARY

Wilma Mankiller was born in 1945 in Tahle-
quah, Oklahoma, the capital of the Cherokee
Nation. The sixth of eleven children of a full-
blooded Cherokee father and a Dutch-Irish

mother, she spent much of her childhood on a tract of land given to her grandfather by the government as part of a settlement for brutally forcing the Cherokee to move to Oklahoma. When she was ten years old, the government relocated her family to California; Wilma was heartbroken. Years later, she wrote in her autobiography: "I wept tears that came from deep within the Cherokee part of me . . . tears from my history, from my tribe's past."

As a teenager, Wilma found her home away from home at the San Francisco Indian Center. She married a month before her eighteenth birthday and had two daughters. The traditional role her husband expected her to play clashed with the social change she saw all around her in California in the 1960s: the women's movement, the anti–Vietnam War movement, and the civil rights movement. When a group of Native Americans occupied the abandoned Alcatraz prison and claimed Alcatraz Island in San Francisco Bay "in the name of all Indian tribes" in 1969, Wilma's life changed forever. "Just as seeing women speak up had an impact on me, seeing native people on the 6 o'clock news challenge the United States government — go and take over an island, and talk about treaty rights and the need for education and health care — had a profound impact," she said.

Throughout the nineteen months that the group occupied the prison, Wilma brought

supplies and helped raise funds and awareness. It was a turning point for Wilma; the
more she did, the more involved she wanted
to be with Native American issues. "When
Alcatraz occurred, I became aware of what
needed to be done to let the rest of the world
know that Indians had rights, too. Alcatraz
articulated my own feelings about being an
Indian." She started taking college classes in
social work. She bought her first car, a symbol
of independence. She would dance with her
daughters to her favorite song, Aretha Franklin's "Respect."

Wilma's husband demanded that she remain a traditional housewife — a tension she
resolved by divorcing him and moving back to
her grandfather's land in Oklahoma with her
daughters. Once back on the Cherokee reservation, she suffered two physical setbacks. In
1979, she was severely injured in a car accident. The driver of the other car — tragically
her best friend — was killed. Wilma required
nearly a year of recovery. She spent that time
reflecting on her future and immersed herself
in Cherokee traditions, embracing the idea
of "being of good mind." For her, that meant
fighting to keep a positive outlook, even when
it wasn't easy, and searching for ways to serve.
"After that," she said, "I knew I'd lost the fear
of death and the fear of challenges in my life."
Once she recovered from the accident, she
was diagnosed with a neuromuscular disease

that made moving difficult. Still, she never wavered from her commitment to advocating for her community.

As she put her life back together, Wilma organized a self-help project in the small village of Bell, Oklahoma, on the reservation. She engaged the community in identifying its own problems and, through their own work and Wilma's fundraising, devising a plan to solve them. In Bell, she supervised the construction of a water system and the upgrade and renovation of substandard housing. Because of this work, *Ms.* magazine named her Woman of the Year in 1987. She also enrolled in courses in community development at the University of Arkansas to further her skills.

During this time, she met her second husband, a Cherokee man who supported her entry into politics. Based on her proven organizing and management skills, she was recruited to run for deputy principal chief in 1983, the first woman to vie for that position. "I expected my politics to be the issue," she said. "They weren't. The issue was my being a woman, and I wouldn't have it. I simply told myself that it was a foolish issue, and I wouldn't argue with a fool." She overcame opposition, harsh criticism, and death threats to win the election.

When the principal chief resigned in 1985, Wilma ascended to chief. Two years later, she ran to be elected in her own right. Once again, she faced sexist attacks. The hostility she endured surprised her because traditional Cherokee societies, families, and clans were organized through the maternal side. To deal with the sexism, she called on the traditions of Cherokee culture where women's councils historically had participated in making social and political decisions for the tribe. In her autobiography, *Mankiller: A Chief and Her People,* she writes about how Cherokee and Native American women had been respected before the conquest of Native American tribes and that the imposition of the conquering culture altered the balance between men and women.

Under her leadership, the Cherokee government built new health clinics and created early education, adult learning, and job-training programs. She negotiated an agreement with the United States government to allow the tribe to manage its own finances, increased the number of enrolled members of the tribe, and improved its budget by developing factories, restaurants, and bingo operations. She also stressed the importance of caring for the environment. She was tireless in working to

---

"I've run into more discrimination as a woman than as an Indian."

— WILMA MANKILLER

---

improve respect for Native Americans across the country. When she retired, she stayed active promoting women's rights, tribal sovereignty, cancer awareness, and other issues.

When writing about Wilma, I can't help but think about her tenacity. No matter how many times she got knocked down, she always got back up. She didn't let anything stand in the way of serving and advocating for her community. Through it all, she kept a sense of humor, sometimes joking that her last name came from her reputation (it's actually a Cherokee military term for a village guard). On April 29, 1994, she came to the White House for a historic meeting of Native American leaders. At that meeting, Wilma presented me with a piece of pottery on behalf

---

"The happiest people I've ever met, regardless of their profession, their social standing, or their economic status, are people that are fully engaged in the world around them. The most fulfilled people are the ones who get up every morning and stand for something larger than themselves. They are the people who care about others, who will extend a helping hand to someone in need or will speak up about an injustice when they see it."

— WILMA MANKILLER

---

of all the tribes assembled. She was committed to strengthening the relationships between the Cherokee people and the United States government. In 1998, my husband awarded her the Presidential Medal of Freedom, and I was proud to be there cheering her on.

Not content to simply pursue individual success, Wilma was also dedicated to inspiring future generations and helping them to succeed. She took part in a program through the American Association of University Women that matched Cherokee girls with career mentors in order to help raise their self-confidence and open up opportunities. "Suddenly you hear young Cherokee girls talking about becoming leaders," she wrote. "And in Cherokee families, there is more encouragement of girls." She understood from her own experience that celebrating tradition and looking to the future can and should go hand in hand.

MICHELLE BACHELET

HILLARY AND CHELSEA

In 1975, at the age of twenty-three, Michelle Bachelet, then a medical student at the University of Chile, was arrested, imprisoned, and tortured by the secret security agency of the military dictatorship of Augusto Pinochet. Her mother, an archaeologist, was sent with her to the secret prison; her father, an air force general, had died in prison the year before. Their crime was opposing the coup that brought Pinochet to power against the elected president, Salvador Allende.

After a few weeks, Michelle was released into exile — first to Australia, then to East Germany. She continued her medical education, married another Chilean exile, had her first child, and then returned to Chile. She graduated as a surgeon in 1982 and started practicing medicine, including treating children whose parents had been tortured or were missing. She had her second child in 1984, after which she and her husband separated.

Chelsea

When Chile returned to democracy in 1990, Michelle worked in various public health roles. She also had her third child with a physician who had supported Pinochet. (Now that's a complicated story!) For four years, she worked in the Ministry of Health, began studying military strategy, and started taking courses at the Inter-American Defense College in Washington. She was ultimately appointed Minister of Health, a position she used to confront inequality throughout the country. Michelle expanded health care coverage and made the public hospital system more efficient. She also authorized free distribution of the morning-after pill at state-run hospitals for victims of sexual abuse — a gutsy decision in what was then one of the most socially conservative countries in South America.

Hillary

In 2002, she was appointed Minister of National Defense, the first woman to hold this position in a Latin American country and one of the few in the world at the time. She used her position to help reconcile the military and victims of the Pinochet years, and modernize equipment. I will never forget the most striking image from that time: Michelle, in the midst of a serious flood, leading rescue operations from the top of a military tank.

When I heard Michelle had become the Socialist Party's candidate for president, I was delighted. She had experienced the brutality of dictatorship firsthand, but never lost hope in the people of her nation or the promise of democracy. I remember thinking how wonderful it would be for a woman to break through yet another barrier, and help her country break through barriers, too. When we met in January 2005 during her campaign, she spoke with deep passion and even deeper expertise on the challenges facing her nation, from modernizing the military to finishing her work on the health care system.

Chelsea

After a runoff election on January 15, 2006, Michelle became Chile's first female elected president. One of her first actions was appointing a cabinet with equal numbers of men and women. During her first term, she stressed the economic and social well-being of poor and low-income families. She championed equal pay, maternity care, and — once again — access to emergency contraception pills with no parental consent requirements. She drew fury from the Catholic Church, but didn't back down. She simply explained that because "not everyone is equal and not everyone has the same possibilities," it was her job "to guarantee that all Chileans have real options in this area, as in others." She built a system to provide social services to at-risk children, distributing briefcases filled with books to hundreds of thousands of families

---

"We simply can no longer afford to deny the full potential of one half of the population. The world needs to tap into the talent and wisdom of women. Whether the issue is food security, economic recovery, health, or peace and security, the participation of women is needed now more than ever."

— MICHELLE BACHELET

---

and computers to poor seventh graders with good grades. When students organized massive protests demanding better education, she responded by passing reform measures to improve it. She also never forgot the wrongs of Chile's past; when Pinochet died in 2006, she denied him a state funeral and refused to attend his services, saying it would be "a violation of [her] conscience." In 2010, she opened the Museum of Memory and Human Rights in Santiago to document the brutal abuses of Pinochet's long dictatorship. Proving her commitment to looking forward as well as back, she created a National Institute for Human Rights.

Hillary

On February 27, 2010, when Michelle was less than two weeks from leaving office, Chile was devastated by an 8.8-magnitude earthquake that killed five hundred people and caused massive property damage. I visited her when she was in the midst of the relief and recovery operations to deliver aid from the United States government and show support in the midst of such a catastrophe.

On March 27, 2013, she announced she would run again for president. Polls at the time showed strong support for her, and she won, becoming the first president of Chile to be reelected since 1932.

Chelsea

In her second term, Michelle proposed free university education. She ran into problems from both the right, which wanted to know how it would be funded, and the left, which argued it didn't go far enough. Eventually, she worked out a compromise that sent 200,000 students from low-income families to college at no cost to them. She reformed the tax system by shifting taxes from individuals to corporations, created new national parks and marine reserves, and taxed carbon emissions. Michelle also passed a civil union law for LGBTQ couples and sent a bill legalizing marriage equality to Congress — though it has yet to become law. And she legalized abortion under certain circumstances. Her second term, though, was marred by corruption allegations involving her son and daughter-in-law's business dealings. Michelle denied knowing about their activities and appointed an independent commission to investigate those charges and recommend new reforms to guard Chile against corruption. She carried out the reforms, but her approval rate never fully recovered to its previously high levels.

Hillary

After leaving office, she became the United Nations High Commissioner for Human Rights, a position she has used to criticize abuses by governments from China to Saudi

Arabia to the United States. "I have been a political detainee and the daughter of political detainees," she said in her first speech. "I have been a refugee and a physician — including for children who experienced torture and the enforced disappearance of their parents." For her, human rights is personal; it should be for the rest of us, too.

DANICA ROEM

CHELSEA

The night Danica Roem made history in Virginia in 2017 as the first openly transgender person elected to a state legislature, she climbed up on a table and delivered her victory speech. She dedicated her win "to every person who's ever been singled out, who's ever been stigmatized, who's ever been the misfit, who's ever been the kid in the corner." And then she went on to talk about one of her core campaign promises: fixing congestion on Route 28 in Fairfax County. "That's why I got in this race," she said. "Because I'm fed up with the frickin' road over in my hometown." The crowd went wild.

Throughout her campaign, Danica had reiterated the crucial points of her story to her dedicated team of volunteers: She was a thirty-three-year-old stepmom, she had lived in her district of Manassas nearly her entire life, and she had worked as a journalist covering local public policy issues. (The fact that she had also been a vocalist in a metal band didn't make the top three list, but it definitely helped pique national interest in her campaign.) Those volunteers delivered her message to her future constituents, knocking on more than seventy-five thousand doors in the district and talking about what Danica saw as the most important issue in the race: traffic. "When people see me doing this, they're going to be like, 'Wow, she's transgender, I don't get that,'" she said in an interview. "'She's a metalhead, I don't get that; and she's weird, I don't get it. But she's really, really focused on improving my commute, and I do get that.'"

Meanwhile, she was up against an incumbent

> *"I don't have to pretend to be someone else. I still listen to the same music I did before, still love to play guitar, and I still love to see shows. I want to make sure that when people see me, they go: 'Yeah, she's transgender, and she's a really, really good policy wonk. Yeah, she's transgender, and she has a really good bill to fix Route 28.' It's not trans but. It's trans and."*
>
> — DANICA ROEM

who had held his seat in the Virginia House of Delegates for a quarter century and called himself Virginia's "chief homophobe." He had sponsored a cruel and mean-spirited "bathroom bill" intended to bully and shame the transgender community, supported a proposal to ban LGBTQ people from serving in the Virginia National Guard, and written a constitutional amendment defining marriage as between a man and a woman. He refused to debate Danica, and he incorrectly and insultingly referred to her with male pronouns.

"I understand the national implications of my race," Danica said. "I mean, I'm not stupid." But she refused to let her opponent drag her down to his level. She was going to run on her terms, not his. As she reminded voters, "I've always seen my role as a public servant. And public servant in this case means upholding myself with the same ethics and integrity that I did as a reporter for ten and a half years." When she was asked to comment on her opponent on election night, her response was simple, elegant, and honorable: "I don't attack my constituents. Bob is my constituent now."

HILLARY

One of my favorite parts of Danica's story is that she was an early candidate supported by Run for Something, which was started by a staff member and a volunteer from my 2016 campaign. They're working hard to elect young progressives to office, and changing the face of politics in America. Danica is a great example of someone whose potential they spotted early on!

After Danica and her fellow members of the Virginia House of Delegates were sworn in in January 2018, they got to work. They passed Medicaid expansion and voted to raise teacher pay. During her second session in the House of Delegates, she passed three pieces of her own legislation. Two were requests from her constituents. "You have to realize as a delegate that your number one job is still to represent eighty-three thousand people back home, to legislate on their behalf, to get bills passed on their behalf, and to vote on their behalf," she said in an interview. And she

> *"What I hope people across the country are able to see in [our victories] is that transgender people can be really good at doing their jobs in elected office; we can make really good legislators. Just by being in office, our mere presence fundamentally changes the equation."*
>
> — DANICA ROEM

never forgot her core campaign promise to tackle congestion. Route 28 is currently under construction, being widened from four lanes to six — but as Danica reminds her constituents and colleagues, there's still a lot of work to do.

Danica Roem has the kind of laser focus and wisdom we should demand from all our elected officials. She is vibrant, eloquent, and cool. As she has said: "No matter what you look like, where you come from, how you worship, who you love, or how you identify, if you've got good ideas, you can bring those ideas to the table." That's the government and the country we should all aspire to build and support.

■ ■ ■ ■

GROUNDBREAKERS

■ ■ ■ ■

FRANCES PERKINS

HILLARY

Every month, sixty-four million Americans receive benefits from Social Security. Tens of millions go home after an eight-hour work-day. Others who have lost their jobs can rely on unemployment insurance. Children go to school instead of working in factories. Fire alarms and sprinkler systems are a fact of life. And while it's still far too low, we have a federal minimum wage, mandated and enforced by law. All of these facts of modern working life are thanks in no small part to the efforts of one woman: Frances Perkins.

Frances was "the first" to do many things: The first woman named to a seat on New York's powerful Industrial Commission, where her eight-thousand-dollar annual salary made her the highest-paid woman in state government. And the first ever "madam secretary," when she led the federal Department of Labor for Franklin Delano Roosevelt.

Born in Massachusetts in 1880 to a middle-class family, young Fannie, as she was known then, grew up comfortably. She attended Mount Holyoke, where a course on American economic history exposed her to how the vast majority of American workers lived: constantly

---

"I had a kind of duty to other women to walk in and sit down on the chair that was offered, and so establish the rights of others long hence and far distant in geography to sit in the high seats."

— FRANCES PERKINS

---

at risk that a mistake at work could cost them their health, their job, or even their life. After college, she spent time at Hull House, the innovative settlement founded by Jane Addams in Chicago; took a dangerous job working to prevent young women from falling victim to sex trafficking in Philadelphia; and literally stood on soapboxes to advocate for women's suffrage.

Like many young women of her social status and era, she assumed that when she married, her activism would take the form of board seats and charity fund-raisers. That all changed on March 25, 1911. Frances had moved to New York City, where she worked at the National Consumers League and was friends with a group of young social reformers. The group was sitting down to tea near Washington Square Park when they heard the clanging of fire sirens. Just a few blocks away, the building housing the Triangle Shirtwaist Factory was in flames. One in a sea of thousands of onlookers, Frances watched in horror as the fire ladders proved too short to reach the upper stories where the factory was housed. Workers crowded against the windows until, one by one, many chose to jump rather than burn to death.

One hundred and forty-six people died in the fire, mostly young Italian and Jewish immigrant women. Many were doomed by the fact that the factory's doors were locked during working hours in order to prevent employees from taking unauthorized breaks or smuggling out scraps of material. It was the worst industrial accident in the history of New York City and one of the worst ever in the United States. The Triangle Shirtwaist fire changed the course of American labor history — and the course of Frances Perkins's life.

Frances became executive secretary of a new citizen's committee on industrial safety, where she threw herself into learning about fire escapes, building construction, and insurance policies. Over the next four years, New York State adopted dozens of laws with Frances's fingerprints all over them: mandating fire drills and escapes, requiring automatic sprinklers, banning smoking in factories, setting occupancy limits, and other seemingly commonsense measures that we take for granted today. Through that work, Frances learned a lesson that she would carry with her through decades of public service: A small group of dedicated, creative reformers could come together and make a difference.

During this time, Frances married Paul Wilson, another progressive reformer, in his thirties. She worried that getting married would cost her the name recognition and personal identity she had painstakingly built. "I was very puffed up, I suppose, about the fact that I could sign a letter and my name meant something to the labor commissioner of California," she said later. "If I were Mrs. Paul C. Wilson, I was just somebody's wife." Although she sometimes referred to herself socially as Mrs. Paul Wilson, Frances didn't change her last name — a decision that was so far outside the norm in 1913 that at least one newspaper reporter showed up on the newlyweds' doorstep to demand the full story.

Over the years, Frances held multiple positions in New York State government. She was confirmed to the Industrial Commission by Governor Al Smith in 1919, a year before women across America won the vote, making her one of the first female commissioners in New York. When Franklin Roosevelt became governor of New York in 1929, he appointed Frances as the state industrial commissioner. During that time, she supervised an agency with eighteen hundred employees, raised the minimum wage, and worked to end child labor.

In 1933, with the country in the grips of the Great Depression and one in four Americans unemployed, President-elect Franklin Roosevelt asked Frances Perkins to be his secretary of labor. On the campaign trail, FDR had promised a "new deal for the American people," but Frances knew that there wasn't a concrete plan. So, like many women, she made a list: putting millions to work through public employment, providing direct aid to states to help the destitute, setting a forty-hour workweek and a federal minimum wage, banning child labor, creating unemployment insurance and workers' compensation systems, establishing Social Security and universal health insurance.

Frances's list was staggeringly ambitious, a complete rewriting of the social contract between government, employers, and workers. In some cases, her list took reforms she had helped introduce in New York and expanded them to more reluctant corners of a vast nation. In others, she was proposing an entirely untested path. She was also deeply conflicted about becoming the first woman to head a federal department, knowing that she would face more than her share of criticism for being a woman in a "man's job." But once FDR signed off on her list of proposed policies, Frances's mind was made up. She signed up to join his Cabinet.

Item by item, Frances's list became the law of the land. The National Industrial Recovery Act banned child labor and created the first ever national minimum wage. The Federal Emergency Relief Administration authorized unprecedented transfers of federal money to

"I came to work for God, FDR, and the millions of forgotten, plain, common workingmen."
— FRANCES PERKINS

states to help the needy. The Civilian Conservation Corps and the Works Progress Administration put hundreds of thousands of people to work. And the Social Security Act created both a national unemployment insurance system and federal pensions for the elderly.

Frances's breakneck pace on behalf of the American people belied profound struggles in her home life. She and Paul had a daughter, Susanna, in 1916, who would struggle throughout her life with mental illness. Soon after her birth, Paul began suffering from a series of mental health crises. In manic states, he would squander the money he had inherited from his family; then, plunging into deep depressions, he would be institutionalized. Even as Frances climbed through the ranks of New York State government and, later, became labor secretary, most of her earnings went to paying for her husband's care in a series of expensive sanitariums.

The day the Social Security Act was signed into law, Frances received word that Paul had escaped the facility where he was living. After the signing ceremony, where she was photographed standing behind President Roosevelt, Frances rushed to New York to search for her husband. She found him hours later, confused and wandering the streets. She had to work all her life to support Paul and Susanna, and she constantly struggled to keep them out of the public eye.

As the New Deal rescued the American economy, the rising tide of fascism in Europe began eroding progressive political will in the United States. As labor secretary, Frances also oversaw the nation's immigration office. She argued in favor of expanding visa allotments for labor activists, Jews, and other persecuted people from Germany and Austria. Although she was able to intervene in some individual cases, her larger efforts were blocked by the State Department. In 1940, FDR approved a plan to move the immigration bureau, as it was known then, from the Department of Labor to the Department of Justice, cutting Frances out entirely. And, as we know all too painfully, the last item on Frances's 1933 list of New Deal programs — universal health insurance — did not come to pass then. Though the Affordable Care Act brought us closer than ever, we still have work to do over eight decades later.

Frances Perkins served throughout all twelve years of FDR's presidency, and she continued briefly as labor secretary under President Harry Truman. She had been decried as a Communist, survived an impeachment attempt by her enemies in Congress, and struggled privately with her husband's illness — all while weaving together many of the strongest strands of America's social safety net. The creator of Social Security worked until just a few weeks before she died, in 1965. Despite the immense challenges she faced in her personal and professional life, Frances's tenacity and vision allowed her to make a difference in the lives of countless people across the generations. To me, she has always embodied the highest ideals of public service.

KATHARINE GRAHAM

HILLARY

"Frightened and tense, I took a big gulp and said, 'Go ahead, go ahead, go ahead. Let's go. Let's publish.' And I hung up. So the decision was made."

That's how Katharine Graham described one of the most pivotal moments in the history of American journalism: her choice, as publisher of the *Washington Post,* to publish the Pentagon Papers, a collection of classified documents about the Vietnam War that contradicted much of what the government had said publicly. The Nixon administration had already won an injunction to stop the *New York Times,* which had already begun printing excerpts from the papers, from publishing the rest. The *Post*'s lawyers, and many of Katharine's friends and advisers, had urged her not to publish. There was a chance, they reminded her, that the paper could be prosecuted by the government under the Espionage Act. But Katharine knew that, in a time of national emergency, she had an obligation to defend the Constitution and promote the highest standards of journalism. For that brave act, and the many more that followed, I called her "Mother Courage" in a speech celebrating press freedom at the American Society of News Editors in 2001.

After college and a brief stint working as a reporter for the *San Francisco News,* she joined the staff of the *Washington Post,* the paper her father owned, in 1939. The next year, she married Philip Graham, a Supreme Court law clerk. Soon after, she gave up her career to fulfill her duties — which she always said she enjoyed — as a wife, mother, and self-described socialite.

When the time came for her father to hand over the paper to the next generation, he passed it not to Katharine but to her husband. "No man should be in the position of working for his wife," he explained to her. At the time, it didn't occur to her to object. She claims she was perfectly happy with her life as it was — until her husband's affair, depression, and mental health challenges created many unhappy years during which Katharine struggled to keep her family together and prevent her husband from hurting himself or anyone else. He died by suicide in 1963.

After Philip's death, Katharine stepped up to lead the *Post,* despite her hesitations about her lack of qualifications. (" 'Me?' I exclaimed. 'That's impossible. I couldn't possibly do it,' " she recounted later, echoing a familiar refrain of generations of women confronted with a daunting new chapter in their career.) Under her leadership, and with the help of executive editor Ben Bradlee, whom she brought on board, the paper became known for its unflinching investigative reporting. Though films like *All the President's Men* leave out this detail, it was Katharine as well as Ben who authorized Bob Woodward and Carl Bernstein to report on the Watergate scandal, providing a much-needed check on an out-of-control president. When she took over as the

> *"There was always the most acute discomfort and self-consciousness about my presence in a room. One speaker after another used to start his presentations coyly by saying 'Lady and gentlemen' or 'Gentlemen and Mrs. Graham,' always with slight giggles or snickers. It made me extremely uncomfortable, and I longed to be omitted, or at least not singled out."*
> — KATHARINE GRAHAM

CEO of the Washington Post Corporation in 1972, she became the first woman CEO of a Fortune 500 company.

But it was more than her professional success that made Katharine such a source of courage to so many of us. Her autobiography, *Personal History,* is regarded as one of the gold standards of the Washington memoir. Even before the book won the Pulitzer Prize, the great Nora Ephron reviewed it in the *New York Times:* "Am I making clear how extraordinary this book is?" she asked. "Kay Graham has lived in a world so circumscribed that her candor and forthrightness are all the more affecting." Katharine detailed her husband's infidelity, the miserable reality of coping with his mental illness, and the trauma and guilt she felt after his death. Equally moving are her descriptions of growing up in an era when women were assumed to be inferior to men, and the unique challenge of being forced to come into her own professionally at age forty-six. She was also open about the painful process of changing not just the mind-sets of people around her but her own. "Women traditionally also have suffered — and many still do — from an exaggerated desire to please, a syndrome so instilled in women of my generation that it inhibited my behavior for many years, and in ways still does," she confessed. She wrote about her friendship with Gloria Steinem and her relationships with younger women colleagues who helped change her views on her own place in the world.

Katharine exemplified the importance of the press as a force for accountability in democracy. It's not always comfortable — in fact, as someone who has been on the receiving end of good press and bad, I can say with absolute certainty that it can be downright uncomfortable. But our future depends not only on a free press but on a fearless one. We need a fourth estate willing to risk criticism, condemnation, and retaliation in order to expose the truth, just as Katharine did.

CONSTANCE BAKER MOTLEY

HILLARY

In 1936, fifteen-year-old Constance Baker Motley was turned away from a public beach in Milford, Connecticut, because she was black. She had never experienced such outright racism before; it left an impression that would stay with her for the rest of her life.

The daughter of immigrants from the Caribbean island of Nevis, Constance grew up in New Haven, Connecticut. Her father worked as a chef for student groups at Yale University. Her great-grandmothers had been enslaved in the West Indies, something her parents seemed loath to talk about. Constance and her eleven siblings attended New Haven's integrated public schools, and even from a young age, her love of learning was evident. "I grew up in a house where nobody had to tell me to go to school every day and do my homework," she later wrote.

Constance had studied the writings of W. E. B. Du Bois and other black writers in Sunday school. After the incident at the beach, she dove into other books on black history. The more she read, she recounted, the more she "began consciously to identify with black America." Soon she decided it wasn't enough to read about the struggle for civil rights; she wanted to be part of it. Her mother

---

"Lack of encouragement never deterred me. I was the kind of person who would not be put down."
— CONSTANCE BAKER MOTLEY

---

was a founder of the New Haven NAACP, and while she was in high school, Constance became president of the organization's Youth Council. Around this time she reportedly read Abraham Lincoln's descriptions of the legal profession as one of the hardest jobs, which led her to decide that it was the career for her. The fact that there was only a small handful of black women practicing law at the time didn't deter her. Neither did her parents' repeated suggestions that she become a hairdresser — a seemingly more attainable occupation. Her family's inability to pay for college, however, was a bigger obstacle.

After graduating from high school, Constance found a job helping with a building reconstruction project and continued her activism. One night, at a public discussion of a community center ostensibly created to serve the black population in New Haven, Constance "caused a stir" by pointing out that "all of the people on the board were from Yale, and, therefore, the black community had no real input into what was going on." The next day, a wealthy white man who'd been at the meeting asked to see her and offered to pay her college tuition.

With his support, she enrolled at Fisk University, a historically black university in Nashville, Tennessee. On her first trip to the campus in 1941, as the train crossed the border from Ohio into Kentucky, she would later recall, "I had to disembark while the train employees put another passenger car behind the engine. It was older and rustier than the other cars on the train. When I went to get back on, a black porter said to me: 'You have to go in this car,' pointing to the one that had just been added. It had a sign reading COLORED on the coach door inside. Although I had known this would happen, I was both frightened and humiliated." Constance ultimately transferred to New York University (NYU), where she graduated with a bachelor's degree in economics.

In 1944, she became the second black woman to attend Columbia Law School. By this time she was working for a wartime agency that supported family members of servicemen. When she told her supervisor at work why she was leaving, he scoffed, echoing a refrain she would hear throughout her life: "Women don't get anywhere in the law. . . . That's the dumbest thing I ever heard, a complete waste of time."

While in law school, Constance joined the NAACP's Legal Defense and Education Fund. After graduation, she was hired to work as a law clerk for Thurgood Marshall, then the NAACP's chief counsel and a future Supreme Court justice. There, she helped write briefs for the Supreme Court case *Brown v. Board of Education*. Three years after *Brown*, she argued and won the right of the Little

Rock Nine to attend the previously all-white Central High. She defended protesters arrested during the Freedom Rides of the 1960s and students who were expelled from school in Birmingham, Alabama, for taking part in public demonstrations. She also served as lead counsel on a case to allow a high school student named James Meredith to gain admission to the University of Mississippi, likely becoming the first black woman to argue before the Supreme Court in modern times. Over the course of the case, she made twenty-two trips to the state. She would later describe the day Meredith accepted his diploma from Ole Miss — the first black student to graduate from the institution — as the most thrilling day of her life. Of the ten cases she argued before the highest court in the land, she won nine.

She was ironclad in her convictions and always positive, though part of her strength was how gracious she was in her arguments. When a reporter once wrote that she had "demanded" something in court, she corrected: "What do you mean 'I demanded the court'? You don't demand, you pray for relief or move for some action."

Constance's quiet activism was evident in the courtroom and beyond. "She visited the Rev. Dr. Martin Luther King Jr. in jail, sang freedom songs in churches that had been bombed, and spent a night under armed guard with Medgar Evers, the civil rights leader who was later murdered," wrote the *New York Times* in her obituary. In 1964, at the age of forty-three, Constance entered politics. She accepted a nomination to run for the New York State Senate on one condition: that serving in office would not interfere with her work for the NAACP. She became the first black woman to serve in the state Senate, then the first to serve as Manhattan borough president — a position for which she was unanimously chosen by the city council to fill a vacancy. She was later elected to a full four-year term with bipartisan support. As borough president, she worked to revitalize Harlem and improve housing and schools. Her work captured national attention, and President Lyndon B. Johnson soon appointed her as the first black woman to serve as a federal judge. Throughout her nearly forty years on the bench, she earned a reputation for being fair-minded.

By the time of her death in 2005, Constance had earned eight honorary college degrees. She hadn't simply overcome the injustice she experienced as a child; she dedicated her life to correcting it on a grand scale, giving other people of color and other women opportunities she could only dream of as a little girl. "Her métier was in the quieter, painstaking preparation and presentation of lawsuits that paved the way to fuller societal participation by blacks," wrote the *New York Times*. "She dressed elegantly, spoke in a low, lilting voice and, in case after case, earned a reputation as the chief courtroom tactician of the Civil Rights Movement." In her autobiography, *Equal Justice Under Law,* she explained that setbacks in the struggle for civil rights and progress could not be abided. "We all believed that our time had come and that we had to go forward," she said. Generations of lawyers and Americans are glad she did.

EDIE WINDSOR

HILLARY AND CHELSEA

Chelsea

Edie Windsor didn't set out to change the course of American history. Born in 1929, she grew up at a time when a woman was generally expected to settle down, get married, and let her husband support her. Instead, at twenty-three years old, Edie was divorced, living on her own in New York City, and supporting herself. But Edie didn't let that stop her. She got her master's degree in math and became a computer programmer at IBM in the 1950s and '60s, when women were still very much in the minority across the company. The photos from the time show Edie looking determined, standing in front of a computer the size of a room; or sitting behind a desk, in charge, and clearly loving it. When Maya Angelou declared, "Each time a woman stands up for herself, without knowing it, possibly without claiming it, she stands up for all women," she could have been describing Edie.

While Edie was making history in her professional life, she was also in the process of making history in her personal life. In 1963, she met a graduate student named Thea Spyer, and the two danced all night. Over the next two years, they fell in love. Before Stonewall, before Pride parades, before two women could legally marry anywhere in the world, their devotion to each other was its own quiet, revolutionary act. They loved each other through good times and hard times — including the hardest time of all, Thea's diagnosis of progressive multiple sclerosis. For decades, Edie gladly took care of Thea.

After being told in 2007 that Thea had no longer than a year to live, they flew to Canada and were legally married. When Thea died two years later, Edie was overcome with grief. That grief was compounded by the realization that she owed hundreds of thousands of dollars in taxes she wouldn't have had to pay if she had been married to a man — as Edie used to say, "if Thea had been Theo." She knew she had two choices: Accept this painful injustice or fight back. She chose to fight, all the way to the highest court in the land. With her brilliant lawyer, Roberta "Robbie" Kaplan, by her side, they made the case for her marriage, indeed the case for equality, forcefully and poignantly.

Hillary

Through it all, Edie's strength never wavered, though she did confess to one moment of panic: the day she saw her name in print as *"United States v. Windsor."* It's only fitting to know that's how she will be immortalized in history books, in a landmark decision synonymous with equal rights and dignity under the law.

Edie's battle affirmed the fact that progress — especially in a vibrant pluralistic society like America — takes a whole lot of persistence. True to form, after Edie won her fight, she didn't quit. She kept on fighting for others. She mentored and supported women in technology. She assiduously corrected misinformation about MS, because she couldn't stand the thought of causing more fear and uncertainty for anyone living with the disease, or for their loved ones. She was a source of inspiration and friendship for Jim Obergefell, who later brought his own case to the Supreme Court, which made marriage equality the law of the land in every state. The LGBTQ community had given Edie the strength to live her truth, and she dedicated her life to paying it forward.

Chelsea

I'll never forget joining advocates back in 2011 during the ultimately successful fight to pass marriage equality in New York; we had failed to pass it in 2009. Marc and I had gotten married in 2010, and it was the happiest day of my life to be able to marry my best friend. It also renewed my commitment to marriage equality. It seemed obvious that every New Yorker — every American — should have the same right I had. I was very proud in 2013 when the Supreme Court ruled that the Defense of Marriage Act (DOMA) was unconstitutional. My father had signed DOMA in 1996. It never should have become law and I will always be grateful to Edie for helping ensure it didn't stay law.

Edie felt strongly that as necessary as it was, marriage was just the beginning — and she was right. She talked often about how wrong it was that LGBTQ Americans in many parts of the country can be married on Saturday, evicted from their home on Sunday, and fired on Monday simply because of who they are. She also spoke out about laws passed at the state level that treated LGBTQ Americans as second-class citizens; about LGBTQ youth homelessness; about the cruel and inhumane practice of so-called conversion therapy, which is child abuse by another name; and about the crisis of violence against the transgender community — especially transgender women of color. "It's been the joy of a lifetime to see the world change for the better for LGBT Americans before my very eyes," she said. "But even though I'm not so young anymore, I'm not willing to stop fighting."

Hillary

It was hard to say goodbye to Edie in 2017, but she left us with so much. She pushed us all to be better, stand taller, dream bigger. She didn't just want us to say the right thing, she wanted us to do the right thing. She embodied the words of Mary Oliver: "There is nothing more pathetic than caution / when headlong might save a life, / even, possibly, your own." Edie did everything headlong, including fall in love again — something even she never thought was possible, until she met her second wife, Judith Kasen-Windsor.

Because of Edie, people came out, marched in their first Pride parade, married the love of their life. Women followed in her footsteps in science, technology, engineering, and math, shattering stereotypes and breaking barriers of their own. Advocates and activists watched her stand up to injustice and found renewed determination to wage their own battles. After she died, people took to social media to share their favorite memories — everyone from friends to fans to a fact-checker who once worked on a profile of her. (All hail the fact-checkers!) One man told the story of running up to Edie at the Container Store on Sixth Avenue, with a little encouragement from his then boyfriend, now fiancé. He thanked her and told her that she and Thea had changed his life. Edie grabbed his arm, winked, and said, "Don't thank me. Just get married. It's the most magical feeling to wake up married."

The magic of Edie Windsor was simple but powerful: She had a fierce belief in the value of being true to yourself. Whether she was reminding friends of her and Thea's credo, "Don't postpone joy," or standing before the Supreme Court, Edie Windsor was always exactly herself and no less. When her lawyer, Robbie, asked her to make fewer references to her love life with Thea in order to make herself more palatable to the Supreme Court, Edie reluctantly agreed, on one condition: that their deal expire the moment the case was over. (And, as Robbie tells it, expire it did.) In her final days at a hospital in Manhattan,

Edie still insisted on having her nails manicured and hair set, even if the only visitors she saw that day were her nurse and her wife.

Edie was brave, endlessly determined, the kind of person you always want in your corner. It meant the world to me to have her support in my campaign. During some of the toughest days of the election — and the days that followed — I thought about Edie and her long struggle. I thought about how she never got discouraged. How she experienced loss, grief, and injustice, but how that only made her more generous, more openhearted, and more fearless in her fight. She refused to give up on the promise of America, and she refused to shrink any part of herself in order to fit into the America she dreamed of. Through determination and sheer force of will, and by being the most honest version of herself that she could imagine, she brought us one step closer to that more perfect union.

Ela Bhatt

Hillary

On my first trip to India in 1995, I met one of the twentieth century's most effective political and labor organizers, Ela Ramesh Bhatt. Following Gandhi's example, she founded the

Self Employed Women's Association (SEWA) in 1971.

Both a trade union and a women's movement, SEWA had more than 140,000 members when I visited, including some of the poorest, least educated, and most shunned women in India. It has now grown to more than one million members. Many of the SEWA members had entered into arranged marriages and then lived in their husbands' households under the watchful eyes of their mothers-in-law. Some had lived in purdah — the enforced isolation within their own homes that is applied to certain Hindu and Muslim women in South Asia — until their husbands died, were disabled, or left, and they had to support their families; all struggled day-to-day to survive. SEWA offered small loans to enable them to earn their own income and also provided basic literacy and business education training. When I visited SEWA headquarters in Ahmedabad, Ela showed me the large books kept in SEWA's one-room office that recorded the loans and repayments. Through this system of microfinance, SEWA was providing employment for thousands of individual women and changing deeply held attitudes about women's roles.

Ela received a bachelor of arts in English and a law degree and then joined the legal department of the Textile Labour Association, where she headed its women's wing. Thousands of women worked in the textile industry, but most were self-employed at home rather than working in factories, so the labor laws did not apply to them. Ela decided to organize them and to seek better working conditions and income for them. She encountered stiff opposition from businesses and governments but kept pressing her mission and became known as the "gentle revolutionary."

Ela, a practitioner of Gandhian nonviolence, stresses the centrality of the peaceful struggle against injustice. When I was secretary of state, I proudly gave her the Global Fairness Initiative's Fairness Award for helping more than one million poor women in India to greater dignity, independence, and self-sufficiency. I have often referred to her as one of my personal heroes because of her life's example and SEWA's achievements. I have stayed in touch with Ela and her successors over the years, and I visit SEWA members and stores when I go to India. But the memory of that first visit is indelible.

Word of my visit had spread through the nearby villages in Gujarat, and nearly one thousand women flocked to the meeting, some of them walking nine or ten hours along hot, dusty paths through the countryside. Tears filled my eyes when I saw them waiting for me under a large tent. Fanning themselves in their sapphire-, emerald-, and ruby-colored saris, they looked like an undulating human rainbow. They were Muslim and Hindu, including untouchables, the lowest Hindu caste. There were kite makers, scrap pickers, and vegetable vendors. While I sat in front, Chelsea sat down among the women in the audience.

One by one, women stood up to share how SEWA had changed their lives, not only because of the small loans they'd received and the help SEWA had given them in their businesses, but also because of the solidarity they felt with other struggling women. One woman struck a common chord when she explained that she was no longer afraid of her mother-in-law. In the culture many of the SEWA women shared, the mother-in-law typically exerts rigid control over her son's wife as soon as the couple marry and move in with his family. Having her own market stall and her own income gave this woman welcome independence. She added that she was no longer afraid of the police, either, because a group of SEWA-sponsored vendors now protected her from harassment by overbearing officers in the market. The dignified bearing, chiseled faces, and kohl-rimmed eyes of the speakers belied their difficult lives.

Finally, I was asked to make closing remarks. After I finished, Ela took the microphone and announced that the women wanted to express their gratitude for my visit from America. In a stunning flash of moving

> *"A woman who tends a small plot of land, grows vegetables, weaves cloth, and provides for the family and the market, while caring for the financial, social, educational and emotional needs of her family is a multifunctional worker and the builder of a stable society."*
>
> — ELA BHATT

color, they all sprang to their feet and began singing "We Shall Overcome" in Gujarati. In that moment, the thread connecting Gandhi's principles of nonviolence to the American civil rights movement came full circle, back to India. I was overwhelmed and uplifted to be in the midst of women who were working to overcome their own hardships as well as centuries of oppression. For me, they and Ela were a living affirmation of the importance of women's rights.

TEMPLE GRANDIN

CHELSEA

As a toddler, Mary Temple, as she was known then, didn't speak. The doctors her parents brought her to in their hometown of Boston didn't think anything could be done to help her. Her parents were advised to institutionalize her, an all-too-common practice even in the 1950s. But her mother, Eustacia, refused to accept that verdict. First she found a doctor who suggested speech therapy, which worked. Then she sent Temple to school, even though it was sometimes challenging for her to be in a classroom because she didn't learn or communicate the way other kids did. When Temple was fifteen years old, she went to her aunt's ranch, where she had a life-changing realization: The animals she saw there felt the same intense fear and sensitivity to sound and touch that she did.

Temple Grandin has spent her life working to improve the living conditions of livestock in a male-dominated industry. Despite the challenges she faced, Temple never doubted her mission, her training, or her unique qualifications. After studying human psychology in college, she completed a master's degree and a PhD in animal science. She went on to design facilities around the world that lead to fewer animal injuries and less stress, and she has helped come up with more effective stunning methods so animals are killed more humanely, with less pain. Over time, she won over an industry that was skeptical of her approach and rife with sexism. Temple's scoring system to assess how the livestock industry treats the animals that ultimately wind up as steaks, burgers, chops, and bacon is now the standard assessment tool for most of the

> *"When I started my career in the early '70s, no women worked in the cattle yards. The guys didn't like me being there, but I didn't pick up on the subtle social cues; what I cared about was working with the animals and studying the cattle chutes. Being autistic was an advantage, because all the hostility didn't affect me as much."*
>
> — TEMPLE GRANDIN

livestock industry in the United States and Europe.

I first learned about Temple from my Grandma Dorothy. It was over the holidays one year when I was in high school, and she had just read Temple's book, *Thinking in Pictures*. My grandmother raved about Temple's brilliance and how well she explained what it was like to think in pictures. I promptly borrowed the book and began to follow her work through interviews and other writing. Years later, my grandma and I watched a movie about her life. The more I learned, the more interested I became in Temple and her work. She links her ability to think in pictures — including her ability to innovate humane livestock handling designs in her mind before she ever commits them to paper — to her autism.

Temple is not a hands-off researcher. She

goes into the physical spaces where animals are kept, as well as the corrals and chutes they're forced through; she has even stood in stun boxes where animals are killed. Her physical experience of an animal's journey led to two of her signature designs. Her curved loading chute prevents cattle from seeing where they're headed, so they are less likely to become stressed or injure themselves trying to escape. Her center-track restrainer holds cattle steady during slaughter so that they're stunned without accidental injury. There is no need for an animal to suffer for anyone's breakfast, lunch, or dinner. Even McDonald's agrees: They hired Temple to improve animal welfare in the slaughterhouses that supply their hamburger meat, and she trained the first wave of auditors to ensure that the new standards were being respected.

Though animal welfare is what she's best known for today, it's just one area where Temple is a trailblazer. When she was in college, science professor William Carlock supported her work building the first major design for a hug box, a deep-pressure machine to help calm hypersensitive people who may not be receptive to being hugged by another person. Temple used her version for decades until she became comfortable hugging people. Since then, Temple's hug box and other related designs have helped countless others on the autism spectrum grow comfortable hugging and being hugged.

Temple's impact on raising awareness about autism and the value of supporting people who think, learn, and communicate in different ways is hard to measure. She has never hidden how her autism has shaped her life, or let the discomfort of others limit her. Temple has described the way her mind works as "literally movies in your head." Research suggests that animals also think in pictures, helping to explain Temple's empathy and extraordinary gift for understanding how to lessen their fear and pain; her realization as a teenager that animals experience the world the way she does was spot-on. The woman some doctors gave up on when she was two years old has helped transform how we think about animals and ourselves.

ELLEN DeGeneres

HILLARY

Just thinking about Ellen DeGeneres puts a smile on my face. Not only is she hilarious — I can't think of anyone else who can reduce people to tears of laughter by talking about yogurt or pharmaceutical side effects — she is brave and compassionate. Not only that, she is a human being: imperfect, flawed, and honest.

Ellen was in born in Metairie, Louisiana, in 1958, the daughter of an insurance salesman father and a speech pathologist mother. Her brother, Vance, was four years older. Growing up in the Christian Science faith, Ellen later said she often felt out of place. Her family struggled with poverty, and her parents divorced when she was a teenager. To help her mom through painful times, Ellen made her laugh.

An animal lover from the very beginning, a young Ellen dreamed of being a veterinarian. Fearing she wasn't "book smart" enough, she dropped out of the University of New Orleans after a semester and worked odd jobs: painting houses, selling vacuum cleaners, waiting tables, and shucking oysters.

In her early twenties, she started performing comedy, first for friends, then at local

---

"It's our challenges and obstacles that give us layers of depth and make us interesting. Are they fun when they happen? No. But they are what make us unique."
— ELLEN DEGENERES

---

coffeehouses and comedy clubs. In 1982, Ellen entered a Showtime contest to be the "Funniest Person in America." She won; it was her breakthrough moment. Despite the recognition, she battled nerves every time she took the stage. "I would choke," she later said. "My material was strong, but I just wasn't ready." She kept at it, and at twenty-eight years old, she snagged a coveted stand-up spot on *The Tonight Show Starring Johnny Carson.* During his show, Carson often invited comedians to sit with him on the couch and talk after their set. He had never extended the invitation to a female comedian, but Ellen's mind was made up: She was going to bring down the house with her set and perform so well that he would have no choice but to call her over. And that's exactly what happened.

Ellen's hard work and talent were getting noticed. In 1994, she landed a starring role as Ellen Morgan on the television sitcom *These Friends of Mine,* which was later renamed *Ellen.* After three seasons, rumors started to spread that Ellen's character was preparing to come out as a lesbian — and so was the real-life Ellen. She had spent years working to keep her private life and her public life separate. ("I never thought it was anybody's business, who I am and who I am with. So I thought, 'Why do people need to know?'" she would tell Oprah in an interview.) Before the episode aired, Ellen put the speculation to rest with a 1997 *Time* magazine cover that bravely declared "Yep, I'm Gay."

Meanwhile, Ellen was fighting a behind-the-scenes battle with her network and her show's sponsors. There weren't many openly LGBTQ characters on television — if any — and coming out on the show was seen as a risky move. But Ellen won, and in the show's fourth season her character came out as a lesbian — a milestone in television history. "The Puppy Episode" was the show's highest-rated episode, with around forty-four million viewers tuning in. It later won an Emmy Award, and *Ellen* was renewed for a fifth season.

CHELSEA

It was perfect that Oprah, another hardworking, trailblazing woman in television who broke so many barriers of her own, guest starred as Ellen's therapist on the coming-out episode of her show. After the show aired, Oprah encountered a backlash that was, she said, like nothing she had ever experienced before. But she never questioned her decision to stand by her friend. "I did it because she asked me to do it and I wanted to support her," Oprah said later. "Being able to be free, literally, and to express herself in a way that she can be 100 percent truthful with the audience has allowed them to fall in love with her."

Ellen learned firsthand that breaking down barriers, while important, can also be painful. Today her coming-out episode is recognized and celebrated for helping change hearts and minds and bringing long-overdue visibility to LGBTQ people on-screen. But she faced a difficult backlash at the time. Advertisers pulled their ads from the show, and religious groups called for a boycott. In season five, ABC began some episodes — absurdly — with a parental warning, which she was strongly against. The network canceled her show the next season, and Ellen battled with depression. She later joked about the "meerkat closet," which was her funny way of describing other LGBTQ celebrities popping their heads out of their dens to see what happened after she came out, then diving back into hiding when they witnessed the aftermath.

It's fitting, though, that Ellen had the last laugh. In 2003, she began hosting *The Ellen DeGeneres Show,* a talk show that's now in its sixteenth season. Besides her successful television talk show, Ellen is also a bestselling author, a voice actor, and was the first openly gay person to host the Academy Awards ceremony, in 2007. In 2012, she won the prestigious Mark Twain Prize for humor. She has a new television show called *Ellen's Game of Games* and a game called Heads Up! (a favorite pastime on our campaign plane in 2016).

I've visited my fair share of talk shows over

> *"Most comedy is based on getting a laugh at somebody else's expense. And I find that that's just a form of bullying in a major way. So I want to be an example that you can be funny and be kind, and make people laugh without hurting somebody else's feelings."*
>
> — ELLEN DEGENERES

the years. They are some of my favorite stops, and none more than *The Ellen DeGeneres Show,* which I first visited in October 2005 as senator from New York. I promised Ellen I would show her around Staten Island, and a month later, we were riding the ferry together. One of my all-time favorite episodes involved the phenomenally talented Kate McKinnon doing impressions of Ellen and me — they were spot-on! Best of all, Ellen ends every show by encouraging audiences to "be kind to one another."

Besides Ellen's historic career, she has also used her voice for good causes. In 2011, as secretary of state, I named Ellen the U.S. Special Envoy for Global AIDS Awareness. She brought to the effort not only her sharp wit and her big heart but also her impressive TV audience and social media following. She has raised awareness and donated millions to charities and people in need, from supporting sick children and their families to wildlife conservation efforts. Along with her wife, Portia de Rossi, she has helped to send a message to LGBTQ young people that the future ahead of them is a hopeful, accepting one. When President Obama awarded Ellen the Presidential Medal of Freedom in 2016, she was overwhelmed with emotion, and so were the rest of us. Seeing her earn such a well-deserved and hard-won recognition was a poignant reminder of the power of a single voice to spark immense change.

In recent years, she has spoken candidly about how hard it is to embrace her full, complex self in the public eye — to choose not to dance when she's not in the mood, to tackle tough topics, and to care less and less about being liked. Even the title of her latest comedy special, *Relatable,* is a tongue-in-cheek affirmation that sometimes the bravest — and hardest — thing we can be is true to ourselves.

MAYA LIN

CHELSEA

Growing up in Ohio, Maya Lin loved working in her father's ceramics studio, casting bronzes in her school's foundry, and building miniature towns. She took those passions to college, studying sculpture and architecture. When she was a senior at Yale, she had the confidence to enter the Vietnam Veterans Memorial Fund's national competition for the design of a new monument on Washington, D.C.'s National Mall to honor those who had fought and died in the Vietnam War. In 1981, the selection committee chose Maya's proposal out of more than fourteen hundred submissions. Her design was simple. Two black granite walls, each close to two hundred and fifty feet long, standing at their highest above ten feet and sloping down to under a foot, all sunk below ground level. There are more than fifty-eight thousand names on the walls.

The Vietnam Veterans Memorial has received countless accolades from veterans' groups and architectural critics alike over time, including the prestigious Twenty-five Year Award from the American Institute of Architects. But when its design was chosen, it was surrounded by controversy for its simplicity, its color, and its artist — a mix of sexism, racism, and doubts that anyone so young could be charged with such an important task. But Maya believed in her design, and the selection committee stayed firm in its choice. When the Vietnam Veterans Memorial officially opened in late 1982, Maya was twenty-three years old. It is now one of the most visited memorials in Washington, D.C. Standing in front of the walls, as I have done, enables the viewer to see one's reflection. It is a haunting and moving experience.

HILLARY

When I saw photos of the memorial, I couldn't imagine its power. But when I first visited in the 1980s, I felt it all around me. Being surrounded by the names of the fallen and the visitors searching for their lost friends and family members is an overwhelming emotional experience. I used to visit there when I'd leave the White House, wearing a baseball cap and casual clothes for incognito walks around the Mall.

After finishing her graduate studies, Maya continued creating important public art pieces. The Women's Table at Yale chronicles the number of women at that institution from its founding in 1701 until 1993, the year the sculpture was completed; women's enrollment would surpass men's in the first-year class for the first time two years later, in 1995. The Civil Rights Memorial in Montgomery, Alabama, is a memorial fountain with the names of forty people killed from 1954 to 1968 while courageously fighting for civil rights in the United States. It includes the name of Dr. Martin Luther King Jr., and his iconic quote "Until justice rolls down like water and righteousness like a mighty stream." In my early twenties, I took a friend who was planning to do a PhD in history on a road trip across the South. The Civil Rights Memorial was one of many stops in Montgomery, and one of the most memorable and moving of our trip.

Maya has said her virtual memorial, What Is Missing?, will be her last memorial. What Is Missing? aims to raise awareness about the growing number of endangered species around the world and the growing crisis of a sixth extinction (the argument that we are in the middle of a man-made mass extinction event). It is poignant and appropriately alarming; I hope it is also galvanizing.

HILLARY

Ever since Chelsea was a little girl, she has worried about what happens to endangered animals like whales and elephants. Inspired by a whaling trip when she was seven, she asked for a membership to Greenpeace as a Christmas present. And in 2019, she wrote a children's book about species going extinct: *Don't Let Them Disappear.*

Maya's interest in environmental conservation started at a young age; in elementary school, she promoted a boycott of Japan to oppose their whaling practices and dreamed of being a zoologist. Today, in addition to What Is Missing?, she is part of the Confluence Project, an effort to connect people to the Columbia River ecosystem in the Pacific

Northwest through indigenous communities and voices. She has said she hopes to help stop us from degrading our planet and is optimistic that art can change the way people think, including, presumably, how we think of our relationship and responsibility to nature. That conviction is also evident in her "wavefields," which are exactly as they sound, stunning waves built out of grass and soil. On a trip to the Storm King Art Center in New York, I was mesmerized and disoriented by the seven almost-four-hundred-feet-long ripples of earth seeming to form waves in motion. All I could do was wonder: How did the ocean merge with solid ground?

For almost my entire life, Maya's work has given us different ways to look at the world, confront our past, and imagine a different, healthier, more sustainable and just future. With guts, humility, and compassion, Maya poses a question to all of us: What more can, and must, we do?

SALLY YATES

HILLARY

Like many Americans, I got my first sense of Sally Yates's courage through a breaking news alert.

"CNN, January 30, 2017: Trump fires

Acting Attorney General Sally Yates for 'refusing to enforce a legal order' on immigration."

That didn't take long.

Ten days earlier, Donald Trump had been sworn in as president. Seven days after that, the White House ordered its notorious, bigoted travel ban. Among other things, the ban would prevent more than 218 million people from seven Muslim-majority countries from entering the United States for the next three months. And it banned all refugees worldwide from entering the U.S. for four months, with an exception made for persecuted religious minorities, specifically Syrian Christians. As a candidate, Trump had threatened "a total and complete shutdown of Muslims entering the United States." Now it looked like he was following through.

Sally Yates was running the Justice Department in the early days of the Trump administration. And it turned out she was exactly who America needed there and then.

Usually, attorney general is a political appointment. That wasn't the case for Sally. She had been a lawyer for the government for nearly thirty years — ever since she made the jump to public service as a young lawyer in Georgia. She had been working at a distinguished Atlanta firm that had a history stretching back over a century, a job that offered a path to a life of wealth and prestige. But Sally had walked away.

Instead, she went to work for the United States of America.

As an assistant U.S. attorney, Sally prosecuted white-collar fraud and political corruption cases, eventually becoming chief of that section in the Justice Department. She was also the lead prosecutor in the trial of Eric Rudolph, the domestic terrorist who bombed the 1996 Olympic Games, two abortion clinics, and a lesbian bar. Sally was exceptional at her job: She got promotion after promotion under both Republican and Democratic presidents. Politics didn't matter. What mattered was the law — and the Constitution above all.

President Barack Obama nominated Sally to be U.S. attorney of the Northern District of Georgia. She was the first woman ever to hold that position. A few years later, he nominated her to be deputy attorney general of the United States — the second-highest position at the Justice Department. It was during her Senate confirmation hearings for that role that this prophetic exchange occurred.

JEFF SESSIONS: Do you think the attorney general has the responsibility to say no to the president if he asks for something that's improper?

SALLY YATES: Senator, I believe the attorney general or the deputy attorney general has an obligation to follow the law and the Constitution, and to give their independent legal advice to the president.

Soon she showed the world what that obligation meant.

When President Obama left office, Loretta Lynch stepped down as attorney general, leaving Sally running the Justice Department temporarily until a new attorney general was confirmed. Sally no doubt planned on a quiet week or two at the office, keeping everything running smoothly, making no news, then tendering her resignation after a long and distinguished career — and maybe heading somewhere sunny for a well-deserved break.

Instead, Trump's Muslim ban happened.

After Trump's executive order was announced late on Friday, Sally spent the weekend thinking about the ban, then showed up at work on Monday, ready to figure out whether it was constitutional. There were two major problems. First, by banning people from Muslim-majority countries while giving preferential treatment to Syrian Christians, the order appeared to violate the Establishment Clause of the First Amendment: "Congress shall make no law respecting an establishment of religion, or prohibiting the free exercise thereof. . . ." Our government must not favor one religion over another — yet this executive order clearly seemed to favor Christians over Muslims. Add to that Trump's repeated pledge on the campaign trail to ban Muslims from entering America, and the religious intent of this executive order seemed even clearer.

Second, by imposing a sweeping ban on everyone from those seven countries — including people with legal visas and those who had already established legal residency in the U.S. — the order presented a due-process problem. The Constitution promises — in two different places — that no one should be "deprived of life, liberty, or property, without due process of law." The provision applies to citizens and noncitizens alike. It means you can't just take valid visas and green cards away from people arbitrarily. Everyone deserves due process — for example, a hearing where people would have a chance to make a case as to why they couldn't return to their country. But Trump's ban didn't allow for that. It just said, Keep them out — and if they're here already, throw them out.

At the Justice Department that Monday, Sally Yates considered all of this. She read the executive order carefully. She convened a meeting of government lawyers, including several appointed by Trump, and asked them to give their best possible defenses of the ban. She reflected on the Constitution and the oath she'd sworn to uphold it. She thought about what the Establishment Clause means to a country founded on religious freedom, and what due process represents in a country that believes all people are created equal and that promises equal justice to all. She decided that she could not defend the legality of the ban.

Then she made an extraordinarily courageous decision.

Sally could have resigned. She could have walked away from the whole mess and let the next guy deal with it. The message would have been clear: "My conscience won't let me be a part of this for even one day more." But what would that mean for the institution to which Sally had devoted nearly her entire professional life? As she put it later, "Resignation would have protected my own personal integrity. . . . But I believed that I had an obligation to also protect the integrity of the Department of Justice."

She didn't want to see the Justice Department defend an illegal and unconstitutional order. And though she couldn't prevent that from happening indefinitely, she could prevent it right then. She had that power, because she was in charge.

So Sally Yates wrote a statement: "For as long as I am the Acting Attorney General, the Department of Justice will not present arguments in defense of the Executive Order, unless and until I become convinced that it is appropriate to do so." Then she sent the statement to Justice Department employees across the country and to the White House. And she sat back and waited for what she knew would happen next.

Four hours later, a letter arrived from the White House. After nearly three decades of faithfully serving the American people and defending the U.S. Constitution, Sally Yates had been fired.

Since that day, she has continued to comport herself with dignity and integrity. Her appearance before the Senate Judiciary Committee a few months later was a master class in remaining composed and respectful even in the face of bluster and bullying. (As someone who once spent eleven hours in that hot seat, I know how tough that is to pull off.) She testified persuasively about not only her decision on the Muslim ban but also her attempts to alert the White House to how National Security Advisor Michael Flynn had been compromised by the Russians. At a time when it seems like the people in charge care far less about our national security and the integrity of our institutions than about their own political fortunes, Sally reminded us that a different way is possible.

Sally reminds me of so many dedicated civil and foreign service officers I've worked with over the years who put country and Constitution above everything else, including themselves. They're the best of America, and we're lucky to have them.

Now that she's a private citizen, working as a partner in a law firm and speaking out about her experiences in government, people often ask Sally to consider running for office. So far, she's demurred — but she hasn't ruled it out. I hope she does run. She'd be great at holding office. But whether she does or not, future generations of public servants will always have her to look up to. And we're all the better for it.

KIMBERLY BRYANT AND RESHMA SAUJANI

KIMBERLY BRYANT

RESHMA SAUJANI

CHELSEA

Kimberly Bryant loved math and science as a kid. She was an unapologetic, self-proclaimed nerd. As someone who has always thought it absurd and wrong that "nerd" is sometimes used as an insult or a bad word, I love that Kimberly reclaimed it. In the early 1980s, she embraced her love of "nerdy" subjects and joined the math team at Memphis Central

High School in Tennessee. She was always searching for role models who looked like her, and not finding many. After high school, she studied electrical engineering at Vanderbilt. As excited as she was by all of the innovation happening in her field, she couldn't help but notice, again, that she was one of the few women, and the only black woman, in most of her lectures and discussions. "Few of my classmates looked like me," she later observed.

She was working as a project manager for a tech company in San Francisco when her ten-year-old daughter, Kai, signed up for summer coding classes at Stanford. Kai couldn't wait for the first day; she loved video games and wanted to become a coder when she grew up. But when Kimberly dropped her off, she had a startling realization: Twenty years after her own college experiences, her daughter had no classmates who looked like her.

Kimberly knew she had to do something. She left corporate America in 2010 to start a new organization, Black Girls Code. Now their camps and classes reach eight thousand black, Latina, and Native American girls across the U.S. She has also extended her work to include girls in Johannesburg, South Africa. As girls in the Black Girls Code programs learn how to build their own app, or understand more about robotics and artificial intelligence, Kimberly has said she can see their confidence growing in front of her. Building a diverse pipeline of talent isn't just the right thing to do, she has repeatedly pointed out — it's the smart thing for companies who want to compete and win in the future. "Imagine the impact these curious, creative minds could have on the world with the guidance and encouragement others take for granted," she rightly said. Soon we won't have to imagine. As the Black Girls Code graduates go through college, graduate school, and their careers, the world will see what they build, create, and then help others imagine.

When Reshma Saujani ran for Congress in 2010, she had a moment of reckoning somewhat reminiscent of Kimberly's at the Stanford code camp drop-off. As Reshma campaigned in New York City, she didn't meet many women working at the tech companies she spoke to. When she visited computer science classes, she saw a familiar sight everywhere she went: computer labs full of boys learning to code. She didn't win that election or her next. But along the way, she found a new and powerful calling: working to close the gender gap in tech.

I was lucky enough to visit one of Reshma's early summer coding programs. The energy and enthusiasm were infectious, the environment full of optimism. The girls were from all across New York City and building apps they wanted to use to chase opportunities or solve problems they had identified. Reshma knew the statistics: huge numbers of girls who are interested in math and science in elementary school lose interest by age fifteen. She also knew how formative those early school years had been in her own life.

Reshma's family was expelled from Uganda in 1972, after Idi Amin's government ordered all Ugandans of South Asian descent to leave within ninety days. Her parents ultimately immigrated to Illinois. The bigotry her family had encountered didn't stop in their new country. In middle school, Reshma endured hateful, racist bullying. She worked hard, determined to do everything perfectly. That goal, in itself, taught her a lesson about what happens to girls in middle and high school. In her words: "We're raising our girls to be perfect, and we're raising our boys to be brave."

She finished college in three years and set her sights on an ambitious goal: going to Yale Law School. The first time she applied, she was rejected. And the second time. And the third. She refused to give up, and on her fourth try, she got in. Once again, she worked hard to do everything perfectly. It wasn't until she left her job at a big-name investment firm to run for office that she finally felt free to go after the risks she had always been afraid to take. "It turns out when you get a taste for being brave, it's hard to stop," she said. That realization also helped inspire the title of Reshma's terrific book, *Brave, Not Perfect*.

From a summer program started in 2012, her program Girls Who Code has since worked with tens of thousands of girls across all fifty states. It now runs after-school programs along with its summer programs, and it developed open-source curriculum and guides that anyone, anywhere, can use to learn to imagine, code, and build. Reshma has built a behemoth to tackle a massive problem. Not only is she equipping girls with the skills for their future careers, she's teaching them that it's okay to take risks, get things wrong, make mistakes, and try again.

Black Girls Code and Girls Who Code are not alone in teaching that lesson. There are now numerous groups focused on teaching girls how to code — from summer camps where girls come together to build their own apps to organizations that hold meetups and hackathons to programs focused on the intersection of technology, entrepreneurship, and social impact. Even the Girl Scouts are now helping girls learn to code: There are badges in robotics, website design, cybersecurity, and creating algorithms.

With their energy, innovation, and problem-solving, Reshma and Kimberly are part of a group of women who are transforming an entire field from the inside out — and helping to build a brighter future for all of us in the process.

■ ■ ■ ■

WOMEN'S RIGHTS CHAMPIONS

■ ■ ■ ■

ROSA MAY BILLINGHURST

CHELSEA

In high school, we studied the traditional story of women's suffrage: the Declaration of Sentiments from the 1848 women's rights convention in Seneca Falls onward, as well as

Mary Wollstonecraft's famous manifesto, *A Vindication of the Rights of Women*. But much of what I knew about suffrage and women's rights I learned from my mom, her friends, and our travels. I thought it bizarre that I hadn't learned more about the women from around the world to whom we owed so much, and I decided to start seeking out their stories on my own — from Kate Sheppard, who led the women's suffrage movement in New Zealand, the first country in the world to grant suffrage to all women, including indigenous Maori women, to the tough and determined Rosa May Billinghurst in England.

After surviving polio as a child in London, May, as she was known, decided that the use of her legs would be the only thing that disease would take from her. She had to confront the horrible prejudices that were all too common in the United Kingdom of the late nineteenth century against people with disabilities. In her twenties, May taught Sunday school, worked to raise awareness about the horrors of contemporary poverty in her community and around the country, and supported the temperance movement. Another cause she took up as a young woman would become a defining part of her life: women's suffrage.

In 1910, when she was in her midthirties, May took part in a protest against Prime Minister H. H. Asquith, who had blocked a bill that would have enfranchised one million

> "The government authorities may further maim my body by the torture of forcible feeding as they are torturing weak women in prison at the present time. They may even kill me in the process for I am not strong, but they cannot take away my freedom of spirit or my determination to fight this good fight to the end."
>
> — ROSA MAY BILLINGHURST

women in Britain and Ireland. She was able to attend demonstrations and participate in protests because of her hand tricycle, which enabled her to use her arms to power herself, all while sitting or reclining. Hundreds of women were brutally assaulted by police that day, which became known as Black Friday. May was one of them. She recounted the event in the newspaper afterward: "At first the police threw me out of the machine and on to the ground in a very brutal manner. Secondly, when on the machine again they tried to push me along with my arms twisted behind me in a very painful position. . . . Thirdly, they took me down a side road and left me in the middle of a hooligan crowd, first taking all the valves out of the wheels and pocketing them so that I could not move the machine."

May's treatment by the police made her that

much more determined to fight. Soon she was back at another protest, where she was arrested for attempting to use her wheelchair to ram through the crowd in London's Parliament Square. In 1912, May was arrested again, and not for the last time, for her participation in the window smashing campaign, a coordinated protest against Parliament's repeated failure to pass proposed legislation to grant women the right to vote. She was sentenced to hard labor, wheelchair and all. Her numerous arrests drew significant attention, with the press and even some of her fellow suffragettes pointing to her as a "cripple." She didn't shy away from the spotlight, as long as it furthered her cause; she once chained herself to the railing in front of Buckingham Palace.

May was force-fed in prison, as were many suffragettes who were arrested while protesting for their fundamental right to vote. None of this deterred her, and she continued to work for suffrage until 1918, when the UK granted property-owning women thirty and older the right to vote. Women in the UK wouldn't receive the same voting rights as men until 1928, when voting rights were extended to all people twenty-one and older. May, along with many other courageous women, helped make that possible, even inevitable.

May's political activism lessened after her cause was won, though she did continue to support other feminist efforts throughout her life. Her obituary in the Women's Freedom League bulletin described her as having "a strong sense of humor, even perhaps, a mischievous one . . . full of life and courage and not to mention jollity." A fierce believer in reincarnation, she thought "of this life as but one of many." She proved, again and again, that she was ready to sacrifice her physical safety, even her life, for the cause she believed in. Though her story is too often forgotten, even in histories of the suffrage movement, her personal fortitude and dedication make her a standout in an era of fierce women.

THE SUFFRAGISTS

HILLARY

The history of women's suffrage in the United States is too often taught as the story of a few brave women — a few brave *white* women, to be precise. Those who were fortunate enough to learn about the fight to grant "Votes for Women" in school may know the names of

Susan B. Anthony and Elizabeth Cady Stanton. They may even have studied the rift between the suffragists and abolitionists that occurred when Congress granted black men the right to vote but left women of any race behind, and discussed the fact that even after the Nineteenth Amendment was ratified in 1920, it would take decades for women of color to win the right to vote.

But the story of how women in the United States won the right to vote starts long before the Nineteenth Amendment was ratified, nearly one hundred years ago. It goes back almost one thousand years to the Iroquois Confederacy in what is now upstate New York, where it was women who elected and deposed male leaders. It carries forward through the rights of some women in the original colonies to vote until the Constitution and new state and local laws systematically stripped away that right. It is accelerated by defiant women like Angelina Grimké and her sister, Sarah, who famously said: "I ask no favors for my sex. . . . All I ask of our brethren is that they will take their feet from off our necks and permit us to stand upright." It continues through the decades-long effort of Native Americans to win voting rights state by state and through the civil rights movement's efforts to enforce voting rights nationally and locally — struggles that, as evidenced by the 2018 efforts to strip away voting rights and access in North

Dakota, Georgia, and elsewhere, wage on today.

One of the most important chapters in this story was written in 1848. At the famous Seneca Falls Convention in upstate New York, one hundred women and men signed their names to the Declaration of Sentiments, rewriting the Declaration of Independence to boldly assert: "We hold these truths to be self-evident: that all men and women are created equal." They faced criticism and derision; they were called "mannish women," old maids, and fanatics. One paper said granting rights to women would result in "a monstrous injury to all mankind." Only one of the signatories — Charlotte Woodward, a nineteen-year-old glove maker from Waterloo, New York — would live to see women cast ballots in a presidential election.

After the Civil War, black women assumed prominent roles in the struggle to achieve equality for both their race and sex. If you open an American passport, you will see this quote: "The cause of freedom is not the cause of a race or a sect, a party or a class — it is the cause of humankind, the very birthright of humanity." Yet few people know the author of those words: Anna Julia Haywood Cooper.

A teacher, scholar, and staunch supporter of suffrage through her writing and speaking, Anna was born into slavery in North Carolina in 1858. After Emancipation, she enrolled at a school for freed slaves. Her awakening came when she realized that her male classmates were studying a harder curriculum than she and the other girls at the school. She defiantly enrolled in the same classes they were taking.

Anna went on to graduate from Oberlin College with bachelor's and master's degrees. She then got involved with the black women's club movement becoming a well-known speaker on issues of women's rights. One of her most famous speeches was delivered at the World's Congress of Representative Women in Chicago in May 1893. She described the plight of enslaved women, like her own mother, and then ended with this stirring call for justice: "The colored woman feels that woman's cause is one and universal; and that not till the image of God, whether in parian [white marble] or ebony, is sacred and inviolable; not till race, color, sex, and condition are seen as the accidents, and not the substance of life; not till the universal title of humanity to life, liberty, and the pursuit of happiness is conceded to be inalienable to all; not till then is woman's lesson taught and woman's cause won — not the white woman's, nor the black woman's, not the red woman's, but the cause of every man and of every woman who has writhed silently under a mighty wrong."

Midge Wilson and Kathy Russell wrote in *Divided Sisters: Bridging the Gap Between Black Women & White Women,* "Among Black women who were staunch suffragists was Anna Julia Cooper, best known for her statement: 'Only the BLACK WOMAN can say when and where I enter the quiet, undisputed dignity of my womanhood, without violence or special patronage; then and there the whole Negro race enters with me.' Cooper was particularly effective in emphasizing to Black women that they required the ballot to counter the belief that 'Black men's' experiences and needs were the same as theirs." Her 1892 book, *A Voice from the South,* is considered the first published work of a black feminist.

Widowed by age twenty-one Anna became principal of the M Street Colored High School in Washington, D.C., the first public high school for black students in the country. Anna raised the school's standards for students and, with her at the helm, several were accepted to Ivy League colleges.

Anna's approach to providing a comprehensive education for black students was not universally appreciated; she had high-profile critics, including Booker T. Washington, who favored vocational education for black Americans. When the D.C. Board of Education refused to renew her contract — possibly due to her innovative practices — she left to teach in Missouri until she was rehired at M Street five years later.

Anna received a PhD in history from the Sorbonne in 1925, writing her dissertation on slavery and becoming the fourth black woman from the United States to earn a doctoral degree. She went on to spend more than a decade as the president of Frelinghuysen University for working-class adults. Anna believed that, for black Americans living in poverty, education was a "doctor and unfailing remedy." She died at 105 years old in 1964, mere months before the passage of the Civil Rights Act.

Like Anna, Mary Church Terrell also understood that the rights of women and the rights of people of color could not be separated. Born in Memphis in 1863, Mary was the daughter of Robert Reed Church, a former enslaved person and one of the first black millionaires in the South. She graduated from Oberlin College in 1884 and earned a master's degree four years later. She taught at Wilberforce University and at the M Street Colored High School alongside fellow teacher Anna Julia Cooper. ("While most girls run away from home to marry, I ran away to teach," she wrote later.) After she married Robert Heberton Terrell, she was forced to resign, since married women at that time were prohibited from teaching at the school.

The following year, Mary's childhood friend Tom Moss from Memphis — also a friend of Ida B. Wells — was lynched over his grocery store's business competition with a white-owned store. Mary joined with Frederick

Douglass to petition President Benjamin Harrison to condemn lynching; Harrison refused.

In 1895, Mary became the first black woman appointed to the D.C. Board of Education. In 1896, she became the first president of the newly organized National Association of Colored Women's Clubs, an organization whose founders included Harriet Tubman, Ida B. Wells, and poet and advocate Frances E. W. Harper. They adopted the motto "Lifting as we climb" in an effort to reassure "an ignorant and suspicious world that our aims and interests are identical with those of all good aspiring women."

In 1898, Mary delivered an impassioned speech on "The Progress of Colored Women." In 1900, in the face of rising white supremacy within the suffrage movement, she reiterated her commitment to suffrage for all women. "As a nation we professed long ago to have abandoned the principle that might makes right," she said. "Before the world we pose today as a government whose citizens have the right to life, liberty and the pursuit of happiness. And yet, in spite of these lofty professions and noble sentiments, the present policy of the government is to hold one-half of its citizens in legal subjection to the other, without being able to assign good and sufficient reasons for such a flagrant violation of the very principles upon which it was founded."

In 1940, Mary published her autobiography,

> *"With courage, born of success achieved in the past, with a keen sense of the responsibility which we shall continue to assume, we look forward to a future larger with promise and hope. Seeking no favors because of our color, nor patronage because of our needs, we knock at the bar of justice, asking an equal chance."*
>
> — MARY CHURCH TERRELL

A Colored Woman in a White World. She declared her intent to stay active in the fight for racial and gender equality as she aged, and that's just what she did. In 1950, at the age of eighty-seven, she was a plaintiff against a Washington, D.C., restaurant that refused to serve her and others because of their race. She helped organize pickets and business boycotts. Her efforts paid off in 1953 when the court declared segregation in our nation's capital unconstitutional. She died the following year, right before the Supreme Court decision in *Brown v. Board of Education* struck down the doctrine of "separate but equal."

Another gutsy woman whose name is too often overlooked in the history books is Alice Paul. Alice was born in New Jersey in 1885 into a Quaker family whose roots stretched back to the colonies. Her mother was a suffragist and member of the National American Woman Suffrage Association (NAWSA) who would sometimes take Alice to suffrage meetings, introducing her at an early age to the struggle for women's rights and social justice.

Alice went away to Swarthmore College, then moved to New York City after graduation to pursue social work. Her letters home showed a young woman searching for a way to confront injustice. She found one after graduating in 1905, when she traveled to England and heard the suffragette Christabel Pankhurst speak. ("Suffragette" was the term there, but American activists preferred "suffragist" because it sounded less diminutive.) Christabel's speech inspired Alice to join the Women's Social and Political Union (WSPU), the militant suffrage group led by Christabel and her mother, Emmeline Pankhurst.

Alice and her cohorts were relentless and creative. On November 9, 1909, the Lord Mayor of London hosted a banquet for cabinet ministers in Guild Hall. Alice and another suffragette, Amelia Brown, disguised themselves as cleaning women to sneak into the event. They hid themselves until the prime minister stood to speak, at which point Brown threw her shoe through a window and she and Alice yelled "Votes for women!" They were arrested and sentenced to one month of hard labor after refusing to pay fines and damages.

Alice returned to the United States in 1910, by then a celebrated suffragist with the goal of achieving recognition of women as equal citizens to men. She earned a PhD from the University of Pennsylvania; her dissertation was titled "The Legal Position of Women in Pennsylvania," which argued that suffrage was the key goal in achieving women's equality. She called for a campaign to achieve a federal suffrage amendment — an effort that directly contradicted the then strategy of NAWSA, which argued for the more gradual strategy of passing legislation state by state.

In 1913, the day before President Wilson's inauguration, Alice organized a massive women's suffrage parade. She proved to be not only an effective agitator but also a formidable organizer. Leading the parade was labor lawyer Inez Milholland, dressed in white, astride a horse, followed by bands, floats, and more than five thousand women from across the country. (It was in this parade that Ida B. Wells famously — and heroically — refused to follow Alice's directive that black women march on their own in the back, and instead marched at the front.) At least half a million spectators showed up — a bigger crowd than at Wilson's inauguration — and the crowd became unruly with some marchers being attacked and injured while the police stood by. The drama of the event raised the visibility of Alice's goal.

Alice eventually formed her own group, the National Woman's Party (NWP). In 1917, the NWP organized the first-ever picketing of the White House. The picketing continued, controversially, after World War I started. The so-called Silent Sentinels carried banners pointing out the president's hypocrisy in championing democracy around the world while denying women their rights in his own country. "Kaiser Wilson, have you forgotten your sympathy with the poor Germans because they were not self-governed?" demanded one banner. "20,000,000 American women are not self-governed. Take the beam out of your own eye."

All of this infuriated President Wilson; he had not supported suffrage in his 1912 presidential campaign against Theodore Roosevelt, who had. Wilson had no choice but to pass by the banners outside the White House that implored: "Mr. President, how long must women wait for liberty?"

The final sprint began on August 28, 1917, when suffragists protesting in front of the White House were arrested. As new groups of women showed up to picket, the arrests continued. On November 14, 1917, a group of thirty-three suffragists being held

---

"There will never be a new world order until women are part of it."

— ALICE PAUL

---

at the Occoquan Workhouse in Virginia were beaten and clubbed by guards in what became known as the "Night of Terror."

Alice herself had also been arrested. She began a hunger strike in jail, refusing to eat in protest. She was force-fed through a feeding tube inserted through her nose and down her throat, a procedure that amounted to torture. At one point, the superintendent of a local hospital interviewed Alice in an attempt to have her committed; he found her to be not only sane but "perfectly calm, yet determined." She later described the brutal treatment the suffragists endured and reflected on the motives behind it: "It was shocking that a government of men could look with such extreme contempt on a movement that was asking nothing except such a simple little thing as the right to vote."

The treatment of the suffragists in jail sparked national outrage, which marked a turning point in the struggle. Under public pressure, Wilson finally agreed to support a constitutional amendment for suffrage. It passed the United States House of Representatives on May 21, 1919, and the Senate on June 4, 1919.

After Congress passed the amendment, it had to go to the states to be ratified by the votes of legislatures in thirty-six out of the forty-eight states. That's when Carrie Chapman Catt began to work in earnest.

Carrie was born in 1859 and grew up in Iowa. After graduating from high school, she enrolled in college against her father's wishes, where she excelled and became an advocate for women's participation in everything from debate to military drills. When she graduated from Iowa State Agricultural College, she became a teacher and then the first female superintendent of the Mason City, Iowa, school district.

She became involved in the Iowa Woman Suffrage Association, and, in 1892, Susan B. Anthony asked her to address Congress on a proposed woman's suffrage amendment. Carrie began climbing up the ladder of the NAWSA and succeeded Anthony as president in 1900, but resigned after her first term to care for her sick husband. After becoming the organization's president again in 1915, she unveiled a plan to obtain support for suffrage in the states; two years later, under her leadership, NAWSA led a successful campaign for suffrage in New York State. Once the United States entered World War I, although she was a committed pacifist, Carrie made the difficult decision to support the war in hopes that her show of patriotism would help the cause of suffrage.

In her efforts to obtain suffrage state by state, Carrie sometimes appealed to the prejudices of her time — and, sadly, of our own. She denigrated Native Americans, immigrants, and black Americans, arguing that their citizenship should not be seen as equivalent to that of white women. Sally Roesch Wagner, the distinguished women's history scholar, sums it up aptly in *The Women's Suffrage Movement:* "This has been a journey of courage and cowardice; of principle and capitulation; of allies and racists. Examining our heroes and heras up close can be a painful process."

While Alice Paul was engaging in civil disobedience, Carrie Chapman Catt was pressuring Congress to pass the amendment and convincing states to ratify it. Thirty-five states did so. By the spring of 1920, Alice Paul and Carrie Chapman Catt, the final architects of congressional action and state ratification, were focused on Nashville, where the deciding vote took place in the Tennessee House on August 18, 1920.

The fight for that Tennessee victory, dramatically told in *The Woman's Hour* by Elaine Weiss, came down to one young legislator, Harry Burn. On the eve of the vote, he planned to oppose women's suffrage. But that morning, he received a letter from his mother, Phoebe Ensminger Burn: "Dear Son: Hurrah, and vote for suffrage and don't keep them in doubt . . . Don't forget to be a good boy and help Mrs. Catt . . . With lots of love, Mama." After reading the letter, Burn switched sides and cast the deciding vote.

Six months before the ratification of the Nineteenth Amendment, Carrie Chapman Catt founded the League of Women Voters in 1920 with the intent of educating and encouraging women to use their vote — an organization whose work continues to this day. Alice Paul drafted the Equal Rights Amendment and would spend the rest of her life advocating — as yet, unsuccessfully — for its passage. Her story is celebrated at the Belmont-Paul Women's Equality National Monument in Washington and the Alice Paul Institute at her family home in New Jersey, which provides leadership training to new generations of young women.

Reading the words of the Nineteenth Amendment today, it's hard not to wonder why it took so long: "The right of citizens of the United States to vote shall not be denied or abridged by the United States or by any State on account of sex. Congress shall have the power to enforce this article by appropriate legislation." But, of course, it was a long struggle because it was about so much more than the right of women to vote. It was about race, class, and deeply held cultural and religious views about women's subordinate roles to men in society. It was about men's — and some women's — insecurities and fears of the unknown. These challenges are still present today.

The franchise — the basic right of citizenship

— is still being fought over between those of us who believe every citizen should be able to vote and have that vote counted, and those who want to restrict the vote by erecting barriers against people, largely still based on race.

Our charge today is to continue the work these heroes and so many others — sung and unsung — began. We must ask ourselves how we can do better; how we can keep expanding the circle of rights and opportunities and make that more perfect union a reality not just on paper, but in practice.

SOPHIA DULEEP SINGH

CHELSEA

Sophia Duleep Singh was born to a prestigious family in England, the daughter of the last maharaja of the Sikh Empire on the

Indian subcontinent and the goddaughter of Queen Victoria. Her immense privilege protected her in many ways, though not in every way. Her father, deeply unhappy over being forced to abdicate his kingdom in Northern India and his subsequent exile to England by the British Raj, abandoned his family. Her mother suffered from alcoholism and died while taking care of an ill eleven-year-old Sophia. Still, given her wealth and position, few people would likely have guessed then that Princess Sophia would one day become a leader in the suffrage movement — probably least of all Sophia herself.

Growing up in the late 1880s in England, Sophia immersed herself in her studies with private tutors and focused her free time on her two passions: fashion and dogs. As a young woman on one overseas voyage, Sophia insisted on traveling with her dogs close at hand, feeding them "fine cuts of meat and the occasional nip of brandy." She posed for newspaper photographers, danced at debutante balls, and rode a bicycle in public, scandalizing the rest of the aristocracy as one of the few women to do so at the time.

But then, as Anita Anand, author of *Sophia: Princess, Suffragette, Revolutionary,* said, something changed. In 1903, at the age of twenty-seven, Sophia traveled to India and saw for the first time the brutality of life under the British Raj. She was shocked by the racism, famine,

> *"Taxation without representation is a tyranny. . . . I am unable to pay money to the state as I am not allowed to exercise any control over its expenditure."*
> — SOPHIA DULEEP SINGH

and poverty. Though she hadn't understood what life was like in India for the vast majority of people, her paternal grandmother, Jind Kaur — a gutsy woman in her own right — had spent her life organizing the Sikh resistance to British rule and was even imprisoned for her political activities. As for Sophia, she returned to England "with this sense of fire in her," as Anand said, and had made up her mind "that it is not right to have equals treated as underclasses, be they brown or be they female." At the time, British suffragettes were ramping up their organizing to demand votes for women, and expanding their use of more aggressive tactics: throwing rocks and bricks through windows, tossing nails under tires in the streets, interrupting speeches by political figures. In 1908, Sophia met Una Dugdale, a member of the Women's Social and Political Union, a group founded five years earlier by suffragette Emmeline Pankhurst. Sophia signed up as a member the same day. Within a year, she had become one of the organization's "tax resisters," refusing to pay taxes to a government that denied women representation. (Their slogan was straight to the point: "No vote, no tax.") As a result, some of her possessions were confiscated and sold, only to be bought back for Sophia by her fellow suffragettes.

Sophia joined Emmeline and hundreds of other suffragettes as they stormed the House of Commons in 1910 on a day that would become known as Black Friday. It wasn't the suffragettes' actions that earned the moniker: Police and bystanders attacked the suffragettes for six hours; more than two dozen women reported being sexually assaulted. Sophia leaped in between a petite woman and a police officer, shouting at him to let her go. Once the police officer recognized the woman who was screaming at him, he tried to slip away into the crowd. Sophia chased after him, demanding that he tell her his badge number. He refused, but she saw it and memorized it. She wrote to the home secretary at the time, Winston Churchill, demanding the officer be taken off duty. After exchanging multiple letters, he left a note on her file: "Send no further reply to her."

While other suffragettes were being sent to prison, Sophia took part in one demonstration after another but couldn't seem to get herself charged with a crime, likely because of her relationship to the royal family. In 1911, Sophia was arrested after she threw her body at the prime minister's car, carrying a banner that read "Give Women the Vote," but no police officer wanted to be responsible for mistreating Queen Victoria's goddaughter. Over and over, she was released without being charged, even though she was more than willing to join the other suffragettes who were going on hunger strikes in prison, risking their lives for the cause.

Sophia brought the fight for voting rights to her own home, often standing outside her Hampton Court apartment (given to her by Queen Victoria), selling copies of *The Suffragette*. (After seeing Sophia's photo in the magazine, one high-ranking aristocrat wondered whether anything would be done to "stop her.") Other suffragettes saw the potential publicity they could gain from having a princess as a member, and urged Sophia to take a more prominent role, but she refused, not wanting her privilege to further protect her or her celebrity to obscure their mission. When she was asked to speak at a glitzy suffrage fund-raiser, she agreed only after the organizers' repeated insistence. "I will come on the 9th to the meeting with pleasure," she wrote. "I hope you have found someone else to support the resolution, if not I will do so, but very much prefer not to and I shall only say about 5 words!" When it came to the cause to which she dedicated her life, she preferred to stay out of the spotlight and in the crowds. That's exactly where she was in February 1918, when the Representation of the People Act was passed, giving property-owning British women over thirty the right to vote, and again in 1928, when another piece of legislation enfranchised every British citizen age twenty-one and older.

Sophia's advocacy extended beyond suffrage. During World War I, she raised money to buy good-quality uniforms for Indian soldiers and advocated for their rights. She also volunteered as a nurse, caring for the wounded on the home front. But after the war and success in securing voting rights, when her "sister suffragettes" returned to their lives, Sophia felt lost, lonely, aimless, and in search of another cause. She struggled with depression for decades, finding another calling only after World War II broke out, when she began caring for her goddaughter (her housekeeper's child) and three refugee children she'd taken in.

It wasn't just Sophia's reluctance that kept her out of the public spotlight or out of history books. The British government worked hard to keep her name out of the headlines, in order to avoid embarrassing the monarchy, and much of the British suffrage movement was led by white British women, for white British women. Still, Sophia was far from the only British Indian woman who worked to enfranchise women in the UK. And while she often went unrecognized for her activism during her life, her name now appears on a monument in Parliament Square, alongside her fellow suffragettes. The monument was unveiled in 2018, one hundred years after the first British women could vote and 108 years after Sophia and other suffragettes were harassed, beaten, and assaulted nearby.

FRAIDY REISS

CHELSEA

Until recently, few people talked about the scourge of child marriage in the United States. Even fewer were actively campaigning to raise the minimum marriage age to eighteen and protect girls and women who had been child brides. Fraidy Reiss, herself a survivor of forced marriage with an abusive husband, is working to change this. Unchained At Last, the organization Fraidy founded after escaping her marriage, focuses on ending forced marriage — whether in a religious or secular context — in the United States. She considers any marriage of a minor forced because no child is of legal age to consent. She's right.

No child should be married, and yet so many are, all over the world. Over 650 million women alive today were married before eighteen, an estimated 12 million girls every year. Wherever it happens, it is a violation of a child's human rights and their rights to health, education, and self-determination. Girls who are married are less likely to finish school, more likely to give birth before their bodies are ready, and more likely to die prematurely, including in childbirth. Their children are more likely to be born at low birth weights and to die in the first month of life. In some countries, the majority of women were married before eighteen. In Niger, it's more than three in four; in Bangladesh, it's more than half.

Yet the magnitude of the child marriage crisis in parts of the world does not invalidate that it is a challenge everywhere in the world. Child brides are found across the globe, including in the United States. Child marriage is not a problem that happens in other places, to other people. In the U.S., part of what makes child marriage inevitably forced, as Fraidy often points out, is that if a child bride leaves her husband, she is considered a runaway. Many shelters will not take in minors traveling on their own — even those escaping forced marriages — because of concerns about criminal liability. In many states, children cannot enter into contracts on their own, meaning that a child bride often cannot hire her own lawyer, even to file for a divorce. It strikes me as a fundamental cruelty that a girl can be considered old enough to be forced into marriage but not old enough to decide to get a divorce.

From 2000 to 2015, an estimated two hundred thousand children were married in the United States. While many were sixteen or seventeen, some were as young as eleven or twelve. While a few were boys, and some marriages occurred between two minors, the overwhelming majority of child marriages involved girls married to adult men. No child — not an eleven-year-old or a seventeen-year-old — should be married. That this is still being debated — and not a practice being eliminated — is something I find unconscionable.

Fraidy never shies away from a debate or a demonstration. Her courage is particularly tangible when she shares her own story of how she wasn't told she had other options in her community, to not marry, to set her own course in life. And, as she would come to painfully know, no laws, religious or secular, were there for her or for minors forced into marriage. (She was nineteen on her wedding day.) She had no recourse in her Orthodox Judaism — only her husband could have divorced her, not the other way around. Even though it meant leaving her community, she decided to leave her violent, abusive husband. To do that, she developed a five-year plan that included going to college at Rutgers (where she graduated as valedictorian) and getting a job. Having financial independence enabled her to finally escape and take her children with her. Years later, most of her family continues to shun her. But Fraidy has never doubted that she made the right choices: to leave her forced marriage, help other women leave theirs, and work toward ensuring that one day, only women, not girls, are married in the United States.

Until 2018, and before Fraidy started her work to advocate for raising the minimum marriage age, no state had a no-exceptions ban on child marriage. Still today, many states have no minimum age for marriage, and others have abysmally low ages — including twelve or fourteen — even if they also require parental consent or a court to agree. But when parents are the ones doing the coercing, their consent offers scant to no protection for children. Why is this still so wrenchingly true in the twenty-first century? Partly because of the legacy of stigma around unwed mothers, partly because of a failure to appreciate how devastating child marriage is for girls, partly because of deference to conservative religious forces, and all wrapped up, I'd argue, in the tyranny of sexism. Thankfully, in 2018, in large part because of Fraidy's efforts, Delaware became the first state to ban child marriage without exception, and New Jersey followed a few months later. That means no parents can choose marriage for their child and no child can be forced into marriage. Fraidy worked on those two bills for years.

There is no federal law prohibiting child marriage, largely because marriage is governed at the state level. What the federal government could do is institute a federal minimum age for foreign spouses. This still hasn't happened, though it is an area Fraidy is advocating for while simultaneously working across multiple states to persuade legislators to ensure that no child is married before adulthood. Fraidy knows deeply that while we need to change laws, we also need to change our culture so that we value our girls and so that no parent, no person, thinks it is acceptable for a child to marry. This is why she leads "chain-ins," where people are dressed in bridal gowns with tape over their mouths and their wrists chained together. These events send a powerful signal that child marriage takes away a girl's voice and agency. Until we confront and end this shameful practice, girls will be forced into marriage when they should be focused on school, their friends, and their own dreams for their lives.

MANAL AL-SHARIF

HILLARY

In Saudi Arabia in 2011, it wasn't technically illegal for women to drive, but it *was* forbidden by Saudi custom, and that ban was enforced by the Saudi religious police. So even though Manal al-Sharif was thirty-two years old, and even though she had a car and knew how to drive, she couldn't. "Saudi women rely on drivers, usually foreign men, some of whom have never taken a driving test or had any kind of professional instruction to ferry them from place to place," she would later explain. "We are at their mercy."

One evening, she found herself walking along the side of the road, trying and failing to find a taxi to take her home after a doctor's appointment. Men harassed her from their cars; one followed her for so long she was scared for her safety. "Why do I have to be humiliated?" she started asking herself. "Why can't I drive when I have a car and a license? Why do I have to ask my colleagues to give me a ride, or my brother, or look for a driver to drive my own car?" Simply raising those questions was an act of defiance.

In school in the 1980s, Manal had been, as she put it, "brought up to follow the rules and listen to the man." At twenty-five, she got married, then had a son. Her husband was controlling and violent; after he beat her, she got a divorce. She went back to work as a cybersecurity engineer, and was sent by her employer to the United States, where she saw what seemed like a different world. She could open a bank account, go where she wanted, and get behind the wheel of a car. She learned the rules of the road and got her driver's license. For Manal, driving was a path to economic opportunity. It made it possible for her to shop for groceries, run errands, and go to the doctor. She longed to have that same freedom in her own country.

Back in Saudi Arabia, Manal al-Sharif captured the world's attention in May 2011 with a brave act of civil disobedience: She filmed herself driving and posted the video on YouTube and Facebook. In twenty-four hours, the video had 700,000 views. But then, at two a.m., the secret police showed up at her house while her five-year-old son slept. They arrested her, and charged her with "driving while female." She was held in a cockroach-infested jail for nine days. After a massive outcry in Saudi Arabia and around the world, she was released on the condition that she refrain from driving or speaking to the media. Instead, at the height of the Arab Spring protests, she launched the Women2Drive campaign, organizing others to join her in a day of action.

Manal was condemned for her activism; some even suggested she was a foreign spy.

"Exercise your rights. Never take them for granted. That's the day they're taken away from you. Living in a democracy is not a privilege. Living in a democracy is a huge responsibility. If you have a voice, honor it and use it."

— MANAL AL-SHARIF

Her brother, who had been in the passenger seat while she filmed herself driving, was subjected to so much harassment that his family was forced to leave the country. Manal was pressured to resign from her job. She lost custody of her son and left Saudi Arabia. But she refused to be silenced.

As secretary of state, I was moved by Manal's courage, and the courage of the women who stood with her. At a press conference in June 2011, I publicly declared the United States' support for lifting the ban in Saudi Arabia. "What these women are doing is brave and what they are seeking is right," I said. "We have raised this issue at the highest level of the Saudi government. We've made clear our views that women everywhere, including women in the Kingdom, have the right to make decisions about their lives and their futures." When another group of women protested the ban again on October 26, 2013, some opponents of lifting the ban pointed to the date — my birthday — as evidence that the protests had been organized by the United States. They hadn't, of course. This was not about the United States; it was about the women of Saudi Arabia.

In 2017, Manal wrote a book about her journey to become what she called an "accidental activist": *Daring to Drive: A Saudi Woman's Awakening*. In 2018, in part because of Manal's persistence, Saudi Arabia lifted the "unofficial" ban on women drivers. When Manal heard the news, she cried tears of joy. "Saudi women will be free not only to drive their own cars but also to be the drivers of their own lives," she said at the time. Then she learned she couldn't go home to celebrate the victory; women activists were being detained and imprisoned with little to no explanation. "The recent arrests dilute and tarnish the progress that has been made in lifting the ban," she wrote in the *Washington Post*. "The activists were arrested despite their love for Saudi Arabia — for in an absolute monarchy, dissidents are the true patriots."

There is still a long road ahead, but Manal's willingness to risk so much to demand freedom and opportunity should inspire women everywhere.

NADIA MURAD

HILLARY

When Nadia Murad was a teenager, she wanted to be a teacher or open a beauty salon. At her family's home in Kocho, Iraq, she kept a photo album with pictures of hairstyles and

734

makeup that inspired her. When she wasn't at school or dreaming about her future, she was helping her family on their farm and spending time with the other women in her village.

That changed in an instant in August 2014, when the Islamic State attacked her community. Hundreds were killed simply for practicing their religion, Yazidism. Her mother was one of eighty older women executed and left in an unmarked grave. Six of her brothers were among the six hundred Yazidi men murdered that day. Nadia was separated from her family and taken captive. She was sold by ISIS into sex slavery, where she was brutally raped, beaten, and sold again.

After three months of living in a nightmare, and a thwarted escape attempt that resulted in horrific punishment, Nadia found an unlocked door in the house where she was being held. Risking her life, knowing the torture that awaited her if she got caught, she fled. She made her way to a family who helped her to a refugee camp. She had freed herself.

In 2015, she spoke at a UN forum on minority issues, the first time she would tell her story in front of an audience. That same year she was asked to speak to the UN Security Council on human trafficking. "I wanted to talk about everything," she said. "The children who died of dehydration fleeing ISIS, the families still stranded on the mountain, the thousands of women and children who

> *"I assumed that Hajji Amr had left me alone in the house with the door unlocked and no guards not because he had forgotten. He wasn't stupid. He did that because he thought at this point, having been abused for so long and being so weak from sickness and hunger, I wouldn't think of trying to escape. They thought they had me forever. They are wrong, I thought."*
>
> — NADIA MURAD

remained in captivity, and what my brothers saw at the site of the massacre." And that's what she did. "Deciding to be honest was one of the hardest decisions I have ever made, and also the most important," she said later.

In 2016, Nadia was appointed UN goodwill ambassador for the dignity of survivors of human trafficking. She is currently working with human rights lawyer Amal Clooney to bring ISIS to justice before the International Criminal Court. Amal and Nadia were in the audience, sitting side by side, when the UN Security Council unanimously adopted a resolution to create an investigation team to build a case against ISIS. In 2017, she published her courageous memoir, *The Last Girl: My Story of Captivity, and My Fight Against the Islamic State.*

The dedication page of Nadia's memoir

reads: "This book is written for every Yazidi." Nadia knew that even though she was able to escape, others were not. She has dedicated her life to fighting on behalf of those who remain captive. Nadia's work is especially close to my heart because I have worked for decades against human trafficking — as first lady, as a U.S. senator, as secretary of state, and now, as a private citizen. Her story underscores the importance of human rights, the rule of law, due process, judicial systems, and international organizations in holding people accountable and serving as places of recourse for the Nadias of the world.

From the moment she escaped, Nadia has refused to hide her face in shame. Instead, she has forced the world to confront the atrocities committed against the Yazidis and the horror of sexual violence as a weapon of war. I was thrilled when, in 2018, Nadia was awarded the Nobel Peace Prize, alongside pioneering Congolese gynecologist Dr. Denis Mukwege, who has treated survivors of wartime sexual

---

"Those who thought that by their cruelty they could silence her were wrong. Nadia Murad's spirit is not broken, and her voice will not be muted."

— AMAL CLOONEY

---

violence. What Nadia deserves even more than an award is to see her message turned into action everywhere that women's human rights are threatened so that the attackers are brought to justice.

EPILOGUE

It's hard to read the news and not feel grateful for brave, resilient women around the world. That's been true throughout history, and it's especially true today.

We wanted to cheer and scream at the same time when Olympic athletes Alysia Montaño, Kara Goucher, and Allyson Felix broke their nondisclosure agreements to tell the *New York Times* about being paid less by their sponsor, Nike, after they gave birth. We *only* wanted to scream when white male legislators in Alabama and other states voted to effectively ban abortion. Thousands of women came forward in response to publicly share their own experiences of ending a pregnancy — but why should it fall to women to share their most personal stories in order to defend a right we've had in America for more than forty-five years? What's more, why are legislators focused on limiting reproductive choices rather than solving the real challenges pregnant women confront? A woman in America today is 50 percent more likely to die from pregnancy, childbirth, or related complications than her own mother, and black women are three to four times more likely than white women to die from pregnancy-related complications. Why aren't these legislators concerned about keeping women alive?

Meanwhile, around the world, efforts to dictate what women can wear continue. The speaker of the Tanzanian parliament banned women members from wearing nail and eyelash extensions. The Japanese health and labor minister defended employers who require women to wear high heels, calling the practice "necessary and appropriate." More than a few countries currently either restrict what religious clothing women wear in public or require women to wear religious clothing in public. And it's not only governments policing women's attire and accessories. In 2018, the U.S. Open chastised professional tennis player Alizé Cornet for changing her shirt during a break in a match, and Serena Williams was told by French Open officials that she couldn't wear her black catsuit, even though it was helping prevent life-threatening blood clots.

As we said in the introduction, ensuring the rights, opportunities, and full participation of all women and girls remains a big piece of the unfinished business of the twenty-first century. But sometimes it seems even more unfinished than we'd hoped. Even though women in the United States have graduated from college in higher numbers than men for decades, there's still a woeful lack of women in the upper reaches of science and technology, business and education, not to mention politics and government. Women's representation in the current administration in Washington is the lowest it's been in a generation, and women hold just a quarter of computing jobs in the U.S. — a percentage that has gone down instead of up since the mid-1980s.

For too many women, especially low-wage workers, a livable wage or predictable work schedules or affordable child care are still far out of reach; less than 20 percent of American workers have access to paid family leave, and those benefits are concentrated among the highest-income workers. One in three women in the United States and worldwide has experienced physical or sexual violence. Every year globally, more than two million girls under fourteen give birth.

Yet, we have made progress. Around the world, child marriage rates are declining. So, too, is teenage pregnancy. Brave women in India, Canada, South Korea, the United States, and elsewhere are shining a brighter light on sexual assault and harassment. More women are making their own reproductive health choices in more places, even as we lose ground in America. Women are running countries and cities across the globe. They're leading Fortune 500 companies and starting their own enterprises. They're making award-winning films and theater, shattering records in sports, and inventing revolutionary technologies.

For the first time ever, there are more than one hundred women in the U.S. Congress — the most diverse class in history. We've watched the first woman Speaker of the House, Nancy Pelosi, face off with a president who embodies misogyny. A century ago, most women in America couldn't vote; today we have enough women running for president of the United States to field a basketball team.

While writing this book, we have loved thinking back across our own lives to remember the women who inspired, educated, and challenged us. Some we've had the gift of knowing; others we've never met. Some come from politics and public service. Many don't; running for office is one great way to make a difference, but it's far from the *only* way. Some of their names are famous, others are unknown. To us, they are all gutsy women — leaders with the courage to stand up to the status quo, ask hard questions, and get the job done. Many have done heroic things, but they are not superheroes. They are complex, flawed, and imperfect human beings. They all made the world better. We draw strength from these women, and we hope you will too. Because if history shows one thing, it's that the world has always needed gutsy women — and we know it always will.

ACKNOWLEDGMENTS

We are both thankful for the many people who helped us visualize, research, and produce this book. It's been an adventure and labor of love for us to work together.

First and foremost, we could not have done it without the indispensable Lauren Peterson, our intrepid collaborator. Her writing skills and love of the subject are unmatched, and her good humor in navigating between our different working styles (one of us still writes longhand) deserves special recognition, as does her help in the painful process of moving from our initial count of more than 200 essays to the 105 we share in this book. We are also grateful to all of the teachers, historians, writers, and librarians who helped shape and guide our thinking and writing over the years, including for this book.

Opal Vadhan provided invaluable contributions in deciphering Hillary's handwriting and researching our endless arcane inquiries; her efforts added immeasurably to our own.

She was ably assisted by Harshil Bansal, Nina Emilie Bechmann, Charles Burton-Callegari, Jessica Grubesic, Olivia Hartman, Sara Hussain, Alana Jennis, Ashley Kawakami, Anna Matefy, Valia Mitsakis, Dylan Mott, Maria Julia Pieraccioni, Madison Sidwell, Ekum Sohal, Millie Todd, Olivia Weathers, and Aija Zamurs.

We were very lucky that Ruby Shamir, an author with whom we have both worked before, led our fact-checking efforts, and that the indefatigable Joy Secuban took on the formidable challenge of finding all the photographs we needed, tracking them down, and securing permissions. Both of their efforts made this book stronger and more vibrant.

As always, we appreciate the help we received from our teams and friends who offered advice along the way: Huma Abedin, Allida Black, Kristina Costa, Bari Lurie, Nick Merrill, Laura Olin, Megan Rooney, Robert Russo, Dan Schwerin, Ella Serrano, Lona Valmoro, Melanne Verveer, Shanna Weathersby, Emily Young, and Liz Zaretsky. A special thank you to Marc, a wonderful husband and son-in-law who is also a wonderful reader. And, as always, thanks to Bill/Dad for offering comments.

A heartfelt thank-you to Jonathan Karp, Priscilla Painton, Elizabeth Breeden, Annie Craig, Amar Deol, Paul Dippolito, Lisa Erwin, Jonathan Evans, Elizabeth Gay, Cary

Goldstein, Kimberly Goldstein, Yvette Grant, Kayley Hoffman, Megan Hogan, Irene Kheradi, Sara Kitchen, Ruth Lee-Mui, Richard Rhorer, Elise Ringo, and Jackie Seow at Simon & Schuster, who believed in this book and stayed with us through all the ups and downs. And we both value the continuing support of our respective lawyers, Bob Barnett and Tara Kole.

We will be donating a portion of the proceeds from this book to organizations that support the work and legacies of the women spotlighted within it.

Finally, we want to thank Charlotte and Aidan for providing endless joy and laughter throughout this process, as throughout all days.

INDEX

Note: Page numbers in *italics* refer to illustrations.

American Red Cross, 15, 287, 291–92
Americans with Disabilities Act, 392
amfAR, 310
Amin, Idi, 690
Amma, G. Devaki, 214
Anand, Anita, 717–18
Anderson, Marian, 453
Angelou, Maya, 421–25, *521,* 651
Antheil, George, 263
Anthony, Susan B., 45, 701, 712
Ardern, Jacinda, 14
Artemis (goddess of the hunt), 28
Ascend Afghanistan, 353
Asquith, H. H., 696
Athena (goddess of wisdom and war), 27
ATTENTIONTheatre, 549
Atwood, Margaret, 32
Auld, Sara, 295, 296

Babbage, Charles, 239
Bachelet, Michelle, 614–20, *614*
Baden-Powell, Lord Robert, 121
Balanchine, George, 535–5, 56
Bancroft, Margaret, 114–18, *114*
Bangura, Zainab, 16
Barnett, Ferdinand, 422
Barton, Clara (Clarissa Harlowe), 15, 287,
        288–92, *288*
Bates, Daisy, 148–54, *148*
Bates, Lucius Christopher (L. C.), 149–50,
        153

PHOTO CREDITS

Page 22: (top and bottom) Authors' Collection

Page 37: Benjamin Powelson/Library of Congress

Page 47: (top, left to right) Museum of London/Heritage Images/Getty Images; Hulton Archive/Getty Images; (bottom, left to right) Jack Mitchell/Getty Images; Dance Theatre of Harlem, Marbeth

Page 58: Hulton Archive/Getty Images

Page 66: Robert W. Kelley/The LIFE Images Collection via Getty Images/Getty Images

Page 75: Margaret Bourke-White/The LIFE Picture Collection via Getty Images/Getty Images

Page 83: George Konig/Keystone Features/Getty Images

Page 90: Anne Frank Fonds-Basel via Getty Images

Page 95: JOHAN ORDONEZ/AFP/Getty Images

Page 102: (left) Mike Powell/Allsport/Getty Images; (right) Andy Hayt/Sports Illustrated via Getty Images

Page 109: DeAgostini/Getty Images
Page 114: Courtesy of Bancroft NeuroHealth
Page 119: Bettmann via Getty Images
Page 126: (top) Popperfoto via Getty Images/ Getty Images; (bottom) Dustin Harris/ Getty Images
Page 134: Hulton Archive/Getty Images
Page 143: Michelle VIGNES/Gamma-Rapho via Getty Images
Page 148: Thomas D. McAvoy/The LIFE Picture Collection via /Getty Images/Getty Images
Page 155: (top, left to right) Bettmann via Getty Images; Photograph NWC'77 99-27n copyright © by Jo Freeman; (bottom) Oregonian/Advance Media
Page 167: AP Photo
Page 172: John Russo/Contour by Getty Images
Page 179: AP Photo/Jim Kerlin
Page 184: Alfred Eisenstaedt/The LIFE Picture Collection via Getty Images/Getty Images
Page 190: (left) © Ruth Orkin; (right) WE ACT for Environmental Justice/Glamour Magazine
Page 198: SUMY SADURNI/AFP/Getty Images
Page 207: GIANLUIGI GUERICA/AFP/ Getty Images
Page 215: Adam Schultz/Clinton Foundation
Page 222: Photograph by Michael Campanella

Page 452: Arnold Michaelis/Pix Inc./The LIFE Picture Collection via Getty Images

Page 461: Arthur Schatz/The LIFE Picture Collection via Getty Images/Getty Images

Page 469: (top, left to right) ALAN LEWIS/AFP/Getty Images; Robin Holland/Corbis via Getty Images; (bottom, left to right) Paul Faith-PA Images/PA Images via Getty Images; Jonathan Saruk/Getty Images

Page 478: The 1860 Heritage Centre

Page 482: Courtesy of Ai-jen Poo

Page 489: (top, left to right) Ken Lubas/Los Angeles Times via Getty Images; Daniel Acker/Bloomberg via Getty Images; Al Drago/Bloomberg via Getty Images; (bottom, left to right) LMG Photography; Noam Galai/Getty Images

Page 502: (clockwise from top left) Slaven Vlasic/Getty Images; Emilee McGovern/SOPA Images/LightRocket via Getty Images; Mike Coppola/Getty Images for Tory Burch Foundation; © Everytown for Gun Safety Action Fund, 2019; Cindy Ord/Getty Images for Teen Vogue; Paul Morigi/Getty Images for March For Our Lives

Page 513: Photograph by Bill Bernstein

Page 521: Patrick Fraser/Corbis via Getty Images

Page 526: Manuel Vazquez/Contour by Getty Images

Page 531: GDA via AP Images

ABOUT THE AUTHORS

Hillary Rodham Clinton is the first woman in U.S. history to become the presidential nominee of a major political party. She served as the 67th Secretary of State after nearly four decades in public service advocating on behalf of children and families as an attorney, First Lady, and U.S. Senator. She is a wife, mother, and grandmother.

Chelsea Clinton is a champion for girls and women through her advocacy, writing, and work at the Clinton Foundation. She is also an adjunct assistant professor at Columbia University's Mailman School of Public Health. She lives in New York City with her husband, their children, and their dog.